T0386116

The Book of Travels

Volume Two

LIBRARY OF ARABIC LITERATURE

GENERAL EDITOR
Philip F. Kennedy, New York University

EXECUTIVE EDITORS
James E. Montgomery, University of Cambridge
Shawkat M. Toorawa, Yale University

EDITORIAL DIRECTOR
Chip Rossetti

ASSISTANT EDITOR
Lucie Taylor

EDITORS
Sean Anthony, The Ohio State University
Huda Fakhreddine, University of Pennsylvania
Lara Harb, Princeton University
Maya Kesrouany, New York University Abu Dhabi
Enass Khansa, American University of Beirut
Bilal Orfali, American University of Beirut
Maurice Pomerantz, New York University Abu Dhabi
Mohammed Rustom, Carleton University

CONSULTING EDITORS
Julia Bray    Michael Cooperson    Joseph E. Lowry
Tahera Qutbuddin    Devin J. Stewart

DIGITAL PRODUCTION MANAGER
Stuart Brown

PAPERBACK DESIGNER
Nicole Hayward

FELLOWSHIP PROGRAM COORDINATOR
Amani Al-Zoubi

# Letter from the General Editor

The Library of Arabic Literature makes available Arabic editions and English translations of significant works of Arabic literature, with an emphasis on the seventh to nineteenth centuries. The Library of Arabic Literature thus includes texts from the pre-Islamic era to the cusp of the modern period, and encompasses a wide range of genres, including poetry, poetics, fiction, religion, philosophy, law, science, travel writing, history, and historiography.

Books in the series are edited and translated by internationally recognized scholars. They are published as hardcovers in parallel-text format with Arabic and English on facing pages, as English-only paperbacks, and as downloadable Arabic editions. For some texts, the series also publishes separate scholarly editions with full critical apparatus.

The Library encourages scholars to produce authoritative Arabic editions, accompanied by modern, lucid English translations, with the ultimate goal of introducing Arabic's rich literary heritage to a general audience of readers as well as to scholars and students.

The publications of the Library of Arabic Literature are generously supported by Tamkeen under the NYU Abu Dhabi Research Institute Award G1003 and are published by NYU Press.

Philip F. Kennedy
*General Editor, Library of Arabic Literature*

# كتاب السياحة

## حنّا دياب

### المجلّد الثاني

LIBRARY OF
المكتبة
ARABIC
العربية
LITERATURE

# The Book of Travels

## ḤANNĀ DIYĀB

## Volume Two

Edited by
JOHANNES STEPHAN

Translated by
ELIAS MUHANNA

Afterword by
PAULO LEMOS HORTA

Volume editor
MICHAEL COOPERSON

NEW YORK UNIVERSITY PRESS
*New York*

NEW YORK UNIVERSITY PRESS
*New York*

Copyright © 2021 by New York University

All rights reserved

Library of Congress Cataloging-in-Publication Data

Names: Diyāb, Ḥannā, approximately 1687, author. | Diyāb, Ḥannā,
approximately 1687. Kitāb al-Siyāḥah. | Diyāb, Ḥannā,
approximately 1687. Kitāb al-Siyāḥah English. | Stephan, Johannes,
1966- editor. | Muhanna, Elias, translator.
Title: The book of travels = Kitāb al-Siyāḥah / Ḥannā Diyāb ; edited
by Johannes Stephen ; translated by Elias Muhanna.
Other titles: Kitāb al-Siyāḥah
Description: New York : New York University Press, [2021] | Title and
statement of responsibility appear on pages | Includes bibliographical
references and index. | Contents: v. 1. The book of travels: volume one
-- v. 2. The book of travels: volume two | Includes text in Arabic; with
English translation on opposite pages. | Summary: "Ḥannā Diyāb's
account of his travels as a young man from his hometown of Aleppo to the
court of Versailles and back again"-- Provided by publisher.
Identifiers: LCCN 2020054531 | ISBN 9781479810949 (set) | ISBN
9781479892303 (v. 1 ; cloth) | ISBN 9781479806300 (v. 2 ; cloth) | ISBN
9781479849475 (v. 1 ; ebook) | ISBN 9781479837274 (v. 1 ; ebook) | ISBN
9781479806263 (v. 2 ; ebook) | ISBN 9781479806270 (v. 2 ; ebook)
Subjects: LCSH: Diyāb, Ḥannā, approximately 1687--Travel. | Aleppo
(Syria)--Description and travel--Early works to 1800. | Paris
(France)--Description and travel--Early works to 1800. | Travelers'
writings, Arabic--Translations into English. | Travelers' writings,
Arabic--History and criticism. | Lucas, Paul, 1664-1737. |
Maronites--Syria--Biography. | Aleppo (Syria)--Biography.
Classification: LCC DS47.2 .D59 2021 | DDC 910.9182/209033--dc23

LC record available at https://lccn.loc.gov/2020054531


New York University Press books are printed on acid-free paper,
and their binding materials are chosen for strength and durability.

Series design by Titus Nemeth.

Typeset in Tasmeem, using DecoType Naskh and Emiri.

Typesetting and digitization by Stuart Brown.

Manufactured in the United States of America
c 10 9 8 7 6 5 4 3 2 1

# Table of Contents

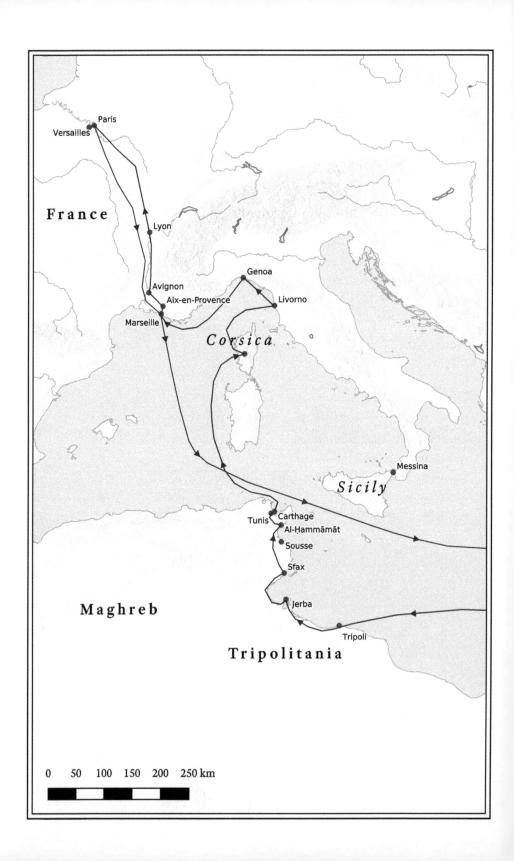

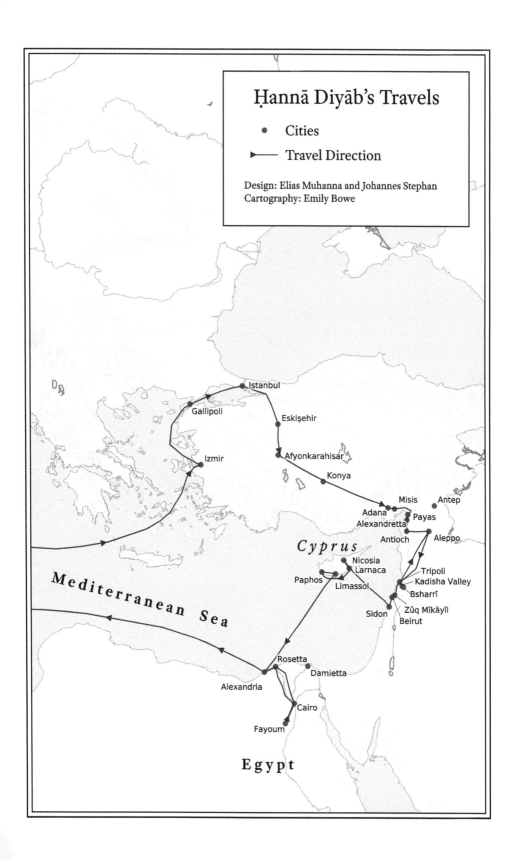

كتاب السياحة

المجلّد الثاني

# The Book of Travels

## Volume Two

# الفصل التاسع[1]

## وكان دخولنا الي مدينة بهريس في شهر شباط سنه ١٧٠٩

٩.١ فاستقمنــا مدة ايام في بيت ذلك الرجل الي حين ما هيا معلمي اشغاله وفصل له بدله ثمينه في الغايه وارسل الي المطبعه طبع كتاب سياحته التي ساحها بالتدقيق وفي جميع بلاد التي دخلها وجميع الذي راه وسمعه من الاخبار والفرج لانه كان يكتب كل يوم الامور التي يراها ويسمعها واخيرًا امر بتنجير قصص مكلف لتلك الوحوش المر ذكرهم وكان بقي منهم اثنين لا غير .

٩.٢ فبعدما كملت جميع ما احتاج اليه معلمي حينٍ امرني باني البس بدلت حوايجي التي كنت ارسلت وجهتها من حلب وهي طوله بترا وغنري الاجه شاميه وحجور لوندرين وزنار مكلف وسكين مفضضه وشاش وقاووق وما يشبه ذلك من كسوة بلاد الشرق فبعدما لبست حوايجي ما عدا الشاش والقاووق لبست قلبق مثل قلابق السمور الذي كان اشتره معلمي من مدينة مصر منشاني وهو قلبق جميل .

٩.٣ اخيرًا ركبنا في عربانه وقصدنا قرية ورساليا حيث صرايا سلطان فرنسا وهي بعيده عن مدينة بهريس حكم ساعه ونصف ولما قربنا الي ورساليا رايت عن بعد لميع ببهر النضر فسالت معلمي ما هذا اللميع الذي براه فاجابني بان هذا اخور خيل الملك ولما وصلنا اليه فرايت وهي عماره مكلفه مشيده واسطحتها[2] مرصوفه من ذلك الحجر الاسود الذي بينكتب عليه ومداخن تلك العماير قووعها مدهبه ولما بتشرق الشمس

---

١ لم يرد رقم لهذا الفصل في الأصل. ٢ الأصل: واسطحتها.

# Chapter Nine[1]

## Our Arrival in Paris, in October 1708[2]

We remained at the home of my master's friend for a few days, until my master    9.1
had sorted out his affairs. He had an expensive suit tailored for himself, and
sent his book off to the printer. The book described in great detail the journey
he had undertaken, the lands he had visited, and all the stories and sights he
had seen and heard, which he had recorded every day. And he had a fine cage
built for those animals I mentioned previously, of which only two remained.[3]

Once my master had secured all that he needed, he told me to put on the    9.2
clothes I'd sent for from Aleppo. They included a short reddish-brown over-
coat made of Damascene *alājah* fabric, some *jakhjūr* trousers made of *londrin*,
a fine belt, a silver-plated dagger, a turban cloth and cap, and other such pieces
of Eastern clothing. I put on all the clothes, but instead of the turban I wore a
calpac similar to the ones made of sable fur my master had purchased for me in
Cairo. It was a beautiful calpac.

We climbed into a carriage and set off for the town of Versailles and the    9.3
king's palace. It was an hour and a half from Paris. As we approached Versailles, I perceived something glittering in the distance, so bright it dazzled
the eye.

"What's that I see?" I asked my master.

"The king's stables," he replied.

As we drew near, I saw that it was a splendid, imposing building, roofed
with those black stones that people write on.[4] The chimneys had gilded fun-
nels, and when the sun shone it was impossible to fix your gaze upon them,

ما بتقدر تحقق النضر فيها من شده لميعها فاستقمنا نمشي في طول ذلك الاخور نحو نصف ساعه وبعده وصلنا الي ورسايلا.

٤،٩ فلما شرفنا علي صراية الملك رايت قدام السرايا فسحه كبيره متسعه في الغايه وما يدورها درابزون من حديد بعلو قامه ومده ايد بروس محرفه مثل الرماح وفي الوسط باب الذي بيندخل منه الي تلك الفسحه من حديد وواقفين جنود طويلين القامه وفي ايدهم الطبارات والحراب ويبهمروا كالنوره وما يدعوا احد يدخل الا الذين بيعرفوهم انهم معروفين من الدوله فلما وصلنا الي ذلك الباب فارادوا يصدونا عن الدخول فاعطاهم معلي اشاره المعروفه عندهم فاطلقوا سبيلنا.

٥،٩ حينذٍ دخلنا في تلك الساحه وسرنا الي ان وصلنا الي باب صراية الملك وفي ذلك المكان ايضاً واقفين جنود مثل الاولين وجالس قبجي مكلف وامامه جمله من الخدام وهو مهيب وجميل المنظر فاتقدم اليه معلي وخاطبه وبين له ذاته فاسترحب فيه وكرمه واذن له في الدخول. حينذٍ صعدنا في درج عريض متسع من حجر فلما انتهينا الي اعلا المكان توجهنا نحو صراية الوزير الذي يسما بونشطرين وهو وزير الشرق فبعدما اخذنا اذن دخلنا صحبة القبجي امام حضرة الوزير.

٦،٩ فلما امتثلنا امامه حينذٍ عمل معلي تمني اللايق لحضرته واعلمه بوصوله من سياحته الي بهريس بالسلامه واعطاه القايمه الموجوده في السبع سناديق الذي كان اشتراهم في سياحته الي حضرة الملك الذي ذكرناهم سابقاً فلما قرا تلك الجريده فعاد استرحب فيه وهناه علي سلامته من تلك الاهوال الذي قاساها في سفره والفقير كت واقف من بعد عنهم في يدي قفص الوحوش فالتفت الوزير فراني واقفاً وفي يدي القفص.

٧،٩ فسال معلي ما هذا الغلام وما الذي في يده فاجابه قايلاً هذا الغلام كان ترجماني في سفري ولما كنا في بلاد الصعيد فوجدت بعض وحوش غريبي الشكل والمنظر وما رايت لهم وجود في ساير بلاد التي درتها فاخدت منهم سبعة الذي بالجهد حتي قدروا الصيادين ان يمسكوهم فوضعتهم في قفص وجبتهم معي ولكن في الطريق مات منهم خمسه فيبقي منهم اثنين فان كان حضرتك بتريد تراهم ها هم داخل القفص.

as they gleamed so brightly. We spent half an hour driving by those stables before arriving at Versailles.

As we approached the king's palace, I could see that there was a vast open space before it, surrounded by an iron fence as tall as a man with his arm outstretched, and topped with points as sharp as spears. At the center was a gate that opened onto the space, flanked by tall soldiers carrying battle-axes and spears, and snarling like panthers. They allowed no one to pass except those they recognized to be known at court. When we approached the gate, the soldiers tried to turn us away, but my master gave them a password and they let us through.

We entered the square and walked across it to the gates of the king's palace. There were soldiers there just like the ones we'd seen earlier, along with a seated chamberlain wearing an ornate uniform. He was a handsome man of dignified bearing, attended by a group of servants. When my master stepped forward and introduced himself, the man welcomed him in most cordially. We climbed a grand set of stone stairs, then headed to the pavilion of the minister known as Pontchartrain, who was minister for the Orient. We received permission to enter, and presented ourselves before His Excellency the minister, accompanied by the chamberlain.

My master bowed ceremoniously and announced that he'd returned safely to Paris from his voyage. He presented the minister with an inventory of the seven trunks' worth of goods he had purchased for His Majesty the king during his travels. The minister read the inventory and repeated his greetings, congratulating my master on returning home safely despite all the frightful things he'd surely encountered during his voyage. I stood at some distance from the two men, holding the cage with the animals inside. The minister spotted me.

"Who's that, and what's he carrying?" he asked my master.

"This young man served as my dragoman during the voyage," he replied. "When we were in Upper Egypt, I discovered some peculiar animals, which I'd never seen in all the lands I'd visited. I managed to procure seven of them, despite the fact that it's very difficult to catch them. I put them in a cage to transport them home, but five perished along the way and only two survived. If Your Excellency would like to see them, they're in this cage."

9.4

9.5

9.6

9.7

٨٠٩ فامر الوزير بان يدخلوني امامه واتخذوا القفص من يدي واعرضوا علي حضرة الوزير فلما راء تينك الوحوش وفي خلقتهم العجيبه فقال الي معلمي انا بريد افرج الملك علي هذه الحيوانات في الغد لان فات وقت خروجه الي الصيد[١] وفي الحال امر بان يعطونا منزول في صرايته فادخلونا الي منزول مفروش وقدموا لنا من اكل وشرب وما نحتاج اليه علي غاية ما يكون.

٩٠٩ فاستقمنا في ذلك المنزول الي ثاني يوم الي قبل الذهر بساعتين. حينذٍ امر الوزير في حضورنا امامه وسار بنا الي ديوان الملك فلما وصلنا فدخل الوزير ونحن استقمنا خارج الي حين ما خرج الملك من قصره ودخل الي الديوان فاعلمه الوزير في وصول معلمي وطلب منه اذن في دخولنا فدخلونا فرايت الملك واقف ومن علي يمينه وشماله مصطفين اكبر دولته بغاية التهيب والاتضاع وهو طويل القامه بهي المنظر ومن شدة هيبته ما بيقدر الانسان يحقق النظر فيه. حينذٍ امتثل معلمي امامه وعمل له مطايبه ودعا له بدوام الملك والكماله من ما يقال في مقابلة الملوك فسمعت من الملك خطاب ذات لين ومحبه الي معلمي تاويله بانه بيستكتر بخيره علي اتعابه التي اصرفها في خدمته.

١٠٠٩ اخيرًا اتقدم الوزير وسال الملك ان كان بيريد يتفرج علي تلك الوحوش فامر الملك باحضارهم امامه. حينذٍ اخذوا من يدي القفص ووضعوه امام الملك فلما راء الوحوش تعجب من خلقتهم فسال معلمي في اي بلاد وجدهم فاجابه في بلاد الصعيد فساله ايضا هل انهم انثي وذكر فاجابه يا سيدي كانوا سبعه وكان موجود فيهم ذكر وانثي والان ما عدت اعرف انكان موجود فيهم انثي وذكر فساله ايضًا ما اسمهم في بلادهم فخجل معلمي وما كان بيعرف اسمهم اوانه نسي فالتفت اليّ وقال لحضرة الملك بان هل غلام الذي معي بيعرف اساميهم.

١١٠٩ حينذٍ التفت الملك وكل اكبار الدوله نحوي وسالني واحد منهم عن اسم هذه الوحوش فقلت له بان في بلادهم بيسما جربوع فامر الملك بان يقدموا لي قلم وقرطاز

---

١ «في الغد . . . الي الصيد» في الهامش و«الصيد» مطموس في الأصل.

The minister gave an order to have me brought before him, and the cage    9.8
was taken from me and presented to His Excellency.

"I'm going to show these animals to the king tomorrow," he said when he
saw the curious creatures. "It's too late to go now, since he's already left for the
hunt."[5] The minister then ordered some lodgings to be prepared for us at the
palace. We were taken to a furnished residence, and offered food and drink of
the finest kind.

We remained in that residence until the next day. Two hours before noon,    9.9
the minister summoned us, and took us to the king's council room. The minister
entered first. We remained outside and waited for the king to emerge from his
pavilion and enter the council room. Once he had, the minister informed him
of my master's arrival and asked permission for us to enter. We were brought
into the room, and I saw the king standing there, with the notables of his realm
lined up to his right and left looking extremely prim and proper.

The king was tall and splendid to behold. His presence inspired such awe
that it was impossible to fix one's gaze upon him for long. My master presented
himself before the king and saluted him with due reverence, praying that his
reign would endure, and expressing all the formulas appropriate for the greeting of kings. I heard the king address my master tenderly and affectionately,
thanking him for the effort he'd expended in his service.

The minister then stepped forward and asked if the king would like to see    9.10
the animals, and the king ordered them to be brought forward. They took the
cage from me and set it before him. When he saw the creatures, he was astonished by their appearance and asked my master where he'd found them.

"In Upper Egypt," he replied.

"Is there one female and one male?"

"Sire, there were originally seven, both male and female," my master
explained.[6] "At present, however, I no longer know whether they're female
or male."

"What are the animals called in their country?" the king asked.

My master, who didn't know the name, or perhaps had forgotten it, looked
embarrassed, and turned to me.

"Your Majesty, the young man who accompanied me knows what they're
called."

The king and all his nobles turned to face me. Someone asked me what the    9.11
animals were called. I replied that, in the lands where it is found, the animal

حتى اكتب اسمهم بلساني فلما قدموا لي القرظاز فكتبت اسمهم بلسان العربي وكتبته
ايضاً بلسان الفرنساوي لاني اعرف اقوي واكتب بالفرنساوي فبعدما كتبت اسمهم
كما ذكرنا واعرضوه لحضرة الملك فتفرس في الملك وسال معلمي ما هو هذا الغلام ومن
اي بلاد هو فاجابه معلمي وهو هاني هامه للارض بان يا سيدي هذا الغلام من
بلاد سوريا من ارض المقدسه وهو من طايفة الموارنه الذين استقاموا في الكنيسه
البطرسيه من عهد الرسل وما انشقوا منها الي الان.

١٢٠٩    وفي ذلك الوقت دخل منسينور الدلفين ابن الملك وهو رجل مربوع القامه عفي
من الرجال وهذا كان يقال عنه بان ابوه ملك وابنه البكر ملك اصبانيا وما هو
ملك فاتقدم واتفرج علي تلك الوحوش فلما راهم اتعجب من خلقتهم وكان عنده
صوره كبيره عظيمه مصور فيها جميع الوحوش الموجودين في الدنيا باسرها ما عدا
هذا الوحش. حينذٍ امر باحضار حكيم الملك الذي اسمه موسه فكو وهذا رجل
عالم ومعلم وما له مثيل في ساير الدنيا في علم الطب والطبيعيات وما شاكل ذلك
من العلوم.

١٣٠٩    فلما حضر موسه فكو المذكور واتفرج علي تلك الوحوش فساله ابن الملك المذكور
قايلاً له هل ما خبره فيهم اوانهم مذكورين في كتب الطبيعيات فاجابه بان ما راء لهم
ذكر ولا صوره. حينذٍ ارسل واحضر المصور حتي يصورهم داخل صورة الوحوش
التي عنده وبعده امر الملك للوزير بان يبقي هل وحوش وحاملهم في مكان ولا يدع
احديراهم الي حين ما ترجع مادام دبركونيو من الصيد التي هي كت الملك مرت ابن
الملك يدعا دوك لدبركونيو وكان الملك يحبها غاية المحبه ويسميها بنته وهذه اول مره
الذي تشرفت في رويت الملك المذكور في ديوانه اعني به سلطان فرنسا لويز الرابع
عشر من هذا الاسم وجميع الذي ذكرته الان هو بغاية التحقيق من غير زود ولا نقص
اما كتبته بالمقتصر ليلا يتوهم القاري باني بحلم في كلامي لاني رايت اشيا كثيره وما
كتبتها ولا بقت في بالي منذ اربعة وخمسين سنه لاني لما كتبت هل سياحه وهذا

is called a *jarbūʿ*.[7] Then the king ordered his attendants to give me a pen and paper so that I could write the name down in my language. I took the paper and wrote the name in Arabic as well as French, for I knew how to read and write in French. After I'd written the words and they'd showed them to His Majesty the king, he studied me carefully.

"Who is this young man?" he asked my master. "What country is he from?"

"My lord, this young man is from Syria, in the Holy Land," my master said, looking down. "He belongs to the Maronite sect, which has been part of the Church of Saint Peter since the time of the apostles, from which it has never diverged, even to the present day."[8]

At that moment, Monseigneur the Dauphin, the king's son, entered the room. He was of medium height and quite rotund. People liked to point out that although both his father and firstborn son were kings—the latter being the king of Spain—the dauphin was not a king himself. He came forward to examine the animals and was amazed. He had an enormous drawing in which all the animals in the world were represented, with the exception of these particular ones. He summoned the king's physician, Monsieur Fagon, a learned man whose knowledge of medicine, natural science, and other such disciplines was unrivaled in all the world.

9.12

Monsieur Fagon appeared and looked at the animals, and the king's son asked him if he knew anything about them.

9.13

"Are they mentioned in any books of natural science?" he asked, and the physician replied that he'd never heard of such creatures, nor seen a drawing of them. Monseigneur the Dauphin called for an artist to add them to his illustration of wild beasts, and the king ordered the minister to hold the animals and their keeper in a place where they wouldn't be seen, until such time as Madame de Bourgogne returned from the hunt. She was the king's daughter-in-law—the wife of his son, the Duke of Bourgogne[9]—and the king loved her like a daughter.

That was the first time I had the great honor of seeing King Louis XIV, the sultan of France, in his council room, and I've faithfully recounted everything that took place, without any additions or omissions. But I've also been brief about it, so the reader won't suspect that I dreamt all of this up. After all, I witnessed many things on my journey that I haven't set down in writing, and that haven't remained in my memory these past fifty-four years. As I now write this

الحَبر كان في سنت ١٧٦٣ وانا كنت موجود في مدينة بهريس سنه ١٧٠٩ هل عاد يجي في بالي جميع الذي رايته وسمعته بالتمام كلا .

٩.١٤  فلنرجع الي ما كنا في صدده فخرجنا من ديوان الملك صحبة الوزير ودخلنا الي منزولنا وامر الوزير للقبجيه بان لا يدعوا احد يدخل لعندنا من اماره وغيرهم ليلا يتفرجوا علي الوحوش قبل ما تراهم كت الملك المذكوره كما امر حضرة الملك فاستقمنا الي حين ما صارة الساعه في العشره اعني قبل نصف الليل بساعتين. حينذٍ امر الوزير في حضورنا امامه فلما حضرنا مشي وامامه اربعة فنوده شمع الي ان وصلنا الي صراية مادام دبركوّنيا المذكوره كت الملك.

٩.١٥  حينذٍ دق الوزير وارسل ياخد اذن منها في الدخول وبعد هنيهه خرج من عندها سريتين وكلفوا الوزير بالدخول فدخل الوزير واحكي لها عن الوحوش وكيف ان الملك امر لا يراهم قبلك فامرت في احضارنا امامها فخرجوا السريات وادخلونا فلما دخلنا فرايت الملكه جالسه علي كرسي وامامها اولاد الاماره جالسين ايضًا علي الكراسي يلعبوا في الورق وامام كل واحد منهم كومة دهب وحولهم من السريات كنهم اقمار ولابسين عليهم الديباج المدهب الثمين فلما امتثلنا امام الاميره المذكوره وهي بالحسن والملبوس تفوق الجميع فاندارت وتفرجت علي الوحوش ونهضوا تلك الاماره ايضًا تفرجوا.

٩.١٦  اخيرًا صاروا يتفرجوا عليّ وعلي ملبوسي ويكشفوا ديالي ومنهم يمد يده الي صدري ومنهم يرفع قلبقي ويكشف راسي فتركوا فرجت الوحوش وصاروا يتفرجوا عليّ وعلي ملبوسي ويتضحكوا. اخيرًا سالت الاميره الي معلي ما هذا الغلام ومن اي بلاد فاحكي لها كما ذكرنا فقالت له ليش له دقن اعني شوارب فاجابها بان هذه عادة بلادهم ما يحلقوا شواربهم.

٩.١٧  فاستقمنا عند هذه الاميره مقدار نصف ساعه. اخيرًا خرجنا من عندها ومضينا صحبة الوزير وفيما نحن ماضيين تعارضة لنا بنت جميلة المنضر ولابسه ردا

account of my voyage, it is the year 1763. I visited Paris in 1709. Is it possible I could have retained everything I saw and heard in perfect detail? Surely not.

Let's get back to the story. We left the king's council room with the minister and went to our chambers. The minister told the chamberlains not to let anyone enter, royals or otherwise, so that they wouldn't see the animals before the king's daughter-in-law did, as His Majesty the king had ordered. We remained there until ten—that is, until two hours before midnight, at which point the minister summoned us. Once we'd joined him, he set off with us in tow, preceded by four men carrying candles. We arrived at the residence of Madame de Bourgogne, the king's daughter-in-law. **9.14**

The minister knocked and asked for permission to enter. A few moments later, two attendants emerged and invited the minister in. He went inside and spoke to Madame de Bourgogne, telling her about the animals, and how the king had ordered that no one was to see them before she did. She ordered us to enter. **9.15**

Her attendants emerged from the room and brought us inside. As we entered, I saw the princess seated on a chair. Before her sat all the young princes, playing cards. Each had a pile of gold coins before him. The princes were surrounded by attendants as radiant as moons, wearing sumptuous clothes embroidered with gold thread. We presented ourselves before the princess, who surpassed everyone in beauty and finery, and she turned to observe the animals. All the princes also got up to come and look.

Then they turned to study me and my costume. They lifted the hems of my outfit, and one reached out to touch my chest, while another took the calpac off my head. No longer interested in the animals, they gazed upon me and my clothes instead, laughing. **9.16**

"Who is this young man and what country does he comes from?" the princess asked my master. He explained who I was.

"Why does he have a beard?" she asked, meaning a mustache.

"This is the custom of their country," he replied. "The men do not shave their mustaches."

We stayed with the princess for half an hour, then left with the minister. On our way, we encountered a beautiful young girl wearing a royal cloak of embroidered silk. On her head was a spellbinding crown, encrusted with fine **9.17**

ملوكي من الديباج وفي راسها اكليل مرصع بجار كريمه مثل الماس وياقوت وزمرد شي يخطف النضر وحولها اربع سريات بثياب فاخره وحسن وجمال لخال لي بانها بنت الملك فلما راها الوزير وقف وعمل لها تمني بغاية الادب والاحتشام. حينذٍ سالته عنّا فاحكي لها قضية الوحوش التي معنا فامرته بانه يفرجها عليهم فاجابها سمعاً وطاعه وفي الحال اخدوا القفص من يدي الخدام وقدموه امامها. حينذٍ كشف الوزير الغطي من علي القفص وصار يفرجها فلما نضرت الي الوحوش فارتعدت وفزت هاربه فسعي الوزير في اثارها حتي يجرعها ويعاودها حتي تتفرج فما امكنه انه ترجع.

حينذٍ عاود الوزير وامرنا المسير الي صرايته فما لحقنا خطينا كام خطوه والا جانا الطلب من عند حضرة الملك مع سريتين من خواص سراياته وامروا الوزير من قبل الملك بانه يرسل ققص الوحوش والذي حامله فامرنا الوزير بالرجوع الي ان دخلنا قصر الملك فرايت واقفين ارجال ابطال طويلين القامه كانهم ارهاض مقدار اربعين بطل وهذا الرجال حراس ذات الملك في قصره. اخيراً دخلنا الي مخدع وهو منامة الملك. حينذٍ دخلوا السريات واخدوني صحبتهم واستقام الوزير ومعلمي خارج المقصوره. ١٨،٩

فلما انتهيت الي داخل رايت الملك جالس علي كرسي وامامه شمعتين وفي يده كتّاب بيقرا فيه ورايت من جانب الاخر سرير مجلل بالديباج وداخله اميره متكيه والبنت التي رايناها في الدرب واقفه من جانب السرير في الحال قدموني السريات امام تلك الاميره وجعلوا القفص فوق كرسي حتي تتفرج الاميره علي الوحوش وفي ذلك الوقت نهض الملك من علي الكرسي واجا الي طرفنا وفي يده شمعدان الدهب وصار يفرج الي تلك الاميره المذكور علي الوحوش وكت الفقير واقف بجانب الملك وعلي قلة عقلي وسداجتي تناولت الشمعدان من يد الملك ومن زيادة حلم الملك فاعطاني هو بعلمه باني فعلت هل امر بسداجه من غير معرفه لان الذي فعلته امر غريب لان من له جراعه يمد يده الي الملك وياخد الذي في يده وكان معلمي يحكي في بهريس ويقول هل غلام اخد الشمعدان من يد الملك. ١٩،٩

jewels like diamonds, rubies, and emeralds, and her entourage consisted of four beautiful attendants wearing sumptuous clothes. It struck me that she must be the king's daughter. When the minister saw her, he halted in his tracks and saluted her most cordially. The girl asked him who we were, and he explained the matter of the animals we had with us. She wanted to see them.

"With pleasure," he replied.

The attendants took the cage from me and placed it before the princess, and the minister removed the cover to show her the animals. When she saw them, she took fright and ran. The minister strode off in pursuit, encouraging her to come and see them, but he was unable to persuade her to return.

When the minister returned, he invited us to his residence. We hadn't taken more than a few steps in that direction when we received a summons from His Majesty, borne by two of his personal attendants. They ordered the minister to send the cage with the animals to the king, along with their bearer. So we turned around and headed back to the king's palace. Standing before it were forty tall, strapping men: the king's palace guards. Eventually we arrived at the king's bedroom. The attendants took me inside with them while the minister and my master remained outside the bedroom.

I saw the king seated on a chair. Before him were two candles, and he held a book in his hand, which he was reading. On the other side of the room was a bed surrounded by embroidered silk drapes. A princess was reclining on it; beside the bed stood the young girl I'd seen earlier. The attendants ushered me forward to the princess and placed the cage on a chair for her to see. The king rose, came over to us carrying a golden candelabrum, and showed the animals to the princess.

There I was, standing beside the king. Not knowing any better, I reached out to take the candelabrum from his hand. The king was magnanimous and handed it to me, knowing all too well that I'd acted out of inexperience, unaware of what I was doing. For it turned out that I had done something most extraordinary! Who would dare to reach out and take something from the king's hand? Later on, my master would tell everyone in Paris that this young man once took a candelabrum out of the hand of the king!

9.18

9.19

٢٠٠٩ اخيراً بعدما تفرجت الاميره فعاود الملك الي مكانه فاعطوني القفص فخرجت من
ذلك المكان فرايت الوزير ومعلمي واقفين في استنداري. حينئذٍ سرنا صحبة الوزير
الي ان وصلنا الي محلنا فرأينا سريتين مرسلين من قبل مادامه دوريان وهي من بنات
الملوك فامروا الوزير بان يرسل قفص الوحوش والذي حامله فامرني الوزير بالمضي
معهم ولما انتهيت الي قصرها رايت عندها جملة من الاميرات حتي يتفرجوا
علي الوحوش والذي حاملهم فلما تفرجوا علي الوحوش وعليّ ايضاً فارسلوني ايضاً
الي عند اميرة اخره ومن هناك الي عند غير اميره ولا زل ياخذوني من مكان الي
مكان حتي مضي ساعتين بعد نصف الليل. اخيراً عاودوني الي منزول الذي نحن
قاطنين فيه وكان معلمي في استنضاري فاستقمنا تلك الليله الي ان اصبح الصباح
ونحن في ارغد عيش.

٢١٠٩ فاتفق بان مادامه دوبركونيا التي هي كنت الملك الذي مركها اصبحت بجازها
منحرف من تعبها في الصيد القنص التي عانته قبل بيوم كما ذكرنا فاجتمعوا عندها نسا
الاماره حتي يسلوها وهي متكيه في سريرها وكان بينهم اميره سمعت خبر الوحوش
فزادة تراهم فاستمنت مادامه المذكوره كنت الملك بانها تامر في احضارهم امامها حتي
تتفرج عليهم ففي الحين ارسلت من قبلها خادم الي عند الوزير المذكور تامره بانه يرسل
قفص الوحوش والشرقي حامل القفص فلما وصل المرسال الي عند الوزير فامره في
الامر المذكور في الحال ارسل فاحضرنا امامه وامرنا بالمضي مع ذلك الخادم.

٢٢٠٩ فلما انتهينا الي قصر الاميره فدخلوني وحدي وانا حامل القفص الي مقصورة
الاميره ومكان منامتها فلما دخلت رايت ذلك السرير الملوكي وهو مجلل بالديباج الثمين
وداخله متكيه تلك الاميره التي هي فريدة عصرها من الحسن والجمال وحول السرير
جالسين نسا الاماره كانهم الاقمار ولابسين حلل ما بقدر اوصف لميعهم من كثرة
الجواهر والحجار الثمينه المرصعه فيهم.

٢٣٠٩ اخيراً قدموني امام الاميره المتكيه داخل السرير فلما امثلت امامها تركت القفص
من يدي وانحنيت الي الارض وعملت لها ثمني مثل ما علمني معلمي ولما انحنيت تباين

Once the princess had finished observing the animals and the king returned    **9.20**
to his seat, they gave me the cage and I took my leave. I found the minister
and my master waiting for me. We went back to our residence with the minister and found two attendants waiting there. They had been sent by Madame
d'Orléans, a princess. The attendants asked the minister to send the cage with
the animals to her, along with their keeper. The minister told me to go with
them. Once I arrived at the palace, I saw that there was a gathering of princesses. They'd all come to see the animals and their keeper!

When they were done scrutinizing the animals—and me as well—they sent
me off to see another princess, and from her to yet another one. I kept being
taken from place to place until two o'clock in the morning! Finally, they took
me back to our residence, where I found my master waiting, and we passed a
most comfortable night.

It so happened that Madame de Bourgogne, the daughter-in-law of the    **9.21**
king, had woken up that morning feeling unwell, following the strenuous
efforts of the previous day's hunt. So the wives of the princes all gathered at
her residence to keep her company while she lay in bed. Among them was a
princess who'd heard about the animals and wanted to see them. She begged
Madame de Bourgogne to have the animals brought in. So they sent off a
servant right away to find the minister, asking him to send the cage with the
animals, along with the Oriental porter. The minister accordingly sent for us.
When we appeared, he ordered us to go with the servant.

When we arrived at the princess's palace, they brought me alone with the    **9.22**
cage to her private residence and bedroom. I went in and saw the royal bed
draped with fine brocade curtains. Reclining on it was the princess, whose
beauty was without peer among all the women of her epoch. Seated around
her were the wives of the princes, as radiant as moons, wearing dresses that
glittered luminously from all the jewels set in them. The sight was simply
indescribable.

They ushered me forward toward the princess reclining on the bed. I pre-    **9.23**
sented myself, put the cage down, and bowed deeply, greeting the princess
with the deference my master had taught me. As I was leaning forward, one of
the princesses noticed the point of the silver-plated dagger I'd slipped into my
belt. She reached out and grasped it.

الي واحده من الاميرات طرف السكين المفضضه التي كنت شاكها فمدت يدها
ومسكت السكين وقالت للحاضرين تعالوا تفرجوا علي سيف المسلم فلما سمعت منها
هل كلام في الحال كشفت ديل الجوخه وقلت لها لا يا سيدتي ما هو سيف الذي
بتريه هذه سكينه فلما سمعت باسم سكينه في الحال ابعدت عني وتغيرة الوانها لكن ما
عطت الشي بالشي واستقاموا الاميرات يتفرجوا علي الوحوش وعلي ملبسي.

٢٤.٩ اخيرًا اطلقوني فحلت القفص وخرجت من ذلك المكان فرأيت معلمي واقف من
بعد وشاهد الحاليه فلما تقدمت الي عنده نضر اليّ بعين الزجر والغضب وما راد
يكلمني من شدة غضبه ولما وصلنا الي منزولنا مد يده الي زناري واخد السكينه
وخبطها في الارض وراد يكسرها.

٢٥.٩ والتفت اليّ وصار يوبخني علي فعلي وقلت عقلي بقوله لي بان اول مره تواقحت
واخدت الشمعدان من يد الملك وهذه جساره عظيمه ما سبقت لواحد غيرك لكن
حضرة ملكًا حليم ولزياده حلمه ترك الشمعدان حتي تاخده من يده والان ثاني وقاحه
التي صدرت منك بقولك للاميره بان ما هو سيف هذه سكينه اما بتعرف بان الحاكم
منبه ومقرط تقريط كلي حتي الملك نفسه بان كل من انوجد معه سكينه براس او
بنيار يرسلوه الي مركب الجرا عني الكبيره يستقيم مابد وبعضهم يحكموا عليهم بالقتل
اذا كانوا مشبوهين بقولهم بان السكينه والبنيار عدو محني خلاف السيخ مشهور
بيتوقي الانسان من صاحبه الذي حامله ولكن السكينه او البنيار يمكنك تقرب الي
عدوك وتضربه بغير انه يعرف وما هو مستحضر منك ولاجل هل سبب امروا الحكام
بان لا احد يحمل معه سكينته او بنيار بحرف. حينٍ قلي انكان هل تنبيه والتقريط
ساير في مدينة بهريس كم بالحري في صراية سلطان فرأنسا بان وقع مثلك يدخل
الي بيت منامته وهو حامل سكين محرفه مثل هذه لكن الله نجاك ونجاني من هل
مصيبه وللوقت اخد السكين وكسر حرفها وابقاها معه. اخيرًا استعدرت منه بقولي
له ما كنت بعرف فقلي لاجل انك فعلت هذا عن غشم الله نجاك وحضرة الملك
ما واخدك.

"Come and see the Muslim's sword!" she cried to everyone in attendance.[10]

Hearing these words, I drew back the tail of my coat and said, "No, my lady. What you see here isn't a sword but a dagger."

Upon hearing me utter the word "dagger," she drew back from me and the color of her face changed. But she paid the dagger no more regard, and the other princesses gazed upon the animals and at my clothes.

Eventually, they let me go and I picked up the cage and left. My master, who arrived after I did and had seen what happened, was waiting for me. As I approached, he glared at me furiously and was so angry that he refused to say a word to me. Once we'd arrived at our residence, he reached out to my belt, seized the dagger, and threw it to the ground, attempting to break it!

Then he turned to me and began scolding me for my actions and my heedlessness. "First, you have the audacity to swipe a candelabrum right out of the king's hand!" he said. "I've never heard of anyone behaving so outrageously! Thank goodness our king is so magnanimous, and deigned to permit you to take the candelabrum from his hand. But now you've gone and done it again! You told the princess that this isn't a sword but a dagger! Don't you know that there's an absolute prohibition—which applies even to the king himself—which states that anyone found carrying a dagger or a poniard will be sent to the galleys, where he'll spend the rest of his life? Some have even been sentenced to death if they were merely suspected of being criminals."

My master explained, "It's often said that daggers and poniards are a hidden enemy, unlike a foil, which is there in plain sight, after all. You can always be on your guard when someone is carrying a foil, but a dagger or poniard? They give you the element of surprise against your enemy. That's why the authorities have forbidden anyone from carrying them!

"With this prohibition in effect across all of Paris, who would have the nerve to march right into the palace, into the king's bedroom no less, brandishing a pointed blade?" he demanded. "Somehow God saved you—and saved me as well—from a real predicament!"

He broke off the blade of the dagger and took it away.

"But I didn't know!" I offered by way of apology.

"It's only because you didn't know any better that God saved you, and that His Majesty didn't hold you to account!"

9.24

9.25

٢٦،٩ حينذٍ سرت اساله عن تلك الاماكن التي دخلناها وعن تلك الاميره التي رايتها في حجرة الملك والبنت التي كانت واقفه بجانبها التي تعارضت لنا في الدرب لعلها بنت الملك قال لا ولكن هذه قصه طويله بريد اعرفك فيها حتي تعرف وتحكي بالذي رايته فان سالت عن الاميره التي في حجرة الملك وبيت منامته هذه تسما ماضامه دميتنون وهي زوجة الملك والبنت التي رايتها هي تربايه الملكة المذكوره جاعلتها بنتها بالتربيه فسالت معلي هل هذه هي زوجة الملك وهي خاليه من كل حسن وهيبه وما عليها من اشارة ملكه .

٢٧،٩ فاجابني بان هذه قصتها طويله عجيبه والملك اخدها له زوجه لحسن عقلها العجيب الذي ما له مثيل في كل مملكته ولاجل هذا عشقها الملك وكان السبب انها كانت سريه من سريات ماضامه دريان وهذه الاميره المذكوره كان يحبها الملك قوي كثير وكان يتردد لعندها كثير من الاوقات وكان يراء هل بنت المذكوره عندها وينبسط من الفاظها العدبه واحتشامها وحسن اخلاقها وعقلها الرفيع .

٢٨،٩ فذات يوم من الايام ارسل مكتوب الي هذه الاميره ودعاها بانه تحضر لعنده فلما وصلتها المشرفه من يد الملك فحارت في امرها كيف ترد جواب لحضرة الملك وتستعدر منه لانها انوجدت في ذلك الوقت مزاجها منحرف قوي كثير وما امكها بانه ترد جواب لحضرة الملك . حينذٍ امرت الي سريتها مادامه مينتنون المذكوره بان ترد الجواب لحضرة الملك وتستعدر منه في تاخير مضيها لعند عزته فباشرة تلك السريه في تكمل امر سيدتها وكتبت مكتوب ونضمت فيه ديباجه لحضرة الملك واستعدار عظيم منظوم من الفاظ عدبه ذات معاني رقيقه ياخد خاطر الملك حتي لما قوي الملك ذلك المكتوب اندهش من حسن الفاظه ومعانيه فزاد حبه في تلك البنت السريه الذي مر ذكرها وراد يجيبها لعنده ويعلي منازلها فما رضيت زوجته الملكه ليلا يصدر بسببها شك للغير لانها كانت امراه خايفة الله قديسه .

٢٩،٩ فبعد كام سنه توفت الملكة[1] وانتقلت الي رحمة الله وصار لها جناز محتفل عظيم ودقت جميع نواقيس بهريس حتي دقوا ناقوز الكبير الذي بينسمع رنته من سبع ساعات

---

١ الأصل: الملك.

I asked him about the various places we'd visited and about the princess I'd    9.26
seen in the king's chamber, as well as the young girl standing beside her whom
we'd met on our walk with the minister. Was she perhaps the king's daughter?

"No," he replied. "It's a long story, but let me tell it to you so you know
what you're talking about when you tell the story yourself. The princess in the
king's bedroom is called Madame de Maintenon, and is the wife of the king.
The young girl you saw is the ward of the queen, who raised her as her own
daughter and educated her."

"*That* was the king's wife?" I asked my master. "But she wasn't beautiful or
majestic at all, and she wasn't wearing any royal tokens."

"Hers is a long and peculiar story," he replied. "The king took her as his    9.27
wife because of her remarkable intelligence, which has no equal in the whole
kingdom. That's why, in fact, he fell in love with her. She'd been an attendant of
Madame d'Orléans, the princess with whom the king was in love.[11] He would
visit the princess often, and would find this young woman with her. Her conversation skills, fine manners, and keen wit delighted the king."

One day, the king sent a letter to the princess, summoning her to visit    9.28
him.[12] The princess, who was feeling quite unwell at the time, could not accept
the invitation, but had no idea how to decline it politely. So she ordered her
attendant Madame de Maintenon to reply to His Majesty the king, begging his
forgiveness for delaying her visit. The young woman set about fulfilling her
mistress's request. She wrote a letter conveying her regrets, which began with
an overture to the king, followed by a grand, versified apology composed in
beautiful language and using refined expressions. The king was dazzled by the
letter, and his love for the princess's attendant grew. He wished to bring her to
his court and elevate her station. But his wife, the queen, wouldn't consent.
She was a saintly woman who feared God, and didn't want any suspicions to
arise from the matter.

After a few years, the queen passed away. A great funeral was held for    9.29
her, and all the church bells of Paris tolled, including the great bell, whose
sound can be heard in places as far as seven hours away from the city. The
queen's body was transferred to the Church of Saint-Denis, which houses the

مسافه. اخيراً نقلوا جسدها الي كنيسة القديس ديونيسيوس حيث مقبره ملوك فرنسا جميعهم والفقير زرت قبرها وقبور كل الملوك الفرنساويه المدفونين هناك.

٣٠٩ فمن بعدما مضي من وفاتها اربعين يوماً حينذٍ تشاوروا مدبرين الملك حتي يزوجوا الملك وبما ان ملوك المسيحيين مسوحين وما بيزوج لهم بانهم يتزوجوا مرتين فارسلوا واخدوا اذن من الحبر الروماني في زيجة ملكهم الضروريه لاجل النسل فبعدما وصلهم الاذن تقدموا الي حضرة الملك وطلبوا منه بانه يتزوج وكانوا افتكروا في اميره بديعة الحسن والجمال وهي من نسل ملوك شريفة الاصل والنسب فلما اخبروه عنها فابا وما قبل في الزيجه مع تلك الاميره وقال لهم انا باخد ماضامه مينتنون المذكوره زوجة لي.

٣١٩ فلما سمعوا منه هل كلام بهتوا وارتموا علي اقدامه وقالوا له كيف سيدنا وملكا بترضي بانك تتزوج بواحده خدامه وهي غربت البلاد وما منعرف اصلها لانها من بلاد صوايا وتلك البلاد هن اعدا لسيادتك وايش بيقلوا عنك الملوك لما بيسمعوا بانك تزوجة بواحده مثل هذه مقدوفه فاجابهم الملك بوجه مغضب وقال كل من عنده[١] كلام يلمه فارتموا علي اقدامه ثاني مره واتوسلوا اليه بانه يغير نيته فما امكن واستقام علي قوله فلما راواه مستقيم الملك علي رايه فقالوا له يا ملكا وولي نعمتنا انكان حضرتك رضيت بان تكون هذه زوجتك نحن ما منرضي بان تكون علينا ملكه فاحتد الملك بالغضب وتهددهم بالنفي انكان ما بيرضوا بذلك الامر الذي نفذ من فمه فخرجوا من امامه حتي يتشاوروا ويردوا له الجواب.

٣٢٩ فما راواء الا فهم يرتموا علي ابن الملك الدوفين حتي يمنع والده عن هل الامر ويصلحهم مع الملك فدخل مون سنير الدوفين علي والده وصار يترجاه بانه يغير نيته عن هل امر الفظيع فاجابه والده علي الفور روح الزم قلعتك اعني امرعليه بالحبس وبعده اجتمعت اكابر مدينة بهريس وكتبوا عرض حال للملك بانهم ما بيقبلوا بان تكون هذه الغريه عليهم ملكه فلما راء الملك بان قامت اهل البلد والقواد واكابر

١ الأصل: عند.

mausoleum of the kings of France—I myself visited her tomb, as well as the tombs of all the French kings there.

Forty days after her death, the king's ministers held a council to discuss the matter of the king's marriage. Because Christian kings are anointed by God, they're not permitted to remarry. The ministers had to seek the permission of the pope to sanction the marriage, an action necessary to preserve the royal lineage. Once they received the pope's permission, the ministers went before His Majesty and asked him to consider remarrying. They had in mind a splendidly beautiful princess whose lineage included kings of great nobility. But when they suggested her to the king, he refused. 9.30

"I will take Madame de Maintenon as my wife."

Baffled, the ministers threw themselves at the king's feet in protest. 9.31

"Sire, how could you consent to marry a serving girl, and a foreigner to boot?" they asked. "We don't know anything about her except that she comes from Savoy, a country hostile to your realm. And what will all the other kings say when they learn you've married a servant?"

The king glowered, and told them to keep their advice to themselves. The ministers threw themselves down at his feet once again, begging him to reconsider. But the king refused. When the ministers saw that he wouldn't change his mind, they addressed him once again.

"Your Majesty, you are our king and benefactor," they began. "Yet, even if Your Majesty should consent to let this woman be your wife, we will not accept her as our queen!"

Furious, the king threatened to send them into exile if they did not accept his decree. They then left to consult with one another about how to respond.

The ministers felt they had no choice but to turn to the king's son, the dauphin, hoping he could dissuade his father and reconcile the ministers with their king. So Monseigneur the Dauphin went to see the king and begged him to change his mind about this scandalous matter. 9.32

"Go back to your palace and stay there!" the king retorted, putting him under house arrest.

After that, the dignitaries of the city of Paris gathered to draft a statement declaring that they would never accept the stranger as their queen. Seeing that the townspeople, the military officers, and the nobles of the realm were all of

الدوله علي رأي راي وما رادوا بان الملك يتزوج بهذه البنت الغريبه حينذٍ انثني عن رايه وابان لهم بانه عدل عن زِبحتها وهمدت الامور وبطل القال والقيل ورجع كل شي لاصله.

٣٣،٩ واستقام الملك بغير زِبحه عام كامل وفي تلك الايام باشر في عمارة ورساليا وبنا فيها صرايا ما لها مثيل في ساير الاقاليم بساتين وروضات ومتنزهات شتي شي بيفوق الوصف وخبرها مشهور عند ساير الملوك المسيحيه والامر الغريب هو ان نهر السينا وهو نهر كبير مثل نهر الفراه فايت من وري ورساليا وما بينهم جبل عالي فراد الملك بان يدخل ذلك النهر الي ورساليا لِجمع جميع المعلمين وامرهم بان يدخلوا ذلك النهر ويجروه داخل تلك البساتين الذي نصبوها داير صرايا الملك في ورساليا فتشاوروا المعلمين فما راوا لها منفد الا ان يقطعوا الجبل ويجروها.

٣٤،٩ فلما اعرضوا ذلك علي حضرة الملك فاجابهم ما الفايده اذا كان النهر جاري في وطاه انا بريد بان الماء يجري من علو حطي يتسلط علي البساتين والاراضي نحاروا المعلمين في امرهم وردوا جواب للملك بان هذا شي ما يمكن والامر لله ثم اليك واظهروا العجز بين اياديه فانحصر الملك من مقولهم بانه ما يمكن. حينذٍ تقدم رجل معلم وباس ديل الملك وقال له يا سيدي انا بحضر لك الماء من فوق اعلي الجبل الا بيتكلف عليك شي كثير من الدراهم فلما سمع الملك منه هل خطاب فامر بان يكتبوا له امر مرسوم في جميع الذي يصرفه وامضاه بخط يده وقله ان كمت الذي قلته الك ما تتمنا علي وتطلب ما تريده.

٣٥،٩ فقبل الارض امام الملك وخرج وابتدا يباشر في ذلك الصنيع العجيب فاولاً امر في سكب طرنبات من الحديد علي جنس الطواب يكونوا طوال ودواليب من البولاد ومرقات بولاد ايضاً فبعدما كملوا علي رسم الذي رسمه لهم حينذٍ ارسل فاحضر البنايين وامرهم بان يحفروا حفره غميقه بجانب النهر وبجانبها حفره ايضاً غميقه وهلم جرا حتي وصلوا الي قمت الجبل وبعده بتعمير حايطين من جانب تلك الحفره وركب اول دولاب وبجانب الدولاب طرنبه.

the same mind, opposed to his marriage to the foreign girl, the king reversed course and made it clear to them that he'd decided not to marry her after all. Things then settled down, the gossip ceased, and everything went back to normal.

The king remained unwed for a whole year. During that time, he initiated the construction of Versailles, building a palace unequaled in any part of the world. He decorated it with all sorts of indescribable gardens, parks, and promenades. The palace is renowned among all the Christian kings.

9.33

A curious aspect of Versailles's construction concerns the fact that the River Seine, a great river like the Euphrates, passes behind Versailles, separated from it by a tall mountain. The king wanted to bring the river to Versailles, so he gathered all the engineers and ordered them to channel the river into the gardens surrounding the palace. The engineers consulted among themselves, and agreed that the only way to achieve this was to cut a channel through the mountain.

They presented this idea to His Majesty the king.

9.34

"What would be the point of the river flowing from the *base* of the mountain?" he said. "I want the water to descend from the *top* of the mountain onto the gardens and grounds!" The engineers were baffled, and told the king such a thing was impossible.

"There's nothing we can do," they said, cowering meekly before him. At this, the king grew angry. Suddenly, one of the engineers came forward and kissed the hem of his robe.

"Sire, I'll bring the water down from the top of the mountain," he said. "But it'll cost you a pretty penny."

When the king heard this, he ordered an edict to be drafted, granting the engineer the necessary funds. "If you are true to your word, I'll give you whatever you wish," said the king, signing the edict. "Name your price."

The man kissed the ground before the king and set off to embark upon this wondrous construction.[13] First, he ordered some long iron pumps to be cast, in the style of cannons. He also called for some steel waterwheels and pistons. Once they'd been fashioned according to his design, he summoned some builders and ordered them to dig a deep trench alongside the river. A second trench was then dug beside the first, and this was repeated all the way to the summit of the mountain. He then had a wall built on either side of each trench, installed the first waterwheel, and placed a pump beside it.

9.35

٣٦٠٩ وجري الما علي ذلك الدولاب فلما دار الدولاب فصار يدخل المزق في الطرنبه ويخرج الي ان انتلت الطرنبه ودفعت الماء الي حفرت الثانيه التي هي اعلي من الاولي بقامتين ولما انتلت الحفرة الثانيه ولها شيب مثل شيب الطاحون يسكب علي ثاني دلاب واذا دار الدلاب يشتغل المزق الذي في الطرنبا[1] وبيدفع الماء الي ثالث حفره ومن ثالث حفره الي الرابعه وهلم جرا حتي اتصل الماء الي قمت الجبل وانحدر علي بساتين الملك ماء وافر .

٣٧٠٩ حينٍ امر الملك بتعمير برك بكار وسنبيلات من حجر يشبه ادراج تجري المياه من فوقهم وتنحدر الي الاسفل ونصبوا اشجار رارنج وليمون وبكاد وغير فواكي كلها مصنوعه من تنك ولها كوزين بيدخلها الماء حتي كل ورقه من هذه الاشجار يخرج منها الماء وكذلك تحت تلك الاشجار مرج وفي داخل المرج كوزين رفاع يخرج منهم الماء ومن اجله صاغين ممشا عريض بيسع اربع زلام اذا تمشوا فيه بالعرض وطوله حكم مايتين دراع وتخرج المياه من جانبيه بتنحدر مياة اليمين علي الشمال ومياه الشمال علي اليمين وبتلتم المياه في بعضها وبتبقي كانها قبو من الماء والذين بيسيروا تحته ما بتنقط عليهم ولا نقطة ماء وكل هذا من عزم الماء الذي قايمه منحدر من علو الجبل .

٣٨٠٩ وفايض هذا الماء جاري في نهر زغير في البستان ويخرج من ورساليا وبيلتم في النهر الذي جاري من خلف ذلك الجبل وبعد كل هذا ناصبين اشجار مغبقه في بعضها البعض وصايره كمثل الحرش وناصبين له سياجات من الجانبين من جنس سجر بيلف علي بعضه وبيورق وبيحبك حتي اذا ضربت عود النشاب ما بيخرق وراخيين في ذلك الحرش من ارانب وغزلان وما يشبه ذلك من الوحوش وهذا لاجل الصيد والقنص وطول هذا الحرش مسيرة سفر يوم واكثر وهذه الوحوش بيولدوا وبينمو وبيكتروا الي يومنا هذا الدواليب بتشتغل والماء بينحدر من قمة الجبل وان سالت عن محاسن هل مكان شي شتي بيفوق الوصف وما كتبت منه الا القليل من الكثير .

٣٩٠٩ ونرجع فيما كا في صدده فلما كملت جميع تلك العماير والصرايات المكلفه المشيده والبستان وجري الماء كما ذكرنا وكل شي صار علي غاية المراد حينٍ امر الملك بان ينقلوا

---

١ الأصل: الطرنبا.

The water flowed through the waterwheel and, as the wheel turned, the    9.36
piston would enter the pump, fill it with water, and push that water into the
second trench, which was two fathoms higher than the first. When that trench,
which sloped downward like a millrace, had filled up with water, it would spill
onto the second wheel. When the wheel turned, it would work the piston in
the pump, pushing the water into the third trench. From there, it flowed into
the fourth, and so on and so forth until it reached the summit of the mountain,
whereupon the water coursed down copiously into the king's gardens.

The king ordered the construction of some large pools and stone fountains    9.37
resembling terraces, and the water flowed down over them. They also erected
tin fountains in the shapes of various fruit trees, such as orange, lemon, and
citron. Water flowed to each tree through a pair of pipes, and spouted out of
every leaf![14] Beneath each tree was a meadow with a couple of thin pipes that
also sprayed water. There was a broad walkway, as wide as four men walking side by side, and two hundred cubits in length. Water spouted over the
walkway from both sides: The fountains on the left side sprayed water to the
right side and the fountains on the right side sprayed water to the left side.
The streams met in the middle, forming a watery vault! And yet, those who
walked beneath it didn't feel a single drop, thanks to the power of the water
descending from the top of the mountain.

The excess water flowed into a small river that ran through the gardens    9.38
and then left Versailles and rejoined the river running behind the mountain.
In addition to all of this, a great number of trees were planted in a dense fashion, creating a sort of forest. On its borders, there was a hedge formed out of a
certain species of tree that coils endlessly upon itself, sprouting so many leaves
and tangled branches that even an arrow shot at it wouldn't pass through.
Inside the forest, they let loose rabbits, gazelles, and other wild animals to be
hunted. The forest extended for a day's journey by foot from one end to the
other, and the animals soon proliferated throughout.

The waterwheels continue to work to this day, and the water still comes
down that mountain. The glories of the place are simply indescribable.
I haven't done them justice with this humble account.

Let us return to our story. Once the construction was complete and the    9.39
plans had come to fruition—the splendid and lofty palaces, the garden, the
watercourses—the king ordered all his things transferred from his palace in

جميع الموجود في صرايته التي هي في بهريس الي الصرايه التي في ورساليا ووضع كرسيه في مكان يليق بالملوك وجمع جميع اكابر دولته ووزراه وحواشيه في ورساليا واروي الي اهل بهريس الحرد عليهم بما انهم ما قبلوا بان مادامه دمنتينون تكون ملكه عليهم ولاجل هذا ارسل فاجابها الي صرايته وتزوج بها بزنبحه مسيحيه بجميع شروطها واستقام في ورساليا الي الممات وما عاد دخل الي مدينة بهريس وهذا الذي احكالي معلي عن خبر هذه الملكه التي ريتها متكيه في السرير في حجرة الملك.

٩،٤٠ اخيرًا استقمت انا الفقير في صراية الملك ثمانية ايام الي حين ما كمل القفص الذي امر في عملانه دلفين ابن الملك ودخلوا تلك الوحوش الي ذلك القفص وفي تلك الثانية ايام كنت ادور في صراية الملك وما احد يتعارضني وبعده رجعت الي مدينة بهريس وكان معلي استكرا بيت علي خصيته فقطنا في ذلك البيت الذي هو فوق جسر مار ميخاييل وكانوا يزورونه اناس كثير من اكابر بهريس وهو يزورهم وياخذني معه حتي اتفرج علي صراياتهم واماكنهم المكلفه وحسن نظامهم.

٩،٤١ فيوم من الايام دخلنا الي بيت رجل امير فرايت في صدر الساله صورة رجل وماسك بيده طير ولكن يبتبين للناظر كان يده خارجه من الصوره مع الطير فلما تاملت الفقير في هذه الصوره فتيقن عندي بان يده خارجه فقالولي الحاضرين بان هذا تصور فما قدرت اصدق حتي واحد منهم تعلا ولمس الصوره بيده. حيندٍ صدقت وشكرت ذلك المعلم الذي صور هذه الصورة العجيبه ثم احكولي بان هذه الصوره نسخة تصور معلم بيترو المصور وهذه مشتراتها بخمسماية غرش.

٩،٤٢ وخبر هذا المعلم غرب عجيب لان هذا المعلم في زمان صبوته كان اجير نغال وزري المنظر فاتفق له يوم من الايام فنظر الي بنت احد الامرا وكانت بديعه في الحسن والجمال فريدة عصرها فلما نظرها وهي بتتمشا مع اولاد الاماره فصار يتشخص فيها وتملك قلبه بحبها بهذا المقدار حتي صار يتبعها من مكان الي مكان حتي وصلت الي صرايه ابوها وغابت عن نظره فصار يترصد خروجها من الصرايا لاجل التنزه كهادة تلك

Paris to the palace in Versailles.[15] He placed his throne in Versailles in a suitably august setting and brought all the dignitaries of his realm, the ministers, and the courtiers to Versailles, in order to punish the people of Paris for not accepting Madame de Maintenon as their queen. That was why he brought her to his palace in Versailles and married her there in a Christian wedding, all of its conditions fulfilled.[16] The king remained in Versailles until his death, and never returned to Paris.

This is the story my master told me about the queen I saw reclining in the king's room.

I spent eight days at the king's palace, during which time the cage ordered by the king's son, the dauphin, was completed and the animals were placed inside. During those eight days, I toured the palace freely; no one prevented me from going wherever I wanted. Finally, I returned to Paris, where my master had rented a house at his own expense. We resided in that house, which was above Pont Saint-Michel. We were visited by many of Paris's dignitaries, and my master would also visit them, bringing me along to see their lavish mansions and well-designed properties. 9.40

One day, we visited the home of a prince. At the rear of the salon, I saw a painting of a man holding a bird in his hand. From the onlooker's perspective, however, it seemed as though the man's hand and the bird protruded out of the picture. I studied the painting and was convinced his hand was outside the frame, but those present told me it was nothing but a picture. I wouldn't believe it until one of them rose and touched the painting with his hand. Finally convinced, I praised the master who had produced that remarkable painting, which, I was told, was a copy of an original by the artist Pietro.[17] It had been purchased for five hundred piasters. 9.41

The story of that artist is extraordinary indeed. During his youth, he was a cobbler's apprentice, and an ugly one at that. One day, he spied the daughter of a prince, whose beauty was unrivaled by any other maiden. She was out for a walk with some other royals, and as he stared at her, his heart was overcome with love. So much so, in fact, that he followed her from one place to another until she arrived at her father's palace and disappeared from sight. The youth began to lie in wait near the palace, waiting for her to emerge every now and then when she would go for a walk, as was the custom in those lands. When she did, he'd follow her and gaze at her. 9.42

البلاد فكان يتبعها وينظر اليها وهذا صدر منه كام مره والبنت ما علي بالها منه الي
ان اولاد الاماره الذين كانوا يتمشوا معها صاروا يهنواها علي هذا العاشق الزريف
المحسن الذي ما له نظير .

٤٣،٩ وفاغتاظة البنت غاية الغيظ ومضت احكت للامير والدها في فعل هذا الصبي
وكيف انه حيث ما مضت بيتبعها وبينظر اليها وصارة معيره لاولاد الاماره فغضب
الامير وارسل فاحضر الغلام امامه وساله بوجه مغضب ما بالك بتتبع بنتي الاميره
حيث ما مضت ايش هو قصدك منها فاجابه الغلام علي الفور اني حبيتها فلما سمع
الامير منه هذا الكلام اتضحك علي قلت عقله وصار يلاطفه بالكلام قايلاً له هل
بتريد تتزوجها فقال له نعم . حيندٍ قال له الامير ماذا تعطي نقضها فاجابه الغلام
اطلب مني ما تريد فقال له الامير بريد منك بان تصور لي صورتها بيدك وان
اتممت هذا الامر انا بعطيك بنتي تكون زوجه لك ولكن بشرط ان عدت تتبعتها
بعمل علي شنقك .

٤٤،٩ فرضي الغلام في هذا الشرط وخرج من عند الامير وهو فرحان وصار يتشخوط
في الحيطان لعله بيقدر يصور في الحيط صورة تلك البنت فما امكنه ياتي بحركه في
هل صناعه فاتطر بانه يخدم عند احد المصورين ويصحن دهانات فاستقام مده
من الزمان عند ذلك المصور وهو يطلع علي شغل معلمه وكيف انه بيرسم وبيركب
الدهانات فابتدي يرسم من عقله صورة تلك البنت لانها كانت مصوره في عقله من
شدة العشق الذي كان له .

٤٥،٩ اخيرًا اتقن صورتها بغاية الكمال فلما كمت الصوره مضي الي عند الامير واعطاه
تلك الصوره فلما تقرس فيها الامير فتجب من حسن تصويرها وصناعة التي فيها فما
سدق بان الغلام صورها فساله من هو الذي صور هذه الصوره فاجابه الغلام هذه
تصوير يدي كما اشرطت علي فما اعتقد في كلامه وراد يعرف حقيقة الامر فارسل
واحضر الي عنده اربع معلمين مصورين وارواهم تلك الصوره وسالهم هل تعرفوا

This happened several times without the girl taking any notice. But then the children of the other princes who accompanied her on her walks began to congratulate her on having such a charming and handsome admirer.

This made her angry, and so she went to speak to her father about the young man, telling him how he followed her everywhere, staring constantly, and making her into a laughingstock among the prince's other descendants. The prince was furious and had the young man brought before him. 9.43

"Who do you think you are, following my daughter the princess wherever she goes?" he asked angrily. "What do you want with her?"

"I love her," the young man replied.

Hearing these words, the prince laughed aloud at the boy's ignorance.

"Would you like to marry her?" he asked sweetly.

"Yes."

"And what will you offer as her dowry?"

"Ask what you wish," the young man said.

To this, the prince said, "I wish for you to paint her portrait. If you do that, I'll let you marry her, on the condition that if you continue to follow her, I'll have you hanged."

The young man agreed to this condition, and left the prince's house in a state of elation. He set about scribbling on walls, trying to sketch the girl's portrait, but failed to make any headway. So he was compelled to work for a period as apprentice to an artist, grinding paints while he studied the master at work, learning his techniques of drawing and his methods for composing different paints. Eventually, he set about drawing the portrait of the girl from memory, as her image was emblazoned in his mind, so deep was his longing for her. 9.44

At last, the young man perfected the portrait. He went to see the prince and presented him with the painting. The prince studied it and was astonished by its fine craftsmanship. He couldn't believe it was the work of that young man. 9.45

"Who painted this?" he asked him.

"This is the work of my own hand," the young man replied. "Just as you stipulated."

The prince refused to believe him and wanted to hear the truth. He summoned four master artists and showed them the painting.

"Do you know the artist who painted this?" he asked them.

هذه تصوير اينا معلم فاجابوه ما في هل بلاد معلم بيقدر يصور مثل هذه الصوره ولا في الهند ولا هي تصوير انسان يا ملاك يا شيطان.

فبعدما تحقق الامير منهم حقيقة الامر رفع منها ان تصور ذلك الغلام. حينٍ دعاه امامه وعاد يستخبر منه هل هو صور تلك الصوره بالتحقيق فاجابه الغلام قايلاً الخص يا سيدي انكان احد من المصورين بيقدر يصور مثلها يكون انا الكاذب فقله الامير صدقت يا ابني ولكن قلت لاجل تصديقي بانك بتقدر تصور صوره بنتي انا زوجتها وان ردت بعطيك اختها لاجل اقراري لك.

فلما سمع الغلام بان البنت تزوجة في الحال زاغ عقله وتلهوز وخرج من امامه وهو كالمجنون وما عاد يعقل علي شي من شدة غرامه وعشقه لتلك البنت وصار يسوح في البراري والقفار فلما مضه الجوع والعري دخل الي مدينه من المدن وخدم عند رجل مصور يصحن دهانات باللقمه فاستقام عنده مده من الزمان فراه معتني بصوره جميله فريده وراد بذلك ياخد الاباحه علي باقيت المصورين فلما كملت تلك الصوره صمدها في سدر مكان ومضي يدعي المعلمين حتي يجوا يرو تلك الصوره ويشهدوا له بالمعلميه فلما مضي المعلم المذكور حتي يدعوا المعلمين فنهض نكولا راز اجيره الذي مر ذكره وصور فوق انف ذلك الشخص ذبانه وتركها وجلس يصحن الدهانات.

فبعد قليل من الزمان اتي المعلم صحبة المعلمين وجلسوا علي الكراسي. حينٍ قدم المعلم تلك الصوره امام المعلمين يروها فراو تلك الذبانه كانها علقت في الصوره فمد يده وكشها فما طارت. حينٍ تفرس فيها فراها تصوير فخجل لانه انغش والتفت الي اجيره وساله قايلاً من هو الذي دخل الي هاهنا وصور هذه الذبانه فاجابه اجيره ما احد دخل غير نيكولا المجنون اجيرك وهو الذي صور هذه الذبانه.

فلما سمعوا المعلمين باسمه وكان انشهر صيته في تلك البلاد نهضوا جميعهم واستقبلوه باكرام وقالوا له لماذا عامل في حالك هكذا وانت رجل معلم في هل صناعه

"No one could paint a portrait like this," they said. "Not in this country, and not in India either. No human being painted this. It must have been an angel or a demon!"

Faced with this evidence, the prince now realized that the painting had to be, in fact, the young man's work. So he summoned him once again, and asked if he was indeed the true painter of the portrait.                                   9.46

"My lord, why not investigate the matter?" the young man replied. "If any other artist can produce a painting like this, then I'm a liar."

"You've spoken well, my son. But I've already married my daughter off, because I never believed that you could produce her portrait," the prince said. "As for my vow, I offer you her sister instead."

When the young man heard that the girl was married, he lost his senses and began to hallucinate. He fled the prince's house like a madman, his passion for the girl having stripped him of all reason. He set about wandering through wilderness and wasteland. Eventually, tormented by his hunger and miserably bedraggled state, he stopped in a city and found work as an artist's servant, grinding paint in exchange for food.                                          9.47

At that time, the artist was at work on a glorious portrait, which he hoped would win him recognition as the finest of all painters. When it was finished, he set the painting in a place of honor and went to invite all the master artists to come see his work and to declare him a great master. After he left, the apprentice—whose name was Nicholas—stood up, painted a fly on the nose of the person in the portrait, then sat down again and went on grinding paint.

A little while later, his master returned in the company of the other artists. They sat down on some chairs and the master presented his portrait to them. Seeing what appeared to be a fly on the surface of the painting, he reached out to shoo it away, but it didn't budge. Scrutinizing it carefully, the master realized that it was in fact painted on! He whirled around to face his apprentice, embarrassed at having been fooled.                                          9.48

"Who came in here and painted this fly?" he demanded.

"Nobody came in besides Crazy Nicholas, your apprentice," he said. "It was *he* who painted the fly!"[18]

When the assembled artists heard that the painter was none other than Nicholas—who had acquired no small amount of notoriety in those lands—they rose to their feet in his honor.                                          9.49

اجلس عندنا ونحن كنا منصير تلاميذك فما قبل ولا اعطاهم التفاته وراد الخروج من هناك. حينئذٍ قله معلمه استقيم عندي حتي اتباحص انا واياك في التصوير فاجابه اجيره المذكور ما مرادك في مقامتي عندك فاجابه المعلم قايلًا انا بصور صوره وبعدي انت صور صوره والتي بتجب للمعلمين اكثر بيكون هو المعلم.

٥٠،٩

فرضي نيكولا بهذا الشرط امام المعلمين. اخيرًا مضوا المعلمين في حال سبيلهم وابتدي ذلك المعلم يصور صوره فلما انتهت تلك الصوره فارسل دعي تلك المعلمين وظهر لهم الصوره وهي صورة فواكي ودوالي عنب مدلاين من الدوالي وعلقها في الصخره فالتمت الطيور وصاروا ينقروا الصوره كانهم بينقروا من الفواكي والعنب مغشوشين فلما راوا المعلمين ذلك فشهدوا لمعلميته لانه غش الطيور. اخيرًا التفتوا الي نيكولا وقالوا له بقا عليك انت الاخر تصور صوره حتي نحكم بالحق علي الصورتين فاجابهم نيكولا اعطوني جره حتي اجلس وحدي واصور الصوره ولا احد يدخل لعندي الي حينما تكمل في مده شهر كامل فرضيوا المعلمين واعطوه جره والت التصوير ومضوا عنه.

٥١،٩

فاستقام نيكولا يصور الصوره فكمها يوم واحد لكن قصده يروي المعلمين بانه بيتعوق في تصويرها لاجل كثرة صناعتها فبعدما مضت الايام المذكوره بادروا المعلمين الي ذلك المكان حتي يروا تلك الصوره بعلمهم بانها تكون فريده عجيبه. حينئذٍ قالوا للمذكور افتح جرتك حتي نراء هل صوره فاعطي المفتاح الي معلمه فلما فتحوا الجره فراء في صدر الجره صوره مغطاه بستر فمد يده معلمه وراد يرفع الستر من علي الصوره فضرب يده والحيط وكان ذلك الجرجف مصور في الحيط فخجل المعلم لانه اغتش ثاني مره. حينئذٍ التفت نيكولا الي معلمه قايلًا ما هي شطاره انك تغش الطيور الشطاره للذي بيغش المعلمين الذين متلك ومضي وخلاهم باهتين في ذلك الستار وصناعة التي فيه.

"As a master of this art, why are you treating yourself in this way?" they asked him. "Come join us, and we'll be *your* students!"

But he didn't accept, nor did he pay them any mind. He turned to leave.

"Why don't you stay here with me now, and we can explore the subject of painting together?" his master persisted.

"Why?" the apprentice Nicholas asked. "What's your purpose in keeping me around?"

"I'll paint a picture, and then you paint a picture," his master proposed. "Whoever paints the finer one, in the judgment of these artists, will be the master."

Nicholas agreed to the challenge. The artists all went on their way, and his master began to paint. When his painting was complete, he invited the artists back to show them his work. It was an image of fruits and grapes hanging from a trellis. He hung it outside, and the birds were fooled, flocking around and pecking at the painting as though the fruits and grapes were real! Witnessing this scene, the assembled artists attested to his mastery, for he had managed to deceive the birds.

9.50

"Now it's your turn," they said, turning to Nicholas. "Paint us a picture so that we can judge them both accurately."

"Give me a room to myself so that I may paint alone," Nicholas replied. "No one may come in until I'm finished, one month from now."

The artists agreed. They gave him a room and some painting supplies, and left him alone.

Nicholas began his painting, and completed it within a day. His plan, though, was to give the artists the impression that he'd taken much longer to finish it because of the great craft it demanded. After a month had passed, the artists hurried over to see the painting, convinced that it would be a unique masterpiece.

9.51

"Open the room so we may see the painting!" they demanded.

Nicholas handed the key to his master. Opening the door, they spied a painting at the back of the room, covered by a draped cloth. Nicholas's master reached out to lift the cloth, but his hand struck the wall: The cloth had been painted directly upon it! The master was embarrassed, as he'd been fooled a second time.

"It doesn't take much skill to fool a few birds," said Nicholas, turning to his master. "Fooling a master painter like you? That takes some doing!"

He turned and walked away, leaving them all flabbergasted by the cloth and its artistry.

وهذا لما كان يدخل الي استريه يستقيم يومين ثلاثه ياكل ويشرب ولما صاحب ٩،٥٢
الاستريه يطلب منه حق الاكل يقله اتيني بقرظاز علي رسم عليه شكل ويقول الي
صاحب الاستريه خد هل قرظاز الي عند معلم مصور واطلب منه حقها خمسة
دهب وانما اعطاك ارجع فيها لعندي فيروح الرجل ويعطي ذلك الرسم الي معلم من
المصورين ويطلب حقها خمسه دهب فيدفع له ثلاثه فيرجع حتي يشاوره فياخدها
من يده ويشقها ويرسم غيرها اشرف منها واصنع ويقول له لا تاخد حقها الا عشرة
دهب فيروح ذلك الرجل ويطلب حقها عشره دهب فيخرج يعطيه في الحال خمسة
دهب فيرجع حتي يشاوره فيراه مضي من الاستريه وما عاد رجع كانه حرد واصرف
مدة حياته علي هذا النسق حامل خرجه علي كتفه وساحب معه كلبه ووالي الان
موجود من تصويره ورسمه يينباع بثمن غزير وهذه حكايته بالمقتصر .

فنرجع الان ونكتب محاسن مدينة بهريس وحسن نظامها اولاً موجود في هل ٩،٥٣
مدينه ثمانماية كنيسه من غير الاديرة الرهبان والراهبات وفي كل كنيسه جملة سناديق
منهم الي فقرات الصايح ومنهم منشان الفقره المستحيين الذين كانوا سابقاً في نعمه
وثروه وفيما بعد مسهم الفقر والعازه وهولاء ما بيقدروا يتشحدوا ولا بيقدروا يبينوا علي
حالهم انهم معتازين ولاجل هذا لهم في كل كنسه سندوق مخصص لهم واثنين من
الجوارنه موكلين في توزيع هل معبور لهم من غير احد يعرف من هولاء المستحيين[1]
وسناديق فقرات الصايح لاجل الفقره الموجدين في ذلك الصايح منهم عميان ومنهم
مقعدين ومنهم شيوخ وهرومه ومنهم ارامل ذات اعيال اطفال وهل سناديق
موكل عليهم وكيلين من امائل الصايح بيوزعوا علي كل منهم علي قدر احتياجه ومدونين
اسماهم في دفتر .

والفقير ما قشعت قط شحاد بيتوسل ويطلب حسنه من احد بالكليه غير اني ٩،٥٤
رايت فد واحد جندي سقط فد رجل جماعة الحاكم بيضربوه ضرب عنيف بغير
رحمه فسالت واحد من الحاضرين لاي سبب جماعة الحاكم بيضربوا ذلك الجندي

---

١ الأصل: المستحتين.

Whenever this fellow would check into an inn, he'd stay for two or three days, eating and drinking his fill. And when the innkeeper would ask him to settle his bill, Nicholas would tell him to bring him some paper to draw on.

"Take this paper to a master painter and offer to sell it for five gold pieces," he told the innkeeper. "If he doesn't pay you, bring it back to me."

The man would go off and present the drawing to one of the master artists, asking for five gold pieces. The artist would offer three, so the innkeeper would return with the drawing to consult with Nicholas, who'd grab his work and rip it in half. Then he'd make another drawing, this one even more sublime and masterful.

"Don't take less than ten gold pieces for this one."

The innkeeper would set off again and ask for ten gold pieces, receiving a counteroffer of five. He'd return to the inn and find that Nicholas had left and not come back, as though he were angry. Nicholas spent the rest of his life in this way, traveling with a sack on his shoulder and his dog trotting behind him. His paintings and drawings continue to fetch high prices even today. So ends this summary of his story.

Let's return to our account of the admirable public works of Paris. First, there are eight hundred churches in this city, not counting the monasteries and convents. Each church contains several collection chests, some reserved for the poor people of the quarter, and some for those who'd come down in the world, having once led a life of ease before sinking into poverty and need. These last are too proud to beg, or to admit to being indigent, so each church keeps a collection chest just for them. Two priests are assigned to disburse the collected funds in a discreet manner, so that no one knows who the recipients are.

The other collection chests are reserved for the poor people of the quarter, including the blind, the housebound, the elderly, the senile, and widows with children. Two upstanding residents of the quarter are put in charge of disbursing the funds from the collection chests according to the needs of each recipient. The names of the recipients are registered in a ledger.

I never saw a single person begging for alms in Paris. In fact, I once saw a one-legged soldier being beaten violently and mercilessly by some of the governor's men, and when I asked an onlooker why they were beating him, he replied that they'd seen him begging. I was astonished.

فاجابني انهم راوه بيشحد فتعجبت وقلت له هل في بلادكم الذي بيشحد بيقتلوه لا
سيما رجل مثل هذا سقط ما بيقدر بيشتغل هل يجوز هذا فاجابني ذلك الرجل
بانه مستاهل الضرب لان الملك الله يحفظه كافيهم في كل لوازمهم ومعاشهم
وما بينقصهم شي يضطرهم للشحاده وهذا لقة نام لعزته.

٩،٥٥ فعدت استفهمت منه وما هي حكايت هل جنود فاجابني بان الملك معمر لهولا
الجنود الذين بيرجعوا من الحرب مجرحين او مقطوعين الايدي والرجلين مرستان متسع
في الغايه وداخله حكما وجراحاتيه وكنيسه وكهنة اعتراف وجعل لهم مايده لغداهم
وعشاهم وكل واحد منهم له سرير لمنامته وراحته وما يشبه ذلك هل بقا لهم عدر
بانهم يشحدوا انما بتكون شحادتهم للشراهه ولاجل هذا من راوه بيشحد بينتقموا
منه في مكان الذي بيروه بيشحد وهناك في المارستان بيبطحوه علي فرض من دف
ويجلدوه علي لواياه بعصاب البرقحتي يتدب غيره.

٩،٥٦ وسنذق اخرالي مرستان ذلك الصالح ومن بعد كل كنايس المذكوره في مدينة
بهريس موجود كنيسه العذري وهي كنيسه عظيمه متسعه ولها ناقوز كبير بمقدار قبه
زغيره وهو مركب في علو مادنه عاليه وهو مركب علي اربع عواميد وسماكته مقدار
شبر الاشوبه ومدلا في وسطه بيضه من الحديد ولها بكرات وحبال مدلاين الي
اسفل الكنيسه واذا رادوا يدقوه بعزم اثني عشر رجل بيسحبوا[1] الحبال وبالجهد حتي
تصل البيضه الي حفة الناقوز وحين بيتدق الناقوز بيصير له صدا ورنه بتوهم اهل
المدينه من ضجيجها وبتتصل رنته الي مسافه سبع ساعات وهذا ما بيندق الا في
النادر لاجل موت ملك اوامير او كردينال وما يشبه ذلك.

٩،٥٧ وهذه الكنيسه موجود فيها ثمانين هيكل وكل هيكل بمقدر كنيسه زغيره وفي
الوسط هيكل كبير بوجين ولها سبعة ابواب وكل باب بينفد علي صايح من صوايح
بهريس وكل صايح بقدر مدينة حلب الجواني وهذه ما هي مبالغه لان علي راي
السواح بان مدينة بهريس بقدر مدينة اسطنبول وسبع مرات لان سقاقات سفر
ساعه للمجد السير والذي مروس علي هل الكنيسه كردينال مرسل من عند سيدنا الپاپا

_____
١ الأصل: بيسبحوا.

"In your country, would they really beat up someone just for begging?" I asked him. "Even a man like that, without a leg, who can't work? How is that allowed?"

"That man deserves it," he replied. "After all, the king—may God save him—takes care of war invalids and pays them a pension. Anything they need, they get free of charge, so they have no excuse to beg. It's a slap in the king's face!"

I asked to hear more.                                                                                          9.55

"There's a big hospital," I was told, "for invalids and crippled soldiers, built by the king. They have physicians, surgeons, a chapel, and priests to receive confessions. Lunch and dinner are prepared every day, and there's a bed for every man to sleep in, and other comforts of that sort. So, what excuse would an invalid have to go out begging? The only reason is greed! That's why anyone caught begging is punished on the spot. And at the hospital, they make an example of beggars by stretching them out on a wooden plank and flogging them on the buttocks with a bull-pizzle whip."

Each church also has a collection chest dedicated to the hospital in its quar-     9.56
ter. In addition to the aforementioned churches in the city of Paris, there is the Church of Notre-Dame. It is a very imposing church with a large bell, about the size of a small dome. The bell is situated at the top of a tall minaret and supported by four pillars, and is nearly a handspan thick. In the center of the bell is an iron ringer, which is attached to pulleys and ropes that dangle down to the church's lower level. To ring the bell with any force, it takes a team of twelve men to pull on the ropes. It takes some effort to make the ringer strike the side of the bell, but when it does, it clangs loudly enough to frighten the citizens, and you can hear it from seven miles away. They only ring it on rare occasions, such as when a king, prince, cardinal, or other important figure dies.

Inside Notre-Dame are eighty chapels, each the size of a small church. In     9.57
the center of the church is a grand altar that can be approached from two sides. Each of the church's seven doors opens onto a different quarter of Paris—every one of the quarters as large as the walled city of Aleppo. Be assured that this is no exaggeration. Travelers have reported that Paris is seven times as large as Istanbul; it has some streets that would take a vigorous walker a whole hour to travel from beginning to end. The head of this church is a cardinal sent by His Holiness the pope, vested with powers similar to those of a second pope over the region of France.

ومعطي سلطانه كانه بابا ثاني في اقليم فرنسا وكان عند الكردينال رجل يسما كرستوفلو اخو باولو چلبي في حلب وهو اغا من اغاوات الكردينال في اكبر بايه من الجميع وهو كان كاخيته.

٥٨.٩ وفي تلك الايام حكم عيد الجسد ومن عادة اهل بهريس بيزيحوا الجسد ثلاث مرات مرة الاوله يوم الخميس الذي هو العيد ويوم الاحد الذي بعده ويوم الخميس الثاني ايضاً ويوم الزناح يبحلوا الحيطان والبواب والدكاكين بافخر القماشات والتحف الموجوده عندهم وبيرشوا الزقات بالزهور وفي راس كل زقاق بينصبوا تحت شكل هيكل ولما يصلوا الي ذلك الهيكل بيصمدوا الجسد وبيقولوا الطلبه والتراتيل وما يشبه ذلك من الصلوات الخشوعيه.

٥٩.٩ وذلك اليوم صار زياح كنيسة العذري ومرالزناح من حارة الفقير الذي ساكنها فوقفت في الشباك اتفرج علي ذلك الزناح العظيم الموجود فيه اكثر من خمسماية كاهن[١] وشماس وكلهم لابسين بدلات كسر التون وفي ايديهم الشموع الكافور والصلبان الدهب وبعدما مروا تلك الكهنه والشمامسه وصل الكردينال ويعلوه خيمه كبيره وسيعه باثني عشر عامود محموله باثني عشر رجل وداخل الخيمه الكردينال ماسك الشعاع الموجود فيه جسد الرب.

٦٠.٩ فلما تفرست في ذلك الشعاع فرايت كانه الشمس ما بيقدر الانسان يحقق النظر فيه من كثرة الجواهر المرصعه فيه من الماص وياقوت وزمرد وغيرجار ممتنه وما يشبه ذلك شي يخطف النظر وفيما انا شاخص ومدهول في هذا المنظر اجا لعندي معلي وقال لي اقرا هل كتابه التي فوق الخيمه فلما نظرت الي تلك الكتابه فرايت جراجف حمر كتبي ومكتوب عليهم احرف بيض من بيز ابيض لا اله الا الله والكتابه فبهت من هذه الكتابه وهي تعلوا تلك الخيمه.

٦١.٩ فسالني معلي ما هي هذه الكتابه فاحكيت له بالذي مكتوب فتعجب وما صدق. حينذٍ امرني باني اسبق واروح الي بيت الجيران واتفرس مليح بالكتابه من تلك

----
١الأصل: كان.

Among the cardinal's men was one named Christofalo, who was the brother of Paulo Çelebi in Aleppo. He was one of the cardinal's senior officers, occupying a rank higher than the others and serving as his chief steward.

When I was there, it happened to be the Feast of Corpus Christi. The custom of the Parisians is to hold three processions of the Blessed Sacrament. The first takes place on the day of the feast itself, which is a Thursday. The second is on the Sunday, and the third is on the following Thursday. On the day of the procession, people decorate their walls, doors, and shops with their finest fabrics and adornments, and scatter flowers in the streets. At each intersection, a platform is set up in the shape of an altar. When the procession reaches the altar, they expose the Blessed Sacrament and recite some litanies, hymns, and other supplications. 9.58

On the day of the grand procession from the Church of Notre-Dame, which passed through the quarter in which I was living, I stood at the window, watching it go by. There were more than five hundred priests and deacons, all wearing vestments of gold brocade, and carrying camphor candles and gold crucifixes. Following the priests and deacons came the cardinal himself, who stood beneath a large canopy supported by twelve poles carried by twelve men. Under the canopy, the cardinal held the ostensorium, the vessel that holds the Blessed Sacrament. 9.59

As I stared at the ostensorium, I felt as though I were looking at the sun! The sheer number of diamonds, rubies, emeralds, and other precious jewels covering it made it so dazzling that you could hardly train your gaze upon it. And yet you couldn't look away either. As I stood there gaping in astonishment at this spectacle, my master came over to my side.[19] 9.60

"Read me what's written on that canopy," he said.

I looked closer and made out some white baize letters appliquéd on dark-red cloth. They read: "There is no God but God . . ." and the rest of it.[20] I was shocked to see such an inscription upon the canopy.

"What does it say?" my master asked. 9.61

I told him, and he was appalled. Refusing to believe it, he ordered me to go over to the neighbors' house to get a better look at the inscription from their window. I did as he asked and scrutinized the inscription again, and found that I'd read it correctly the first time. I returned to my master to confirm my observation.

الشبابيك فمضيت كما امرني ونظرت الي تلك الكتابه فرايتها كما هي في الاول فرجعت
واخبرته بصحة الامر وقلت له ما يمكن اني اكون غلطان لان الجرجف احمر والاحرف
من بيز ابيض كيف يمكن اني غلطان فلما معلمي تحقق مني صحة الكتابه حينذٍ امرني باني
امضي الي عند الكردينال واحكيله بالذي نضرته وقلي بيصير لك من الكردينال اكرام
وافر وبخششيش.

٦٢،٩ فاصطبرت حتي فات الذهر بساعتين فمضيت الي صراية الكردينال فلما دخلت
الي تلك الصرايه فسالوني الحجاب الذين في باب الصرايا ماذا تريد فقلت لهم بان لي
كلام مع حضرة الكردينال فسالوني ما هو كلامك وماذا بتريد فقلت لهم ماني
مامور اني احكي هل كلام الا لحضرة الكردينال.

٦٣،٩ حينذٍ ارسلوا معي واحد من الحجاب فمضي بي الي داخل الصرايه حيث محل
حضرة الكردينال وفي ذلك الوقت اتي واحد من الغلمان ودعاني اروح معه
فمضيت معه فصعدنا الي مكان عالي فدخلني الي حجره فلما دخلت رايت رجل
مهيب جالس علي كرسي فتفرس في وسالني من تكون انت ومن اي بلاد فاجبته
انا من بلاد سوريا من مدينة حلب فسالني بلسان العربي الفصيح من اي طايفه
تكون فاجبته انا من طايفة الموارنه فقلي السلامه في ابن بلادي واسترحب في قوي
كثير وسالني قايلاً هل بتعرفني فقلت له لا يا سيدي فقلي انا من بيت زماريا واخي
الكبير اسمه باولو چلبي واخي الاخر اسمه يوسف واكبرنا كلنا اسمه زماريا وهو
وكيل القدس في اسطنبول قاطن عند الالجي فاجبته انا بعرف خواجه باولو چلبي
واخيه يوسف في حلب واسمهم مشهور عند الجميع في حسن الصيت والسمعه.

اخيراً سالني ما سبب دخولك الي هاهنا لاني رايتك من الشباك داخل مع واحد
من الحجاب الي محل حضرة الكردينال هل لك حاجه عنده قلي انا بقضيلك هي علي
مرادك فقلته ادام الله بقاك يا سيدي ما لي حاجه لكن معي كلام بريد اطلعه علي
حضرة الكردينال فاجابني ما هو الكلام قلي لاني انا كاخيت الكردينال وما احد
بيدخل لعنده بغير اذني.

"I can't be mistaken, because the cloth is red and the letters are in white baize," I said. "How could I be wrong?"

Convinced, my master ordered me to go visit the cardinal and relate to him what I'd seen.

"The cardinal is certain to treat you most honorably for this service," my master said, "and will also reward you with some money."

I waited until two o'clock in the afternoon and went to the cardinal's palace.   9.62

"What is your business?" the gatekeepers asked me. I explained that I had a message for His Holiness the cardinal.

"What is your message?" they asked.

"I've been ordered to convey it to His Holiness alone."

A gatekeeper was delegated to accompany me into the palace to the car-   9.63 dinal's quarters. There, a servant boy invited me to follow him. We climbed to a higher floor and entered a room, where I saw an imposing man sitting on a chair.

"Who are you, and what country are you from?" he asked, scrutinizing me.

"I'm from Syria," I replied. "The city of Aleppo."

"To which community do you belong?" he asked me—in refined Arabic!

"I'm from the Maronite community," I replied.

"Greetings, countryman!" he proclaimed, welcoming me with great warmth. "Do you know who I am?"

"No, sir."

"I belong to the Zamāriyā family.[21] My older brother's name is Paulo Çelebi, and I have another brother named Yūsuf. The head of the family is Zamāriyā, the procurator of Jerusalem in Istanbul, where he lives with the ambassador."

"I know *khawājah* Paulo Çelebi and his brother Yūsuf of Aleppo!" I said. "Everyone does. They have a fine reputation."

"What brings you here?" he asked. "I spotted you from my window as you were coming in with one of the chamberlains to see His Holiness the cardinal. Do you have any business with him? If you tell me what it is, I'll take care of it for you."

"God save you, sir! There's nothing I need myself, but I have a message for His Holiness."

"And what's the message? I'm his steward, and no one may see him without my permission."

٩،٦٤ فلما سمعت منه هل كلام التزمت اني احكي له بالذي نضرته من تلك الكتابة فلما سمع مني هل كلام بهت واتعجب وعاد علي العباره هل هذا صحيح فقلته نعم وهذا شي يكون ماكك عند حضرتك. حينذٍ قلي ما بيلزم انك تدخل عند الكردينال انا بخص عن هل امر ونهار غدي تعال لعندي وأنا بنبيك انكان هل شي صحيح ام لا. اخيرًا بدخلك عند الكردينال.

٩،٦٥ فمضي ذلك النهار فمضيت ثاني يوم الي عنده فاجابني بان الذي اخبرتني فيه صحيح واخبرت به الي حضرة سيدنا الكردينال في الحال ارسل واحضر السكرستيان امامه وامره بانه يجيب تلك الجراجف الذين كانوا فوق خيمة الجسد فلما جابهم فراوا تلك الكتابة المذكوره. حينذٍ سال حضرة الكردينال لذلك الرجل ما هذه الجراجف فاجابه يا سيدي هذه الجراجف قدم وهن بيارق الاعدا المغاربه موضوعين في خزانه السكرستيا فجلت فيهم اعلا الخيمه حضرًا ليلا يسقط علي الخيمه طراب من الاسطحا. حينذٍ امر الكردينال بان يحرقوهم في الحال وسبب وجود هل بيارق في كنيسة العذري المذكوره هو ان لما كان ينتصروا ملوك فانسا علي المغاربه فياخدوا بيارقهم ويضعوهم في الكنيسه لاجل التذكره ويصلوا صلوة الشكر وهذا هو السبب فلما فرغ من كلامه قلي ما بقا بيلزم بانك تدخل الي عند الكردينال واطلقني بعد انه اوصاني بان ازوره دايمًا.

٩،٦٦ وفي صايح هل كنيسه موجود مارستان كبير يسما اوتيل دو ديه اعني هيكل الله لانه يقبل لكل من اراد يدخل اليه ومن اي ملة كان من غير فحص فقير كان او غني او رجبال. المراد يقبل الجميع علي حد سوي فلنشرح الان حسن نظام هل مارستان والخير العظيم الموجود فيه اولًا لما يقبل المريض الي هذا المكان بيجد في الباب جالس رجل مكلف عليه هيبه ووقار وحوله من الخدام واقفين لخدمته فيسال ذلك المريض هل هو غريب ام من اهل المدينه وايش بلغ من العمر وهل معه ورقة معموديته ثانيًا يساله هل انه مسيحي او من غير مله فبعدما يكون اخبره المريض بجميع ما ساله عنه بيكتب اسمه وبيارخ ذلك اليوم وموجود في جريده معلقه مكتوب فيها اسامي[1] المرضي

―――――――――
١ الأصل: اسمامي.

I felt compelled to tell him about the inscription I'd seen. When I did, he    9.64
was astonished.

"Is this really true?" he demanded, repeating the question over and again.

"Yes sir! Your Excellency can see it for yourself," I replied.

"There's no need for you to see the cardinal," he replied. "Let me look into the matter myself. Come back and see me tomorrow, and I'll let you know if you were right about what you saw. Then we can go see the cardinal."

The rest of the day passed without incident. The next day, I went back.    9.65

"What you told me was true!" he said. "I went to tell His Holiness about your message. Right away he called for the sacristan and ordered him to bring the cloths that were draped over the canopy of the Blessed Sacrament."

Now, when the sacristan brought the cloths and they saw the inscription written upon them, the cardinal demanded that the sacristan explain where the cloths had come from.

"Your Holiness, these are antique banners taken from our enemies in the Maghreb," said the sacristan. "They were deposited in the storeroom of the sacristy. I used them to cover the top of the canopy to keep it from being smudged by the dirt falling from the rooftops."

The cardinal ordered them to burn the cloths right away. But why were the banners in the Church of Notre-Dame in the first place? The reason was that when the French kings would win a war against the Maghrebis, they would take their banners and display them in the church as a memorial, offering prayers of thanksgiving.

"There's no longer any need for you to see the cardinal," the steward said after he finished recounting what had happened. He insisted that I come back to visit him regularly, and sent me on my way.

In the quarter of the Church of Notre-Dame, there is a large hospital named    9.66
Hôtel de Dieu, which means "Altar of God."[22] It was so called because it admitted all who came to it, no matter what community they belonged to, no questions asked, whether they were poor or rich or just a simple laborer. In other words, it accepted all people on an equal basis. I shall now describe the excellent organization of this hospital and the wonderful care it provided.

First, when an invalid arrives at the hospital, he encounters a man of dignified bearing seated at the door, surrounded by servants at his beck and call.

الموجودين ينوف عن الف وخمسمايه واوقات ما بتزيد بتزيد دايمًا[1] وبيرسله مع احد خدامه الي داخل المكان وهناك بيجد كنيسه وداخلها كهنه معملين اعتراف فيتسلمه واحد من الكهنه وبيدخله الي قلايته وبينبهه علي الاعتراف ثم بيعرفه اعتراف عام وبعده بيعطيه الحله وبيطلقه مع واحد الي عند الحكيم باشي حتي يراه ما هو مرضه.

٦٧،٩ فعدما بيحفظه الحكيم باشي بيسلمه ليد واحد من الحكما الموجودين تحت يده حتي يتعلموا الحكمه وبيامره بان يدعه في تلك الساله الموجود فيها من ذلك المرض لان في ذلك المكان موجود سالات شتي اعني رواقات وكل رواق منهم مخصوص بمرض وداخل هل رواق علي الصفين تخوته مجللين بجوخ احمر وفي صفحة التخت مكبوب رقم باحرف بيز ابيض عدد لا غير بيسما نمره وبينوجد علي الصفين مقدار مايتين تخت وفي صدر الساله هيكل علي اسم قديس وبيتقدم كل يوم باكر قداس علي اسم المرضي الموجودين في ذلك الرواق.

٦٨،٩ فلنرجع فيما كنا في صدده فيتسلمه ذلك الحكيم وبيدخله الي قاعه واسعه وداخلها بيوتات اعني طوق وكل طاقه داخلها بدله من بدلات المارستان فبيشلحوا ذلك المريض ثيابه وبيلبسوه تلك البدله وبيصروا ثيابه وبيضعوها في تلك الطاقه وبيكتبوا اسم ذلك المريض علي الطاقه حتي انه بعدما يشفي يلبس ثيابه ويمضي بسلام واذا راد واحد يزور احد من اهله او اصدقاه في ذلك المارستان ما بيمكنه يراه بغير انه يكشف علي دفتر الحكيم باشي. حينٍذ بيدله بقوله له امضي الي سالة الثالثه او الرابعه او الخامسه وانضر العدد الفلاني المكبوب علي تلك التخوت فتري مريضك هناك في ذلك العدد ومن غير هذا اذا استقام ثلاثة ايام يفتنش ما بيقدر يراه.

٦٩،٩ وفي كل ساله موكل حكيم بيفرق عليهم الادويه صباحًا ومساءً وكل يوم بعد القداس بيفرقوا عليهم الشوربه وايضًا الدهر والمساء فرأيت لما بيفرقوا الشوربه وهو انهم واضعين حله فوق عربانه وساحبها واحد وايضًا ثاني عربانه وعليها سندوق طويل وداخله شاكاسات من قزديل والخدام بتسكب من تلك الشوربه وبيناولوا للمرضه حتي ينتهوا الي اخر الساله وكت اري ايضًا كثير من نسا الاكابر جلوس عند

---

He asks the invalid if he is a foreigner or a native of the city, how old he is, and whether he has a baptismal certificate with him.

Next, he asks whether the invalid is a Christian or belongs to a different religion. Once he has answered all the questions, the man registers his name and the date on a ledger hanging on the wall, which contains a list of all 1,500 patients in the hospital at the time, a figure that fluctuates. He then admits the invalid, accompanied by one of his servants, into the building. There, the patient comes upon a chapel with priests taking confession. One of the priests receives him, brings him into his cell, and prepares him for confession. After hearing his general confession, the priest absolves him of his sins and sends him to see the chief doctor to be diagnosed.

Following the examination, the patient is handed off to one of the apprentice doctors supervised by the chief doctor, with an order to move the patient into the ward reserved for people with the same illness. There are many wards in the building, by which I mean halls, each one dedicated to a specific illness. On either side of a given gallery, there are beds covered with red broadcloth. A unique number—which they call *numéro*—is appliquéd in white cloth at the foot of every bed. There are about two hundred beds on the two sides of the ward, and at the back is an altar dedicated to a saint. Each day, a morning mass is held for the ward's patients. 9.67

As I was saying, when the doctor takes charge of his new patient, he brings him into a large room containing many cubbyholes, or lockers. Each contains a hospital gown. They have the patient change out of his clothes, which he places in a locker, and into a gown. The patient's name is written on the locker so he can find his clothes again once he has recovered from his illness and is about to leave the hospital. And whenever someone wishes to visit a relative or friend in the hospital, he first has to check the chief doctor's ledger. 9.68

"Go to the third or fourth or fifth hall," they tell him. "Search for bed number such and such, and you'll find your patient there."

In the absence of such a system, one could spend three days searching the hospital for a person without finding them!

In each hall, a doctor is designated to distribute medicines to the patients every morning and evening. Following mass each morning, the patients are served soup, and again at lunch and dinner. I witnessed a soup service. 9.69

روس تلك المرضي يخدموهم ويسلوهم واذا المريض طلب منهم شي بيرسلوا يحضروا لهم ذلك الشي مع خدامهم.

٧٠،٩ ورايت بعضهم اذا المريض راد يقضي حاجة الطبيعه فتلك الست بتجلسه وتمضي بالانا بتكبه ومع انه موجود معها اربع خمس خدامات ما بتريد احد منهم يخدم ذلك المريض غيرهي بيدها بتقضي ما يحتاج اليه من الخدم المستكره والروايح المنتنه ورايت ايضاً اذا واحد من هل مرضه حط في النزاع واشرف علي الموت في الحال يحضروا له كاهن يعطيه مسحة الاخيره وكل من مرمن ذلك المكان بيقف بيصلي ويتضرع لاجله واذا مات بيجنزوه في مكانه ويحلوه الي المقبره التي هي قريه من ذلك المكان.

٧١،٩ ومن جانب هل مرستان مرستان اخرللنسا ما احد بيدخل اليه غير الكهنه والحكماء لا غير وهو نظير مرستان الرجال المذكور وفي اسفل هل مكان دير راهبات موجود فيه مقدار مايتين او ثلاثمائة راهبه مندورين لاجل خسيل ثياب المرضي وخياطة حوايجهم وترقيعهم وايضاً لاجل عجينهم وخبزهم ومن جانب الدير جاري نهر كبير الذي هو جاري من وسط مدينة بهريز والفقير نضرتهم يخسلوا حوايج المرضي.

٧٢،٩ واحكولي ايضاً عن مكان مخفي داخل هل مارستان وهو لاجل البنات الذين تورطوا في خطيت الدنس وقبل ما يبظهر فيهم الحبل بيرسلوهم اهلهم الي ذلك المكان من غير ان يعرف فيهم احد فبستقيموا هناك الي حين ما توضع تلك البنت فيباخدوا منها الجنين ويعطوه للمرضعات ويطلقوا سبيلها والجنين بيربوه الي حين ما يكبر بيضعوه عند معلم حتي يتعلم كار وكثير من هل اولاد صاروا معلمين ماهرين ومنهم ارتقوا الي مراتب ساميه ومنهم صاروا مدبرين ومنهم دخلوا الديوره وترهبوا وصار منهم روسا وقديسين.

٧٣،٩ وهذا هو الخير العظيم الذي ينتج من هل مارستان المبارك والفقير كتبت القليل[١] من الكثير الذي نضرته وسمعته عن هل مكان الذي يسما بالفرنساوي اوتيل ده ديه

---

١ الأصل: القيل.

A man pulls a cart that has a large pot sitting on it. A second cart carries a long, narrow case containing tin bowls. The servants ladle soup into the bowls and hand them to the patients, proceeding down to the end of the ward. I also saw many noblewomen sitting beside the patients, serving them and keeping their spirits up. If a patient needs anything, the women send a servant to fetch it.

When a patient needs to answer the call of nature, the woman tending him seats him on the chamber pot and, afterward, goes and empties it. Even though she has four or five servants at her disposal, she doesn't allow a single one to tend to her patient. She sees to his every need, enduring every filthy service and foul odor. I also witnessed that when an invalid is on the verge of death and fighting for his life, they quickly summon a priest to administer the extreme unction. All who pass by his bed stop to offer prayers and supplications on behalf of the patient. If he dies, they hold a funeral service right there, then transport his body to the cemetery nearby.   9.70

Right next door to the hospital is a second hospital reserved for women. The only men permitted to enter are priests and doctors. It matches exactly the hospital I just described. On the lower level is a convent of about two or three hundred nuns, devoted to serving the sick. They clean, sew, and patch their clothes, and knead and bake their own bread. A great river runs by the hospital—the one that runs through the middle of Paris—and I saw them there, laundering the patients' clothes.   9.71

I was told that there is a hidden area inside the women's hospital devoted to girls who fall into disgrace. Before the signs of their pregnancy become visible, their families send them there without anyone's knowledge. As soon as a girl delivers her baby, it is taken from her and given to the wet nurses. The girl is released, and they raise the newborn. Once grown, it is apprenticed to an artisan to learn a craft. Many of these children have become skilled master artisans themselves. Some have risen to lofty positions and others have become officials. Still others have entered monasteries, becoming monks, and in some cases abbots and even saints.   9.72

The blessed hospital is responsible for all of these many works of charity. I've recorded just a small portion of what I witnessed and heard about this place called Hôtel de Dieu in French, or "Altar of God."   9.73

اعني هيكل الله وهذا المكان له اوقاف شتي منها ضيع واراضي ومساكن ودكاكين شي يفوق الوصف وايضاً مدخول من السناديق الذين موضوعين في جميع كايس بهريز لان كل انسان بيري في سندوقهم حسنه وكثير من البازركان[1] والاكابر يكتبوا في ورقة وصيتهم لهذا المارستان مبلغ من الدراهم. المراد له مدخول عظيم بيفيض عن المصروف شي كثير.

٧٤،٩ وفي مدينه بهريس مارستان لاجل الاولاد الفجر وهو داخل دير رهبان مضطرف عن المدينه فرحت الفقير الي ذلك الدير ودخلوني الي المكان المسجونين فيه تلك الاولاد فرايت وهو ساله طوله وممدود في تلك الساله جسر خشب طويل علي طول المكان وداقتين سكك حديد ومقيدين الولاد بجنزير معلق في تلك السكه وبعيد الواحد عن اخرشي انه لا يصل الواحد الي رفيقه وكل واحد تحته قطعة حصيره وعمال بيشتغل في اشيا بتخص الدير وماكلهم الخبز والماء وكل يوم بيجلدوهم مرتين علي لواياهم وهن مبطوحين علي فرس من دف وكل منهم بيستقيم في هذا المكان الي حين ما يرضي والده او والدته في خروجه والا بيستقيم دايماً وفي مدينة بهريس موجود مدارس لجميع العلوم والفنون الموجوده في ساير الدنيا لان سلطان فرنسا كان ارسل لجاب معلمين من ساير الاقاليم يعلموا في فرنسا بعلوم ما هي موجود في مملكته.

٧٥،٩ وفي ذلك الزمان عرض الي الملك عارض عجيب وهو بان من ليله من الليالي لما كان متكي في مضجعه فدخل عليه الوهم وصار له قلق عظيم فما امكنه انه يستقيم في فراشه فنهض وهو موهوم ومرعوب وخرج الي خارج المقصوره فراء الحراس كهادتهم واقفين لحراسه وهذا دايماً الملك له حراس اربعين واحد من الاطال يحرسوا اقنومه ليل ونهار وهذا شي قديم لكل الملوك فلما نضر اليهم وتقرس فيهم ليلا يكون بينهم غريب فما راء شي من هذا. حينذٍ سالهم من دخل الي هذا المكان غريب فاجابوه يا سيدنا من له قدره يدخل الي هذا المكان فامرهم بان يشعلوا الفنوده ويفتشوا الصرايه لعلهم يجدوا احد ففعلوا كما امرهم وفتشوا جميع الاماكن والملك صحبتهم فما راوا احد فرجعوا والملك معهم. اخيراً دخل الملك الي مقصورته وانتكي في فراشه.

The hospital is supported by the income from various charitable trusts and properties, which include a vast number of villages, plots of land, houses, and shops. It also receives funds from donation chests in all the churches, supplied by everyone who leaves cash in the offering boxes. Many merchants and city nobles leave sums of money to the hospital in their wills. All this is to say that its sources of funding surpass its expenses by a considerable margin.

In Paris, there is also a hospital devoted to delinquent children.[23] It is located in a monastery just outside the city. I visited the monastery, and they brought me in to see the place where the children were held. It was a long room, with a wooden beam traversing the entire length of it. Iron stakes had been pounded into the beam, and the children were tied to the stakes with a chain. They were separated from each other in such a way that none could quite reach his neighbor, and they sat on straw mats, at work on one thing or another for the monastery. They received bread and water by way of nourishment, and twice a day they were stretched out on a whipping frame made of planks and flogged across the buttocks. Each remains at the hospital until the father or mother consents to let them leave. Otherwise, they stay for good.

9.74

In Paris, there are schools for every science and branch of knowledge found anywhere in the world. This is because the king, when a particular science was unknown, would send to distant climes for experts to come and teach that subject in France.

During my time there, a curious incident befell the king. One night, as he was lying in bed, he was seized by an uncanny foreboding, making him profoundly anxious. Terrified, he was unable to remain in bed, and he got up and left his bedchamber. Outside, his sentries stood guard as usual. The king always had a personal guard of forty strapping men to watch over his sacred person day and night, as was the ancient custom. The king scrutinized his guards to see if there were any interlopers among them, but didn't see one.

9.75

"Did a stranger enter my quarters?" he asked.

"How could anyone have, sire?" they replied.

He ordered them to light some candles and search the palace. They did as he instructed, searching everywhere, accompanied by the king, but found no one. They returned together, and the king went back to his pavilion and lay down in his bed.

٧٦.٩ فزاد عليه الوهم الطاق تنين فنهض وخرج ثانياً وقال للحراس موجود في هل مكان عدو واخبروني بالصحيح فارتموا علي رجليه وقالوا له يا سيدنا ها قد فتشنا جميع الاماكن فما راينا احد وابواب الصرايا مغلقه والحراس واقفين منين بيدخل الغريب او العدو ونخار الملك في امره وبالهام الاهي امرهم بان يدخلوا معه الي بستان القصر اعني بستان النزه وفشعلوا ايضاً الفنوده ودخلوا مع الملك الي داخل القصر وفتحوا ذلك الباب الذي بينزل منه الي البستان فداروا في البستان والفنوده متقده وفتشوا ما بين الاشجار وفي جميع زوايا البستان فما راوا احد فعادوا راجعين الي القصر .

٧٧.٩ فواحد من الحراس وفي يده فند وهو عمال بيتفرس في الاشجار فراء شبح في سجرة السرو فوقف ورفع الفند الي فوق فراء واحد مخبا في تلك السجره فاعلم به للملك فامر الملك في تنزيله من السجر فلما نزله وامتثل امام الملك فراه شب متسلح فامر الملك بان يرفعوا منه الصلاح وبعده فساله الملك ما حاجتك في هل مكان وما هو مقصودك قول الصحيح وامان الله عليك فاجابه ذلك الشاب ان سالت عني يا ملك الزمان انا عدوك المميت ودخلت واختبيت في هذا المكان حتي اقتلك في فراشك لا غير .

٧٨.٩ فاجابه الملك وايش هو الذي الجاك لقتلي وما هو الذي فعلته معك من السوحتي اردت قتلي فاجابه ذلك الشاب بان ديني بيلزمني اني اقتلك لانك عدو وديانتنا فلما سمع الملك منه هل كلام فقله ان كان دينك النجس بيامرك في قتلي من غير دنب انا ديني المقدس بيامرني باني اعفي عنك روح احكي الي جماعتك. حينذٍ امر الملك باطلاقه فاطلقوه خارج الصرايا ورجع الملك الي مقصورته واتكي في فراشه وما عاد صار له ذلك الوهم وربنا نجاه من ذلك العطب بعجيبه ظاهره.

٧٩.٩ فلما اشتهر هل خبر في مدينة بهريس حينذٍ اجتمعت اكابر الدوله والمدبرين الي عند الملك وهنوه علي سلامته من ذلك الخطر الذي وقع فيه ثم سالوه بانه يامر بعقد ديوان عام حتي الاساقفه وروسا الديوره ولما احتبك الديوان اصفطوا الجميع كل من هو في مقامه. حينذٍ تقدم دوك درليان واخبر الملك بان موجود في مملكة فرنسا

But his anxiety-filled delusions returned, twice as vivid. He got up again and went outside. 9.76

"Is there an enemy here?" he cried out to the guards. "Tell me the truth!"

"Sire, we just searched every room and found no one," they said, throwing themselves at his feet. "The palace gates are shut and guards are standing watch. How could a stranger or an enemy get in?"

The king was at a loss. Guided by a divine inspiration, he ordered them to accompany him into the palace gardens. They relit the candles and followed the king into the palace again. They opened the gate that led into the gardens, and toured them with their candles blazing, searching among the trees and in every nook and cranny. Once again they found no one, and turned to head back to the palace.

Then one of the king's guards, candle in hand, spotted a shadow in a cypress tree. He stopped, raised the candle, and saw a man hiding in the tree. He told the king, who ordered them to bring the man down. It turned out to be a young man, heavily armed. The king ordered them to take his weapons away. 9.77

"What are you doing here?" he asked the young man. "What is your purpose? Speak truthfully, and as God is my witness I will do you no harm."

"I'm your mortal enemy, king of the age!" the young man replied. "I snuck in and hid here to kill you in your bed!"

"What has driven you to try to murder me?" the king asked. "What did I ever do to harm you?" 9.78

"My religion compels me to kill you—you are the enemy of our faith," the young man replied.

"Yours may be a vile faith that compels you to murder me for no fault at all, but mine is a holy faith that compels me to forgive you," the king said. "Go, and tell your people so."

The king ordered them to let the man go, and they set him free outside the palace. Then the king went back to his private chambers and lay in bed. He no longer felt that sense of foreboding, for God had saved him from death through a manifest miracle.

Once this news had spread throughout Paris, the nobles and state officials all came before the king to congratulate him on his deliverance from the danger he had faced. They requested that he convene a general council, 9.79

كثير من الكنوت اعني هراتقه وهن اعدا الايمان الكاثوليكي وفسدوا كثير من الرعيه السدج ولا زال بيفسدوا ومخاف يا ملكا بان مع المدا ليلا يتبوا ارتقتهم في جميع بلاد فرنسا.

٨٠،٩ فلما سمع الملك هذا الكلام وتحقق عنده هذا الخبر حينذٍ امر بان يكتب امر ملوكي ويتنادا فيه في جميع مملكته بان من الان الي مضيت ستة اشهر¹ كل من التقي في مملكتي من الكنوت يقتل ويضطبط ماله للسلطنه وكل من له دين يستوفيه وان كان عليه دين يوفه وان كان له ملك من بيوت او حقول او بساتين وما يشبه ذلك يبيعه من غير جبر وبعد هل مده كل من هو خطيته عليه وامر ايضاً للمطارين والخوارنه وروسا الديوره بانهم يكتبوا الي ساير بلاد فرنسا بامر كردينال بهريس بان كل من عرف احد من هولاي الكنوت يخبر فيه الي حاكم البلد والذي يخالف يكون محروم ومقطوع من الكنيسه وعلي هذا النسق كتبوا الجميع الي مطارنت جميع البلاد حتي كل مطران ينبه في ابرشيته في هذا الامر.

٨١،٩ وايضاً امر الملك بان في جميع نوافد فرنسا يجلس قبجي من قبل الملك يمنع الهراتقه عن الدخول في ملكه والذي ما بيلتقا معه ورقة عماده يمنعوا عن الدخول فصاروا الكنوت ينتقلوا ناس بعد ناس الي منتها الستة اشهر ومنهم من يروح الي بلاد الانكيز ومنهم راحوا الي بلاد الفلامنك ومنهم تفرقوا في بلاد ايطاليا ومنهم راحوا الي بلاد النمسا والي غير مدن الي ان نضفت بلاد فرنسا منهم بالكليه.

٨٢،٩ فبعد مده من الزمان اتفق ان رجل سكاف في مدينة بهريس وهو راجع من سهرته الي بيته فرأ اثنين غريبي الزي دخلوا في باب فظن بانهم لصوص فدخل الي بيته والتجي في شباك وصار يرقب المكان فرأ دخلوا ايضاً ثلاثه وبعدهم دخلوا ثلاثه اربعه ولا زال ينتقلوا ناس بعد ناس الي ان صار الوقت نصف الليل فتعجب الرجل من هذا المنظر وعلمه بان هذا المكان مهجور من قديم فقال في باله ارقب هل مكان لعلي اعرف الداخلين اليه من يكونوا فاستقام في ذلك الشباك الي ان مضي

---

¹ «اشهر» لم ترد في الأصل.

including all the bishops and the abbots of the monasteries. Once all had gathered for the council and assumed their appropriate places, the Duke of Orléans came forward and informed the king that there were many Huguenots in the kingdom of France, heretics who were enemies of the Catholic faith. They'd managed to corrupt many guileless people of the flock, and were working to corrupt more.

"Sire, we fear they'll spread their heresy throughout all of France," he said.

When the king heard the duke's words and had his report confirmed, he ordered a royal edict drawn up then and there, to be proclaimed throughout France.

**9.80**

"Six months from today, any Huguenots found in my kingdom will be killed, and their property seized by the monarchy," the edict announced. "Let them all settle their loans and debts, and freely sell their homes, plots of land, orchards, and other properties. Once this period has elapsed, those who remain do so at their own risk."

The king further ordered the bishops, priests, and abbots to send letters throughout France proclaiming the edict of the cardinal of Paris, which stated that anyone who was aware of the presence of a Huguenot should report this to the local authority, on pain of excommunication. And so they wrote to all the bishoprics so that each bishop could inform his flock about the edict.[24]

The king also ordered that a royal gatekeeper be stationed at every point of entry to French lands, to prevent any heretics from entering the kingdom. Anyone without a certificate of baptism would be turned away. For the next six months, the Huguenots began to leave France, one group after another. Some went to English lands, others to Flemish lands, and still others dispersed throughout Italy. Some went to Germany and cities elsewhere, until France was entirely cleansed of them.

**9.81**

Some time later, a shoemaker in Paris was returning home after an evening out when he saw two strangely dressed people entering a doorway. He thought they might be thieves, so he went into his own house and repaired to a window to spy on the place they'd entered. Three more people entered as he watched. Then another three or four. People kept arriving until midnight. This sight surprised the shoemaker, particularly since the building they'd entered had been abandoned for a long time.

**9.82**

بعد نصف الليل ثلاثة ساعات فما راء الا صاروا يخرجوا ناس بعد ناس الان انتهوا وما بقا احد من داخل واغلقوا الباب.

٨٣،٩ فلما اصبح الصباح مضي ذلك الرجل السكاف الي عند الحاكم واخبره بالذي رااه في تلك الليله من دخول تلك الاوادم وخروجهم في الليل فلما سمع الحاكم هذا الخبر امر الرجل بان لا يحكي لاحد بالذي رااه انما يعاود لعنده عشيه فلما عاود ارسل معه اثنين من جماعته وامرهم بانهم يكمنوا في بيت ذلك الرجل ونضروا هل قول ذلك الرجل صحيح ام لا ولا يقولوا لاحد شي فلما اختفوا في بيت ذلك الرجل الي ان صار الوقت فصاروا يجوا ناس بعد ناس ويدخلوا لذلك البيت فاستقاموا جماعة الحاكم الي محل خروجهم فصاروا ايضاً يخرجوا ناس بعد ناس واغلقوا الباب كما ذكر ذلك الرجل للحاكم.

٨٤،٩ حينذٍ مضوا واخبروا الحاكم بالذي راوه. حينذٍ ارسل الحكم جواسيس من قبله ينقبوا علي تلك الاوادم فبعد حين عرفوا ذلك المكان وتلك الاوادم سادقين بان هل مكان لما كانوا الكنوت موجودين في مدينه بهريس كانوا يجتمعوا في هل مكان لاجل المشوره في الشهر مره او مرتين فلما تحقق الحاكم هذا الامر فاخبر به حضرة الملك بعد الفحص والتدقيق الكلي. حينذٍ امر الملك بان يرقبوهم حين يدخلوا جميعهم يسدوا الباب عليهم ويصعدوا[1] الي اعلا ذلك البيت . . . . .[2] يهدموه عليهم وان كان احدهم خلص من الردم فيقتلوه حالاً ويحرقوا ذلك المكان بالسكه والفدان ويبقوه بلا رصف حجاره حتي يصير تدكره جيل بعد جيل وكان عدد المقتولين خمسمايه رجل وضبطوا مالهم للسلطنه.

٨٥،٩ والفقير ومعي رجل من اهل بهريز مرينا في ذلك المكان فلما رايت ذلك المكان ما هو مرصوف تعجبت فسالت ذلك الرجل الذي كان معي عن سبب هذا المكان انه بغير رصف وان مدينة بهريس جميع زقاقها مرصوفه بحجر اسود فاحكالي هذا الخبر ولاجل هذا السبب ابقوه بلا رصف لاجل التدكار.

---

١ الأصل: يصعودوا.  ٢ مطموس في الأصل.

"I'm going to keep an eye on this place to find out who these people are," he said to himself.

He stayed by the window until three o'clock in the morning. Suddenly, he saw some people leave the building, followed by some others. This went on until the last people to leave shut the door behind them.

When morning came, the shoemaker went to see the governor and told him about the people he'd seen coming and going during the night. After hearing his story, the governor ordered the shoemaker to come back that evening, and not to tell a soul about what he'd witnessed in the meantime. When the shoemaker returned, the governor ordered two of his men to accompany him and hide in his house to find out if he was telling the truth. They weren't to breathe a word to anyone.    9.83

As they hid in the shoemaker's home later that night, groups of people began arriving at the abandoned house once again. The governor's men waited to see them emerge, and sure enough, the people eventually came out of the house and closed the door behind them, just as the shoemaker had told the governor.

They returned to the governor and reported what they'd seen. Immediately, the governor sent spies to make peepholes in the walls. After a while, they figured out what the place was and who was meeting there. When the Huguenots had lived in Paris, they would gather once or twice a month at that place and hold council. When the governor realized that this was still going on, he carried out a thorough investigation and reported his findings to the king. The king gave an order to have the Huguenots followed, up to the moment they entered the house. Then they were to be locked inside. Meanwhile, the king's men were to climb to the roof and . . . bring the building down on their heads. If anyone survived, they were to be killed on the spot. The house was to be razed to the ground and the lot was to be left unpaved as a reminder to future generations. In the end, five hundred men were killed, and their property was seized by the monarchy.    9.84

I once passed by that place, accompanied by a Parisian. When I saw the unpaved lot, I was surprised, and asked my companion why every street in Paris was paved with black stones except that one. He told me this story, explaining that the lot was left unpaved as a memorial.    9.85

وفي تلك الايام قدم الجي من اسطنبول مرسل من قبل حضرة سلطان احمد الي
حضرة سلطان فرنسا في طلب ثمانين مرسايه لانه كان عمرهسة مراكب بكلك
فاستقبلوه بغاية الاكرام ودخلوه الي مدينة بهريس بالاي محتفل وفرشوا له صرايا من
صراية الملك وعينوا له خدم وطباخين وسخيره واوه وهوكان معه اربعين جوخدار من
غير الخدم وعين الملك له ترجمان من تراجمينه وبعد كام يوم قابلوه مع حضرة الوزير
بونشطرين وزير الشرق فاتلقاه باكرام زايد وعمل له وليمه مكلفه.

وبعدما اكل الوليمه امرالملك بان يفرجوه علي مقاصف ورسايا وعلي بستان الملك
ورخواله الماء الذي بينفد من الاشجار ومن البرك والسنبيلات وخصوصاً ذلك القبو
من الماء الذي كا ذكرناه سابقاً. المراد من بعد تلك الفرج عاد راجعاً الي بهريس ودخل
الي سراته المعينه له. حينذٍ صارت اكابرالمدينه يزوروه ويهنوه بالسلامه وايضاً نسا
الاكابر والاماره ايضاً يزوروه لاجل الفرجه.

والفقير كنت كل يوم اروح الي صرايته واجلس مع الجوخداريه وكثير اوقات ما
يكون حاضرالترجمان كت اترجم ما بين الالجي وبعض من نسا الاكابر وكان الالجي
يتعجب من احتشام تلك النساء وحسن الفاظهم العذبه وسرعة جواباتهم المسدده
وكان يقول بان نسا بلاد الافرنج عندهم ادب واحتشام اكثر من نساء بلاده. اخيراً
بعدما زاروا اكابرالمدينه صار هو ايضاً يزورهم ويتفرج علي اماكنهم وحسن نظامهم
وتدبيرهم وعيشتهم الهنيه فراء فوق عظيم ما بين نظام بلاد الفرنجيه وبين نظام
بلاده المملوه من السبس والاضطراب والظم وجور الحكام علي الرعيه وكان يقول
هذا الي جوخداريته بالخني وكانوا يحكولي بالذي يقوله لهم لان كان رايهم مطابق
راي اغتهم.

اخيراً بعد كام يوم امرالوزير للترجمان والي كام واحد من اكابر الدوله بان يفرجوا
الالجي علي لوبراه وهومكان بيصير فيه ملاعيب غريه عجيه في فصل الشتا وبيدخلوا
اليه في الاسبوع مرتين فكلف الترجمان الي الالجي من قبل الوزير بانه يروح يتفرج

While I was in Paris, an ambassador arrived from Istanbul. He had been     9.86
dispatched by His Majesty Sultan Aḥmad to request eight anchors from His
Majesty the sultan of France, as he had recently constructed five ships for the
sultan's fleet. The ambassador was received most honorably and welcomed
into Paris with a great procession. One of the king's palaces was prepared as a
residence for him, furnished with a staff of cooks and an ample pantry. He had
forty officials in his retinue, as well as many servants. The king appointed one
of his own interpreters to serve him, and after a few days granted the ambassador an audience in the company of Pontchartrain, minister for the Orient.
The king showered the ambassador with honors and prepared a sumptuous
banquet for him.

After they'd dined, the king had the ambassador shown around the beauti-     9.87
ful grounds of Versailles. He was shown the royal gardens and the water spouting from the trees, the pools, the fountains, and especially that arching vault
made of water, which I described previously. After taking in all these sights,
the ambassador returned to the palace that had been prepared for him in Paris.
The nobles of the city began to pay him visits, congratulating him on his safe
arrival. The wives of nobles and princes also came along for curiosity's sake.

Each day, I'd go to the ambassador's palace and sit with his officials. Often,     9.88
the interpreter wasn't present, so I would interpret for the ambassador and
some of the nobles' wives. The ambassador was astounded by the gracious
modesty of these women, their refined and pleasant conversation, and their
sparkling repartee. He mused that the women of Frankish lands had far better
manners and were more respectable than the women of his own country.

Once the city's nobles were done calling on the ambassador, he began to
repay their visits. He gazed upon their homes, with their orderliness and good
management, and their comfortable way of life. It struck him that there was a
notable difference between the law and order in Frankish countries and law
and order in his own land, which was beset with tumult, trouble, oppression,
and tyrannical leaders who lorded over their subjects.[25] He would privately
confess all this to his officials, who would tell me what he'd said, as they were
in agreement with him.

After a few days, the minister told the interpreter and some senior gov-     9.89
ernment officials to take the ambassador to l'Opéra. This was a place where
extraordinary and wondrous plays took place during the wintertime. People

علي ذلك المكان تلك الليله فقبل الالجي بالرواح والفقير كت موجود وقتيدٍ[1] في سرايةِ
الالجي فلما بلغني هذا الخبر فرحت ومضيت اخبرت معلمي واخدت منه اذن باني
امضي مع جماعة الالجي حتي اتفرج فبعدما اخدت منه اذن رجعت الي سراية الالجي
واستقمت عندهم الي حين ما صار الوقت.

فحضر وقتيدٍ ناس من قبل حضرة الوزير وكلفوا الالجي بالرواح الي ذلك المكان
المذكور . حينذٍ خرج الالجي من الصرايه صحبة جماعته والفقير معهم فدخلوه الي
عرابانه ملوكيه ومضو به الي ذلك المكان فدخلنا جميعنا صحبة الالجي فرايت وهو
مكان متسع عالي الاركان برواقين في كل جانب رواق طويل ومقسمين الرواق قسم
وكل قسم بيسع ثمانية انفار لا غير وهو كمثل المقصوره وله باب وداخل المقصور
درابزون وخوانات من خشب الجوز تنجير مكلف .

وكل مقصوره لها ثمن اعني اول جزء من المقاصير الذين هن في اخرالرواق علي كل
واحد غرش تاني جزء الذين هم اعلا واقرب الي مكان الملعوب علي كل واحد غرشين
وثالث جزء الذي هو مقابيل مكان الملعوب كل واحد بواحد دهب والذين بريدوا
يروحوا يحضروا الملعوب انكانوا ثمانيه او خمسه او ثلاثه او واحد فيبروح واحد منهم
قبل بيوم الي عند وكيل هل مكان وبيقبضه علي عدد الانفار انكان في اول جزء او في
الثاني او الثالث كما ذكرنا فبعدما يقبض منه بيعطيه طسكره من يده في عدد الانفار
الذي قبض عنهم وبشير في اينا جزء يدخلوا فلما بيروحوا تلك الرجال بيعطوا الطسكره
للذي موكل علي ذلك المكان فبيدخلهم الي مكان الماشره في الطسكره وبيقفل الباب
عليه حتي لا احد يدخل لعنده .

فدخلوا الالجي الي اول مقصوره وهي اشرف مكان واقرب الي مكان الملعوب
ودخلوا جماعته في ثاني مقصوره وابقوا الابواب مفتحه لاجل الوسعه فلما جلسنا
ما رايت الا ستار منصوب علي عرض ذلك المكان حصه من الزمان فبدا داخل
الستار يضي بضيا عظيم حتي خمنت بان الشمس اشرقت من داخل وبعد قليل
من الزمان ما رايت الا ارتفع ذلك الستار وتبين من داخل شي بيدهش العقل

_____

would go there twice a week. The interpreter, acting on behalf of the minister, invited the ambassador to go that very evening, and he accepted the invitation.

I happened to be at the ambassador's palace at the time. When I heard the news, I was overjoyed. I went to tell my master about it, and begged his permission to let me join the ambassador's retinue and witness the spectacle. I received his permission and headed back to the ambassador's palace to wait until the appointed hour.

The representatives of His Excellency the minister arrived and invited the ambassador to accompany them. He left the palace with his entourage, and I joined them. The ambassador and the minister's men climbed into a royal carriage and headed off to the opera. We all entered together. It was a vast space with tall columns and two long galleries—one on each side. The galleries were divided into small sections, each of which could accommodate no more than eight people. The sections were like boxes, and each had its own door. Inside each box were a balustrade and benches made of ornately carved walnut. 9.90

Each box had a price. For example, a seat in the first set of boxes, which was at the very end of the gallery, cost a piaster.[26] The second set of boxes was higher up and closer to the stage; a seat in one of those boxes cost two piasters. The third set of boxes, which directly faced the stage, had a price of one gold piece per seat. Whoever wished to attend a play—either alone or in a group of eight or five or three people—had to visit the opera the day before to see the agent, who would sell him a ticket for the number of people attending and the category of box in which they wished to sit. Once he'd received the money, the agent would write out a ticket in his own hand, certifying that he had received payment for a specific number of people, and indicating which box they were permitted to enter. The people, upon arriving at the opera, would hand their ticket to the usher, who would lead them to the seats indicated on the ticket. Then the door to their box would be locked so no one could go in. 9.91

They brought the ambassador into the first box, the place of honor, and the closest to the stage. His retinue were given the second box, and the doors were kept open for the sake of space. When we sat down, all I could see was a curtain hanging across the width of the stage. After a few moments, a great white light began to glow behind the curtain. It was so bright it seemed to me the sun itself was shining on it. A moment later, the curtain rose, revealing an 9.92

اولاً في سدر ذلك المكان رايت مثل جبل وفيه اشجار كثيره وفلاحين ماشيين بين تلك الاشجار مع حميرهم وفي ديل ذلك الجبل ضيعه والفلاحين داخلين وخارجين من بيوتهم مع نسا‏هم وقرب الضيعه بوش من غنم بقر ومعزه ورعاه وما يشبه ذلك وبعدما رايت هذا كله وتحققت ان كل الذين رايتهم من اوادم وبهايم صحيحين ما هن خيالات ولا اشباح لكن اوادم ذي نفس وجسد من غير ريب.

وبعد هنيهه اقتم المكان ونزل من الجو غيمه كبيره وركزت علي الارض وخرج من تلك الغيمه رجل طويل القامه بلحيه بيضا وفي راسه تاج ملوكي وفي يده عكاز معكوف وهو مهيب ما بيشبع النظر منه فابتدا يلفظ الفاظ غويزه غير مفهومه فا رايت الا خرج من ذاخل اثني عشر صبيه واثني عشر غلام وكل منهم عمره من دون الاربعة عشر عام ولابسين حلل مدهبه ملوكيه وطلعتهم كالاقمار واصطفوا يمين وشمال. حينٍ بدت الالات الموسيقيه وتبعوهم تلك الغلمان والصبايا باصوات مثل سلك الذهب مطابقين اصواتهم مع تلك الالات شي بيدهش العقل بهذا المقدار حتي الفقير غبت عن حواسي.

فاستقامة النوبه مقدار نصف ساعه. اخيراً سكتت الالات وابتدا ذلك الاختيار يترنم بالاشعار بصوت رخيم فصاروا يتقدموا اليه اثنين بعد اثنين من تينك الغلمان والصبايا وبردوا عليه ايضاً بالشعر بنغم نديذ شي بيرضي الملوك ولما كملوا من تلك الاشعار بدة ايضاً النوبه كالاول واستقامة كملت الساعه. اخيراً ركب ذلك الاختيار تلك الغيمه وارتفع الي الجو وما عاد بان وفي ارتفاعه علي لحصة عين ارتفع جميع الذي كان موجود وظهر مكانهم صرايا عظيمه عالية الاركان ذات قصور وديواخانات وشبابيك بلور وما يشبه ذلك من المحاسن شبيه صراية سلطان فرانسا.

ولها باب مقنطر مبني من رخام ابيض واسود وخرج من ذلك الباب ملك متوج ولابس البرفيل وعليه هيبة الملوك وقضيب الملك في يده وحوله حواشيه من وزرا¹ واكابر الدوله الي ان وصل الي المكان المعين. حينٍ خرجوا الي ملاقاته تلك الغلمان والصبايا وقبلوا الارض امامه ورجعوا اصطفوا كالاول. حينٍ بدت الالات الموسيقيه

---

١ الأصل: وزر.

astonishing scene. First, there was what appeared to be a mountain in the very center of the stage. It was covered with trees, among which peasants walked with their donkeys. And at the foot of the mountain was a village, where peasants, men and women alike, bustled in and out of their houses. A group of cows, goats, and other animals stood nearby, together with some shepherds. I had to look twice to confirm that everything I saw—people and beasts alike—were real, and not specters or phantoms. It was unmistakable: They were creatures of flesh and blood!

A few moments later, the stage was plunged into darkness. A large cloud floated down out of thin air and settled on the ground. Inside the cloud was a tall man with a white beard. He wore a royal crown and carried a crooked cane, and was so striking in appearance that you couldn't take your eyes off him. He intoned some obscure and incomprehensible words, and suddenly twelve young girls and twelve young boys emerged from the cloud. Not one could have been older than fourteen. They wore golden royal robes and were as luminous as moons, and they lined up on the right and left sides of the stage. Then the musical instruments began to play, and the boys and girls joined in with voices as pure as gold filament. The harmony of voices and instruments was so mesmerizing that I utterly lost track of time. 9.93

The orchestra played for half an hour. Then it fell silent, and the old man began to chant some verses in a melodious voice. As he did, the boys and girls walked forward to him in pairs, responding with their own verses, set to melodies so beautiful they would charm a king. Once they finished singing, the orchestra began to play again and continued for the rest of the hour. Then the old man climbed into the cloud once again, and it rose into the air and disappeared. Meanwhile, everything else that had been onstage flew up too, and vanished in the blink of an eye! In its place appeared a palace as splendid as the palace of the king of France, complete with towering columns, pavilions, salons, crystal windows, and other beautiful features. 9.94

The palace had an arched entryway made of black and white marble. From it emerged a king in purple robes, a crown upon his head, and emanating a royal aura. He held a scepter in his hand and was surrounded by a retinue of ministers and grandees. The king strode forward to a designated spot, and the boys and girls came out to greet him, kissing the ground before him, then returning to stand in line once more. The instruments began to play again, and 9.95

تشتغل وتعتهم اوليك الصبايا والغلمان باصوات رخيمه ملايكيه الي ان كملت النوبه فاقتم المكان هنيه وانحضر من الجو غيمه كبيره وخرج من داخلها صبيه جميلة الحسن وصحبتها طفلين كانهم ملايكه ولهم اجناح وكل واحد في يده قوص ونشاب .

٩٦،٩ فصارة تلقش مع ذلك الملك والاطفال يضربوه بالنبل من غير حربه ولا زالت تلقش معه وتملقه وهو ينفر منها الي ان تشاجروا بالكلام ونفروا من بعضهم بعض قتبلين انها غضبت عليه ودخلة الي تلك الغيمه صحبه الاطفال وارتفعت الي الجو وغابة وفي ذلك الحين ما رايت الا انشقت الارض وخرج منها شيطان بدنب طويل ملقوت الجلد وفي خروجه نفخ في وجه ذلك الملك بنار ودخان وغاب في الجو وفي تلك الدقيقه ابتدا الملك يخلط ويرغي ويزبد كالجانين .

٩٧،٩ فلما حواشيه راوا ذلك الشيطان والملك اضحي مجنون هربوا جميعهم ليلا يصيبهم ما اصاب الملك فبقي الملك وحده وهو ينظم الاشعار علي ما اصابه ويقول هل هذا جري في المنام او في اليقضا وهو مضيع حواسه فما رايت والا خرج من الارض اربع عواميد تحت وبعده كمل التخت وانفرش ووضع فيه وساده فلما راء الملك ذلك التخت فاتكي ونام ولما نام خرج من الارض اربع اشجار في اربع قواني التخت ولما كانت هل اشجار تنمي وتطول كانت ترمي اغصان مورقه حتي صاروا اشجار كبار وخيموا علي ذلك السرير وهو نايم كانه في روضه .

٩٨،٩ وفي ذلك الوقت رايت خرج من تحت التخت بنات حسنات وفي يديهم شبابات وصاروا يدوروا ما يدور التخت ويصفروا في تلك الشبابات بحس رخيم لديد شي يجلب النوم والنعاس ويلقشوا مع النايم بلغاتهم وبعد حصه انتبه من النوم وغابة جميع تلك الاشيا ورجع ذلك الملك ينظم بالاشعار كالاول وهو في ذلك الحال نزلت ثاني مره تلك الغيمه وخرجت منها تلك الصبيه وصارت تستملقه وتجذبه الي حبها وفي ذلك الوقت دخلت الملكه وراءت هذه الساحره عنده فغضبت وزجرة تلك الامراه في الحال دخلت لغيمتها وولت هاربه الي الجو .

٩٩،٩ والتفتت الملكه الي الملك وصارت توبخه بكلام صارم علي فعله هذا كيف انه قبل قيمه مع امراه صاحره التي سببت له الجنون فلما سمع منها هذا الكلام المنكي غضب

the boys and girls sang along in sweet, angelic voices until the orchestra fell silent and the stage went dark. A moment later, a large cloud floated down from the sky, and a beautiful young maiden emerged from it along with a pair of small children. They looked like angels, as each had wings and carried a bow and arrows.

The maiden began to converse with the king while the children shot blunt arrows at him. When he spurned her attempts to win him over, they quarreled and turned away from each other. Looking furiously at the king, the maiden climbed into the cloud with the two children, and it rose up and disappeared. Suddenly, the ground split open and a demon appeared! He had a long tail and contorted skin, and as he emerged from the earth he spat fire and smoke in the face of the king. Then he vanished into thin air, leaving the king ranting and raving and foaming at the mouth like a madman. 9.96

At the sight of the demon and the mad king, the retinue of ministers and nobles fled in terror, fearing they might suffer the same fate. The king was left alone, reciting verses about what had befallen him and asking himself if he was dreaming or awake, all the while in a state of delirium. Suddenly, four bedposts emerged from the ground, followed by a freshly made bed with a pillow set upon it. Seeing it, the king settled into the bed and fell asleep. After he drifted off, four trees sprang up out of the ground at the four corners of the bed. As the trees grew taller, they sprouted branches thick with foliage and soon towered over the bed, sheltering it like a canopy. The king appeared to be sleeping in a garden. 9.97

Then some beautiful maidens with reed flutes emerged from beneath the king's bed. They began to dance around it, playing soft, sweet lullabies on their flutes as they spoke to the sleeping king in their own languages. A few moments later, he woke up, and everything around him disappeared. He returned to reciting verses as he had before he'd fallen asleep; then the cloud with the maiden descended to the stage once again. She fawned over him, trying to seduce him, but the queen appeared and caught the sorceress weaving her spells upon the king. The angry queen lashed out at the maiden, who climbed into her cloud and escaped into the air. 9.98

The queen then turned to the king and began to reproach him bitterly. How could he debase himself with such a woman, a sorceress who had driven him to madness? At this rebuke, the king flew into a rage, drew his weapon, and 9.99

غضب شديد فاستل سلاحه وضربها في خاصرتها فخرج السنان من جنب الاخر فسقطت مايته فلما نضروا جواريها موت ملكهم فروا هاربين واعلموا ارباب الدوله في الذي جري فالتاموا جميعهم واحضروا الجنود ودخلوا علي الملك وارتقوه وخلعوه من كرسي الملك وصارة الصيحه في السرايا وغاب كل ما كان موجود ما عدا حوط من الرخام الابيض والما خارج من فم سبع رخام وفايض الماء بيصب علي ثاني حوض وفايض الثاني بيصب علي حوض الثالث.

اخيرًا بدت الالات الموسيقيه تدق وخرجوا اوليك الغلمان والصبايا وصاروا ٩،١٠٠ يرقصوا اثنين بعد اثنين برقص محتشم من غير خلاعات وبعدما كملوا من الرقص عملوا تمني للالجي وللحاضرين ومضوا. حينذٍ ارتفع ذلك الحوض والماء وما عاد له اثر البتا فاخدني العجب كيف ان من وقت ما انفتح الستار رايت هل حوض وكل شي تغير وهل حوض ثابت وكت اظن بان الما جاري من كوز او انه نبع. المراد بعد ارتفاعه اقتم المكان وما عاديان شي ابدًا وكل الملعوب والذي دكرّه عن هذا المكان وهذا الملعوب ما هو شي بالنسبي عن النضر والسمع شي بيفوق الوصف.

اخيرًا نهض الالجي ومعه الترجمان واغاوات الوزير وتمشوا نحو الباب وكان واقفين ٩،١٠١ علي الصفين جميع النسا الذين كانوا موجودين في ذلك المكان واكثرُم بنات الاماره ونسا اكابر المدينه واولاد الاماره وما يشبه ذلك ونحن مارين سمعت من واحده من بنات الاماره٢ بتشتم دقن الالجي وبما اني بفهم في لسان الفرنساوي التفت وقلت لها في لسان الفرنساوي لماذا يا ستي بتلفظي في حق اسدادنا هذا اللفظ الناقص فلما سمعت مني باني فهمت قولها اختفت بين النساء من عظم نجلها واستحياها لانها انتبهت علي النقص الذي صدر منها في حق الالجي. المراد جزنا ما بينهم وخرجنا خارج ذلك المكان وكل من ركب عربانته ومضي في حال سبيله والالجي توجه الي صرايته والفقير توجهت الي بيت معلمي.

_____
١ الأصل: وخروجوا.   ٢ الأصل: الامار.

plunged it into the queen's waist! The weapon passed through the queen's body, its point emerging from the other side, and she fell to the ground, dead. At the sight of the dead queen, her servant girls fled in horror and told the nobles what had happened. Rallying together, the nobles summoned some soldiers and climbed onto the throne to depose the king. Then a great cry went up in the palace, and everything on stage disappeared except for a white marble basin, with a marble fountain in the shape of a lion. Water spouted from the lion's mouth into the basin, and overflowed into a second basin, which overflowed into a third.

At last the musical instruments began to play, and the young boys and girls 9.100 emerged on stage again, dancing together in pairs in a respectable manner, without a hint of wantonness. When they finished dancing, they bowed to the ambassador and the rest of the audience, and exited. The marble basin then rose into the air, disappearing without a trace! I was beside myself with wonder. From the moment the curtain had gone up, that basin had remained on stage without moving, while everything else changed. I'd concluded that the basin must have received its water through a pipe or a spring. But that was before it rose into the air! Then the stage went completely dark, and I couldn't see a thing. The play was over.

What I've recounted about the opera house and the play is nothing compared to the experience of seeing and hearing it for oneself. It was simply indescribable!

The ambassador got up from his seat along with the interpreter and the 9.101 minister's men, and they all made their way toward the exit. On either side stood all the women who'd been present at the play, most of them princesses, wives of the city's nobles, and other royals. As we walked by, I heard one of the princesses make fun of the ambassador. I understood French, of course, so I turned to her and replied in the same language.

"My lady, why would you speak ill of my master?"

Realizing that I had understood what she'd said, the princess quickly disappeared into the crowd of women, deeply embarrassed and ashamed of her rudeness. In the meantime, we made our way through the crowd and left the opera. Each climbed into his own carriage and went on his way, the ambassador returning to his palace and I to my master's house.

٩،١٠٢ فلما دخلت رايت كثير من اصحاب معلي في استنظاري حتي يستحكوني ويتضحكوا علي فلما امتثلت امامهم صاروا يسالوني عن الذي رايته وسمعته هل انه عجبني فاجبتهم كل شي الذي رايته وسمعته عجيب لكن اعجب ما رايت هو ذاك الحوض الذي استقام من اول الملعوب الي اخره يجري الماء من فم السبع واخيراً ارتفع الحوض والماء جملة هذا الذي اعتجبت منه اكثر من باقية الملاعيب التي صارت.

٩،١٠٣ فصاروا يتضحكوا وقال لي واحد منهم هذا اهين من جميع التي رايتها فقلته يا سيدي زيل عني الشبهه بحياتك فقلي هذا الحوض هو من دف مدهون شكل الرخام وخلف منه سندوق مزفت ملان من الماء ويعلوه غراف يصب في نفيره ومنه بتدخل الماء في فم السبع ولما بتنهي الي اسفل بترجع لذلك السندوق وهذا الغراف بيديره غلام وجميع هذا الماء بمقدار قربه وما بيتقص منه شي ابداً وله بكرات ومربوط بوتراسود ما بيبان في حكم الليل فلما بيسحبوا تلك الاوتار بيرتفع بقل سهوله وكذلك باقيت الملاعيب علي هذا ..... [1] فسالته عن ذلك الاختيار وتلك الغيه فاجابني هذا يسمي سلطان الجو وذلك الملك يسما باكوس وهذا الملعوب يسما نعاس الملك باكوس وهذا الذي رايته جميعه تحت معاني عن سيرة الملك باكوس.

٩،١٠٤ ثم قلي بان هل مكان مكلف دراهم كثير وكل الذين رايتهم من بنات وغلمان وغيرهم من اوادم كلهم ترباي في هل مكان وشرحلي عن تلك التغيرات واحده فواحده وقطع عقلي وهدا شي بيطول الشرح فاقتصرنا التغيير عنه لانه مشغول بحركات ودواليب مختلفه بصناعة عجيبه حتي في لحصة عين بتغير جميع ما كنت تراه والمكان شاسع من داخل وبعيد عن النظر ولاجل هذا بترا هية الشي لا غير وما بتقدر تشاهد حركاته كيف هي.

٩،١٠٥ وفي مكان اخر يسما كوديه وهو شبه خيال البزار عندنا والذي بيظهر فيه من الملاعيب من المسخنات والمضحكات شي بيفوق الوصف وهو منظوم من اوادم وصاحب الملعوب بيسما اركلين مثل ما عندنا صاحب الملعوب عيواظ وقري كوز

---

[1] «وكذلك باقيت الملاعيب ... هذا .....» في الهامش والكلمة الأخيرة مطموسة.

I found several of my master's friends waiting for me. They were there to   9.102
hear my account of the evening, and to have a laugh at my expense. When I
presented myself before them, they asked me about what I'd seen and heard.
They wanted to know—was I impressed?

"Everything I saw and heard was astounding," I replied. "But the most amaz-
ing thing was the basin with the water spouting out of the lion's mouth from the
beginning of the play to the end, when it just rose up into the air, together with
the water! Of all the illusions I saw, that was what impressed me most."

They all burst into laughter.   9.103

"That was the simplest effect of them all!" one of my master's friends replied.

"Then, for goodness' sake, clear up my confusion, kind sir!" I said.

"The basin is made of wood, painted to look like marble," he explained.
"There's a tank full of water sitting behind it, its interior coated with pitch.
A bucket wheel feeds the water from the tank into a pipe, which flows into the
lion's mouth. When the water reaches the last basin, it goes back into the tank."

The bucket wheel was turned by a young boy, and the entire quantity of
water that circulated through the fountain amounted to no more than a wine-
skin's worth, with scarcely a drop going astray. The basin was attached to some
pulleys and had black cords that were invisible in the darkness. When they
were pulled, the basin would rise easily. All the other theatrical effects made
use of the same mechanism.

"What about the old man in the cloud?" I asked.

"That's the Sultan of the Air, and the king's name is Bacchus," he replied.
"The title of the play is *The Slumber of King Bacchus*, and everything you saw
was related to episodes from that king's life."[27]

He went on to tell me that the opera had cost a great deal of money to   9.104
build. All the young girls and boys I'd seen, along with everyone else on stage,
had been trained there. He explained how each of the set changes took place,
astounding me even more. It would take far too long to explain all of this, as the
changes are operated by an ingenious system of pulleys and wheels that allows
the entire scene to be transformed in the blink of an eye. The area behind the
stage is vast and quite distant from the spectators, which is what permits one to
see the shapes of things but not the mechanisms behind them.

There's another place called the Comédie, which puts on wonderful farces   9.105
and comedic plays similar to the shadow plays we have at home, except they

وكل ملعوبهم يبني عن اشيا صادره في ذلك العصر وعن اناس سكره اشقيا وغيرهم من ذوي الباطولين المعترين وغيرهم من الجنود الجبانين الجزوعين الغير ثابتين في الحروب وما يشبه ذلك وخصوصاً عن النسا الشراشيح الرعنات وجميع هذا منظوم بالفاظ مقنعه مسدده حتي ان السامع بينوعظ من امثال هل جماعات المكروهه والمدمومه من الجميع .

٩.١٠٦ وفي بعض الكنايس في ايام معلومه يصير تعليم الحق من الباطل وهذا اشرف ما وجدته من المحاسن في هذا التعليم الشريف وكثرة فوايده لكل انسان من نسا ورجال عالم كان اوسادج شب كان اواختيار . المراد نافع للجميع اعزب كان اومزوج كاهن كان او راهب وهو ان يقف في المنبر رجل عالم كاهن فيلاسوف ومقابيله في الاسفل ايضاً معلم فيلاسوف عنده من كل شي خبر من لقش العالم وخرافاتهم فيبدي¹ الواعظ من المنبر بيوعظهم² بالحق فيعترضه الثاني بالباطل بكلام اهل العالم المغشوشين من الشيطان عدو الخير .

٩.١٠٧ فالكاروز الفوقاني يفسد كلامه بشهادات من كتاب المقدس وبرويه كيف انه مغشوش في اعتقاده في هل اراء الفاسده التحتاني بيبدا يعترف في الخطايا المشهوره بين الناس فيبرد عليه كاروز الحق وبيفسد اعترافه المملو من الحيل والاعتدارات العنكبوتيه التي بتزيد خطيته خطية اخري وبرويه كيف يعترف بالحق من غير تصنع وتلبسه وخصوصاً في اعترافات النسا العلاكات كانهم بيقصوا قصه الي معلم الاعتراف وهلم جرا .

٩.١٠٨ ونهار الاحد والعيد بيصير في باقية الكنايس تعليم المسيح للاولاد من بعد الظهر بساعه الي وقت العصر من رجل معلم فيلتمو اولاد صايح تلك الكنيسه حتي يتعلموا والذي بيكون من تلك الاولاد حفظ متيلته بيقف في الوسط وبيقول الذي تعلمه من الاحد الماضي واذا قاله علي ما يجب حينٍ المعلم بيعطيه قونه اوصوره وبيعلي منزله عن غير اولاد الذين ما حفظوا متيلتهم ومن جري هذا بتصير غيره في باقت الاولاد

---

١ الأصل: فيبدي. ٢ الأصل: بيوعظم.

are played by real people. These plays have a main character named Harlequin, just as ours have the characters of Iwaẓ and Karagöz.[28] Every one of their plays makes reference to contemporary events, and features miserable drunkards, down-on-their-luck loafers, cowardly and panic-stricken soldiers, and other similar characters, especially foolish and uncouth women. The dialogue is convincing and to the point, making an example of these detestable and blameworthy characters so that the audience might learn from their ways.

In some churches, on specific days, a lesson is given on how to distinguish truth from falsehood. This lesson benefited all sorts of people—women and men, educated and ignorant, young and old, wed and unwed, priest and monk. The best example of a lesson that I encountered proceeded as follows. A wise priest—a philosopher, in fact—would come to the pulpit. Facing him, below the pulpit, was another philosopher who was well versed in all the frivolous chatter of the masses and their superstitions. The priest on the pulpit would begin to preach the truth, and the second would contradict him with falsehoods, reproducing the claims of those people deceived by Satan, enemy of the good.   9.106

Then the priest on the pulpit would refute these words with evidence from the Holy Bible, showing him how he'd been deceived into holding these corrupt views. The priest down below would then begin to confess his sins, recounting only those most common among people. The priest of the truth would reply by invalidating his confession, which was full of tricks and justifications as tangled as a spiderweb, which only added another sin to his record. He'd then teach him how to confess truthfully, without fabrication or ambiguities. This lesson was especially relevant to garrulous women, who were prone to spinning tales to their confessors, and to other similar types.   9.107

In all the other churches, catechism classes were held for children on Sundays and holidays, beginning at one o'clock in the afternoon and continuing until the evening. The children would gather in their neighborhood church along with a learned teacher. The student who had memorized the previous week's lesson would stand in the middle of the assembled group and recite what he'd learned. If he did so faithfully, the teacher would give him a medallion or a picture, setting him apart from those students who hadn't learned their lessons. This would make the others more zealous about doing their work the following week.   9.108

حتي يحفظوا متيلتهم في تلك السبه وكذلك يوم الاحد والعيد يصير مجادلة في جميع المدارس اعني الذين بيدرسوا في الفلسفه بيجلس المعلم وتلاميذه بيتجادلوا مع بعضهم في علم الفلسفه والذي بيطلع رايه احسن من الجميع بيعطيه المعلم قونه من فضه وبيعلي منزله وقول عن علم المنطق وعلم اللاهوت وعلم الفلك وباقيت العلوم علي هذه الصيغه .

١٠٩،٩ والفقير كت دخلت مع رجل مصور الذي كان يعلمني الرسم الي مدرسة المصورين وكان ذلك يوم خميس الكبير ليلة الجمعة العظيمه فلما دخلت فرايت انفرد اربع معلمين وهن المشهورين في صناعة التصوير ودخلوا الي داخل ذلك المكان فدخلت معهم بشفاعة ذلك المصور الذي كان يعلمني الرسم فلما انتهيت فرايت صاله متسعه وما يدورها خوانات وفي الوسط مركوز صليب من خشب عالي طويل وفي اسفله ثلاث درجات فحضر وقتيدٍ شاب كامل القامه والخلقه في سن الثلاثين سنه ونيف وهو عاري بالزط وموزر بحزم ابيض .

١١٠،٩ فامروه المعلمين بانه يصعد الي الصليب فصعد ومسك بيدتيه من خشبة المصلبه مكان النقب من كل جانب حبله وركز رجليته علي مركز مصمر في تلك الخشبه فلما استوي علي الصليب فصاروا المعلمين يتشاوروا في بعضهم حتي وقفوا علي راي وقالوا لذلك الشاب ارخي ذاتك كانك ميت فلما رخا ذاته ورجلاه ثابته علي ذلك المركز انحنت ركبتيه وصار معلقًا بايديه . اخيرًا امروه بانه يحني هامه فاحناه فبقي منظره كمنزر رجل مايت وهذا رسم السيد المسيح لما مات علي خشبة الصليب .

١١١،٩ فبعدما تم الامر علي هذا المنوال ورضيوا الاربع معلمين علي هذا التشخيص حينٍ امروا لجميع التلاميذ بانهم يدخلوا ويرسموا الصلبوت علي هذا الشكل فبعد ما دخلوا وكل منهم اخذ مكانه وصاروا يرسموا باوراق وبقلم رصاص مقدار ساعه وبعده نزل ذلك الشاب من علي الصليب حتي ياخد راحه هنيهه من الزمان ورجع وقف كما كان في الاول واستقام ايضًا مقدار ساعه حتي كملوا التلاميذ الرسم . اخيرًا اوردوا التلاميذ اوراق رسمهم علي المعلمين فتفرسوا فيهم وميزوا الاصنع رسمه من الجميع فاعطوه قونه دهب بجنزيرحتي يضعها في عنقه وجعلوه ريس علي باقية التلاميد .

Similarly, the schools would hold debates on Sundays and holidays for all the students who studied philosophy. Teachers and pupils would sit together and hold debates on philosophical matters, and whoever articulated the finest argument would receive a silver medallion from his teacher and be named head boy. The same went for those who studied logic, theology, astronomy, and similar sciences.

I once visited an art school in the company of an artist who was teaching me **9.109** how to draw. It was Holy Thursday, the eve of Good Friday. As I arrived at the school, I saw four masters of drawing, standing apart from everyone else. They were famous for their skill in illustration, and I accompanied them as they entered the school, as I was there by invitation of my teacher. Once inside, we came to an enormous room furnished with benches on all sides.

A tall wooden cross stood in the center of the room, with three steps at its base. At that moment, a young man appeared. He must have been about thirty years old, and had a perfect physique. He was stark naked except for a white loincloth.

The masters told the young man to go up onto the cross, which he did. **9.110** There were ropes hanging from the two ends of the crossbar, where the nails would have been. Taking a rope in each hand, he placed his feet on a ledge that was nailed to the wooden plank. Once he was settled, the masters began discussing among themselves how to proceed, and soon reached a consensus.

"Lean forward and hang, as though you were dead," they told him.

He slackened his body, bending his knees while leaving his feet planted on the ledge so he was hanging by his hands. Then they told him to loll his head to the side, which he did, looking for all the world like a dead man. He was the very image of Our Lord the Messiah, dead upon the cross.

When everything was prepared and the four masters were satisfied with **9.111** the scene being represented, they instructed all the pupils to enter the room and to draw the crucifix as it was composed before them. All came in, took their places, and spent an hour drawing with pencils on paper. The young man came down off the cross to take a short break before assuming the same pose he had before. After another hour, the pupils had finished their drawings and presented them to their masters, who scrutinized them carefully and chose one as the finest. They gave the pupil who had produced the drawing a gold medallion on a chain to wear around his neck, and declared him to be top of his class.

٩،١١٢ وفي اماكن ايضًا لاجل تعليم مسك السيخ اعني السلاح مثل عندنا لعب الحكم وغير اماكن في تعليم مسك البندقيه ونيشان الرصاص وغيره لاجل تعليم ضرب الطوب وغيره تعليم الخيوله والنتيجه موجود في مدينة بهريس مدارس من جميع العلوم والفنون الموجوده في ساير الدنيا حتي ان موجود اماكن لتعليم الرقص وغيرهم لتعليم الالات الموسوقيه.

٩،١١٣ وموجود في هل مدينه كثيرين من بنات الخطا وبيوتهم معروفه من الاشارة المعلقه علي ابوابهم وهي كبة شوك كبيره وموجود من المحتالين والمحتالات شي كثير ومن جملتهم واحده محتاله لعبت ملعوب بيتارخ وهو انها استكرت بدلت حوايج مكلفه نظير بدلات القاضونوات الاغنيا واستكرت عربانه باربع روس خيل واربع خدام راكبين ورا العربانه وسارت الي دير الذين بيادبوا اولاد البجر العاصيين علي والديهم فلما انتهت الي ذلك الدير دعت الريس واتوسلت اليه بان لها غلام فاجر وانه بيصرف مالهم في الفجور ولعب الورق وان والده مات. اخيرًا طلبت منه بانها تاتي به الي عنده بحيـله فيمسكه ويضع رجليه في القيد ويجلده كل يوم ويقـيته بالخبز والماء كهادتهم الي حين ما يتادب¹ وترجع وتاخده واخرجت اعطته نفقه شهر.

٩،١١٤ وقالت له اياك تنغش من كلام هل غلام لانه حيلي تلبيس لانه بيقول لك انا ابن فلان تاجر وابي ما معه خبر اطلقني حتي امضي لعند ابي وهل امراه ما هي امي فلا تصدقه ابقيه الي حين ما اجي الي عندك في اخر هل شهر وانضر هل عقل ام لا. حينٍ بطلقه ام بقيه فاجابها الريس يكون خاطرك طيب انا بعرف الاولاد المحتالين امضي بسلام.

٩،١١٥ حينٍ ركبت العربانه وامرت الذي بيقيد الخيل بان يمضي بها الي مكان يسماء لوبلي اعني الصرايه وهذا المكان مخصوص بتجار الهند الاغنيا لان بينوجد عندهم من بضاعة الهند شي مكلف من قطع وبرجادات وخاصات رفيعه متمنه وغيرهم

---

¹ الأصل: يتدادب.

Other places were devoted to teaching fencing, which is similar to the  9.112
sport of stick and shield we have here at home. Other places offered instruction in riflery, shooting, cannon firing, and horsemanship. In sum, there were
schools dedicated to every art and discipline in the world, even ones that
taught dance and how to play musical instruments.

There are many ladies of light virtue in Paris. Their homes are each marked  9.113
by a sign hanging on their doors of a large heart made of thorns. There are
also plenty of scoundrels among the citizens, including one woman in particular who played a trick so dastardly that it deserves to be recorded for
all posterity. This is how it went: She rented a beautiful ball gown, fit for a
wealthy lady, and a carriage, drawn by four horses, with some footmen to
ride on the back of it, and drove off to the monastery devoted to the reform
of delinquent children.

Upon arrival, she summoned the abbot and begged him to help her with
her dissolute son, who had squandered the family's money by gambling at
cards and other debaucheries. His father was dead, she explained, and she
planned to bring the young man to the monastery under false pretenses.
Would the abbot help her by seizing him when they arrived, binding his feet,
and flogging him each day? She handed the abbot some money to cover a
month's expenses and told him not to feed her son anything but the usual
bread and water until he was reformed and she returned to pick him up.

"Don't be fooled by anything he tells you, because it's all trickery and lies,"  9.114
she added. "He'll say, 'I'm the son of the merchant so-and-so, and my father
has no idea where I am. Let me go home to him! That woman isn't my mother!'
But don't believe him. Keep him here until I return at the end of the month to
see if he's straightened out or not. I'll decide then whether to free him or keep
him here."

"Don't you worry," the abbot said. "I know a thing or two about delinquent
children. Go right ahead with your plan."

She climbed into her carriage and told her driver to take her to a place  9.115
called Le Palais, which means "the palace." This was a place reserved for the
wealthy merchants of India, who sold expensive Indian merchandise such as
*barjādāt*, fine and costly *khāṣṣāt*, and other types of fabric. Arriving at the
palace, she headed directly to see the chief merchant, a wealthy man, stopping

من القطع وما يشبه ذلك فلما انتهت الي ذلك المكان توجهت الي عند رجل اكبر تجار ذلك المكان فلما انتهت امام حانوت ذلك الغني وقفت الخيل. حينذٍ امر ذلك التاجر خدامه بان يخرجوا لها كرسي للنزول من العربانه ومسكوها من تحت اباطيها ودخلوها الي ذلك الحانوت فاسترحب فيها ذلك التاجر وعمل لها الاكرام الواجب ثم جلست واخرجت مكتوب.

١١٦،٩ وقالت له بان اخي ارسلي هل مكتوب من اصبانيا وطالب مني باني ارسله بعض اغراض هل بينوجد عندك منهم فاجابها ما هن فصارت تسمي له اسماءهم شي بعد شي فقال لها ذلك التاجر كل شي الذي ذكرتيه موجود عندي والذي طلبته الخر ما يكون من قماش الهند واغلي ثمن من غيره فصار يخرج لها شي بعد شي وهي تنقي من العشر طاقات خمسه او سته وترد الباقي ولا زالت تنقي وترد حتي تمت مطلوبها.

١١٧،٩ اخيرًا صارت تفصل معه فصل بازركان وتكتب الذي قطعت ثمنه الي حين ما كملوا الفصل وجمعوا الدراهم يكونها خمسة الاف ونيف من السكوت. اخيرًا بقوا لها تلك القماشات ووضعوها ذاخل العرابانه. حينذٍ نهضة تلك القاضون حتي تروح فقالت لذلك التاجر ارسل معي واحد من غلمانك حتي ارسل لك معه الدراهم فالتفت التاجر وقال لابنه الوحيد امضي يا ولدي مع خالتك واقبض منها هذا المبلغ وراد يركبه في عربانه فما قبلت بل ركبته في عرابنتها وامرت الذي بيقيد الخيل بان يمضي بها الي فلان صايح في فلان محله.

١١٨،٩ فساروا في الطريق ومروا علي ذلك الدير المنسوب لتاديب الاولاد الخرفلما انتهت العرابانه مقابيل باب الدير جدبت القيطانه التي معلق فيها لجم الخيل فوقفت الخيل فانحدرت وقالت لذلك الغلام ابن التاجر بريد اتكلم مع ريس الدير بشي ضروري انزل انت الاخر اتفرج علي هذا الدير وعلي الاولاد الخر المغلولين هاهنا فنزل الغلام ودخل مع تلك القاضون للدير فلما انتهوا في صحن الدير ارسلت دعت الريس فلما حضر

her carriage outside his shop. The merchant ordered his servants to place a footstool at the door to help the lady step down from the carriage. Hoisting her by the upper arms,[29] they whisked her into the shop to meet the merchant, who welcomed her most graciously. The lady sat down and took out a letter.

"My brother sent me this letter from Spain, requesting that I forward him 9.116 some things," she said. "Perhaps you'll have some of what he's looking for."

"Such as?" asked the merchant, and the woman rattled off a list of products.

"I have what you're looking for," the merchant said, as she'd requested the most luxurious and valuable of Indian fabrics. He began to bring out one piece after another, and for every ten things he showed her, she would choose five or six and refuse the rest. She continued in this way until the order was complete.

Then she set about negotiating with him like a seasoned merchant, making 9.117 a note of all the discounted prices she'd bargained for. They concluded the negotiation, added it all up, and arrived at a total of over five thousand ecus. They bundled up the fabrics for her and stowed them in the carriage. Then the lady rose to leave.

"Have one of your servant boys come along with me to collect your money," she said.

The merchant turned to his only son.

"Son, go along with the good lady and pick up the money," he said. The merchant began to prepare a carriage for him, but she refused, insisting that the young man ride in her own carriage. Then she told her driver to take them to an address in a certain quarter of the city.

They set off, and soon passed by the monastery that reformed juvenile 9.118 delinquents. As the carriage drew up alongside the gate of the monastery, the woman pulled the cord attached to the horses' bridles, and they came to a stop. She stepped out of the carriage.

"I wish to speak to the abbot of this monastery about an urgent matter," she told the merchant's son. "Why don't you come along, and have a look at the monastery and all the disobedient children in shackles?"

The boy got out of the carriage and went into the monastery with the lady. As they entered the courtyard, she summoned the abbot.

"This is the boy I was telling you about," she said. They began to chat, and the boy wandered off into the monastery to look at all the children in chains. As soon as he disappeared, the woman bid the abbot farewell. She left the monastery, climbed into her carriage, and set off to the address she'd previously

الريس فصارت تقله ها هو ذا الغلام الذي كنت دكت لك عنه وهن في هل مصاحبه دخل الغلام الي داخل يتفرج علي الاولاد المقيدين وفي ذلك الوقت ودعت الريس وخرجت من الدير وركبت العربانه ومضيت الي حيث ما امرت الذي بيقيد الخيل فلما انتهوا في ذلك الصايح وفي تلك المحله وقفت الخيل عند مفرق دروب وامرت بان يخرجوا البقج من العربانه ويضعوهم في ذلك المكان واعطتهم ما يخصهم من كري العربانه وكراهم وامرتهم بالمسير وهي دخلت الي بيتها ونقلت البقج وما احد عرف في ملعوبها هذا الي الان.

واما الغلام بعدما تفرج راد الخروج فمسكوه وقيدوه مثل الغير فصار يقلهم ١١٩،٩ لماذا بتقيدوني انا مارر درب مع القاضون اخرجوا سالوها فقالوا له اجلس يا شقي يا مبدرق¹ مال ابيك في لعب الورق فبهت الغلام من كلامهم له وصار يقول لهم انا ابن فلان تاجر وهل امراه اشترت من عند ابي قماش الهند وانا ماضي معها حتي اخذ ثمنه فلما سمعوا منه هذا الكلام فراح واحد منهم واخبر الريس بالذي احكاه هذا الغلام فاما الريس بما انه ملقب من امه بانه محتال وتلبيس فقال لهم لا تصدقوه انما زيدوا في عذابه فاستقام الغلام ثلاثة ايام يقتات علي الخبز والما ويجلدوه كل يوم مرتين بغير رحمه وما عادوا سغوا الي قوله.

واما والده استناه الي الدهر فما اجا فقال في باله بتكون القاضون كلفته حتي ١٢٠،٩ يتغدا معها فاستقام الي حكم العصر ما بين منه خبر فاعتجب من عوقته فمضي النهار ودخل الليل فما بان احد. حينذٍ امر خدامه بانهم يطوفوا ويدخلوا بيوت الاكابر والبازركان ويسالوا عن سيدهم لعلهم يروه او ياخدوا خبره فمضوا الخدام كل واحد في صايح فصاروا يفتشوا ويسالوا عنه فما راوا له خبر ولا جنية اثر الليل كله رجعوا الي عند سيدهم واخبروه بانهم داروا مدينة بهريس باسرها فما وجدوا له خبر فاغتم ذلك التاجر وحزن حزناً شديد علي فقدان ابنه والمال واتجه الي عند الحاكم واخبره بالقضيه.

---

¹ الأصل: مبردق.

given her driver. When they arrived, she had the horses stop at the street corner, and told the men to unload the bundles from the carriage and leave them where they'd stopped. She paid them for the hire of the carriage and their services and sent them on their way. Then she brought all the bundles into her house, and no one was the wiser.

As for the boy, when he was done touring the monastery and tried to leave, 9.119 they grabbed him and chained him up like the other children.

"Why are you tying me up? I'm just visiting, along with that lady. Go ask her!"

"Sit down, you miserable wretch," they replied. "Been squandering your father's money at cards, have you?"

The boy was flabbergasted.

"I'm the son of so-and-so, the merchant," he protested. "That woman purchased some Indian fabrics from my father, and I was just going to collect payment for them."

At this, one of the men went off to tell the abbot what the boy had said. But the abbot refused to believe it, having been forewarned by the boy's "mother" that he was a scoundrel and a liar.

"Don't believe him," the abbot replied. "And let's give him a few extra floggings too."

The boy spent three days at the monastery, surviving on bread and water, and receiving a merciless flogging twice a day at the hands of his jailors, who paid no mind to his protestations.

In the meantime, the merchant had spent the morning awaiting his son's 9.120 return.

"The lady must have invited him over for lunch," he thought to himself when the boy hadn't appeared by midday. By late afternoon, there was still no sign of him and the merchant was baffled by his son's tardiness. At nightfall, the boy still hadn't turned up, so his father ordered the servants to go to the homes of all the nobles and chief merchants to inquire as to the whereabouts of their young master. Perhaps they'd find him, or at least discover where he'd gone.

The servants spread out. Each headed to a different quarter of the city and began to snoop around. But the whole night passed without them locating even the ghost of a trace of him. They returned to their master with the bad news that they'd turned Paris upside down but hadn't uncovered a single clue. Distraught over the disappearance of his son and the loss of his property, the merchant went to see the governor of Paris and told him what had happened.

١١٧١.٩ حينذٍ امر الحاكم بان يطبعوا اوراق بصورة الواقعه ويلزقوهم في تصليبات الشوارع والحارات وذكر في تلك الاوراق كل من عرف او اخذ خبر هذه الامراه يكون له الحظ الوافر وكل انسان الذي يعرف فيها وما يجي يخبر عنها يشنق ففعلوا كما امر الحاكم ولزقوا الاوراق في الزوايا كما ذكرنا اول يوم وتاني يوم وفي يوم الثالث اتفق بان خادم ذلك الدير نزل للمدينه حتى يتسوق بعض اغراض للدير فصادف تلك الاوراق فلما قراء واحد منهم علم بان الغلام كلامه حق ورجع في الحال.

١٢٢.٩ واخبر الريس وان المدينه ملهوبه بنار من اجل الغلام الذي فقد والحاكم امر بالشنق لكل من عرف فيه وما يخبر عنه. حينذٍ دخل الريس الي عند الغلام وساله عن قصته فاحكاله الغلام مثل ما مذكور في تلك الوراق. وقتيذٍ صدق الريس كلامه واطلقوه من القيد ومضي به الريس الي عند والده وقص له القصه من اولها الي اخرها كما ذكرنا سابقًا فرجع الغلام الي والده والمال غابة فيه تلك الشقيه وما قدروا ياخدوا لها خبر ابدًا وهذا ما تم من حيلة هذه الشقيه.

١٢٣.٩ ويوم اخر وانا مارر في بعض الشوارع فرايت واحد راكب ويصيح السنطانسه وفي يده وراق مطبوعه والناس عمالين بيشتروا منه كل ورقة بجديدين فاتصدقت[١] الي واحد معارف وسالته ما هذه الاوراق وما هي صنطانساء فاجابني بان هذه الاوراق سجل الذي تسجل علي واحد اثيم بالشنق وصار يحكيلي قضية السجل وهو انه لما بتحكم الشريعه علي رجل بالموت بتكون في الساعة العاشره قبل الظهر بساعتين وهو مدون في ورقة دنب ذلك الرجل وكيف انه علي موجب دنبه استحق الشنق او التكسير او قطع الراس وما يشبه ذلك من الميتات المتنوعه التي يحكموا فيها علي المجرمين وبعد خروج هل سجل من يد قاضي الشريعه ياخدوا تلك ورقة السجل ويطبعوا صورتها في وراق ويدوروا في المدينه بيبيعوهم كل واحده بجديدين.

١٢٤.٩ واما المجرم المسجل عليه القتل بيدخلوه الي كنيسه داخل المحكمه فيتسلمه معلم الاعتراف بيعرفه اعتراف عام وبيستقيم معه في الاعتراف حكم ساعتين الي وقت

١ الأصل: فالتصدقت.

The governor immediately issued an order to have posters printed and 9.121
placed at every street corner stating the facts of the case, adding: "An ample
reward awaits anyone who knows this woman or has heard of her. And anyone
with information who does not come forward will be hanged!" The governor's
order was carried out, and the posters were plastered at every street corner.
Two days passed with no incident. On the third day, it so happened that one
of the servants of the monastery had come into town to purchase some things
for the monastery. As he walked by a poster, he paused to read it. As soon as he
did, it dawned on him that the boy had been telling the truth. He hurried back
to the monastery.

"The city's on fire with the news of a lost boy!" the servant told the abbot. 9.122
"And the governor has vowed to hang anyone who knows something about
him and doesn't come forward." The abbot immediately went off to see the
boy. He asked him for his story, and the boy recounted the very same facts the
posters did. It was only then that the abbot believed him. He set the boy free,
and took him back to his father, explaining the entire affair to him from start
to finish. As for the goods, the damnable woman absconded with them all, and
no one was ever able to figure out who she was. And so it was that the she-devil
swindled the merchant.

One day, as I was walking down the street, I saw someone running by, 9.123
shouting, "*La Sentence!*" He was carrying some printed papers, which he was
selling for two silver coins.

"What are those papers?" I asked a friend. "And what's *la sentence*?"

"They're broadsides that report why a criminal is being hanged," he said,
going on to explain why broadsides were issued. When the courts condemned
a man to death, the execution would always be held at ten o'clock in the morning. The man's crime would be recorded on a piece of paper along with the
punishment necessitated by the crime, be it hanging, decapitation, drawing
and quartering, or whatever capital punishment is typically handed out to
criminals. After the judge issues the sentence, it's printed on sheets of paper
and sold throughout the city for two silver coins apiece.

As for the criminal condemned to death, he is taken to a chapel inside the 9.124
courthouse to meet the chief confessor, who hears his full confession. This lasts
two hours, ending at noon. After leading the condemned man in the act of

الظهر وبعد كالت اعترافه بيندمه وبيعطيه الحله وفي ذلك الوقت بيجيبوا للكاهن
غدا فيتغدا مع ذلك المجرم وبعد خلوصهم الغدا يمضي الكاهن وبيدخل الي عنده
راهب من رهبان مار اوغسطينس حتي يوعضه ويسليه ويجرعه والاخر بيستقيم
عنده الي وقت العصر.

١٢٥.٩ حينٍ بيجي الجلاد وبيدق عليهم الباب وبيدخل وبيضع المرسه في رقبته وبيخرجه
من الكنيسه وبينزلوا كلاهم من درج المحكمه وبيركبوا العرابانه الراهب والمجرم والجلاد
وبيسيروا بهم الي المكان المعين من الحاكم وهناك بيصعد الجلاد في السلم الذي مركب
علي خشبة المشنقه وبيتبعه¹ المجرم بيقف تحت رجلين الجلاد وبعده بيصعد الراهب
وفي يده الصلبوت ورافعه امام عيني المجرم حتي يندمه ويجرعه علي المنيه.

١٢٦.٩ حينٍ الراهب بيلتفت الي الشعب وبيديهم في صلاة النياحه فيبصلوها بعياط
وبعد خلوصها فيبيدوا في ثاني صلوه والكاهن مداوم علي تنبيهه علي الندامة الكامله
فلما بتنتهي ثاني صلوه حينٍ بيلتفت الكاهن الي الشعب وبيحثهم بانهم يطلبوا
من مريم العدري شفيعة الخطاه بانه تخلص هل نفس الخارجه من بينا فيبيبتدي²
الشعب يصلي ببكا ودموع طالبين من مريم العذري بانها تشفع في هل نفس وبعد
انتها الصلوه بيرشمه الكاهن باشارة الصليب المقدس ونزل من علي السلم وفي ذلك
الوقت الجلاد دفع ذلك المجرم والمرسه في رقبته وركب علي كتافه ودخل هامه بين
ساقيه وطوطحه ثلاث مرات ونزل من عليه ونزلوا المشنوق ووضعوه في العرابانه
واشتروه الحكا من الجلاد واخدوه الي مدرستهم حتي يشرحوه ويعلموا التلاميد فبعد
انتها الكلام سالت ذلك الصاحب وماذا عمل حتي تسجل عليه الشنق.

١٢٧.٩ فاجابني بان خبر هذا المسكين غريب عجيب وهوان اوما لي عن رجل تاجر كثير الغنا
وفي طول عمره ما جا له ولد فيوم من ذات الايام دخل الي مارستان البناديق فراء
بينهم ولد جميل المنظر كامل الصوره فجح مهدب في الفاظه ذو عقل رفيع بيفوق علي

---

١ الأصل: يتبعه. ٢ الأصل: فيبتدي.

contrition, the confessor grants him absolution. Lunch is then served, and the priest and the criminal dine together. After lunch, the priest withdraws, and is replaced by a monk from the order of Saint Augustine, who admonishes the condemned man, reconciling him to his fate and giving him courage to face it. The priest returns and remains at the condemned man's side until the evening.

At this point, the executioner arrives. He knocks at the door, enters, and places a noose around the condemned man's neck. The three men leave the chapel, descend the steps of the courthouse, and climb into the wagon together, making their way to the place designated by the authorities for the hanging. The executioner ascends the ladder propped against the gallows, followed by the criminal, who stands a step behind him. The monk comes next, with a crucifix in his hand. He holds it up in front of the criminal's eyes, urging contrition and courage in the face of death. 9.125

The monk then turns to face the assembled crowd, leading them in the prayer of eternal rest. It's a prayer that is practically shouted, and is followed by a second prayer. All the while, the priest continues to urge the condemned man to contrition for all his sins. When the second prayer is complete, the priest turns to the crowd again and exhorts them to ask the Virgin Mary to intercede on behalf of this soul, which will soon be departing from our midst. The crowd begins to pray and weep, begging the Virgin to intervene for the sake of the man's soul. At the end of the prayer, the priest makes the sign of the cross over the criminal and descends the ladder. 9.126

At that moment, the executioner pushes the condemned man off the ladder, the noose tight around his neck, and climbs onto his shoulders, the man's head between his legs. He swings him back and forth three times to snap his neck, then jumps off. Then he takes the body down off the gallows, puts it into the cart, and sells it to the doctors, who take it to their medical school so they can dissect it for the instruction of their students.

After my friend finished explaining all of this, I asked him what this particular man had done to deserve to be hanged.

"The story of this poor man is strange and remarkable indeed," he replied, launching into it. 9.127

There was once a very rich merchant who had no sons. One day, he visited an orphanage for bastard children, and saw a perfectly beautiful child among them. He was precocious, well-spoken, and intelligent, and exceeded all the other children in beauty, manners, and modesty. The merchant was drawn to

جميع الاولاد بالحسن والظرافه والاحتشام فمال قلبه اليه وطلبه من وكيل المارستان حتي ياخده ويربيه عنده مثلما يكون ابنه.

١٢٨،٩ وهناك بيفرقوا هل اولاد علي معلمين الصنايع والكارات اعني كل من تقدم وانتجبوه معلم في كار من الكارات بيلزموه باخد ولد من هل من هل اولاد ويجعله مثل ابنه ويعلمه الكار الي حين ما يكبر ويتعلم الكار مليح. حينذ بيبقا مطلوق الاراده ان راد يستقيم عند معلمه والا يمضي بيشتغل عند غيره اوانه بينتخب معلم وبيشتغل وحده وهذه من جملة المحاسن الموجوده في تلك البلاد.

١٢٩،٩ فتسلم ذلك الرجل التاجر ذلك الولد بوسيقه ومضي به الي بيته فلما راته حرمة ذلك التاجر نحبته محبه عظيمه وهي ورجلها بهذا المقدار حتي انهم كتبوا في ورقة وصيتهم بان هل ولد يكون وريثهم بعد موتهم وصار ذلك التاجر يربيه واوقف له معلم يعلمه القراه والكتابه وبعدما كمل علمه دخله الي مكتبه وعلمه مسك الدفاتر والحسابات الي مده من الزمان حتي انه تعلم وصار يساعد ابوه في البيع والشرا والاخد والعطا حتي انه فاق علي ابوه في كار البازركانيه.

١٣٠،٩ واستقام الي ان بلغ من العمر نحو عشرين سنه ونيف. حينذ اشارة امه الي ابوه بان يخطبوه ويزوجوه علي حيوة عينهم فارتضي ابوه بذلك وخطب له بنت محسنه من بنات التجار وخصص له من ماله مقدار والبنت كذلك خصصها والدها مقدار من الدراهم وكتبوا وثيقه ما بينهم في المحكمه ودونوا في الوثيقه المال الموهوب لهم من والديهم وبعد مده من الزمان هموا في العرس وزوجوهم. حينذ انفرق ذلك الولد من ابوه وفتح له دكان وصار يبيع ويشتري وحده وهذا صار برضا ابوه لانه راه نشط في كار التجاره وصار يكسب في متاجرته.

١٣١،٩ فاستقام في هل حال مده من الزمان فيوم من ذات الايام مضي الي عند ابوه حتي يستشيره عن امر من الامور فما راء ابوه في البيت فدخل المكتب لعله يراه هناك فما راه فماد فؤاد الرجوع فاخدته التفاته فراء تمسكين موضوعين في طاقه

the boy, and asked the director of the orphanage if he could take him home and raise him as a son.

In France, children are fostered by master artisans of different trades. Anyone who advances in his trade and is recognized as a master artisan is required to take on one of these children as an apprentice. He treats him like a son, and teaches him the trade. Once the child has grown up and learned the trade well, he's free to do what he wishes. He may remain with his master, for example, or find another. He might even become recognized as a master artisan himself, working on his own. This practice is one of the many virtues of that country.

So the merchant adopted the child, received a document to this effect, and took him home. When the man's wife saw the boy, she too fell deeply in love with him. They were both so enamored that they amended their will, stipulating that the boy should inherit from them when they died.

The merchant then attended to the boy's education, arranging to have an instructor teach him how to read and write. Once the boy had completed his studies, the merchant involved him in his business and gave him a thorough education in the methods of bookkeeping and accounting. The boy began to assist his father in all of his commercial dealings, from purchases and sales to bargaining and negotiation, and eventually surpassed his father in his trade.

When the young man was about twenty years old, his mother suggested to his father that they marry him off while they were still alive. The father agreed, and arranged an engagement to a fine young lady, the daughter of a fellow merchant. He set aside some of his wealth for his son, the girl's father did the same for her, and they drew up a marriage contract at the courthouse. Recorded on the contract was the sum of money gifted to the betrothed couple by their parents. After a period of time, the wedding was held and they were married.

The young man left his father's business and set up his own shop. He began to operate on his own with the blessing of his father, who could see that his son was a shrewd merchant and had already begun to earn a living from his commerce.

Everything was going well until one day, when the young man went to see his father to ask his advice about a particular matter. His father didn't seem to be home when the young man arrived, so he went by his office to search for him. He wasn't there either. The young man was about to turn around and go home when he noticed something. There were a pair of bond certificates sitting in a cubbyhole at his father's desk. The certificates had been issued by

9.128

9.129

9.130

9.131

من طاقات المكتبه وكانوا هل تمسكين من تمسكات الملك واحد بخمسمايه والاخر بثلاث مايه غرش لان الملك لما تقل عليه الخرجيه فكان يعطي لاجل علايف العسكر تمسكات فكانت روس العسكر ياخدوا هل تمسكات ويبيعوهم الي التجار بناقص شي قليل وياخدوا منهم دراهم ويعطوا العلايف وهذا كان في زمان الحرب وبعد مده تطلع الخزنه وكل منهم يعطي تمسكات التي معه ويقبض دراهم علي المختوم ولما تعوق خروج الخزنه عليهم فكانوا يتاجر في هل تمسكات الموجوده عندهم كمثل ما تكون معارضه مثلاً يشتري التاجر شخص بضاعه بالف وخمسمايه غرش يقول للبايع عندي تمسك بخمسمايه والف غرش نقوض ويصير البازار علي هذا المنوال.

فالغلام لما راء هل تمسكين غره الطمع وقال في باله ابي عدا عن البيع والشرا وما ١٣٢،٩ له حاجه فيهم وربما نسيهم فاخدهم ومضي الي حانوته وما احد عرف في دخوله وخروجه من مكتب ابوه فبعد كام يوم اشتري من واحد بازركان[1] شخص بضاعه ودخل التمسكين في البازار بجاري العاده ومضي كلمن هو في حال سبيله.

فمضي علي ذلك مده من الزمان فيوم من الايام دخل لعند ابوه دلال وقله تحت ١٣٣،٩ يدي شخص بضاعه رخيصه وهي شكار اسمع مني حتي اخد لك هي بثمن مناسب فلما سمع التاجر بثمن مناسب فرضي وقال للدلال عندي تمسكين بثمانية غرش وبعطي الباقي دراهم فرضي الدلال بذلك وكتبوا البازار وعرضه الدلال علي صاحب البضاعه فقبل وارسل البضاعه الي عند ذلك التاجر مع الدلال فلما تسلم التاجر البضاعه فتح سندوقه واخرج الدراهم وعد الذي يخصه من بعد التمسكين ومضي الي مكتبه حتي يجيب التمسكين فما راهم فتعجب.

اخيراً فتش بين الاوراق والدفاتر[2] فما راء شي فاحتار في امره فصار يسال امراته ١٣٤،٩ والخدام من دخل للمكتب فاجابوه ما احد بيدخله غيرك فزاد فيه العجب والتزم بانه

---

١ الأصل: بازكان.  ٢ الأصل: والدفا.

the king, one for five hundred piasters and the other for three hundred. It was customary for the king, when his expenditures had grown onerous, to issue bonds in order to be able to pay the salaries of the military. His generals would take these bonds, sell them to the merchants at a modest discount, and use the money to pay their soldiers.

This was a wartime practice, and once the treasury was flush again, the merchants would present their bonds and receive money in exchange, as was guaranteed by the royal seal. When the treasury was delayed in repaying its debts, the merchants would buy and sell these bonds among themselves, treating them like currency. For example, if a merchant were to buy some goods for 1,500 piasters, he might say to the seller, "I'll give you a bond for five hundred piasters, plus a thousand in cash." The negotiation would proceed along these lines.

Now, when the young man saw the bond certificates, he was overcome with greed. 9.132

"My father isn't in business anymore, and has no need for these bonds," he thought. "In fact, he might even have forgotten all about them!"

The young man pocketed them and returned to his shop without anyone knowing he'd set foot in his father's office. A few days later, while purchasing some merchandise from another merchant, he introduced the two bonds into the negotiation, as was customary. The transaction was completed smoothly, and each man went his way.

Time passed; then one day a broker came to see the father. 9.133

"I've got some cheap merchandise for you, a real steal!" the broker said. "Believe me, I can get it for you at a good price."

Confronted with the prospect of a good deal, the merchant agreed.

"I have some bonds worth eight hundred piasters, and I'll pay the rest in cash," he said.

The broker was satisfied. They drafted an offer, which the broker took to the seller, who accepted it, and sent the goods to the merchant through the broker. Once he'd received delivery, the merchant opened his cashbox and counted out the amount he owed minus the value of the bonds. Then he went into his office to get the bonds, but to his surprise he couldn't find them.

The merchant hunted through his papers and account books, to no avail. 9.134 Bewildered, he turned to his wife and servants, asking them who had entered the office.

"No one ever goes in there besides you," they replied.

يعطي عوض التمسكات دراهم نقوض فغت عليه الامر فبعد التفتيش والفحص الكلي قطع الاياس منهم لكن صار يحكي للتجار عن فقده التمسكين فواحد من التجار قله لا تخف التمسكات بينوجدوا عن قريب انما قلنا عن تاريخهم ولا بد ما بيقعوا في يد واحد منا.

حينذٍ اعطي لكل واحد منهم التاريخ فما مضي شهر من الزمان وصلوا ليد واحد من التجار كان اخدهم بطريق المعارضه فلما تقرس فيهم عرفهم بانهم تمسكات ذلك التاجر المذكور فمضي الي عنده واروه التمسكين فلما راهم التاجر عرفهم ولكن ما الفايده منين بعرف انكان هذا هو الذي نشلهم من مكتبي هذا شي ما بيتصدق عن رجل تاجر اهل عرض ناس ملاح بانه دخل الي مكتبي ونشلهم فاجابه ذلك التاجر امضي اخبر الحاكم في امرك وهو بيحصل الذي نشلهم.

فمضي ذلك التاجر الي الحاكم واخبره في الامر الذي وقع وكيف انهم انوجدوا عند فلان تاجر . حينذٍ الحاكم امرتين من خدامه بانهم يمضوا مع هل تاجر ويستقصوا الجره فمضوا معه الي عند ذلك التاجر وسالوه بامر الحاكم يقول لهم من يد من اخد هل تمسكين فقال من يد فلان تاجر فمضوا عند ذلك ايضاً وسالوه منين له هل تمسكات فدلهم عن رجل تاجر ايضاً فما زالوا يمضوا عند واحد ويدلهم علي غيره حتي انتهوا الي عند الغلام ابن التاجر المذكور .

فلما سالوه فما قدر يقول عن احد بل التجم وصار ابكم فعرفوا بانه هو الذي نشلهم فمضوا به الي عند الحاكم فلما امتثل امام الحاكم وهو مرعوب فساله الحاكم منين اخدت هل تمسكين فما قدر يرد جواب فامر في حبسه تحت العداب حتي يقر بالصحيح . اخيراً قر واعترف بانه هو الذي نشلهم من مكتب ابوه فارسله الحاكم الي الشريعه فحكمت عليه الشريعه بالشنق امام باب بيته لاجل انه امين حتي يتادب غير من الامنا.

As his astonishment grew, he was forced to pay in cash the remainder meant to be covered by the bonds. This rankled him. Meanwhile, he continued to turn his whole office upside down, searching for the bonds, but eventually gave up hope. He did, however, mention the lost certificates to his fellow merchants.

"Don't worry, they'll turn up soon enough," one of them said. "Tell us the date they were issued, and we'll be able to recognize them when, inevitably, they fall into the hands of one of us."

The merchant gave them all the issue dates of the two bond certificates. 9.135 A month later, they turned up in the course of a transaction. When the trader involved studied them, he realized right away that they were the bonds his fellow merchant had lost. He took them to their owner, who immediately recognized them.

"But how does this get me anywhere?" he wondered to himself. "How can I be sure that it wasn't this fellow who pilfered them from my office? On the other hand, I can't believe that an honorable and upstanding merchant would sneak into my office and take my property."

"Why don't you go tell the governor about your situation?" the other merchant suggested. "He'll be able to find the person who stole them."

So the merchant went to see the governor and informed him about the 9.136 matter, telling him how the bonds had been recovered by his colleague. The governor ordered two of his men to retrace the course of events and take the merchant with them. They went to see his colleague and demanded, by authority of the governor, that he tell them where he'd gotten the bonds. He named a certain trader, and they went off to interrogate him in the same way. He in turn pointed them to yet another trader, and the trail continued in this way until they finally arrived at the merchant's son.

When they asked him where he'd gotten the bonds, he was struck dumb. 9.137 That was when they knew they'd found the thief. They escorted him to the governor, to whom the terrified young man presented himself.

"Where did you get these bonds?" the governor asked him.

He was unable to utter a word, and the governor ordered him to be jailed and tortured until he told the truth. Finally, the young man confessed that it was he who had stolen the bonds from his father's office. The governor sent him to court, where he was sentenced to hang in front of his own house, to symbolize his violation of the trust placed in him, and to serve as an example to others who were also invested with people's trust.

١٣٨،٩ فلما بلغ الخبر لابوه ندم علي ما فعل بحيث ما عاد يفيده الندم وفي الحال مضي الي عند الحاكم حتي يتشفع في ابنه بقوله له هذا الغلام ابني بالتربيه ووريثي وما بيني وبينه شي وكل مالي له فاجابه الحاكم اليسانه اخدم بالاختلاس من غير علمك وانت امين منه ولاجل هذا حكمت عليه الشريعه بالشنق فلما خاب امله من قاضي الشريعه التجي الي اشراف المدينه بتوسل عظيم بانهم ينجوا ابنه من الموت فما امكنهم بان يخالفوا الشريعه. حينذٍ اتجه الي بلاط الملك وارتمي علي اكابر الدوله بجمله هدايا فما امكنهم ايضاً ان تخط هل شريعه. اخيراً اتصلت الي الملك نفسه بواسطة الاماره اولاد الملوك فما امكن بانهم يغيروا هذا الحكم المحتوم عليه من الشريعه فخاب امله من الجميع ورجع الي منزله وهو ينتحب ويبكي هو وامراته وما قدر احد يعزيهم في حزنهم الي بعد زمان طويل.

١٣٩،٩ وتم الامر هكذا لاني مضيت الي المحكمه حكم العصر فرايت بقرب الدرج عرابانه فاضيه كشف وكام واحد من الجنود وبلك باشيهم راكبين الخيل وهن في الاستندار وبعد هنيهه نزل الجلاد وقابض علي مرسة المحكوم عليه وهو مكتف من قدام وتبعهم الكاهن فنزلوا من الدرج وركبوا العرابانه والكاهن واضع يده الواحده علي كتفيه ذلك الغلام ويده الاخري قابض فيها الصليب المقدس وواضعه امام وجه الغلام وهو يسجعه ويوعضه ما داموا سايرين في الطريق الي حين ما وصلوا الي المشنقه فلما انتهينا الي هناك فرايت خشبه مركبه علي سيبا وطرفها الواحد خارج عن السيبا وموضوع عليهم سلم فصعد الجلاد الي اعلا السلم وصعد الغلام بعده تحت اقدام الجلاد والمرسه في رقبته قابض عليها الجلاد.

١٤٠،٩ اخيراً صعد الكاهن وفي يده الصلبوت ولكن الغلام مع الصلبوت امام وجهه كانت عيناه مرتفعه الي شباك بيته وهو يبكي وبعد خلوص الصلوات كما ذكرنا وكل الشعب يبكي علي هذا الغلام الذي هو في عنوان شبوبيته وهو حسن الصوره وهو في ثيابه الفاخره ثياب عرسه وعلي ما نقلوا بان له من العمر اثنين وعشرين سنه وهذا

When his father heard this news, he regretted what he'd done, but it was too late for such regrets. He immediately went to see the governor, begging him to intercede.   9.138

"That young man is my adopted son and my heir," he pleaded. "I have no quarrel with him, and all my property belongs to him!"

"Didn't he steal the bonds, taking advantage of your trust by absconding with them without your knowledge?" the governor asked. "That is why he has been sentenced to hang."

Without hope of swaying the judge, the merchant sought out the nobles of the city, begging them to save his son from death, but they could hardly contravene the law. So the merchant made his way to the king's court, throwing himself before the state's high officials and showering them with gifts. They too were powerless to reduce the sentence. Finally, the case reached the king himself by way of some princes, but they too were unable to change the judgment handed down by the court. Having lost all hope, the merchant returned home to weep and wail with his wife. No one was able to console them for a very long time.

And that was that. I went to the courthouse in the evening and saw an empty cart sitting uncovered, parked by the steps. A few soldiers waited on their horses, along with their commander. After a few moments, the executioner emerged from the courthouse holding the noose of the condemned man, who had his hands bound in front of him. The priest followed behind, and they all descended the steps and climbed into the cart. The priest kept one hand on the young man's shoulders and with the other held a crucifix in front of his face. All the way to the gallows, the priest never stopped admonishing the young man and preparing him to face death.   9.139

When they finally arrived, I saw a wooden plank mounted on a tripod, with one end protruding. A ladder was propped up against it. The executioner climbed the ladder, followed by the young man, who ascended a step behind him, the noose around his neck and the other end of the rope in the executioner's hand.

The priest then mounted the ladder, holding the crucifix, and placed it before the face of the young man, who could only stare up at the window of his house as he wept. As the prayers came to an end, everyone in the crowd was crying for this handsome man in the bloom of youth, who stood there in the   9.140

الذي جرح قلوب الشعب الملتم وكنت تسمع حس بكاهم و ضجيجهم كمن كل واحد منهم مات له ولد وحيد محبوب منه ولما انتهت الامور دفعه الجلاد كما ذكرنا ونزلوه في العرابانه وساروا به الحكم اما الجلاد ما قدر ينزل من علي السلم حتي تحاوطوه الجنود خيفتا من الشعب ليلا يقتلوه لان عندهم الجلاد ممقوت مبغوض منهم قوي كثير .

٩.١٤١ ويوم اخر وانا واقف علي جسر مار ميخائيل مكان منزولنا فات ايضا الذين بيبيعوا اوراق السنتانسا اعني السجل وكان تسجل علي اثنين كانوا يقطعوا الدروب يشلحوا ويقتلوا الذين يشلحونهم فرحت قرب العصر الي المحكمه حتي اتفرج فرايت عرابانتين والجنود كما ذكرنا فنزلوا الاثنين مكتفين من ورا والجنود قابضين عليهم ومعهم كاهنين والجلاد فركبوا كل واحد منهم في عربانه ومعه كاهن ماسك الصليب المقدس .

٩.١٤٢ ومضوا بهم الي مكان ساحه فلما انتهينا الي ذلك المكان رايت ناصبين تخت علو نصف قامه وموضوع في الوسط صليب من خشب غليض معكوف مثل صليب ماري بطرس فاصعدوا اول واحد الي اعلا التخت وقابضين عليه الجنود. حينذٍ فكوا كَتّافه ومدوه علي الصليب وهو عريان وربطوا ساعده الواحد في خشبة الصليب رباط متين وساعده الاخر في ثاني خشبه وربطوا ساقيه كل واحد في خشبه وبقي هامه مدلا بين الخشبتين .

٩.١٤٣ فلما انتهوا من رباطه وقف حينذٍ الجلاد وقري علي راس الملا السجل المحكوم عليه وهو تكسير اربعه فلما انتها من القراء[١] اتقدم واحد بيده ساطور طويل سميك وفي ذلك الوقت بدا الكاهن يحث[٢] الشعب علي الصلوه كالمالوف فبعد ان كمة الثلاث صلوات احد الجلاد وضرب ذلك الحرامي المربط علي الصليب علي ساعده الواحد ثلاث ضربات في ذلك الساطور حتي كسر عظامه اربا حتي كنت اسمع تكسير العظام وضربه علي ساعده الثاني ايضا ثلاث ضربات وعلي ساقيه كل واحد ثلاث ضربات الي ما بقا فيه عضو صحيح. اخيرا ضربه علي صرته ضربه واحده ضربه بقوله له هذه انعام من الملك حتي يموت بالعجل. اخيرا فكوه من علي الصليب ووضعوه في

---

١ الأصل: القراء. ٢ الأصل: يحش.

fine suit he had worn to his wedding. I heard he was only twenty-two years old. This was what really stung the hearts of the assembled crowd, who wept and wailed as though each of them were losing a beloved only son.

After the preliminaries were complete, the executioner pushed the young man off the ladder. They then brought his body down to the cart, which was driven away by the doctors. As for the executioner, he wasn't able to come down the ladder until the soldiers surrounded it, out of fear that the mob would lynch him. Executioners are loathed by the French.

Another day, when I was at Pont Saint-Michel, near our house, some 9.141 people walked by selling *La Sentence* papers again—that is, the broadsheet. Two people had been sentenced for highway robbery and for killing the victims they'd robbed. As the evening drew near, I went to the courthouse to watch the proceedings. I saw two carts by the waiting soldiers, as I recounted earlier. The two men were brought out under guard, their hands tied behind their backs. With them were two priests and an executioner. Each of the prisoners was put in a cart and joined by a priest holding a holy crucifix.

They took them to a public square, and when we all arrived, I saw that a 9.142 platform had been set up. It was about waist high, and lying across it was a thick wooden cross, skewed like the cross of Saint Peter.[30] The soldiers took firm hold of the first man, brought him up onto the platform, freed his hands, and stretched him out naked upon the cross. Each of his forearms was tied with stout bindings to a separate arm of the cross, as were each of his legs, leaving his head to hang free between the two planks.

Once the man was tied down, the executioner read his sentence to the 9.143 assembled crowd: He was to have his four limbs broken. Then another man came forward with a long, stout metal truncheon. The priest led the crowd in prayer. When the three prayers were complete, the executioner turned to the robber bound upon the cross and struck one of his forearms with the truncheon three times. With each blow, I could hear the bones shatter. Then he moved to his second forearm and his legs, striking them each three times. The man was left without a single unbroken limb.

The executioner then struck the man across the belly, telling him that this was an act of mercy by the king, so that he would die more quickly. They then untied him from the cross and placed him in a wagon wheel, stuffing his body through it as though it were so much ground-up flesh.[31] They then lifted the

بكرت عربانه وكوموه داخلها حتى بقى كبت لحم ورفعوا تلك البكره ودخلوا في تقبها خشبه بجانب ذلك التخت وتركه ينين وهامه مدلا برات البكره.

٩،١٤٤ اخيرًا اصعدوا الثاني الى ذلك التخت فلما تفرس في رفيقه وراه في هذه الحاله برك على ركبتيه وصار يتوسل الى الكاهن بانه لا يدعهم يميته هذه الميته الصعبه بل يخنقوه قبل التكسير فحن قلب الكاهن عليه والتفت الى الجندي الذي من قبل الحاكم العرفي واتشفع فيه بان يخنقوه قبل التكسير فبالجهد حتى قبل طلبة الكاهن وامر بان يخنقوه فمدوه مثل رفيقه على الصليب وربطوه كالعاده وخربقوا في رقبته حبله ودلوها من تقب التخت ومزوروها بحركه دولاب فاختنق في الحال وعاد الجلاد كسر عظامه كالاول ووضعوه في بكره عربانه مثل رفيقه وابقوهم الى حين ما يموت الاولى وهذا المشهد اثر في قلوب العالم الرعب والكابه. حينذ مضى كلمن سبيله وهن بغاية الانكسار والحزن على ما راوه.

٩،١٤٥ ويوم اخر رايت الناس تتراكم فصرت اركك معهم الى ان وصلنا الى تصليبة زقاق فرايت امراه مربطين سواعدها في اخرعربانة التي يكبوا فيها الزباله وهي عربانه الى نصفها اعنى الى حد الزتار ولما انتهوا الى التصليبه وقفوا العرابانه. حينذ قرى الجلاد سجلها المدون فيه دنبها وهي انها كانت تفسد عقول الشبان وتعرس لهم لنسا جاهلات وغير معروفين بنسا الخطاء ولاجل هذا حكمت عليها الشريعه بانها تجرس في جميع شوارع مدينة بهريس فلما انتها من قراة السجل جلدها اثني عشر جلده بعصب التورحتى كت تراء لحمها مزرق مفزر من ذلك الضرب الاليم وبعد ان كمل الضرب مشية العرابانه وساجتها وهي ماشيه حفيانه وكانت عدمت قواها فصارة العرابانه تجرها عنفاً حتى انها اشرفت على الهلاك فياله من منضر شنيع وخجل فريع لجنس النسا.

٩،١٤٦ ويوم اخرفاتوا باوراق سجل فرحت الى المحكمه حتى اتفرج وفي وصولي رايت منزلين من الدرج صحبة الجلاد والكاهن امراه اختياره في سن السبعين فدخلوها للعرابانه هي والكاهن والجلاد وجنود من قبل الحاكم محتاطين بالعرابانه وساروا بهم الى ان وصلوا حيث منصوبه المشنقه فصعدوا الثلاثه على السلم.

wagon wheel up and hung it on a wooden axle by the platform. There the man was left, with his head dangling out of the wheel, whimpering.

Next, they brought the second man forward to the platform. When he saw 9.144 the state his friend was in, he fell to his knees, begging the priest not to let them execute him in that grisly way, and to let him be strangled before his limbs were broken. The priest felt a pang of sympathy for him, so he turned to the soldier who had been appointed by the judge to carry out the sentence, and interceded on the man's behalf. It was only after a considerable amount of persuasion on the part of the priest that the soldier granted his request and ordered the man to be strangled. They spread him out on the cross like his friend, strapping him down in the same way, and wrapped a rope around his neck. The end of the rope was then pulled through a hole in the platform and tightened by twisting it round and round. He was immediately strangled.

The executioner then set about breaking his bones and putting him in a wagon wheel like his friend. They left the two of them there until the first one died, a sight that horrified and distressed all the onlookers. The crowd then dispersed, and everyone went on their way feeling utterly shattered and dejected by what they'd just witnessed.

Another day, I saw some people running by, and I joined them. We arrived 9.145 at a crossroads, where I saw a woman with her forearms tied to the back of one of the carts used to collect garbage. She was naked to the waist. The cart had stopped at the crossroads and the executioner read out the record of her crime. She was guilty of leading young men astray by procuring for them women who were not registered as prostitutes. For this crime, she was sentenced to be paraded in disgrace through the streets of Paris. After reading the sentence, the executioner flogged her twelve times with a bull-pizzle whip, shredding her flesh. Then the cart lurched forward, pulling her as she stumbled barefoot behind it. The cart continued to drag her along, exhausted, until she nearly died. What a hideous spectacle and humiliating affront to all women!

On another day, I went to the courthouse to observe the proceedings after 9.146 a sentence had been published. There, I saw an old woman in her seventies being escorted down the steps by the executioner and the priest. They all climbed into the cart, which was surrounded by soldiers sent by the authorities. The carriage set off, and soon came to the gallows, where the three of them ascended the ladder.

حينٍ قري الجلاد السجل بان هل امراه كانت خادمه في بيت واحد من الاكابر ٩،١٤٧
مند سنين عديده وكان الرجل وامراته يحبوها لاجل خدمتها وتربيت اولادهم وكان
علي زمان ابو ذلك الرجل الاكابر فقد له اواني فضيه وما امكنهم يروا هل اواني
ولا الذي اغتلسهم من بيته فمضي علي ذلك عده سنين وكان ابو ذلك الرجل توفي
فاتفق بان ذلك الاغا سافر الي مدينة تلوزا فواحد من محبينه عزمه الي عنده فلما
جلسوا علي المايده فراء موجود في المايده بين اواني الفضيه صحن من صونه فعرفه لانه
له علامه في تلك الاواني فبعد كمال الصفره فسال ذلك الرجل صاحب المكان من
من اشترا ذلك الصحن فاجابه بان واحد من اصحابي كنت دكرت لي بان يصيغ لي
بعض اواني في بهريس فارسلي هذا الصحن مع جملة اواني فضيه ومن جملتهم هذا
الصحن وجملة يسيت.

وان سالت عنه وهو فلان تاجر في مدينة بهريس فاستقام ذلك الرجل مده ٩،١٤٨
من الزمان وسافر الي مدينة بهريس واخد معه الصحن وبعض اواني الذي كانوا
فقدوا من بيته فلما وصل الي صرايته وبعد كام يوم ارسل دعا ذلك التاجر وساله
من اين اشترا تلك الاواني الفضيه فدله التاجر عن رجل سايغ وارسل واحضر
السايغ فاوما له عن غير رجل غريب الزي. حينٍ مضي واعلم الحاكم بالامر الذي
جري فارسل الحاكم من قبله اثنين يحفظوا وينقبوا علي الاول الذي باع هل اواني
ويحضروه امامه.

فمضوا جماعته الحاكم يستقصوا الجره الي ان وصلوا الي تلك العزوجه الخادمه ٩،١٤٩
الذي مر ذكرها فلما راوها ما قدره تدل علي احد قبضوا عليها واحضروها امام الحاكم
وقرووها بان هي التي اغتلست هذه الاواني فامرت عليها الشريعه بالشنق ولكن
الجلاد ما قرا كل هذه القصه انما ذكر خيانتها لاستادها وبما انها امينه حكم عليها
بالشنق وكت تري لما كانت واقفه علي السلم كيف انها تتوسل للشعب حتي يصلوا
ويتضرعوا لاجلها. اخيراً شنقوها بكقية المجرمين ولتاديب جميع الخدام المتامنين.١

---

١ الأصل: المتتامنين.

The executioner read aloud the sentence, which began by recounting the story of how this woman had worked for many years as a servant in the home of a particular noble. The husband and wife who employed the old woman loved her dearly, as she had served them and raised their children. Now, the father of that nobleman had once lost some silver vessels. They were never found, and neither was the thief who'd stolen them. Years passed, and the nobleman's father died. Then one day, the nobleman happened to be visiting Toulouse when he was invited to the home of one of his dear friends. As they sat at the table to eat, he spotted one of his own plates among the others, which he recognized by its mark. 9.147

"Who'd you buy that plate from?" the man asked his friend after the meal was over.

"One of my friends," he replied. "I'd asked him to have some plates made for me in Paris, and he sent this one, along with some others."

He gave the nobleman the name of his friend, a merchant in Paris. After some time in Toulouse, the nobleman returned to Paris, bringing the plate with him, along with some other silver plates that had been taken from his house. When he got back to his mansion, he waited a few days before inviting the merchant over and asking him where he'd purchased the silver plates. The man mentioned a certain silversmith, whom the nobleman then summoned. The silversmith, in turn, told him he'd received the plates from yet another person, a man wearing foreign clothes. 9.148

Armed with this information, the nobleman went and reported the incident to the governor, who dispatched two investigators to find and bring in the man who had sold the plates to begin with.

The governor's men set off, following the trail of clues, and eventually arrived at that old servant woman. When it became apparent that she couldn't name anyone else as the source of the plates, they arrested her and brought her before the governor. She was made to confess that she'd stolen the plates, and was sentenced by the courts to hang. 9.149

Now, the executioner didn't read out this whole story. He merely said that she'd betrayed her master. And given that she'd been entrusted with his confidence, she was condemned to hang. As the old woman stood upon the ladder, she begged the assembled crowd to pray and offer supplications on her behalf. In the end, she was made to hang like all the other criminals, as an example to every entrusted servant.

٩.١٥٠ وفي تلك الايام حدث في مدينة بهريس مرض وبايي ومن جراه مات ناس كثير بغير عده والمنصاب بهذا المرض ما بيستقيم اربعة وعشرين ساعه ويموت فارتجة اهل المدينه من هذا الغضب. حينٍ التجوا الي شفيعة بهريس وهي القديسه جنيفيفا واتفقوا بان يزنحوا جسدها في المدينه ويطلبوا شفاعتها لعل الله تعالى يرفع عنهم ضربة الغضب فاشاروا الي مطران كنيستها بان يسمح لهم بان يزنحوا جسد القديسه فابا وما رضي بان يخرجوا جسدها من كنيستها خوفًا ليلا يعصوا في هذه الدخيرة المباركه فلحوا عليه جملة مطارين بهريس وروسا الديوره حتي الكردينال نفسه فا امكن بان يسمح لهم في خروج جسد القديسه.

٩.١٥١ حينٍ اجتمعت جميع اكابر بهريس والقضاه ومضوا الي عند مطران كنيسة القديسه وارتموا عليه بانه يسمح لهم وليلا يخاف بان الكردينال اوغيره يعصوا في الدخيره اعطوه خطوط اياديهم وكفلوها بانهم يرجعوا جسد القديسه الي مكانه وهو تابوت من الفضه وموضوع فوق ثلاث عواميد من الرخام وظهر منه عجايب كثيره حتي انهم بيعلقوا قميص المريض علي قصبه وبيلمسوه في ذلك التابوت بتشفيه من مرضه حسب امانته.

٩.١٥٢ فلما تم الامر علي هذا المنوال رضي المطران وسمح لهم في نزول جسد القديسه. حينٍ ارسل الكردينال الذي هو بابا ثاني في مملكة فرنساء وامر بان تخرج الي الزياح جميع الخوارنه والكهنه والرهبان والاكليريكين الموجودين في جميع كنايس بهريس والديوره من السبع الصوايح التي هي ثمانماية كنيسه ودير وان كلهم يترددا بفخر الثواب التي عندهم وفي ايديهم الشموع ويمشوا في الزياح وامر ايضًا بان في ذلك اليوم لا احد من العوام يشتغل بل يكون نهار عيد عام.

٩.١٥٣ وفي يوم المرسوم خرج الزياح منظوم من كهنه ورهبان وشمامسه متسربلين بفخر البدلات وفي ايديهم الشموع متقده واربع مطارين حاملين علي اكتافهم تابوت جسد القديسه ومروا في شوارع المدينه وكت تري كل فوج من الكهنه ومن الرهبان ومن

Around that same time, Paris was seized by an epidemic, leading to an 9.150
untold number of deaths. Anyone who caught this particular disease would
succumb within twenty-four hours. The city's inhabitants prayed to God to
spare them from His wrath, and sought the intercession of Saint Geneviève, the
city's patron saint. It was then decided that the body of the saint should be carried through the city in a procession while the people prayed to her for mediation. Perhaps, if they did that, the heavy blows of God's wrath would abate. The
people went to consult the bishop of the Church of Saint Geneviève and ask his
permission to let them hold the procession, but he refused to let the body of
the saint leave the church for fear that this blessed treasure might be harmed.
The other bishops of Paris urged him to reconsider, along with the abbots of
the monasteries and even the cardinal himself, but he wouldn't budge.

So the nobles and judges of Paris gathered and together went to see the 9.151
bishop of the Church of Saint Geneviève, imploring him to grant their request.
To allay his fears that the treasure might not be returned by the cardinal or
anyone else, they drafted an edict promising to bring the saint's body to its
resting place, to which each affixed his signature. The body was kept in a silver
coffin, set upon three marble pillars, which had produced many miracles in the
past. It was customary for people to hang the shirt of a sick person on a reed
and suspend it over the coffin, allowing the shirt to brush it. The saint would
then relieve the invalid's distress in proportion to the extent of his faith.

As a result of these efforts, the bishop finally relented and let them bring the 9.152
body of the saint down from its resting place. Then the cardinal, who is a kind
of second pope for the kingdom of France, ordered all the clergy to march in
procession. This included pastors, priests, monks, and higher clerical authorities from all the churches and monasteries in each of the seven quarters of the
city, a total of eight hundred churches and monasteries. The clergy were to don
their finest vestments and carry candles as they marched. He also decreed that
it was to be a general holiday and the masses would not be permitted to work.

On the appointed day, the procession set off with its priests, monks, and 9.153
deacons all decked out in their most magnificent robes, and with candles
ablaze. Four bishops carried the saint's coffin on their shoulders. They passed
through the streets of Paris as wave after wave of priests, monks, and deacons
chanted angelic hymns with stirring voices and beautiful melodies. The procession lasted for two hours, and the number of participants was estimated
at ten thousand. Meanwhile, the laypeople remained in their shops, offering

الشمامسه وهن ماشيين يرتلوا تراتيل ملايكيه باصوات شجيه والحان بهيه فاستقام مرور المذكورين حكم ساعتين حتي انتهي لان بيقدروا بان عدد المذكورين حكم عشرة الاف نفر وجميع العوام واقنين في دكاكيهم يتضرعوا الي الله تعالي بان يقبل شفاعة القديسه ويرفع هل غضب عنهم فاستجاب ربنا دعاهم وانقطع ذلك المرض بالكليه وكت وقيد الفقير في باريس وشاهدت هذا الزياح وتلك العجيبه التي صنعها الله تعالي معهم بشفاعة القديسه جنيفيفه.

١٥٤،٩ ووقفت علي خبرها وهو ان كانت القديسه خادمه عند رجل غني من اكابر بهريس وكانت في بيته كانها راهبه عابده وكانت تحب الفقرا وتتصدق عليهم من علوفتها وشغل يدها ومن فضلات البيت فلما اشتلق عليها اسدادها بانها توزع الصدقات علي الفقر لانه كان بخيل قاسي القلب علي الفقرا وغيرهم من المحتاجين فاتهدد هل اجيره وقال لها يوم الذي براكي بتعطي للفقرا شي ايقني بقتلك واخراجك من بيتي وحرس الخدام بان يرقبوها وان جري منها هذا الشي فيعلموه حتي ينتقم منها فحزنت هل مسكينه وما عادت تقدر تعطي شي للفقرا خيفتاً من اسدادها ولكن كانت تبقي جزو من خبز المعطا لها وتخبيه الي حين ما ترا فرسه وتعطيه للمساكين.

١٥٥،٩ فاتفق يوم بعد خروج اسدادها من البيت فلمت تلك كسر الخبز ووضعتهم في ديلها وخرجت من البيت حتي توزعهم علي الفقرا فاتفق في محل خروجها من باب المنزل واسدادها داخل فراها خارجه ديلها ملان فسالها ما هو الذي في ديلك فارتعشت فرقاً من غضبه وما عادت تعرف ترد عليه جواب ولكن ربنا الحنون انطقها وقالت له هذا ورد وكانت ايام شتا والورد ما له وجود ابداً فبهت اغتها وقال لها اروريني هذا الورد فكشفت ديلها فراء داخله ورد مكبس ولا في اوانه فتعجب والتفت اليها وقال لها اصدقيني منين لك هذا الورد فالتزمت وتقرله الصحيح بان كان في ديلها كسر خبز واني قلت انه ورد بغير وعي وانتباه.

supplications to God Most High to accept the intercession of the saint and to make His anger subside. And this our Lord did, bringing an end to the epidemic. I was in Paris at the time, and I witnessed the procession and the ensuing miracle that God worked through the intercession of the saint.

I also learned something about Saint Geneviève's story. She had once 9.154 worked for a rich nobleman of Paris, in whose home she lived as piously as a nun. She displayed a great love for the poor, offering them charity from her own wages and handiwork, as well as the food discarded by the household. But her master, who was a hard-hearted, uncharitable man, learned of her good works, and threatened her.

"The day I catch you giving anything to the poor will be the day I beat you and toss you out of my house," he snarled. "Be certain of that."

He ordered the other servants to remain vigilant and keep an eye on Geneviève. If they caught her doing it again, they were to inform him so he could punish her. Poor Geneviève was deeply saddened, and had to cease her charitable work, fearing her master's wrath. She did, however, sometimes save a scrap of bread from the food she received for herself, hiding it until she had a chance to give it to the destitute.

One day, after her master had left the house, she collected some scraps of 9.155 bread, bundled them in the gathered folds of her robe, and left the house to distribute these among the poor. As she walked out the door, her master happened to be returning home. He saw that she was carrying something in her robe.

"What do you have there?"

Trembling in fright, she was at a loss for words. But then our merciful Lord caused her to speak, casting words into her mouth!

"Roses," she replied.

As it was winter at the time and there were no roses available, her master was astonished.

"Show me these roses!"

She unwrapped the folds of her robes and uncovered the contents to reveal some double-flowered roses, long out of season. Her master was amazed.

"Tell me the truth," he said. "Wherever did you find these roses?"

Geneviève felt compelled to speak the truth, confessing that her robes had previously been full of scraps of bread.

"I spoke the word 'roses' without being aware of what I was saying," she explained.

١٠٦،٩ فتحقق حينذٍ العجيبه المفعوله لاجلها واعلم المطران بتلك العجيبه فحص المطران عن هل عجيبه فراها حقيه وثبتها. حينذٍ ذلك الغني باشر في تعمير دير راهبات ودخلها فيه وعمر بجانب الديركنيسه واوقف لهم اوقاف تقيم فيهم فاستقامة جنفيفه في الدير واخيرًا انتخبوها ريسه عليهم لحسن عبادتها وقداستها بسيره ملايكيه ولما توفت ظهر من جسدها عجايب كثيره وخبرها مستطيل ولاجل ان جسدها كان يفعل عجايب وضعوه في تابوت من فضه ورفعوه فوق ثلاثة عواميد لاجل المرضي الذين كانوا ياتوا من غير بلاد حتي يزوروا جسدها ويشفوا من امراضهم ومن ذلك الان لقبوها جنفيفه شفيعة بهريس .

It was then that her master realized a miracle had just occurred for the sake    9.156
of his servant. He informed the bishop, who after some investigation was able
to confirm that the miracle was indeed genuine. The wealthy nobleman then
had a convent built, to which he sent his servant Geneviève. Alongside the
convent he built a church, which he endowed with a trust. Geneviève lived
in the convent and was eventually elected Mother Superior on account of
her piety and the saintliness of her angelic conduct. After she died, her body
would work several miracles, whose stories are too long to recount here. It was
because of these miracles that her body was placed in a silver coffin and set
upon three columns, with the aim of allowing invalids from different countries
to visit the saint and to be healed of their maladies. Ever since, she has been
known as Geneviève, the patron saint of Paris.[32]

# الفصل العاشر[1]

## وفي اواخر سـنه ١٧٠٨

١،١٠ في اليوم الخامس عشر من شهر كانون الاول حدث برد شديد بهذا المقدار حتي انه يبس الاشجار وجلد نهر السينا الذي هو جاري من وسط مدينة بهريس والجليد كان بسمك شبر حتي العرابانات كانت تمشي فوقه كانها ماشيه علي ارض محجره يابسه واستقام هل برد والجليد خمسة عشر يوم وفي هل مده ناس من هل برد من سبع صوايح بهريس الذي كل صايح بقد مدينة حلب ثمانين الف الذين اندق لهم ناقوز في الكنيسه ما عدا اولاد الزنار والفقرا والغريبه حتي انهم راوا الحرمه واولادها في فراشهم ميتين والرجل وامراته متعانقين وميتين لان ما واهم في اعلا الطباق لاجل رخص كراهم وبيوت بهريس هي خمسة طبقات وكل بيت الذي هو اعلي من الاخر ارخص كري.

٢،١٠ وايضاً وجدوا اولاد فلاحين بياتوا من الضيع لاجل الخدمه مطمورين في الزبل في الاواخير موتاء وكانت المدينه فاضيه من الاوادم لان كل منهم كان ملتجي في بيته وما يفارق اوضته ووجاقه والفقير كت ملتجي في اوضه وما افارق الوجاق واستمريت خمسة عشر يوم محبوس في تلك الاوضه قبال النار اصتلي والتزموا الكهنه بانهم يضعوا مناقل نار علي المدايح خيفتاً ليلا يجلد المزكا الموضوع هناك وكثير من الناس لما كانوا يولو يجلد البول الخارج منهم ويبس في حليلهم ويسبب لهم الموت وخوابي الذين موضوعين داخل البيوت الذين هن من نحاس فزروا وكانوا يكسروا الخبز بالقداديم ويبلوه بما سخن حتي يقدروا ياكلوه وماذا اقول عن بساتينهم والاشجار

---

[1] لم يرد رقم لهذا الفصل في الأصل.

# Chapter Ten

## The Last Days of 1708

On the fifteenth of December, Paris experienced a bout of cold weather so extreme that the trees froze stiff. So did the Seine—the river that flows through the city. The sheet of ice covering the river was as thick as a handspan and carriages could drive across it as if they were upon dry, rocky ground. The icy weather lasted fifteen days, killing people across the seven quarters of Paris, each as large as the city of Aleppo. In all, eighty thousand people perished, not counting the young children, the poor, and the foreign inhabitants of the city, and the church bells tolled for them all.[33] Women were found huddled in bed with their children, and husbands embracing their wives, frozen to death because their homes were on the higher stories. The buildings of Paris have five stories: The higher up one lives, the cheaper the rent.

The children of peasants who had come from their villages to the city looking for work were found dead on the roads, covered in manure. Paris was a ghost town. Everyone stayed home, confined to a single room, sitting by the fire, as I myself did. I spent fifteen days shut up in my room, warming myself by the fire.

The priests of the city were forced to set up braziers on the altars of their churches to prevent the sacramental wine from freezing. Many people even died while relieving themselves, because the urine froze in their urethras as it left their bodies, and killed them. Indoors, it was so cold that copper casks cracked, and people had to break their bread with adzes and moisten the pieces with hot water in order to eat them.

10.1

10.2

يبسة بالكليه وايضاً كرومهم واشجار زيتونهم يبسة ايضاً وزرعهم في تلك الاراضي يبس بعدما بدروا مرتين وثلاثه وهذا الغضب عم اقليم ﭬرنسا جميعها.

١٠،٣ والفقير خرجت من مخضعي بعد الخمسة عشر يوم ومضيت حتي احلق ومن خروجي من دكان الحلاق الي ان وصلت الي منزلنا تيبست وصرت كاني صنم وسقط شعر شواربي من الجليد وايقنت بالموت ولما انتهيت الي مخضعي وراوني في تلك الحاله فضوا واخبروا معلمي فلما اتي معلمي في الحال امر الخدام بان يعروني من ثيابي ﭬما قدروا يشلحوني توب الفوقاني لان سواعدي يبسة. حينذٍ امرهم بانهم يشقوا كامي.

١٠،٤ فبعدما عروني وبقيت بالزلط كما جابتني امي فاوقدوا النار وكان معنا وعاء دهن النسر الذي اشتريناه من مدينة تونس الغرب فدهنوني من ذلك الدهن من فرقي الي قدمي وقربوني الي النار حتي داب ذلك الدهن علي جسدي. اخيراً احموا ملحفه بيضا ولفوني بها وحملوني اثنين من الغلمان ووضعوني في الفراش وانا كاني صنم ما بقدر احرك يدي عن رجلي وغطوني بثلاث اربع لحف وكروني وبقيت كاني موضوع في جواني الحمام من شدت الحراره.

١٠،٥ وابقوني في الفراش اربعة وعشرين ساعه وبعد تلك المده فقت علي حالي وصرت احرك يداي ورجلاي بغير الم. اخيراً نهضت من الفراش وانا بصحة العافيه ولبست ثيابي وصرت اتمشا في صحن البيت وبعد يومين امر معلمي لاحد الغلمان بان يدوريني في شورع المدينه علي حكم ساعتين جري وما يدعني اقف ابداً حتي سال عرقي لحد اقدامي ومنها تعافيت في غاية ما يكون.

١٠،٦ وبعد تلك الايام بقليل[١] من الزمان صار في المدينه مجاعه وغلا عظيم بهذا المقدار حتي اتطروا مدبرين المدينه بان يكتبوا الانفار الموجوده في البيوت وبامر الحاكم بان يعطوا لكل نفر وقيت خبز لا غير قوت لا يموت وكل عيله مدونه انفارها عند الخباز وجالس في كل ﭬرن رجل من قبل الحاكم وفي يده دفتر العيلات المدونه اسماهم ولاجل هذا الضبط ما يقدر احد ياخد زود تعيته ولا درهم واحد فبعد مدة ايام دقت الفلاحين اهل القره والضيع الي مدينة بهريس حتي يشحدوا ولا يموتوا من الجوع لان

_____

As for the orchards and trees, what can I say? They withered away completely. The same went for the vineyards and olive groves, as well as the crops, which froze after having yielded two or three harvests for the year. This bout of God's wrath struck the entire region of France.

After the fifteen days of cold had passed, I left my room and went to get a  10.3
shave. The freezing walk home from the barbershop left me stiff as a statue. It was so cold that the hairs of my mustache began to fall out, and I was certain I was going to die. When I finally arrived at my room and they saw me in my condition, they ran to tell my master. He came to see me and immediately ordered the servants to strip off my clothes. They were unable to pull off my outer robes because my forearms were frozen stiff, so he told them to slit the sleeves open.

Once my clothes were off and I was naked as the day I was born, they lit the  10.4
fire. We had purchased a flask of eagle fat in the city of Tunis during our travels, and they slathered me with it from top to bottom, moving me close to the fire so the fat would melt all over my body. Then they warmed up a white sheet and wrapped me in it. Two young men picked me up and carried me to my bed. I lay there like a statue, unable to move arm or leg. They covered me with three or four blankets and wrapped me up tightly. I was so hot that it felt as if I were lying in the innermost depths of a bathhouse.

They kept me in bed for twenty-four hours. I then returned to my normal  10.5
self, able to move my arms and legs without pain. I rose from my bed, once again in very good health, put on my clothes, and walked around the house. Two days later, my master commanded one of the servant boys to take me out for a two-hour run through the streets of Paris, and not to let me stop until I was dripping with sweat. That did me good, and I was right as rain again.

A short while later, Paris was struck by a famine, which led to a great rise  10.6
in the cost of food. The city's administrators were compelled to take a count of the number of people in each home, and, by order of the governor, to issue each person a small ration of bread to keep them from starving. The bakers all had lists of the members of each family, and someone representing the city authorities sat at every bakery, armed with a register of all the families and everyone's name. The result of this system was that no one could obtain an ounce more food than that allotted to them. After a few days, peasants began

الفقير رايت ناس كثير مطروحين في الازقا مايتين من الجوع لان ما احد يتشحدهم لان كل واحد له وقيت خبز ما يمكنه بانه يعطي من تلك الوقيه شي للشحاد ولاجل هذا السبب مات كثير منهم من الجوع.

٧،١٠ فلما راوا اكابر المدينه والمطارنه والمدبرين هذه المصيبه افتكروا بل الهموا من ربنا الحنون علي عبيده بانهم يشغلوا هل فلاحين من دراهم اوقاف المدينه وباشروا في عمارة بيوت برات بهريس وكان هناك تله فراموا بان يكبوا ترابها الي غير ناح ويساووا الارض وبعده يبنوا البيوت وكان جا لهم قمح من غير بلاد لكن غاليت الثمن فبنوا فزن في ذلك المكان حتي يخبزوا خبز لتلك الاوادم ويعطوا لكل واحد منهم اعني الرجل وامراته واولاده الذين بيقدروا ينكبوا تراب رغيف خبز وقتين واجره جرقين اعني ثمان عتامنه بتعمل باربع سولديات فاستقاموا يشتغلوا واستراحت اهل المدينه منهم الي حين ما جاهم الفرج وكثر عندهم القمح من بلاد الشرق ومن بلاد المغاربه ومن غير بلاد لان الغلي جلاب.

٨،١٠ ولما رحت الي مرسيليا رايت وصلت اربعة كبيرات من عند سيدنا البابا ومعهم جحاتير ملانه قمح لان في مدينة مرسيليا صار مجاعه اكثر من بهريس لان الاوادم كانت تدحم علي البيوت وينهبوا الموجود عندهم من القوت فالتزم الحاكم بان ينصب في كل حاره مشنقه ووقفوا جنود من قبل الحاكم حتي يصدوا الشعب عن الدخول لبيوت الغير وبعده وصلت المراكب الذي كانوا ارسلوهم الي بلاد الشرق حتي يشتروا قمح من الاضاض والبلاد نحو ثلاثماية مركب وشيطيه فكثر القمح وتفرق في كل اقليم فرنسا وصار الخبز ينوجد لكن صار رطل الخبز علي موجب وزن بلادنا بزلطه اعني بثلاث ارباع واستقام الخبز بهل اثمان حتي طلع مغل الجديد ورجع كل شي لاصله وهذا الذي رايته من خصوص الغلا الذي صار في فرنسا سنة ١٧٠٩.

٩،١٠ وفي تلك الايام¹ صغرة نفسي واتضجرت من السكنه في تلك البلاد وكان يزورنا كثير اوقات رجل اختيار وكان موكل علي خزانت كتب العربيه وكان يقرا مليح بالعربي وينقل كتب عربي الي الفرنساوي ومن الجمله كان في ذلك الحين ينقل كتاب عربي الي

---

¹ الأصل: الايا.

leaving their towns and villages, and streamed into Paris to beg for food so they wouldn't die of hunger. I saw many of them lying in the street, starving to death, for no one could afford to share their own meager ration with them. Many people died of hunger.

Confronted with this catastrophe, the city's nobles, together with its bish- 10.7 ops and officials, puzzled over what to do. Thanks to God's mercy, an inspired solution presented itself: They would put the peasants to work building houses outside Paris, paying them with funds from the city's charitable endowments. There was a hill on the outskirts of Paris that they planned to clear away. Once that was complete, they would level the earth and build upon it.

In the meantime, wheat had begun to arrive from other countries, but the price remained high. They built a bakery in the area to make bread for the workers, giving every man and his wife and children—those of them able to work, that is—a loaf of bread weighing two *ūqiyyah*s, along with a wage of two *jarq*s, which is to say eight *'uthmānī*s, or four soldi. The peasants began to work there, relieving the burden on the city. This was the state of affairs until the crisis finally ended, with shipments of wheat arriving from the lands of the East, the Maghreb, and other places. Demand attracts supply, after all.

Later, when I went to Marseille, I witnessed the arrival of four galleys sent 10.8 by His Holiness the pope. They were accompanied by barges loaded with wheat, as Marseille had experienced a famine even more severe than the one in Paris. It was so extreme that people were breaking into homes and steal-ing all the food they could find. The governor was forced to erect a gallows in every neighborhood, and station soldiers to put an end to breaking and enter-ing. Finally, the ships that had been sent to the East to purchase wheat from the Province of the Islands and various lands arrived in Marseille. There were about three hundred ships and boats in all. Wheat was suddenly plentiful in all the regions of France. Bread became available again, but a *raṭl* of bread now cost a *zolota*, which is to say three quarters of its previous price. That was how it remained until prices rose again and everything returned to normal. This is what I witnessed with regard to the rise of prices in France in the year 1709.

During that time, I became discouraged and discontent with life in those 10.9 parts. An old man, who was assigned to oversee the Arabic Library and could read Arabic well and translate texts into French, would visit us often. At the time, he was translating into French, among other works, the Arabic book

الفرنساوي وهو كتّاب حكاية الف ليله وليله فهذا الرجل كان يستعين في لاجل بعض قضايا ما كان يفهمهم فكنت افهمه اياهم وكان الكتّاب ناقص كام ليله فاحكيت له حكايا الذي كنت بعرفهم فتمم كتّابه من تلك الحكايا فانبسط مني قوي كثير ووعدني بان كان لي مساله حتي يقضيها من كل قلبه.

فيوم من ذات الايام وانا جالس بتحاكا معه قلي بريد افعل معك خير لكن ان ١٠،١٠ حفظت السر فقلتله ما هو الخير الذي بتريد تصنعه معي فقلي نهار غدي برويك الخير الذي بريد اصنعه معك فبعد ما انتهينا من كلام مضي من عندي وثاني يوم اجا وهو يقلي ابشر في الغنيمه ان صح هل امر بيكون في سعادتك. حينذٍ قلتله اجيبني ما هو الخير فاجابني واوما لي عن رجل امير وهو من اكابر الدوله بان كان طلب مني رجل حتي يرسله للسياحة مثل بول لوكاس[1] الذي هو معلي والان خطر في بالي بان اقول له عنك لانك انت سحت وتعرف المطلوب فامرني باني احضرك الي عنده حتي يراك ويلقش معك ونهار غدي بستناك في فلان مكان حتي نروح لعنده جمله ولكن بالك ثم بالك تعطي خبر لمعلمك لانه بيصدك عن الرواح.

فاتفقنا علي هذا الراي ومضي من عندي وثاني يوم مضيت الي ذلك المكان ١١،١٠ فرايته في استنداري فرحت معه حتي وصلنا الي صراية ذلك الامير المذكور فدخل الي عنده وبعد هنيهه امروني الخدام بالدخول فدخلت وامثلت امامه فاسترحب فيّ واناسني وامرني بالجلوس فجلست وبعده صار يسالني عن البلاد التي درناها والاشيا التي وجدناها وهي فلوس قدم واصنام قدم وكتب اخبار الملوك القدم وما يشبه ذلك من الاشيا القديمه التي جلبها معلمي فاجبته نعم يا سيدي كل اشيا انا كنت اشتريها وبعرف فيها لاني تعلمت من معلمي معرفة هل اشيا كلها.

حينذٍ قلي حضرة الامير روح حضر حالك واطلع من عند معلمك وتعال لعندي ١٢،١٠ وانا بوجهك وباخد لك فرمان من الملك نظير فرمان معلمك توصاي فيك للالجي ولجميع القناصر الموجودين في بلاد الشرق وبعطيك مكاتيب توصاي ايضاً ومهما

―――――――――――

١ الأصل: بوللوكاس.

*The Story of the Thousand and One Nights.*[34] He would ask me to help him with things he didn't understand, and I'd explain them to him.

The book was missing some "Nights," so I told him a few stories I knew and he used them to round out his work.[35] He was very appreciative, and promised that if I ever needed anything, he would do his utmost to grant it.

One day, while I was sitting chatting with the old man, he said, "I'd like    10.10
to do something special for you, a favor of sorts. But only if you can keep it a secret."

"What?" I asked.

"You'll find out tomorrow," he said.

After we'd finished chatting, he left.

He returned the next day. "Good news!" he said. "If my plan succeeds, you'll be very happy."

"Tell me," I said, "what is this favor you have in mind?" And he began to tell me about a certain nobleman who was an important figure in the government.[36]

"He asked me if I knew of someone who could be sent on a voyage like the one undertaken by Paul Lucas," the old man explained, referring to my master. "It occurred to me to tell him about you, since you've traveled before and you know what's involved. So he ordered me to bring you to him so that you two could speak. I'll wait for you in such and such a place tomorrow and we can go see him together. But take care not to tell your master or he won't let you go."

We agreed and he left. The next day, I went to the meeting place and found    10.11
him waiting for me. I accompanied him to the nobleman's palace. He went in, and after a little while the servants invited me to enter. I presented myself before the nobleman. He welcomed me courteously and invited me to sit down. Then he began to ask me about the lands we'd toured and the things we'd found: the old coins and carved idols, the books of history about ancient kings, and other such antiquities my master had brought with him.

"Yes, my lord," I replied, "I did buy all these things, and I know a great deal about them. I learned about them all from my master."

"Then go, see to your affairs, and leave your master," the nobleman told    10.12
me. "Afterward, come back to me and I'll send you on a mission. I'll arrange for a royal decree just like your master's mandate, and commission you to all the ambassadors and consuls in the Orient. I will also give you letters of

طلبت من القناصر في دورتك يعطوك ومهما اشتريته تودعه عندهم حتي يرسلوه
الي مرسيليا الي بيت البندر ويكون لك علوفه كل يوم اسكوت من غير مصاريفك
وانت رجعت الي عندي بالسلامه انا بعلي منازلك وبقيمك في وظيفه يكون لها
مدخول عظيم فلما انتهينا من الكلام فقلي امضي وافعل ما قلته لك وعاود لعندي
فخرجت من امامه وانا في حيره كيف اعمل لاني من طرف الواحد انا ضجران من تلك
الاهوال التي جرت علي زهاقي ومن طرف الثاني انا فزعان ليلا ما تصح القضيه التي
تربت فبقيت في حيره بين خايف وراجي.

وكان حكمني بالسابق عارض مهول مرعب في الغاية وهو ان كنت يوم من الايام ١٣،١٠
تصادفت انا ورجل عجمي ارمني يدعا يوسف الجوهرجي وهذا الرجل كان يتعاطه في
مدينة بهريس بيع الجواهر المتمنه مثل الماس وياقوت وزمرد' ولولو وما يشبه ذلك من
الحجار المتمنه فلما راني سلم علي بلسان التركي من غير فني يعرفني فلما سلم علي رديت عليه
السلام فصار يسالني من اي بلاد انا فاجته اني من بلاد سوريا من مدينة حلب
فلما سمع اني من مدينة حلب زاد علي السلام واسترحب في قوي كثير وسالني عن
جماعات وكيف احوالهم ولعلهم طيبين فرديت علي سواله بان فلان طيب وفلان
مات وغير كان مسافر وما يشبه ذلك. اخيرًا صرنا نتمشي حتي وصلت الفقير الي
منزولنا فودعته وصعدت في الدرج فتبعني في ثاني درجه وسالني في اي طبقه انتم
ساكين قلته في الثانيه فتركني ومضي.

فاحكيت الي معلمي عن هل رجل الذي صدفته وانه استرحب في وارواني محبه ١٤،١٠
وصداقه قوي كثير وبما ان هل رجل مسمي في بهريس ومقبول عند جميع الاكابر فقلي
معلمي ليش ما دعيته انه يزورنا وان كان تراه مرة اخري كلفه بانه يجي لعندنا لان بريد
اتلاقش انا وياه في خصوص الجواهر اعني في تجاره الثمينه حتي امتحنه هل انه يعرف
فيهم حد المعرفه لان معلمي كان معلم في علم الجواهر وخواصاتهم واثمانهم في غاية ما
يكون ولاجل هذا السبب راد انه يجتمع معه ويختبره هل علي باله ام لا.

_____
١ الأصل: زمد.

recommendation so that whatever you request from the consuls during your tour will be granted, and whatever you purchase will be conveyed to them for dispatch to the chamber of commerce in Marseille. You will have a daily salary in ecus, and all your expenses paid. And when you return to me safely, I will elevate your standing and establish you in a position with a substantial income." When we were finished talking, he said, "Go now, do as I ask, and come right back."

I left in a state of confusion. What was I to do? On the one hand, I was fed up with all of the nerve-racking frights I'd encountered on this journey. On the other hand, I was worried that this new opportunity wouldn't end in success. So I remained hesitant, somewhere between fear and hope.

I'd been in this sort of frightful situation before. One day, I bumped into 10.13 an Armenian from Persia named Yūsuf the Jeweler, who worked in Paris as a merchant of valuable jewels such as diamonds, rubies, emeralds, pearls, and other expensive stones. Without even knowing who I was, he greeted me in Turkish. I returned the greeting, and he asked me which country I was from.

"Syria," I said. "From the city of Aleppo."

At this, he greeted me again very warmly and asked me about some of his acquaintances and how they were doing, and whether or not they were still alive. I answered all his questions, telling him that so-and-so was alive and that so-and-so had died, while so-and-so had traveled abroad, and that sort of thing. After a while, we set off on a stroll and eventually arrived at our house. I bid him farewell and started up the stairs, but he followed me, asking, "On which floor do you live?"

"The third," I told him, and he went on his way.

I told my master about this man I'd bumped into, and how he'd greeted me 10.14 warmly and showed great affection and friendship. I also told him that Yūsuf was well known in Paris and that he was in the good graces of the city nobles.

"So why didn't you invite him in?" my master asked. "If you see him again, you must insist that he come to our house. I'd like to discuss jewels and precious stones with him so I can determine whether he knows all there is to know about them."

My master was a foremost expert on the science of precious jewels, including their unique properties and values. That was why he wanted to meet Yūsuf and test his knowledge.

١٥،١٠ فبعد مدة ايام في محل ضحوة نهار انطرق الباب وكنت انا ومعلمي لا غير قبال الوجاق بعدما شربنا القهوه جالسين منسطلي فنهضت عاجلاً وفتحت الباب فرايت وهو يوسف الجوهرجي المذكور فاسترحبت فيه وكلفته بانه يدخل ويشرب القهوه عندنا فاجابني في هل وقت ما يمكني اني ادخل لعندكم لان لي شغله ضروريه بريد منك بان تمضي معي وتترجملي بعض كلام عند رجل معلم لاني ما بعرف افهمه قضيتي كمثل ما يجب لان ما لي معرفه بلسان الفرنساوي مليح انا بلقش بالتلياني وهذا الرجل ما بيفهم بالتلياني ولاجل هذا بطلب من فضلك حتي ترجم بيني وبينه. حينذٍ قلتله اصبر هنيهه حتي استازن من معلمي. اخيراً بروح معك.

١٦،١٠ فدخلت الي عند معلمي واحكيت له في ذلك الامر فنهض في الحال وكلفه في الدخول الي عنده من غير تكليف خاطر فما قدر بان يخالفه فدخل وفي الحال هينا له فتور وسقيناه قهوه ووقفنا في واجبه كما يجب من بعد ما كان استرحب فيه معلمي قوي كثير. اخيراً استقاموا يتصامروا مع بعضهم في ما يخص الجواهر حكم ساعه. اخيراً استمن معلمي بان يرسلني معه حتي اترجمله في قضيه ضروريه فساله معلمي ما هي القضيه قلي انا برد لك جوابها فاجابه بان هل قضيه سريه وان كان بتريد اعلم لحضرتك فيها بتعطيني قرار بانك بتكتم[١] السرفاجابه معلمي قول لا تخف سرك محفوض عندي الي الابد.

١٧،١٠ حينذٍ احكاله القضيه بتمامها كما هي واقعه وهو انه خطب بنت وكتب تمسك الخطبه في المحكمه والان جاني ناس وبينولي بان من زريد نخطبلك بنت فلان واعنو لي عن رجل تاجر من تجار الهند غني جداً وهوان له في الهند عدة سنين بيتاجر وما له نيه في الرجوع الي بهريس فعمام البنت وخوالها بيريدوا يزوجوك بالبنت ويرسلوك الي الهند لعند ابو البنت فزعاً ليلا يموت هناك ويتبردق المال لان الرجل كبير في السن وما بيعرفوا اني خطبت والان وقعت في حيره بسالك هل بقدر افكش تلك البنت واخطب هذه فاجابه معلمي بان لها عندي طريقه لكن ما يجوز لك انك تفعلها

---

١ الأصل: بتكم.

One morning several days later, while my master and I were sitting warm-   **10.15**
ing ourselves in front of the fireplace, having had our coffee, there was a knock
at the door. I jumped up to open the door, and it was Yūsuf the Jeweler. I welcomed him and begged him to come in and have coffee with us.

"I can't come in right at this moment," Yūsuf replied. "I have some urgent
business to attend to, and I'd like you to come along and act as an interpreter
between me and a certain gentleman. You see, I just don't know how to make
him understand my particular situation. I don't speak French very well; I do
speak some Italian, but this gentleman doesn't understand Italian. So I'm wondering if you'd be willing to translate for us."

"Wait a moment," I said, "so I can get my master's permission. Then I'll go
with you."

I went in to my master and told him what had happened. He stood up and   **10.16**
insisted that Yūsuf come in, and the man was unable to refuse. He came in
and my master welcomed him with great ceremony. We brought him some
breakfast and coffee, and were attentive to his needs. Then the two of them
sat down and talked about precious stones for about an hour. Afterward, my
master agreed to send me along to translate for Yūsuf in his urgent business.

"What is this matter, exactly?" my master asked him. "If you tell me, I can
tell you what to do about it."

"It's a secret," Yusuf replied. "If you wish me to tell you what it is, sir, give
me your oath that you'll keep the secret."

"Go ahead," my master said. "Don't be afraid. Your secret is forever safe
with me."

Yūsuf told him the story from beginning to end. It so happened that he'd   **10.17**
gotten engaged to a girl and had signed a contract of engagement in court.

"Then some people came to me," said Yusuf, "saying they wanted me to
marry the daughter of a rich merchant in India. He'd been there for many
years, doing business, and had no desire to return to Paris. These people said
to me, 'The girl's uncles want to marry her off to you and send you to her father
in India, because they're afraid that he might die and his money be lost, since
he's very old.'"

"The trouble is," Yūsuf continued, "these people don't know that I'm
already engaged. So I'm at a loss! Can I abandon one girl and marry another?"

"I can think of a solution," my master replied, "but you mustn't pursue it.
It isn't advisable."

ولا بشور عليك بفعلها. حينذٍ لج عليه واتوسل اليه بان يقله فاجابه معلمي بقوله له بتعطيني قرار بانك ما بتفعلها فاعطاه قرار في ذلك .

١٨،١٠ فقله بما انك رجل غريب يمكنك بان تظهر بان جاك مكتوب من اهلك والتزمت في الرواح الي بلادك لاجل امر مخطر او في موت والدك او شريكك وما يشبه ذلك فتقول الي اهل البنت بانك ملتزم في الرواح لا محاله لان امري ضروري جداً ولاجل هذا بتقلهم بانهم يشقوا التمسك ولا ترطبت البنت عن الجازه وان رجعت وبقت بغير زواج باخدها. حينذٍ ما بيقدروا يمنعوك عن الرواح وعن شق التمسك وفنخ الخطبه ولما بيشقوا التمسك اعطي خبر لاهل تلك البنت التي بتريد تخطبها من جديد بان لك دراهم في فلان بلد بروح باخدها وبعد كام يوم برجع وبخطب بنتكم واذا بعد كام يوم[١] رجعت وخطبت الثانيه ما لهم عليك حق ولا احد بيقدر يمانعك عن الخطبه.

١٩،١٠ فلما سمع منه هل كلام استكتر في خيره ومضي في حال سبيله ولكن طمعه في المال ما وقف عند قراره فعمل مثل ما تعلم من معلمي وغاب مده ورجع خطب البنت المذكوره بنت التاجر وكانت ايام صوم الكبير وبما انهم رادوا يزوجوه بالعجل ويرسلوه الي الهند فاخدوا اجازه من الكردينال بان يكللوه في ايام صوم الكبير الذي ما بيزوج الزبجه فيه فلما اعطاهم الكردينال اجازه فباشروا في زبجته وفي تلك البلاد اذا راد الغريب يتزوج فيناودوا عليه في كنيسة الكبيره علي ثلاث احدات وبقول الكاهن بان غريب من بلد الفلانيه بيريد يتزوج وكل من عرف بانه متزوج يعطي خبر للاسقف ويكون تحت حرم قاطع من الكنيسه الذي يعرف وما بيقول.

٢٠،١٠ فناودوا عليه اول احد وثاني احد ما بين عليه شي لكن في ثالث احد انوجد في الكنيسه في محل المناداه رجل كاهن كلداني فمضي الي عند الاسقف وقله انا بعرف هل رجل متزوج في بلاد سوريا في مدينة حلب وهذا صحيح كان متزوج بامراه تسما

---

١ «يوم» لم ترد في الأصل.

Yūsuf insisted, begging that he tell him what it was, and my master said, "Promise me that you will not do it," and Yūsuf promised.

"Seeing that you're a foreigner, you could pretend that you received a letter    10.18
from your family asking you to return home for an urgent matter like the death of your father or one of your business partners—that sort of thing," my master began. "You'd then tell your fiancée's family that you're absolutely bound to return to your country because of this terribly urgent matter and that you want to break off the engagement. The girl would be free to marry someone else, but you could tell them that if you returned unmarried, you'd marry her."

My master continued: "In that case, they wouldn't be able to prevent you from leaving, or from breaking the contract and dissolving the engagement. Now, when they broke the contract, you'd go to the family of the second girl and say that you have some money owed to you in such and such a city and you'd tell them, 'I'll just go collect it and come back after a few days and marry your daughter.' When you eventually returned after some time and married the second girl, no one would have a claim against you, nor would anyone be able to prevent you from getting engaged."

When Yūsuf heard this, he thanked my master profusely and went on his    10.19
way. But his greed got the best of him, and he went and did just what my master had told him. He disappeared for a while, then came back to marry the merchant's daughter.

It was Lent at the time, and because the girl's family wanted them to get married quickly and send Yūsuf off to India, they received permission from the cardinal to do so during Lent, when there are usually no weddings held. The cardinal gave permission and they announced the marriage.

Now, in this country, when a foreigner wants to get married, the impending nuptials are announced in the cathedral on the three preceding Sundays. The priest says, "A person from such and such a country intends to marry. If anyone knows him to be already married, he must inform the bishop." And anyone who knows but doesn't speak up risks being excommunicated by the church.

So they read out the banns on the first Sunday and the second Sunday, and    10.20
nothing turned up. But on the third Sunday, there happened to be a Chaldean priest in the congregation. He went to the bishop and said, "I know that this man is married in Syria, in the city of Aleppo."

In fact, it was true that Yūsuf was married to a woman named Maryam, daughter of Jabbār. He'd fathered a son with her, then traveled abroad. This

مريم بنت جبار وله منها ولد ذكر فتركها وسافر ولقد يكون هذا هولاني لما رجعت الي
حلب سالت هل امراه عن هية رجلها فرايت كما رايته وهو طويل القامه اسمر اللون
رقيق الجسم والله اعلم انكان هو ام لا .

٢١،١٠ فلما شهد هل كاهن وتثبتت شهادته فاعلموا حاكم المدينه في امره ففي الحال امر
الحاكم بامساكه وضبط ماله وانه يشنق فصح من اعطاه الخبر فقط وما عاد بان له اثر
ابد فوقع التفتيش عليه في كل جانب ومكان فما راوا له خبر وبعد ثلاث ايام مضوا الي
منزله حتي يضبطوا ماله فما راوا عنده شي وكان احد من بيوت الاكابر جار متمنه
شي كثير بنا ان يبيعها ويعطي حقها فما وجدوا شي من هذا الا انه سلب المال وهرب
فزاد التفتيش عليه ومسكوا ناس من جيرانه ومن عشراته ووعدوهم بالعداب انكان ما
بيقروا عليه فين مخبا ومن اجله الفقير .

٢٢،١٠ انا ماضي بشغل فما رايت الا اثنين من جماعة الحاكم مسكوني وامروني بالمضي معهم
فانا ارتعبت وسالتهم ماذا بتريدوا اجابوني حتي تحضر امام الحاكم هو بيقلك ايش مزيد
منك فزاد علي الرعب والارتعاش وصرت ساير معهم وانا بغير وعي فمرنا علي دكان
قهوة خواجه اصطفان الشامي وهذا الرجل كان يحبني كثير وبيني وبينه محبه وموده
وسببها لما وصلت الي بهريس امرني معلمي بان اروح اسلم عليه بما انه ابن بلادنا
واحكالي قصته .

٢٣،١٠ انه لما اجا الي بهريس صار يتشحد وما احد يتشحده فالتزم بانه يروح عند خواجه
كريستوفلو زماريا واتوسل اليه بان ياخد له من حضرت الكردينال مشرفه حتي
يقف علي باب كنيسه العذري يتوسل نحن قلبه عليه وبما انه كاخيت الكردينال
ومقبول عنده قوي كثير فاعطاه من يده مشرفه بان يحسنوا اليه بما انه غريب
ومخوص امره بانه فقير ومحتاج فاخد المشرفه ووقف في باب الكنيسه يتوسل
فلما راو معه منشور من الكردينال¹ صاروا يعطوه بسخا حتي صار معه من تلك
الحسنات قرب مايتين غرش .

---

¹ الأصل: الكرديناه.

must have been him, because when I returned to Aleppo myself I asked this woman what her husband looked like, and her description resembled the man I saw in Paris: tall, dark-skinned, and thin. But only God knows whether he really was the same man or not.

When the Chaldean priest testified to this and his claim was confirmed, the governor of the city was informed about the situation. He demanded that Yūsuf be arrested, his money be seized, and that he be hanged. The priest who had informed the governor was telling the truth, so Yūsuf disappeared without a trace. They launched a search for him but there was no sign of him. After three days, they went to his house to seize his property but couldn't find a thing. Apparently he'd taken valuable stones from various nobles' homes with a plan to sell them all, but the governor's men didn't find any of them; he'd simply stolen them and fled. As the search resumed, they arrested some of Yūsuf's neighbors and friends, and threatened to torture them if they didn't reveal where he was hiding. One of those people was me.

While I was out and about on an errand at that time, two of the governor's men suddenly seized me and ordered me to go with them. I was terrified and asked them what they wanted.

"Come see the governor, and he'll tell you what we want!"

I went with them, terrified out of my wits.

We passed by the coffee shop of my dear friend Iṣṭifān the Damascene, a man who was very fond of me.[37] When I first arrived in Paris, my master told me to seek him out because he was my countryman. We had become friends, and he had told me his story.

When Iṣṭifān first came to Paris, he was a beggar, but no one would give him any alms. He decided to go to Monsieur Christofalo Zamāriyā to ask for a letter from the cardinal granting permission to beg for alms at the door of the Church of the Virgin. Christofalo's heart went out to him, and since he was the steward of the cardinal and very close to him, he gave Iṣṭifān what he wanted. That way people would give him charity, because he was a stranger and because he was confirmed to be truly poor and in real need.

Iṣṭifān stood by the door of the church, pleading for assistance. When the people saw that he had an edict from the cardinal, they began lavishing alms on him. He eventually amassed almost two hundred piasters.

10.21

10.22

10.23

١٠،٢٤ فحكم في تلك الايام موسم مار ميخايل لان مدينة بهريس سبعة صواير وكل صاير منهم علي اسم قديس ولما يحكم عيد ذلك القديس بيصير موسم سبعة ايام في مكان فسحه وبيصير في تلك المده بيع وشرا ومفترجات وبياتوا ناس من غير قري لاجل البيع والشرا لان جميع الذي بينباع١ وبينشراء ما بيعطي كمرك ولا مصاريف المعتاده التي بتعطاء في غير اوقات.

١٠،٢٥ والفقير لما حكم موسم مار ميخايل مضيت الي تلك الساحه واتفرجت ومن جملة الفرج تفرجت علي سعدان اسود موضوع في قفص من حديد ورايته قوي بشعه كانه شيطان وايضاً علي تعبان براسين واتنهيت الي هل مكان وبراته واحد بيدق طبل فسالت ما هذا اجابوني بان في هل مكان فرجه عظيمه فردت اتفرج فطلب مني صاحب المكان ربع فرايت طلبه كثير عن غير فرج فما ردت اعطي غير ثمن مثل غير فرج. حينذٍ دخلوا ما بيننا وارضوه باربع شاهيات فازالني بالدخول فلما دخلت فرايت جمل زغير جالس ولا غير فندمت وقلت الي صاحب المكان بان في بلادنا كثير من هولاي الجمال وهذا اصغر ما يكون فيهم بخاطرك لانه كان اخذ مني الربع.

١٠،٢٦ فلنرجع ما كنا في صدده بان بعض ناس محبين الفقرا والغربا شاروا علي ذلك الرجل اصطفان المذكور بان يشتري له ابريقين وكام فنجان وما يعوزه لاجل طبخ القهوه ويمضي الي الموسم وكان ذلك الحين حكم موسم مار ميخايل فعمل الرجل كما شاروا عليه وفتح قهوه في ذلك الموسم وبما انه رجل شرقي غريب فتراكمت الزبونات عليه لان ما في غيره قهواتي وفي ذلك الزمان ما كان انتشا قهوات في بهريس وكل شي جديد حلو فصار ما يلحق في اعطا القهوه واخد له اجاره حتي يساعدوه علي كثره الازتحام الذي صار عليه والنتيجه في تلك السبعة ايام كسب مقدار مايتين غرش ايضاً فبقا معه اربعماية غرش.

١٠،٢٧ فلما انتهي الموسم رجع الي المدينه وفتح دكان قهواتي وكبرته العالم والزبون بهذا المقدار حتي في مده سنه صار معه مبلغ دراهم وانسمي في مدينة بهريس اصطفان القهواتي وكان ياتي لعنده من السبع صواير من اكابر وتجار وغيرهم عالم كثير حتي

---

١ الأصل: بيناع.

Then the feast of Saint Michael came around. The city of Paris has seven 　10.24
quarters, each named after a saint. When a saint's day arrives, a festival is held
in some open space for seven days, full of goods for sale and spectacles to see.
People come from other towns to trade because there are no customs duties
levied on goods bought and sold at that time, unlike the rest of the year.

On the feast of Saint Michael, I went to the square to see the sights. I saw 　10.25
a black monkey in a steel cage who looked as ugly as a devil, and also a two-
headed snake! Eventually I came to a certain building. A man was outside,
beating a drum.

"What's this?" I asked some people. They responded that inside was a wondrous spectacle. I wanted to look at it, and the proprietor asked for a quarter. His price was more expensive than the other entertainments and I didn't
want to give him more money. But some people interceded and convinced the
owner to accept four sovereigns, and he invited me in.

When I went inside, I saw a single little camel. I regretted my decision and
told the owner, "We have plenty of those where I come from, and they're all
bigger than that!"

"That's your problem," he replied, as he had already taken the quarter from
me.

But let's get back to the story. It was suggested to this Iṣṭifān fellow by 　10.26
some charitable people that he buy two kettles and some cups and whatever
else he'd need to make coffee, and go to the festival—that is, the feast of Saint
Michael. The man did as they suggested and opened a café there. And since he
was a foreign man from the East—and because there weren't any other coffee
sellers—he had a lot of customers.

Paris didn't have many cafés in those days, and anything novel was a source
of delight. Soon, Iṣṭifān couldn't keep up with the demand, so he hired assis-
tants to help serve the crowds that descended on him. All in all, he made
another two hundred piasters over seven days, so he'd earned four hundred
piasters in total.

When the festival ended, Iṣṭifān went back to the city and opened a coffee 　10.27
shop. The customers arrived in such numbers that, in the space of a single year,
he had earned a tidy sum and became known throughout Paris as Iṣṭifān the
Coffee Man. People would come to his café from all seven quarters, including
nobles, merchants, and many others. When his fame reached the palace of the

صار له اسم في ورساليا وفي نفس صراية الملك. وقتيدٍ ارسل الوزير وامره بانه يفتح قهوه في ورساليا ليلا تروح اولاد الاماره لعنده في بهريس فعمل بما امره الوزير وفتح قهوه في ورساليا واستقام يسقي قهوه في صراية الملك وصار معلوم اكبر الدوله وصار له نام عظيم.

٢٨،١٠ فاتفق الي امراه ارمله غنيه جدًا صاحبة تروه واملاك رادت تاخذه لها زوج فارسلت ناس بانهم يخاطبوه في هل قضيه فقبل وتزوجها[١] وجا له منها بنت وهذه البنت كان لها مرض ومنه تكرسحة فهذا الرجل ارسل رجل من قبله يخاطبني بهذا الكلام بان خواجه اصطفان التزم بان يفتح قهوه في ورساليا ويستقيم هناك فاد بان يزوجك بنته ويسلمك قهوته التي هي في بهريس وبما انك شرقي الزبون يميل اليك اكثر من اولاد البلد.

٢٩،١٠ فلما سمعت منه هل كلام وكت رايت البنت وهي محسنه لكنها سقط اعني مكرسحه فاجبته علي سواله بانه يعطيني مهله حتي اشاور معلمي وبعده بعطيك الجواب فمضي الرجل علي شرط اني اعطيه الجواب بعد يومين ثلاثه وبعده فشاورت معلمي فما رضي باني اخطب هل بنت لاجل انها مكرسحه فلما عاد اليّ ذلك الرجل حتي ياخد مني الجواب فما اعطيته جواب شافي بقولي له ابق له مساله الي حين حتي اشاور حالي.

٣٠،١٠ وبقيت المساله هكذا اليوم الذي مسكوني فيه جماعة الحاكم كما ذكرنا فلما مرينا من قدام دكانه راني فخرج مسرعًا وسال جماعة الحاكم ما بالكم ماسكين هذا الغلام وما هو دنبه فاجابوه بان قالوا للحاكم بان هذا ايضًا من عشرات يوسف الجوهرجي لعله بيعرف في اي مكان مختبي حتي يقرعليه وان ما قر بالهينه[٢] سوف يتعدب كثير فما قدر خواجه اصطفان يطلقني من ايدي جماعة الحاكم وفي ذلك المحل حضر معلمي لان كان وصله الخبر في مسكي فلما راني ممسوك وانا مرتعب في غاية ما يكون فزجر اوليك الذين ماسكيني وامرني بالمضي الي البيت بقوله لهم اما بتعرفوا بان هل غلام عندي وانا اتيت به من بلاد الشرق لكي يكون في خزانة كتب العربيه التي للملك ماذا تريدوا منه.

---

١ الأصل: وترجها.   ٢ الأصل: بالهين.

king, in Versailles, the king's minister ordered him to open a café there so that the princes wouldn't have to go all the way to his café in Paris. Iṣṭifān did as the minister asked and opened a café in Versailles. He then stayed on, serving coffee at the royal palace. He rubbed shoulders with the grandees of the state, and became quite the celebrity.

It came to pass that a very wealthy widow with many properties set her sights on Iṣṭifān. She sent some people to propose the marriage and he agreed. They were married and she bore a girl who later was afflicted by an illness that crippled her. Her father sent me a message saying that since he had no choice but to remain in Versailles, where he'd opened his café, I should marry his daughter and take over the café in Paris. "You're from the East, so you'll be more popular with the customers than a Frenchman."

10.28

When I heard these words—and had seen the girl, who was beautiful, even if crippled—I responded to his request by asking for some time to discuss it with my master before giving him my answer. The messenger agreed and left, on the condition that I respond within two or three days. I consulted my master, but he didn't consent to me marrying the girl because she was a cripple. When the messenger returned for my answer, I didn't give him a definitive response.

10.29

"Leave me alone for a while so that I have some more time to think about it," I told him.

This was where things stood on the day when the governor's people arrested me, as I recounted earlier. When we passed in front of Iṣṭifān's coffee shop, he saw me and ran out quickly to ask the governor's people, "Why are you holding this young man, and what is his crime?"

10.30

"The governor's been told that he's an associate of Yūsuf the Jeweler," they replied, "and he might know where Yūsuf is hiding. If he doesn't talk, he'll be tortured."

Iṣṭifān couldn't persuade the governor's men to let me go. But then my master appeared, for news had reached him of my arrest. When he saw me in custody and scared out of my wits, he rebuked the men who were holding me prisoner and ordered me to go home.

"Don't you know that this young man works for me and that I brought him from the Orient to work in the king's Arabic Library? What do you want from him?"

فأخبروه عن القضيه' وكيف ان الحاكم بيستقصِ الجره لعله يجده واخبروا الحاكم بان ٣١،١٠
راوا هذا الغلام من قرب كان بيلقش معه ولاجل هذا السبب مسكاه وما معنا علم
بانه هو عندك فاجابهم هذا الغلام هو عندي وانا كفيله وانا برد جواب للحاكم ان لزم
الامر . حينذٍ تركوني جماعة الحاكم ومضوا لكن انا اسرت في الرعبه واتضجرت بالزايد
من تلك البلاد بخزمة على الخروج من بهريس وافعل ما امرني به الامير المذكور حتي
اسافر واسوح سياحة معلمي فصممت النيه على ذلك وطلبت من معلمي اذن حتي
اسافر الي بلادي فلما سمع مني هل كلام بهت.

وقال لي هل ناقصك شي او انك مانك راضي بعيشك معي انا تعبت عليك هل ٣٢،١٠
قدر وجتك الي هذه البلاد حتي اصنع معك خير واقيمك في وظيفه شريفه تكون
تحت نام سلطان فرنسا وتعيش طول عمرك بالهنا والسرور وانت بتريد ترفس هذه
السعاده وترجع يسير للمسلمين كما كنت سابقًا فاسركلامه في وغيرت نيتي عن الرواح
لان دايمًا كان يقلي بان الوزير راسه مشغول من جري الكون الواقع في تلك الايام
لكن لما بيصير الصلح بكمل وعدي معك وبدخلك الي خزانة الكتب.

فضليت في هل امل وعدلت عن الرواح الي عند الامير المذكور فلما اسطبطاني ٣٣،١٠
بعد ثلاثة ايام ارسل دعاني صحبة ذلك الاختيار فلما امتثلت امامه حياني بالسلام
وصار يقلي لماذا تعوقت في مجيك الي عندي وانا في استندارك اجته يا سيدي
ما امكن ان يعطيني اذن معلمي في الخروج من عنده لانه تعب عليّ كثير وجابني
الي هذه البلاد حتي يفعل معي خير ويخلصني من اسر البرابره ولاجل هل سبب
ما بريد افوت خاطره . حينذٍ قلي الامير وانا بريد افعل معك خير واجعلك من
توابعي وتكون دايمًا تحت نام الملك ونامي امضي قول الي معلمك بان جاك مكتوب
من عند اهلك وبتلتزم بالرواح الي بلادك افعل بالذي اقوله لك وهلم لعندي حتي
اجهزك وارسلك.

فلما سمعت منه هل كلام انبكت وما قدرت ارد عليه جواب الا بالسفر فخرجت ٣٤،١٠
من عنده وانا في حيره ولكن الله سبحانه دبرهكذا فرجعت الي معلمي وقلتله يا سيدي

_____

١ الأصل: القضه.

They told him the story of how the governor was hot on Yūsuf's trail and    10.31
that they'd seen me chatting with him.

"That's why we arrested him," they told my master. "We didn't know he
worked for you."

"He's with me," my master replied. "I'll stand surety for him, and if there's
anything the governor needs to know, I'll tell him."

So the governor's men released me and left. But I was still terrified, and
I was suddenly sick and tired of the country. So I resolved to leave Paris and
carry out the nobleman's commission I mentioned earlier, so I could travel
abroad like my master. My mind made up, I asked him for permission to go
back to my country. This request took him quite by surprise.

"Is there anything I haven't given you? Aren't you happy living here with    10.32
me?" he asked. "I've gone to a lot of trouble for your sake, you know. I brought
you to this country as an act of goodwill, so that you could have an honorable
position in the king's service and live a happy and comfortable life. Do you
want to throw that chance away and go back to being a captive of the Muslims
the way you were before?"[38]

Hearing him, I changed my mind about leaving. My master was always telling me, "The minister is busy with what's going on at the moment, but when
peace comes, I'll keep my promise and get you into the Royal Library."

Reassured, I decided not to go to the nobleman. After three days, he sent    10.33
for me and I went, along with the old man I mentioned earlier. He greeted
me and said, "Why have you delayed in coming to see me? I've been waiting
for you!"

"Alas, my master was unable to give me permission to leave him, my lord,"
I said. "He's done so much for me, bringing me to this country for my own
good and saving me from captivity amongst the barbarians. I don't want to
offend him."

"But I too want to help you, and give you a place with me," the nobleman
said. "You will always be under the king's protection and mine. Give word to
your master that you received a letter from your family requiring you to go
back to your country. Do what I tell you, and come back to me so I can prepare
you and send you off."

Upon hearing this. I was dumbstruck and could only nod in assent. I left    10.34
in a state of complete bewilderment, but divine intervention was at work.
I returned home to my master.

انا جاني مكتوب من عند اخوتي وما يمكن بقيت استقيم ههنا فلما سمع مني هذا الكلام غضب وانحصر مني في غاية ما يكون بقوله انتم يا ولاد الشرق قليلين الوفا امضي الي حيث ما تريد لكن بحرد وغيظ شديد واخرج في الحال اعطاني ماية ثلث وقلي روح مع السلامه ولكن سوف تندم حيث ما يفيدك الندم.

٣٥،١٠ وخرج وتركني. حينذٍ لميت حوايجي واودعتهم عند احد جيرانا ومضيت الي بيت الديليجانسا اعني الي مكان عرابانة التي بتساو الي مدينة ليون وهن عرابانتين ولهم ايام معينه للسفر لان في وصول الواحده الي مدينة ليون بتخرج الثانيه من بهريس وهذه العرابه بثمانية روس خيل وبتحمل داخلها ثمانيه انفار وخارج عنها تخت بين الدولابين المتخرات وهذا التخت للخدم المرافقين اسيادهم الذين هن داخلها كراهم كل يوم غرشين والخارجين الذين علي التخت كل يوم كراهم غرش.

٣٦،١٠ وان سالني سايل لماذا الكري غالي بهذا المقدار اجبته بان هذه العرابه كانها قصر مختصر ولها اربع شبابيك بلور نجف وبجلله بجلود السرداق وداخلها اربع خوانات مجللين بجوخ اسقرلات وما بيدخلوا اليها غير ثمانية انفار لا غير وساحبينها ثمانية روس خيل الاقوا وفي كل سفر ساعتين بترا في الطريق واقفين ثمانية روس خيل في استندارها حتي يغيروا علي المكدونين لانها بتسير سفر يومين بيوم.

٣٧،١٠ ومحل الدهر بتصل الي استريا مخصصه لهذه العرابتين لا غير فيينزلو الركابه وبيدخلوا لتلك الاستريه فترا المايده موضوعه بجميع لوازمها وبيقدموا لهم غدا مكلف احسن ما يكون في بيوت الاكابر باكولات مفتخره وخبز كماج وخمر لذيذ واربع خمس من الخدامات ماسكين القداح بيسقوا[1] لكل من طلب منهم وبعدما بيتغدوا هن وتباعهم الذين بياكلوا من اكلهم في ثاني مايده بيركبوا العرابه وبوضعوا لهم داخل العربانه فراغ خمر وكاس وقلة ماء حتي اذا رادوا يشربوا في الطريق يكون موجود عندهم الشرب وكذلك المساء حكم المغرب بيصلوا ايضاً الي استريه التي هي مخصصه الي هذه العرابتين فيدخلوا اليها وبيتعشوا كما ذكرنا باكولات مفتخرة وبيستقيموا يتصامروا الي محل المنامه.

---

١ الأصل: بيسقول.

"My lord," I said, "I have received a letter from my brothers. I can't stay here any longer."

When my master heard these words, he became more furious than he'd ever been.

"You Orientals are a disloyal lot!" he raged. "If you want to leave, go ahead!" Then he handed me a hundred thirds and cried, "Godspeed. You'll regret this one day, but it'll be too late!"

He stormed off, leaving me alone to pack up my things. I left them with one of our neighbors and went to the diligence station, which was where the stagecoaches departed for Lyon. There were two stagecoaches, which left on specific days. As soon as one arrived at Lyon, the second would depart Paris. Each stagecoach was pulled by a team of eight horses and had room for eight passengers inside. An exterior platform between the two rear wheels of the coach was reserved for the servants accompanying their masters. The price for a seat inside was two piasters per day, and for a seat outside one piaster. 10.35

Why is the fare so high? you might ask. Because the carriages are like little palaces, with four crystal windows and leather upholstery. Inside, there are four benches covered in scarlet,[39] which seat no more than eight people. The coach is pulled by eight strong horses, which are relieved every two hours by a fresh team waiting by the side of the road. That way, the length of the journey is halved. 10.36

At noon, it would stop at an inn reserved for the two stagecoaches, and the passengers would disembark and go inside. There, they'd find a table waiting for them, set with all the necessary accoutrements. A sumptuous lunch would be served, including delicacies that wouldn't even appear in nobles' households, along with soft bread and splendid wine. Four or five servant girls carrying goblets served anyone who called for more wine. 10.37

With lunch complete, the passengers and their servants—who ate the same food, but at a separate table—would climb aboard the stagecoach again, now accompanied by a bottle of wine, a glass, and a jug of water for those sitting inside, in case they wanted a drink on the road. At sunset, the coach would pull into another reserved inn, where the passengers would have another splendid dinner. They'd spend the evening together, chatting until it was time to go to sleep.

١٠،٣٨ وبعطوا لكل منهم تخت مجلل بجوخ اذا كان في فصل الشتا وفي فصل الصيف يجللوه بكتان ابيض رفيع وبجانب التخت متكاء وامامه ايقونه وصلبوت لاجل الصلوه ومفروش التخت بثلاثة فرش وبياتوا لكل واحد منهم ملحفتين نظاف ما نام فيهم احد وتخفيفه نظيفه ايضاً ولما يصبح الصباح بيدخلوا الي كنيسة ذلك المكان يحضروا القداس الالهي وبيرجعوا عايدين الي الاستريه بيكون تهيا لهم فطور مثل خبز كج طري وجبنه وخمر طيب فبعدما يكونوا فطروا بيركبوا العرابانه وبيسافروا وكا ذكرنا بيتغدوا في مكان وبيتعشوا وبيناموا في مكان وهلم جرا حتي يصلوا الي مدينة ليون وهي مسافه عشرين يوم بيصلوا اليها بعشرة ايام.

١٠،٣٩ فالفقير لما انتهيت الي ذلك المكان كتبت اسمي وقبضت الكراء علي المعتاد وكان ذلك نهار التلاتاه ومعتاد سفر العرابانه يوم الخميس فاوصوني بان ليلت الخميس انام هناك لانهم بيسافروا من باكر قبل مزوق الشمس وانا كتبت اسمي مع الخارجين عن العرابانه كما ذكرنا ورجعت من هناك الي عند حضرة الامير واخبرته بالذي صنعته واني طلعت من عند معلي ومضيت استكريت في الديليجانسه وقبضت الكري فقلي ليش استعجلت وما جيت لعندي قبل ما تفعل هذا الشي لكن ما في باس.

١٠،٤٠ حينذٍ دعا لعنده يازنجي وامره بان يكتب مكتوب الي واحد من الدوكاوات الذي هو داخل صرايه الملك في ورسايا حتي يعتني بكتب فمان علي موجب ما لخص له في المكتوب وبعدما طوي المكتوب وختمه حينذٍ امرني باني امضي الي ورسايا وادخل الي صرايه الملك واعطي المكتوب لذلك الدوك فاخدت منه المكتوب واستقمت الي حين المساء ليلا يسمع معلي باني رحت الي ورسايا وركبت في قوجيه ومضيت الي ورسايا ودخلت صرايه الملك من غير مانع لان الحراس كانوا عرفوني لما استقمت ثمانية ايام في صرايه الملك لاجل مدارات تلك الوحوش الذي مردكرهم ولاجل هل سبب ما احد صدني عن الدخول.

١٠،٤١ فلما انتهيت داخل الصرايا سالت عن ذلك الدوك فدلوني عليه وهو بيتمشي في صالة الجوانيه داخل الصرايا فلما رايته عملت له تمني واعطيته المكتوب فاخد المكتوب من يدي وقرب الي قرب الشموع المتقده هناك وقري المكتوب فالتف اليّ وانسني

The beds were covered with blankets during the winter months, and thin    10.38
white cotton felt in the summer. A prie-dieu sat by the bed with an icon and
crucifix before it, for prayer. Each bed had three mattresses, and everyone
received two fresh, clean quilts and a clean nightgown. In the morning, all
would go to a church located by the inn and attend mass. By the time they
returned, a breakfast of soft bread, cheese, and sweet wine would have been
prepared for them. Following breakfast, they'd climb into the coach and set
off again. They'd stop for lunch, dinner, and an overnight stay as previously
described; this routine would continue until they arrived at Lyon. The journey, which ordinarily took twenty days, passed in ten.

When I arrived at the way station, I registered my name on the passenger    10.39
list and paid for a fare. It happened to be a Tuesday, and the usual departure
day was Thursday. I was advised to spend Wednesday night there, as the coach
would depart before dawn the next morning. Having written my name on the
list of passengers traveling on the exterior of the carriage, I then went to visit
His Excellency the nobleman, and told him I'd left my master and purchased
a fare on the diligence.

"Why were you in such a hurry? You should have come to see me first," the
nobleman said. "Ah well, that's quite all right."

He summoned his clerk and ordered him to compose a letter to a duke at    10.40
the king's palace in Versailles, asking him to have an edict drawn up according to the stipulations in the letter. He folded the letter, sealed it, and ordered
me to go to Versailles and deliver it to the duke. I took the letter and left, but
decided to wait until the evening to set off for Versailles, as I didn't want my
master to learn of my visit. When evening came, I took a coach to Versailles
and was duly admitted to the royal palace. The guards recognized me from the
time I'd spent eight days there, when we were displaying the animals I mentioned previously, so no one prevented me from entering.

Once inside, I inquired as to the whereabouts of the duke and was taken to    10.41
a room within the palace, where I found him pacing. I bowed before him and
handed him the letter. The duke read it by candlelight, then turned to greet
me cordially.

"Follow me!" he said.

بالكلام ثم قلي اتبعني فمضيت معه الي المكان الذي فيه يكتبوا الفرمانات واوامر الملك وهو مكان متسع وداخله كثير من الكتبه. حينذٍ دعا لعنده ريس ذلك المكان اعني ريس الكتّاب وقري له المكتوب وامره بان يكتب فرمان علي موجب ما هو ماشر في المكتوب فبعد ما امره بذلك تركني ومضي.

واما انا فاستقمت استنظر الفرمان فوقفت حصه طويله وانا في الاستنظار فجاني ريس الكتّاب المذكور وسالني ماذا تريد فاجبته اني بستنا الفرمان فابتسم وقلي ماذا يفيدك الفرمان من غير انه يتعرض علي الملك ويضع اسمه عليه فسالته ايمتا يتم هذا الامر فقلي يوم التنين يصير ديوان وبتتعرض جميع الفرمانات علي الملك فالذي بيجبه بينشنه والذي ما بيجبه بيشقه فلما سمعت منه هل كلام بهت وداقت فيّ الدنيا وندمت لاجل اني استكريت وقضة الكري ولا بد في اني اسافر يوم الخميس فخرجت من الصرايا ودخلت في استريه اتعشيت ونمت هناك ولما اصبح الصباح توجهت الي مدينة بهريس الي عند حضرة الامير.

فلما راني سالني هل اني رحت الي ورساليا فاجبته نعم رحت واعطيت المكتوب لذلك الدوك واحكيته بالذي صار وان الفرمان ما بيطلع الا ليوم التنين وانا يوم الخميس بلتزم اني اسافر فقلي ما في باس امضي الي مرسيليا وانا بعد كام يوم برسلك الفرمان ومكاتيب التوصاي[1] وامر في حضور اليازجي وامره بانه يكتوب مكتوب الي شاهبندر مرسيليا وهو الذي بيتعاطه في امور تجار الشرق الذين بيتاجروا لهذه البلاد.

وامره في المكتوب بان تبقى هل غلام عندك الي حين ما يصل لك مع الولاق الفرمان وتعطيه من يدك مكتوب لجميع قناصر القاطنين في بلاد الشرقيه ومهما طلب منهم يعطوه من الدراهم يعطوه وياخدوا منه وصول وايش ما اودع عندهم يرسلوه الي مرسيليا تحت يد الشاهبندر وايضاً امره في كتب مكتوب الي حضرة الالجي في اسطنبول توصاي فيّ ويطلع لي فرمان من الوزير توصاي لجميع حكام البلاد توصاي فيّ.

_____
١ بعد «التوصاي» جملة مشطوبة في الأصل: خرجت من عنده.

We went to the place where the king's edicts and orders are drawn up. It was a large room full of scribes. Summoning the chief scribe over, the duke read him the letter and ordered him to draw up a corresponding edict, and took his leave.

I remained there, waiting for the completion of the edict. Time passed.   10.42
Finally, the chief scribe came back to see me.

"Can I help you?"

"I'm waiting for the edict," I replied.

"And what use is the edict to you before it is presented to the king for authorization?" the man said, smiling.

"When will that happen?" I asked him.

"Monday," he said. "That's when the council meets and edicts are presented to the king. Those he approves receive the royal seal, and the rest are shredded."

Upon hearing these words, I felt the world crowding in on my miserable self! I regretted my decision to reserve a stagecoach ticket, for I now had no choice but to depart Paris on Thursday. Leaving the palace, I checked in to an inn, where I had dinner and spent the night. The next morning, I returned to Paris to see His Excellency the nobleman.

"Did you go to Versailles?" he asked when he saw me.   10.43

"I did, and I delivered the letter to the duke," I said, recounting what had happened at the palace, and how the edict would not be issued until next Monday even though I was due to depart on Thursday.

"Not to worry," the nobleman said. "Go to Marseille, and I'll send you the edict and your letters of recommendation in a few days."

He summoned his clerk and told him to draw up a letter to the chief merchant of Marseille who oversaw the affairs of those merchants involved in trade with the lands of the East.

"Lodge this young man with you until such time as you receive an edict   10.44
via express courier," the letter read. "In addition, provide him with a letter in your own hand, introducing him to all of the consuls residing in Oriental lands and asking them to grant him any sum of money he requests, in exchange for receipts. Furthermore, whatever goods he entrusts to them should be forwarded to the chief merchant of Marseille."

The nobleman then ordered the clerk to compose a letter of introduction to His Excellency the French ambassador in Istanbul, requesting that he secure an edict for me from the vizier recommending me to all the local governors.[40]

واخيرًا ودعني وخرجت من عنده واخدت المكاتيب ومضيت اخدت حوايجي ٤٥،١٠
من عند الجيران وسلمتهم الي ريس مكان الدليجانسا. اخيرًا رحت ودعت المعارف
والاصدقا ومن جملتهم مضيت ودعت خواجه كريستوفله كاخية حضرة الكردينال
فلما ودعته اعطاني مكتوب الي اخوه خواجه زماريا الذي هو قاطن في اسطنبول
ووظيفته وكليت القدس بخط شريف وهو رجل عالي جناب ودكر له بان يكون
نضره عليّ.

هذا ما تم الي ان سافرت من مدينة بهريس واتوجهنا الي مدينة ليون وفي يوم ٤٦،١٠
العاشر وصلنا الي مدينة المذكوره بغاية الصحه ومن هناك استكريت مع القاطرجيه
الذين يسافروا الي مرسيليا بثمن رخيص لان لهم عرابانات طوال وبيصفوا الفردات
فوقها وبتسحبها ستة كدش وكت الفقير اجلس فوق الفردات براحه عظيمه من غير
تعب طريق وكانوا الدهر يتغدوا في استريه وللمسا يتعشوا ويناموا في غيرها وكت
اهنيهم علي عيشتهم وسفرهم الذي ما يقتضي تحميل افواد ولا تعب وبياكلوا طيب
وبيناموا في تخوته وخدام الاستريه بعتنوا في خدمة دوابهم وتمارهم حتي انهم لما
يصبح الصبح يخرجوا دوابهم من الاستطبل وبيكدنوهم في العرابانه وكل عرابنه
بيصحبها واحد من القاطرجيه لا غير ولا عليهم فزع في الطريق والفقير كت اتعشا
معهم وما كلفوني حق اكل. المراد وصلنا الي مرسيليا بغاية الهنا.

فلما وصلت بالسلامه نزلت في استريت التي كا نزلنا فيها انا ومعلمي لما سافرنا ٤٧،١٠
الي بهريس فاسترحبت في صاحبة الاستريه واعطتني مكان للمنامه وبعد ساعه
من وصولي مضيت الي بيت البندر وطلبت الدخول لعند الشاهبندر فلما امتثلت
امامه اعطيته مكتوب الامير ففتحه وقراه. حيندٍ نهض علي قدميه واسترحب في
وعملي اكرام زايد. اخيرًا قلي بان حضرة الامير كاتب لي بان ابقيك عندي الي حين
ما يرسل لك الفرمان وانا بعطيك مكتوب للقناصر كما اوصاني في مكتوبه هذا.

وانا كان ظني بان الفرمان وصل قبل وصولي الي مرسيليا لان في كل اسبوع ٤٨،١٠
يصل اولاق بمنزل الي مرسيليا. وقيدٍ حسيت بان مسالتي فاشوشه ولاجل

He bid me farewell and I left with the letters, returning home to pick up my   10.45
things from the neighbors' house. I dropped them off with the proprietor of
the way station, then went to say goodbye to all my friends and acquaintances.
Among them was *khawājah* Christofalo, the second-in-command to His
Holiness the cardinal, who gave me a letter to take to his brother, *khawājah*
Zamāriyā, who lived in Istanbul. He was the syndic of Jerusalem, appointed
by the sultan himself, and was a man of very high rank. *Khawājah* Christofalo
asked his brother to keep an eye out for me.

That was how I spent my remaining hours in Paris before setting off for the   10.46
city of Lyon. After a ten-day journey, we arrived safe and sound. I then booked
passage on one of the cheap coaches that travel between Lyon and Marseille.
They were long carriages with bales of goods piled on top of them, pulled by
six cart horses. I stretched out on the bales in utmost comfort, happily spared
from the aches and pains of travel!

We'd stop at noon for lunch at one inn, and at another for dinner and
the overnight stay. I complimented my fellow travelers on this way of life of
theirs—effortless journeys that didn't require carrying a heavy load or suffering any fatigue, during which they ate good food and slept in soft beds. The servants at the inn took care of looking after and feeding the horses, even bringing
them out of the stables in the morning and hitching them up to the carriage.
A single coachman was responsible for driving the carriage, and nobody had
any fear of danger on the roads. I dined with the passengers each night, and no
one charged me for my supper. We made our way to Marseille in this fashion,
traveling in the greatest of ease.

After our safe arrival, I checked in to the same inn where my master and I   10.47
had stayed on our way to Paris. The proprietress of the inn welcomed me and
gave me a place to sleep, and after an hour I went to the chamber of commerce
and asked to see the chief merchant. I presented myself to him and gave him
the nobleman's letter, which he opened and read. Then he jumped to his feet
and greeted me most cordially.

"His Highness the nobleman has asked me to have you stay at my home
until he sends you the edict," the merchant said. "I'll also provide you with a
letter of introduction to the consuls, as he requests in this letter."

Now, I'd assumed that the edict would have reached Marseille before me,   10.48
because the postal horses arrived in the city once a week. It was then that

هذا ما ردت استقيم عند الشابندر بل قلته انا نزلت في استريه بتسما بتي بهريس ولما بيصلك الفرمان ارسل ادعوني الي عندك فقلي علي كيفك فخرجت من عنده وانا سكران بغير خمر واتندمت علي ما فعلت ولكن ايش عاد يفيد الندم وتذكرت كلام معلمي بقوله لي سوف تندم.

ولكن استقمت بين الخوف والرجا الي ثاني سبوع لما وصل المنزل مضيت الي عند الشابندر وسالته هل وصله خبر من ذلك الامير فاجاني ما وصلني منه خبر ولا مكتوب. حينذٍ افتكرت بان ارسله مكتوب وقله هل عاد يرسل الفرمان ام لا فرد علي الجواب بمكتوب من يده وداكر باني معتجب كيف ما وصلك الفرمان الذي كت ارسلته مع واحد من اصحابي الي مرسيليا واعنا لي عن اسمه فدرت فتشت عليه لعلي اراه فا رايت له ذكر في مرسيليا واستقمت ثالث اسبوع ورابع اسبوع فا بين احد. حينذٍ تحققت بان مسالتي مع هذا الامير ما هي تحت خبر .

ولما قطعت الاياس منه كتبت له مكتوب توبيخ وعار علي رجل مثله امير بانه يفصلني من معلمي وبصير في خايب من الطرفين لكن هكذا دبرت العناية الالهيه لخيري وارسلت المكتوب وشلت من بالي هذا الامر .

وفي تلك الايام اتي من مدينة بهريس رجل عابرطريق ونزل في استريت التي نازل الفقير فيها فيوم من ذات الايام لما كت اتسامر انا وياه فسالني عن بلادي وكيف كان قدومي الي تلك البلاد فاحكيت له عن سبب مجيي وهواني جيت مع رجل يسما بول لوكاس¹ من سواح الملك وكيف اني مضيت معه الي بهريس وقصيته بقصتي من اولها الي اخرها وكيف ان الامير الفلاني خوني واخرجني من عند معلمي وكيف انه خرم بوعده معي فقلي صدقت يا اخي ولكن حضرة الامير ما له دنب الدنب الي معلمك وانا بحكيلك بالمجراويه كيف تمت.

---

I began to suspect that my plan was falling apart, so I decided not to stay with the chief merchant.

"I'm staying at an inn called Petit Paris," I told him. "When the edict arrives, let me know and I'll return."

"As you wish."

I stumbled out the door as though I were drunk, though I hadn't had a sip of wine! I regretted what I'd done, but it was too late now. At that moment, I remembered my master telling me, "You'll be sorry!"

I waited until the following week, afraid yet hopeful that my luck would change. When the post arrived, I went to see the chief merchant. 10.49

"Have you received any news from the nobleman?"

"No news, and no letters either," he replied.

It occurred to me then to send the nobleman a letter myself, asking him if he was going to send me the edict or not. This I did, and he soon responded with a letter in his own hand.

"I'm surprised that you never received the edict," it read. "I sent it to Marseille with one of my friends," and gave the name of the individual.

I set about looking for the man, hoping to find a trace of him somewhere in Marseille, but my search turned up nothing. A third week passed with no sign of him, then a fourth. Finally, I came to the conclusion that my arrangement with the nobleman had fallen apart.

My hopes dashed, I wrote a reproachful letter in response, heaping shame on such a man—some nobleman!—who conspired to separate me from my master, dooming us both to failure. And yet, as it would turn out, this was all for my own good, and part of God's plan. I sent the letter and put the whole affair out of my mind. 10.50

It was around that time that a traveler arrived from Paris and checked in to the inn where I was staying. One day, while we were chatting, he asked me where I was from and how I'd come to this country. So I explained how I'd come to France with a man named Paul Lucas, who was one of the king's explorers. I told him how I'd gone to Paris with him, and recounted my story from beginning to end, including my encounter with the nobleman who deceived me and led me to leave my master, and eventually broke the promise he'd made. 10.51

"What you've said is all true, brother," the man said, "but His Excellency the nobleman isn't to blame. The fault rests with your master. Let me tell you how this story came to an end.

١٠،٥٢ فالاختيار الذي كان يزورك هو الذي شوق الامير في ارسالك الي السياحه تحت تلبسه لانه سمع بل تحقق بان معلمك بيريد ياخد لك وظيفة خزنه كتب العربي وخوفاً ليلا تفلت هذه الوظيفه من يده فلعب هذا الملعوب وشوق الامير في ارسالك ولما تم الامر والامير ارسلك الي ورسايا حتي يكتوب لك فرمان من الملك في تلك الليله راءك رجل من اصحاب معلمك واحكي له بانك اعطيت مكتوب الي فلان دوك وكيف ان الدوك واجهك مع ريس الكتّاب حتي يطيلع لك فرمان من الملك توصاي فيك لاجل سياحتك.

١٠،٥٣ فلما سمع معلمك هذا الخبر فمضي الي ورسايا لعند ذلك الدوك واستخبر منه حقيقة الامر فانحصر معلمك بما ان هذه وظيفته عند الملك وهي السياحه فمضي في الحال عند حضرة الامير ووشي عليك بقوله له بالك يا سيدي تسلم امرك الي واحد مثل هذا لان اولاد الشرق خاينين يمكن علي موجب امرك ياخد من القناصر مال ويعصي في بلاده وما بيعود يصير لك مقدره عليه واكراماً لخاطرك انا بنوب عنه ونخدمك هل خدمه وايش ما جنيته برسلك هو فلما سمع الامير من معلمك هذا الكلام تغير عقله ووجه له بانه يسوح علي كيسه.

١٠،٥٤ وهكذا صار لان بعد وصولي الي حلب بمده وصل معلي الي حلب فواجهته وسلمت عليه وعزمته لعندنا ووقفت في واجبه واكرمته غاية الاكرام وبات تلك الليله عندنا وفرشت له فرشه في عليتي فبعد ما مضوا اخوتي وبقيت انا واياه جلسنا نتسامر فصار يعاتبني كيف اني ما اعطيته خبر في اتفاقي مع الامير حتي امضي الي السياحه وقلي هذا انقص جري منك في حقي وما كان املي منك تفعل معي هكذا لان نيتي كانت لك افعل معك خير عظيم الا انك رفست النعمه وبعد كلام مستطيل وعتاب جزيل رقدنا وثاني يوم بعدما فطرنا نزلنا للمدينه وكنت الفقير فاتح دكان جوخ فكان كل يوم يزورني واروح معه كعادتنا في سفرنا نفتش علي فلوس مداليات وتجار ثمينه.

"The old man who used to visit you was the one who tricked the noble-   10.52
man into sending you off on a journey," he continued. "He'd learned that your
master was trying to secure a position for you in the Arabic Library. So, fearing
that the position in the library would slip from his grasp, he played this little
trick and convinced the nobleman to send you away.

"Now, on the night when the nobleman sent you to Versailles to get an edict
from the king, one of your master's friends happened to see you there. He went
and informed your master about how you'd given a letter to a certain duke,
who then took you to meet with the head of the chancery, who in turn drew up
a royal edict recognizing you as a traveler on behalf of the crown.

"When your master learned about all this, he went straight to Versailles to   10.53
see the duke, and extracted the complete story from him. He was furious, for
the position of a traveler appointed by the king was his own! So he went immediately to see His Excellency the nobleman, and defamed you to him.

"'Be careful with these types, my lord!' he said. 'Orientals are a traitorous
lot, and it's quite possible that this fellow will take advantage of your authority to steal from the consuls then vanish to his homeland. And if that happens,
you'll have no power to make him do anything. Permit me instead, as a token
of my esteem for Your Excellency, to replace that man as your servant! In
return, I promise to send you everything I collect during my travels.'

"When he heard that, the nobleman changed his mind and decided to
finance your master's travels instead," the man concluded.

And this was, in fact, how things came to pass. Some time after I returned   10.54
home to Aleppo, my master turned up in the city as well. I went to meet him,
and invited him to pay a visit to my family's home, where I received him most
honorably and put myself at his service. He spent the night at our house, and I
prepared a bed for him in my loft. After my brothers left, my master and I were
left alone. As we sat chatting, he began to reproach me.

"Why didn't you tell me about your agreement with the nobleman to go
on a voyage? That was the lowest thing you could have done to me! I never
expected you'd treat me that way, because I meant to do right by you. But you
threw away your best chance!"

After much discussion and quarreling, we finally fell asleep. The following
day, we had breakfast and went into town together. At the time, I'd opened a
textile shop, and he would visit me each day. We'd go off together to hunt for
old coins, medallions, and precious stones, just like old times.

١٠،٥٥ فيوم من ذات الايام دخلنا الي سوق السياغ فراء داخل ققص جحر مبخوش بلون جحر العقيق فاشتراه بمصريتين واعطاني هو وقلي علقه في عنق امك فتشفا مرضها لان لما كان عندنا في البيت خطر في بالي بان ارويه والدتي لان كان فيها مرض مزمن مند عشرين سنه وعجزت الاطبا وما قدر احد يطيبها من داها فلما ارويناه هي واحكينا له عن مرضها وهو انها ما بتقدر تنام ولا بتلقش ولا بتريد تخرج من الدار حتي تتنزه او تحضر القداس واكلها قوي قليل وبالجهد حتي يقدروا يطعموها حتي قد جسدها وبقت كانه قزمه.

١٠،٥٦ فلما علقنا تلك الجحر في عنقها فتلك الليلة نامت مليح كعادتها وثاني يوم بدلت حوايجها وطلبت انها تروح علي الحمام ورجعت من الحمام وهي بصحة العافيه فتعجبنا جميعنا من فعل هذه الجحر كانها فعلت عجيبه. اخيرًا استخبرت من معلمي عن هذه الجحر وما اسمها اجابني هذه اسمتها في لسان التلياني كرميديه ولها هذا الخواص بتجدب ريح السوداوي في الحال ومرض والدتك ريح سيداوي لاغير.

١٠،٥٧ اخيرًا قلي ذلك الرجل بان الامير وجه الفرمان الي معلمك حتي يطلع يسوح علي كيسه وعدل عنك لا بقيت تامل بشي من هذا. هذا الرجل علي ما اظن انه مرسل من عند الامير حتي يطلعني[١] علي هذا الخبر وهذا ما تم في سبب خروجي من بهريس.

١٠،٥٨ ونرجع بالكلام فاستقمت في مرسيليا في تلك الاستريه الي حين ما يتوجه مركب الي اسكلت اسكندرونه حتي اسافر معه وكنت كل يوم امضي الي بيت البندر حيث بتجتمع التجار هناك من قبل الدهر بساعتين الي حين الدهر ومن بعد الدهر بساعتين الي حين العصر وجميع البيع والشراء بيتم هناك وبيوجد هناك جميع تجار بلاد الشرق والذين بيتاجروا الي ينكي والي بلاد دنيا والي بلاد اصبانيا والي بلاد المغاربه والي غير بلاد وهذه التجار لما بيردوا مركب يرسلو مركب بيعلقوا ورقة داكرين فيها اسم المركب واسم تلك البلد التي ماضي اليها.

---

١ الأصل: يطليني.

One day, we went to the jewelry souk, and he saw a pierced stone, the color   10.55
of carnelian, in a case. He bought it for two *miṣriyyah*s and handed it to me.

"Hang this around your mother's neck, and she'll be cured of her illness."

When he'd stayed at our house, it had occurred to me to let him see my
mother, who had suffered from a chronic illness for the previous twenty
years. No doctor had been able to cure her, so we took her to my master and
explained her symptoms: She couldn't sleep or speak, and never wanted to
leave the house on a walk or to attend mass, and she hardly ate anything. It was
only with great effort that we managed to feed her; as a result, her body had
shriveled to a thin stalk.

We hung the stone around her neck, and that night she slept soundly, as she   10.56
used to do before! The next day, she changed her clothes and asked to be taken
to the bathhouse. When she returned, she was the picture of health. All of us
were astounded by the power of that stone, which seemed to have worked
a miracle! I asked my master to tell me what it was called, and to explain its
powers.

"It's called *cheramide* in Italian," he said. "It has the special property of
instantly drawing out the black humor. Your mother was suffering from melancholy, that's all."

Anyway, the man I met at the inn in Marseille told me that the nobleman   10.57
had sent my edict to my master, allowing him to set off on a voyage at the
nobleman's expense.

"The nobleman isn't interested in you anymore, so you may as well give up
on this whole affair," the man said.

My suspicion is that this man was sent by the nobleman to convey this
information to me. In any case, that's the end of the story of why I left Paris.

Now, back to what I was saying. I remained at the inn in Marseille, waiting   10.58
to catch a ship bound for Alexandretta. Every day, I went to the chamber of
commerce where the merchants gathered from ten in the morning until noon,
and again from two in the afternoon until the early evening. That was where
all of the commercial activity took place. The merchants who had business in
the Eastern lands could be found there, along with those who traded with the
New World, Spain, the Maghreb, and other lands. Whenever these merchants
were planning to dispatch a ship, they'd post a notice with the name of the ship
and its destination.

٥٩،١٠ فيوم من الايام مضيت الى ذلك المكان فرايت معلق ورقه باسم مركب ماضي الى اسكلت اسكندرونه ففرحت ومضيت الى عند خواجه سامطان الذي هواعز اصحابي وهوكان تاجر في مدينة حلب وكان اخي الكبير مخزنجي عنده فهذا الرجل كان يحبني وكثير اوقات يعزمني الى بيته ويضيفني ويقف في واجي فاخبرته بان تهيا مركب الى اسكلت اسكندرونه بريد اروح معه فقلي معي خبر وانا بوصي فيك القبطان وبخلي ياخدك معه بلاش.

٦٠،١٠ فاستكثرت بخيره ومضية حضرة حوايجي١ وبقيت علي نيت السفر ومضيت ودعت خواجكيت حلب المعارف معي وبعدكام يوم تغيرة نية اصحاب المركب وما عادوا يرسلوه فزعاً من القرصان فلما سمعت هل خبر حزنت قوي كثير لاني كنت ضجرت وداقة الدنيا فيّ ورحت الى بيت المضجر لعلي اري مركب ماضي الى السيحل فما رايت غير مركبين متهيين للسفر واحد الى اسطنبول والاخر الي ازمير فسالت عن القبطان الذي بده يسافر الي ازمير فدلوني عليه فطلبت منه بانه ياخدني معه الي ازمير فرضي وطلب مني باني اعطيه في الحال سلف عن كروتي اربعين غرش من غير حق اكلي وشربي وانا في ذلك الوقت ماكان معي غيرعشرة غروش فحرت في امري كيف اعمل.

٦١،١٠ فرحت عند صديقي خواجه سماطان واحكيته بالذي صار فا هان عليه في رواحي الي ازمير وقلي اصبر قليل لعل بيتهيا مركب الى اسكندرونه برسلك معه بلاش فاجته واتوسلت اليه بان ما بقا يمكني الاستقامه في هل بلاد لاني زعلت حالي وما بقا لي صبر بدي اسافرمن كل بد وسبب. حينذٍ قلي بريد اعلمك شي وهو ان اسعد الي بيت القنصر الذي هو فوق بيت البندر واطلب من القنصر بان يامر قبطان المركب بانه ياخدك معه وقله اني رجل غريب وفقير وما لي كار هاهنا حتي اسحب معيشتي فللوقت بيامر القبطان بانه ياخدك معه لا محاله.

٦٢،١٠ ففعلت كما امرني ومضيت الى بيت القنصر من باكر فالبخت وجدت الكاهن تهيا حتي يقدس للقنصر فدخلت في الحال وخدمت للكاهن وبعد خلوص القداس

---

١ بعد «حوايجي» جملة مشطوبة في الأصل: وكتبت مكتوب الي اخي في حلب باني.

One day, I went down to the chamber of commerce and saw a notice posted      10.59
with the name of a ship headed for the port of Alexandretta. I happily went to
see *khawājah* Samatan, who was my very best friend. He had been a merchant
in Aleppo, and my oldest brother had worked as his warehouseman. *Khawājah*
Samatan was very fond of me, and would often invite me to his house and treat
me as a cherished guest. So I told him that a ship was preparing to sail for Alexandretta, and that I planned to be on it.

"I know about the ship," he said. "I'll put in a good word for you with the
captain, and have him take you aboard for free."

I thanked him and wished him well, and went home to pack my things. As I      10.60
was intent on sailing with that ship, I said goodbye to all the foreign gentlemen
of Aleppo I knew. A few days later, however, the owners of the ship changed
their mind and decided not to sail, fearing the threat of pirates. I was devas-
tated when I heard this, as I'd been anxious to leave and was starting to feel at
my wits' end. I went to the chamber of commerce to see if there might be a ship
headed to the Levantine coast.

There were only two: one bound for Istanbul and the other for Izmir. I
made some inquiries about the captain of the Izmir-bound ship, sought him
out, and asked if he would take me aboard. He agreed, but demanded that I pay
my fare of forty piasters—not including food and drink—in advance. All I had
was ten piasters! What was I to do?

I returned to my friend *khawājah* Samatan and told him what had hap-      10.61
pened. He wasn't pleased with my plan to go to Izmir.

"Be patient, and perhaps a ship will be dispatched to Alexandretta soon
enough," he said. "I'll get you on board for free."

"But I can't bear to stay in this country any longer!" I said, pleading with
him. "I'm fed up, and my patience has run out! I absolutely must leave!"

"Let me give you some advice," he replied. "Go upstairs to the consul's residence, which is above the chamber of commerce. Ask the consul to order the
captain of the ship to take you with him. Tell him, 'I'm a penniless foreigner
in this country, and don't have a job to earn a living.' I guarantee you that he'll
order the captain to take you with him."

I did as he advised and went to see the consul early the next morning. As      10.62
luck would have it, I arrived as a priest was preparing to lead a mass at the
consul's residence, so I quickly went inside and began to help the priest. After
the mass, the consul left with several merchants for a walk in the courtyard.

خرج القنصر ومعه جمله من البازركان يتمشوا في صحن المكان. حينئذٍ تقدمت امام القنصر وعملت تمني اللايق بشانه كوايدهم واحكيت معه بلسان الفرنساوي كما علمني خواجه سمطان فلما انتهيت من كلامي فسالني القنصر من اي بلاد انت اجبته باني من بلاد سوريا فقلي ماذا اتيت الي هل بلاد فاجبته اتيت مع رجل فرنساوي ومضيت معه الي مدينة بهريس فعاد تركني والان رجعت من بهريس حتي ارجع الي بلادي والذي كان معي اصرفته في الطريق وما بقا معي شي حتي اتقوت.

٦٣،١٠   فلما انتهينت من كلامي امر واحد من خدامه بانه يمضي ويدعي ذلك القبطان الي عنده والتفت قلي اصبر هاهنا ولا تروح وبعد هنيهه اتي القبطان فامر القنصر بانه ياخدني معه وقال له هذا الغلام بما انه غريب وفقير فنلتزم بان نرسله الي بلاده كجري عوايدنا فاجابه القبطان سمعاً وطاعه والتفت اليّ القبطان وقلي الليله وقت العصر نزل حوايجك في القايق وانت ايضاً روح مع القايق الي المركب لان في الغد باكر بسافر. حينئذٍ استكثرت بخير القنصر والقبطان ومضيت من هناك الي عند خواجه سمطان واحكيت له بالذي صار وشكرت فضله.

٦٤،١٠   حينئذٍ قلي بقا علينا باني اخدك الي عند صاحب المركب واخدلك من يده مكتوب للقبطان توصاي فيك ليلا احد ينكد عليك في الطريق لانك نزلت غرماً عنه فاخدني ومضا الي عند صاحب المركب وكان هذا صاحبه فلما دخلنا لعنده فاسترحب فينا قوي كثير. حينئذٍ قله خواجه سماطان بان هل غلام بريد ارسله مع مركبك وبطلب من فضلك بان تعطيه مكتوب من يدك توصي فيه القبطان يكون نضره عليه في المركب لاجل خاطري فاجابه ذلك علي الراس والعين في الحال كتب مكتوب وامر القبطان بانه يتوصي فيّ ويدير باله عليّ ولا ياخد مني شي البته بل اذا احتشة شي يكون يعطيني وختم المكتوب واعطاني هوثم ودعنا ومضينا.

I followed them, and presented myself before the consul, bowing deeply as custom required. Speaking in French, I told him what *khawājah* Samatan had instructed me to say.

"Where are you from?" he asked when I was done speaking.

"Syria," I replied.

"What brought you to this land?"

"I came with a Frenchman, and traveled with him to Paris," I explained. "When he left me, I came back here to find a way to return to my country. I spent all my money getting back to Marseille, and don't even have a coin to spend on food."

After hearing me out, the consul ordered one of his servants to summon the captain.

10.63

"Wait here," he said, turning to me. "Don't go anywhere."

A few minutes later, the captain appeared, and the consul ordered him to take me with him.

"In keeping with our custom, this man ought to be sent back to his land, as he's a stranger here and has no money," the consul explained.

"Yes sir," the captain replied, and turned to me and said, "Get into a rowboat with your bags this evening and come out to the ship. We sail early tomorrow morning."

I thanked the consul and the captain from the bottom of my heart, and went to tell *khawājah* Samatan what had transpired, and to thank him.

"All that's left for me to do now is to go see the owner of the ship," he said. "We'll need to get a letter from him vouching for you to give the captain, so no one causes any trouble for you on the journey. You were put on the ship against his wishes, after all."

10.64

So he took me to see the shipowner, a friend of his, who greeted us warmly when we arrived.

"I'd like to have this young man travel aboard your ship," *khawājah* Samatan explained. "As a favor to me, would you be willing to write a letter to the ship's captain vouching for the boy and entrusting him to his care?"

"It would be my pleasure," the man replied, and immediately drafted a letter to the captain commending me to his charge. He encouraged the captain to watch over me and not to accept any payment for my expenses. In fact, if I needed anything at all, the captain was to provide me with it. The shipowner sealed the letter and handed it to me, then we bid him farewell and left.

٦٥،١٠ فانا اخدت المكتوب ومضيت الي الاستريه حيث كنت نازل فما رايت الا جاني من عند المذكور زواده وافه بقصمات وجبن وكعده سمك انجيه وفراغ زيتون وبرميل نبيد زغير وهو ايضًا اجا لعندي حتي يودعني فاستكثرت بخيره وشكرت فضله قوي كثير. حينذٍ قلي بلكي القبطان ما يكلفك لسفرته خد معك هل زواده حتي لا تعتاز اليه.

٦٦،١٠ اخيرًا اعطيته مكتوب حتي برسله الي اخي في حلب مع مكاتيب التي بتروح علي اسطنبول في البرواخبرته فيه بان يوم تاريخه سافرت في مركب الذي هو موجه الي ازمير وفيما بعد وصل المكتوب ليد اخي وبعد مده سمعوا بان مركب خارج من ازمير الي اسكندورنه انكسر في الطريق وغرقت جميع الاوادم كانت فيه فصار عند اخوتي واهلي حزن شديد بمعرفتهم باني توجهت من مرسيليا الي ازمير فتاكدوا باني كنت في ذلك المركب وما عاد اخدوا لي خبر لان بعد ذلك المكتوب ما عدت كتبت لهم مكتوب فقطعوا الايس مني وصلوا علي روحي نياحة الموتي.

٦٧،١٠ فنرجع بالكلام فبعدما ودعت المذكور حمّلت حوايجي الي الاسكله ونزلتهم في القايق ونزلت انا ايضًا ومضي فينا القايق الي المركب الذي مرسي برات البوغاز فصعدت الي المركب وهو مركب كبير يسما لكلاطان وفيه اربعة وعشرين طوب وبمقدار ثمانين عسكري من غير النوتيه وكان موسوق نصف وسق فزعًا من القرصان نصفه جنكي ونصفه بازركان فبتنا تلك الليله وثاني يوم من السلام سحب مراسيه وفتح قلوعه وسافر فلما صرنا في دهر البحر حينذٍ اعطيت المكتوب القبطان فلما قراه ابتسم وقلي كون في امان وتركني وما كلفني حتي اكل عنده.

٦٨،١٠ فسافرنا اول يوم وتاني يوم ضحوة نهار فما رايت الا اجتمعوا مدبرين المركب وبدوا يهيوا امور الحرب اعني الطواب والتفنك وكتبوا اوراق وعلقوا علي كل طوب ورقه وكتبوا اسامي الذين يقفوا لاجل ضرب المدافع وايضًا كتبوا اسامي الجنود الذين بيضربوا التفنك فلما انتهوا اليّ فسالوني ما اسمك فقلت ما لكم في اسمي اجابوني لما

With the letter in hand, I returned to the inn where I was staying. No sooner   **10.65**
had I arrived when a delivery appeared for me. It was a sack full of provisions
for the road: hardtack, some cheese, a sack of little dried fish, a jar of olives,
and a small barrel of wine. Then the *khawājah* himself came to wish me farewell. I thanked him dearly for the gift, heaping praise and gratitude upon him.

"The captain might not invite you to dine at his table," the *khawājah* said.
"Take these provisions with you, so you don't have to depend on him."

I gave him a letter to send to my brother in Aleppo via the overland postal   **10.66**
service to Istanbul. The letter, which informed my brother of the date of my
departure by ship from Marseille to Izmir, arrived safely in my brother's hands
some time later. Not long after that, however, my family received news that
a vessel bound from Izmir to Alexandretta had been wrecked, and all aboard
had perished. My brothers and my relatives were overwhelmed with grief, as
they knew I'd traveled from Marseille to Izmir, and felt certain I had been on
the stricken ship. Not receiving word from me—as I'd stopped sending letters
after leaving France—they lost all hope and mourned me, praying for my soul's
eternal rest.

Back to the story. After I said goodbye to the *khawājah*, I had my bags   **10.67**
brought to the harbor and loaded them into a rowboat. I got in, and off we
went to the ship, which was anchored beyond the harbor channel. I climbed
aboard the ship. It was a large vessel named *La Galatane*,[41] and had twenty-
four cannons. There were eighty soldiers on board, not counting the crew. As
a precaution against pirates, the ship held only a half load, so it was really half
warship, half merchant ship.

We spent the night there. Early the next morning, we raised the anchors,
unfurled the sails, and set off. It was only once we were out on the open sea
that I handed the letter to the captain. He read it and smiled.

"Rest easy," he said, then left me to my own devices, and didn't invite me
to dine with him.

We sailed all day without incident. The following morning, I noticed that   **10.68**
the officers had gathered together and were preparing the ship for combat,
readying the cannons and muskets. Each cannon had a notice hung upon it
with the names of the crew members responsible for firing it; there was also a
list of soldiers tasked with firing the muskets. Finally, they came to me.

"Name?" they said.

"What do you want my name for?" I asked.

بيجينا العدو بتلتزم تمسك بندقيه وتقف تحارب مثل غيرك فقلت دعوني انا رجل غريب وما بعرف في امور الحرب ولا في ضرب التفنك فالتفت الي القبطان وقلي بيجي منك لما بترانا نحارب العدو بتنزل للعنبر وبتتخبا ولكن انا بنصحك انا في محل الحرب لا تخبي وجهك لان في ذلك الوقت العسكر بيقتلوك لا محاله.

٦٩،١٠ اخيرًا التزمت بان اكتب اسمي واتجند مثل الغير فمضي ذلك اليوم ايضاً وفي اليوم الثالث راينا من بعيد مركب كبير قرصان وهو لما شافنا اجي علينا بنيت انه يحاربنا وياخدنا ايضاً توجه عليه وفتحوا طوق المدافع واصطفت العسكر وفي ايدهم البندقيات والفقير من جملتهم الي حين ما قربنا من بعضنا نحن والمركب الذي خرج معنا وهو رايح الي اسطنبول هو الاخر تهيا للحرب تجاه ذلك المركب وذاك لما راء مركبين كبار موجهين اليه خاف وعطي كسره فلحقناه ولما حطيناه تحت الضرب رفع بندرية الفرنساويه لانه عرفنا باننا فرنساويه وصار يصوت بالبوق انه فرنساوي. حينذٍ عرفوه انه فرنساوي فمضوا وتركوه. حينذٍ راحت الرعبه من قلبي وشكرت الله تعالي بانه ما كان عدو لاني في ذلك الوقت كت ايست من حالي وايقنت الموت.

٧٠،١٠ فيوم نزلت للعنبر حتي اتعدا فرايت بقربي شاب جميل المنضر لايح عليه اثارات النعمه لكنه مشلح ولابس قباز جوخ عتيق مخزق علي اللحم من غير قميص وهو دليل ومكتاب فوق قلبي عليه وكلفته حتي يتعدا معي فتقدم وتعدي معي فسقيته وقال نبيد وانسته وبعد فوغنا من الغدي اخرجت من قفتي قميص وسدريه وقباز وقلته يلبسهم فتمنع اولاً. اخيرًا استكثر بخيري ولبسهم وجلسنا نتصامر فسالته عن حاله وما هو وامره.

٧١،١٠ فاجابني ان سالت عني انا واحد من جوخدارية الحي فرنسا في اسطنبول فارسلني الايلجي حتي اسافر الي بهريس واعطاني مكاتيب للوزير في امر ضروري وهو ان لما مضي يقابل الملك وهو سلطان احمد بعد ما قدم الهدايا المرسله معه

---

١ الأصل: فرغوننا.  ٢ الأصل: الاجي.  ٣ الأصل: الايجي.

"When the enemy shows up, you'll have to pick up a musket and fight like everyone else!"

"Leave me be," I said. "I'm a foreigner, and I don't know anything about war, or how to fire a musket for that matter."

"I suppose you could go hide in the hold when you see us fighting the enemy," the captain said, turning to me. "But if I were you, I wouldn't disappear in the middle of a battle, because the soldiers won't think twice about killing you!"

So I was forced to put my name down and enlist like everyone else. The day 10.69 passed without event. Then, on our third day at sea, we spotted a large pirate ship in the distance. When it caught sight of us, the ship headed in our direction, dead set on attacking us and seizing our ship. We turned to face them, opening the gunports as the soldiers lined up with their muskets, with poor little me among them!

We drew near the pirate ship, and were followed by a second ship, which had left Marseille with us. It was bound for Istanbul, and it too had prepared for a battle. When the pirates saw two large ships bearing down on them, they turned tail and we gave chase. Realizing that our vessels were French, the pirates raised a French flag once they started taking fire, and hailed us over their bullhorn, announcing that they too were French. Once we determined this to be the case, we left them alone and went on our way. It was only then that my fear dissipated, and I thanked God Almighty that the pirates didn't belong to an enemy nation! For a moment, I'd lost all hope and had been certain I was going to die.

One day, when I went down into the hold of the ship to have lunch, I 10.70 noticed a handsome young man by my side. He bore all the signs of a well-to-do person, yet he scarcely had any clothes on, wearing only a decrepit, ripped old tunic that revealed the flesh beneath, and no shirt. My heart went out to this abject, melancholy young man and I invited him to join me for lunch, which he did. I gave him a jar of wine to drink, and chatted amiably with him. When we'd finished our lunch, I took a shirt, vest, and tunic out of my basket and gave them to him to wear. He refused at first, but finally accepted and put them on, thanking me profusely. We sat down and struck up a conversation, and I asked him what his story was.

"If you'd like to know, I suppose I'll tell you," the young man began. "I'm 10.71 one of the secretaries of the French ambassador in Istanbul.[42] The ambassador

من سلطان فرنسا فدخل صحبة الوزير والترجمان لاجل المقابله فلما دخلوا الي ثالث باب فالعاده الجاريه عندهم من قديم الزمان هو ان لما بيدخل الالجي الي ثالث باب بيتقدم القبجي باشي ويرفع السيخ من علي جنب الالجي احتراماً لحضرة الملك فلما القبجي تقدم حتي يرفع السيخ كالعاده دفشه الالجي الي ورا وما راد انهم يرفعوا السيخ من علي جنبه.

٧٢.١٠ فبهت الوزير من هذا الفعل والترجمان غاب عن صوابه وصار يتوسل الي الالجي بانه يدعهم يرفعوا السيخ علي موجب عوايد القديمه فما امكن انه يرفع السيخ وقال للوزير انا مامور باني ادخل واقابل حضرة الملك بالسيخ فابا الوزير وقال له هذا شي غير ممكن اني ادعك تقابل حضرة الملك بالسيخ. حينذٍ رجع الالجي من غير مقابله ومضي الي صرايته فالوزير كتب مكتوب الي وزير سلطان فرنسا واخبره بالذي صنعه الالجي بغير حق فالالجي ايضاً كتب مكتوب للوزير في هذا الخصوص وارسل المكتوب معي حتي اسلمه في يد الوزير وحرسني بان لا ادع احد يعرف في باني مرسل من عند الالجي.

٧٣.١٠ فاخذت المكتوب منه وسافرت مع مركب فرنساوي انا ومعي اثنين اخر فلما سافرنا طلع علينا مركب قرصان واخد مركبنا وشلحونا واخدوا جميع ما معنا حتي اخذوا ثيابنا بقينا بالزلط فواحد من البحريه حن علي في هذا القنباز المخرق. اخيراً رمونا في اسكلت ليكورنا فطلعنا نشحد وناكل لكن المكتوب استقام معي ولاجل تتميم امر اسدادي فاتدرجت من ليكورنا الي ان وصلت الي مرسيليا والان صار لي جملة ايام في مرسيليا عريان وجوعان ورايت غير ممكن اني اروح الي بهريس في هل حاله وما احد حن قلبه علي غيرك انت الان فالتزمت ارسل المكتوب مع البوسطه وارجع الي عند اسدادي ليلا اهلك في هذه البلاد.

٧٤.١٠ فلما سمعت منه هذا الكلام صرت اتوجع له واسليه واخد بخاطره وبعده وقعت المحبه بيننا وصرنا عشره وانا ايضاً احكيت له بالذي جري علي من الاول الي الاخر

sent me to Paris with some letters for the minister about a very urgent matter, which had to do with an audience with Sultan Aḥmad. After having presented gifts from the king of France, the ambassador prepared to meet the sultan in the company of the grand vizier and the dragoman. They passed through the third gate of the palace.[43] Now, the Ottomans have a very old custom. When an ambassador enters the third gate of the palace, the chief eunuch comes forward to relieve the ambassador of the rapier he wears at his side, out of respect for His Majesty the king. But when the gatekeeper tried to do so, the ambassador pushed him away and refused to let them take his rapier!

"The grand vizier was flabbergasted and the dragoman just about lost his   10.72
senses, pleading with the ambassador to let them take his rapier in accordance with their ancient custom. But he refused to let them lay a hand on it.

"'I've been ordered to greet His Majesty the king wearing my rapier,' he told the grand vizier.

"'Impossible!' the grand vizier replied. 'I cannot allow you to appear before His Majesty with a rapier.'

"So the ambassador left without an audience and returned to his palace. In the meantime, the grand vizier wrote a letter to the French king's minister, apprising him of the ambassador's insolence. As for the ambassador, he wrote his own account of the incident, and handed it to me to deliver personally to the minister. He also warned me not to let anyone know that I was traveling on his behalf.

"I took the letter and boarded a French ship, along with two companions.   10.73
No sooner had we set sail than we were attacked by a pirate ship. They seized our vessel and robbed us of all our possessions! They even stole our clothes, leaving us naked. One of the sailors took pity on me and offered me this ripped tunic. Eventually, they dumped us in the harbor of Livorno and we were reduced to begging for food to stay alive. And yet, I still had the letter.

"I was determined to complete my mission, so I gradually made my way from Livorno to Marseille. But after several days in Marseille with no clothes and no food, I realized that it was all but impossible for me to reach Paris, for no one had taken pity on me as you did. I was compelled to send the letter with the postal service and return home to my superior, so I wouldn't die there."

When I heard this sad story, I consoled the young man and tried to distract   10.74
him from his troubles. In this way, an affectionate bond developed between us and we became close friends. I told him my own story from start to finish.

واستقمنا مسافرين الي ليله من ذات الليالي كنا بقرب جزيره سيليا وهذه الجزيره كانت في يد الفنساء والفنساوين كانوا مع فرنساء حرب وفي مرورنا في ذلك المكان تحصن مركبنا خوفًا ليلا يخرج من الجزيره مركب قرصان وكانت ليله ضوه لان القمر في ليلة الاربعة عشر وفي ذلك الوقت نضروا الكاردي اعني الحراس شايقه كانه خارجه من الجزيره فنبهوا القبطان والطايفه.

٧٥،١٠ ولما راوها لحط مركبنا في اثرها وكذلك المركب الذي خرج معنا من مرسيليا راءها وهو ايضًا حط في اثرها حتي اخذناها في المواسطه وما بقا علينا الا نرسل لها قايق الكبير مع جمله جنود حتي تمسكها فلما راءت الشايقه بانها صارة بين المركبين وما يمكنها الهربه ليلا يضربوا عليها مدافع ويغرقوها لفت قلاعها ووقفت فلما وقفت نزل من عندنا قايق الكبير وجمله من الجنود حتي يمسكوها ويقيدوها معنا فلما قرب منها القايق دارت عليه الشقلوظات فامشعوا عن القرب اليها وفي ذلك المحل فتحت قلوعها وهربت بواسطة الريح كان معها بوبا اعني في ظهرها.

٧٦،١٠ فلما راء مركبنا ومركب الاخر بانها هربت حطوا في اثرها وتحاوطوها ما بينهم ففعلت كما فعلت في الاول وهربت وثالث مره احطاطوها١ وصاروا يرشقوها بالرصاص من الجانبين فزعًا ليلا تهرب ايضًا من يدهم ولما كانوا يرشقوها بالرصاص سمعوا قبطان الشايقه يقول الي جماعته بانهم ينزلوا للعبر ليلا ينصابوا من الرصاص الذي كان نازل عليهم كرخ المطر عرفوا صوته بانه فرنساوي فكفوا عنه الضرب وسالوه بالبوق من تكون فاجابهم انا فلان قبطان. حينذٍ عرفوه وهو الذي طلع معهم من اسكلت مرسيليا حتي يتلجا فيهم فلما سمعوا وتحققوا بانه هو ذلك القبطان فندموا علي فعلهم معه هكذا وصاروا ياخدوا بخاطره.

٦٨،١٠ وثاني يوم ارسلوا له قلاع لان قلاعه جميعها تخرقت من ضرب الرصاص واوصوه بانه لا يفارقهم ومضوا في طريقهم الي ان مركبنا وصل الي قرب مينة ازمير وفي ذلك

١ «ففعلت كما . . . احطاطوها» في الهامش.

One night during our voyage, we drew near the island of Sicily. It was governed by Austria, which was at war with France.[44] The ship was on guard, fearing the possibility of pirates attacking us from the island. The sky was luminous that evening, as the moon was in the fourteenth night of its cycle. Suddenly, the night watch spotted what seemed to be a vessel sailing away from the island, so they woke the captain and the rest of the crew.

When the captain spied the vessel, he ordered our ship to pursue it. Meanwhile, the other ship that had departed Marseille with us also spotted the vessel and likewise set off in pursuit. We soon caught up to the vessel, drawing up on either side of it. All that was left to do was to send a longboat full of soldiers to seize it. When our quarry realized they were caught between two ships and had no way to escape without being fired upon—which could only lead to the sinking of their ship—they lowered their sails and came to a standstill. We put our longboat in the water with the soldiers so we could seize the enemy ship and hitch it to our own, but as soon as the longboat approached them, they swung their cannons up, barring it from coming any closer. Then they hoisted their sails and took off again with the help of a wind gusting over their poop deck, which is to say their stern. **10.75**

At this sight, we set off in hot pursuit together with the other ship, and closed in on it once again. But they pulled the same maneuver as before and escaped a second time! On the third chase, our two ships began to spray the enemy vessel with shot, hoping to prevent it from slipping away again. As soon as the fusillade began, the captain of the enemy ship could be heard telling his crew to go down into the hold so they wouldn't be struck by the shot raining down on them. His voice was recognizably French, so our ships ceased fire. **10.76**

"Identify yourself!" we called out over our bullhorn.

"I'm Captain So-and-So!" he replied.

It was the same captain who had left Marseille with us in order to benefit from our protection.[45] As soon as our crew confirmed that it was indeed that captain, they regretted their action and offered their apologies to the man.

The next day, we sent the ship some new sails, as the old ones had been shredded by our shot, and advised its captain not to stray far from us. Then we set off again, and sailed without incident until we drew near to the port of Izmir. **10.77**

الوقت خرج علينا ريح عاصف شديد من البر فرجعنا الي نواحي اراضي الموره ومن هناك رجعنا وفي رجوعنا صدفنا الريح وموج البحر الشديد ما بين الصخوره التي هي في تلك الرقعه التي هي مقابل اسطنبول فاستقمنا يوم وليله ما بين تلك الصخور وايقنا بكسر مركبنا وهلاكنا وفي يوم الثاني ارسل لنا ربنا ريح من البرحتي قدرنا نخرج من بين تلك الصخور بالسلامه وشكرنا الباري تعالي علي احسانه وجوده معنـا.

A heavy gale then rose up from the land, blowing us back into the vicinity of the Morea. We fought our way back, but the wind and waves tossed us in the direction of Istanbul, where we found ourselves stranded among the reefs. We spent all day and night between the rocks, certain our ship would be wrecked and we'd all perish. But the next day, our Lord sent us a wind from the coast and we were able to sail away from the reef, thankful to the Almighty Creator for His beneficence and grace!

# الفصل الحادي عشر[1]

# في دخولنا الي بلاد الشرق

١،١١ فوصلنا بالسلامه الي مينة ازمير وبعدما رسا مركبنا خرجت من المركب ومعي ذلك الشاب السابق ذكره فلما خرجت من القايق ووضعت رجلي في البر ورايت المسلمين الموجودين في الكمرك فرجف قلبي وانوهمت كاني حصلت في اليسر وندمت علي ما فعلت كيف اني تركت بلاد المسيحيه ورجعت الي يسر المسلمين.

٢،١١ حينذٍ التف الي صاحبي وقلي اتبعني الي حيث ما امضي فتبعته حتي وصلنا الي بيت قنصر الفرنساويه وهو بيت مكلف وفي الباب انجكاريه وتراجمين وخدم وما يشبه ذلك فصعدنا الي اعلا المكان. حينذٍ ذلك الشاب طلب اذن حتي يدخل يقابل حضرة القنصر فبعد اعطا الاذن امتثلنا امام القنصر فصار يحكيه ذلك الشاب كيف ان حضرة الالجي ارسله الي فرنسا وكيف انه تشلحنا من القرصان والان راجعين الي اسطنبول الي عند حضرة الالجي فلما انتهي من كلامه وعرف القنصر حقيقة امره في الحال امر بحضور واحد التراجمين امامه وامره بانه يمضي بنا الي الاستريه ويوصي صاحب الاستريه بانه يقوم في اودنا الي حين ما يتهيا مركب الي اسطنبول يرسلنا معه.

٣،١١ فمضي بنا الترجمان الي الاستريه وهو مكان مكلف بيزلوا فيه القباطين وغيرهم من التجار العابرين الطريق فاعطونا مكان لمنامتنا بفرشات نضيفه وملاحف بيض مثل نظام استريات بلاد الفرنساويه واحسن فاستقمنا ناكل ونشرب في الغدا والعشا

---

١ لم يرد رقم لهذا الفصل في الأصل.

# Chapter Eleven

## In the Lands of the East

We arrived safely in the port of Izmir, and once the ship had dropped anchor   11.1
I disembarked along with the young man I mentioned earlier. As soon as I
got out of the rowboat and set foot on dry land, I saw the Muslim customs
inspectors, and my heart skipped a beat. I was overcome with an awful sense
of foreboding, as though I'd been taken prisoner, and instantly regretted what
I'd done. How could I have left the lands of the Christians to return to being a
prisoner of the Muslims?

My friend turned to me and told me to follow him, and we soon arrived   11.2
at the residence of the French consul. It was a stately house with janissaries
guarding the door, and was full of dragomans, servants, and other attendants.
We went upstairs and the young man asked to be admitted to meet with the
consul. With permission granted, we presented ourselves before him and the
young man set about recounting the story of how he had been dispatched to
France by His Excellency the French ambassador in Istanbul.

"We were robbed by pirates," he explained, "and are now on our way back
to Istanbul to see His Excellency."

Having learned who the young man was, the consul immediately summoned one of his dragomans and ordered him to take us to an inn. The consul
recommended us to the innkeeper, entrusting us to his care until such time as
a ship was ready to depart for Istanbul.

The dragoman brought us to a very fine inn frequented by ship captains   11.3
and traveling merchants, and we were given a place to sleep with clean beds
and fresh white sheets. It was just as orderly as the inns in French lands, if not
more so. We spent the rest of the day there, savoring delicious food and drink
for lunch and dinner, and enjoying the wonderful service.

باكل طيب وخدمه علي الكيف وثاني يوم قلي ذلك الشاب لا بقيت تهلكهم المعيشه
طول مانك معي قوم اتبعني فمشيت معه وتفرجت في دربي علي اماكن ازمير وهي في
قرب الاسكله حاره متسعه طويله وجميع بيوتها قاطنين تجار فرنج وغيرهم من البياعين
والشراين فرنج ونساهم جالسين في الدكاكين¹ نظير بلاد الفرنج وهي تسما حاره الفرنج
والمدينه بعيده عنها مقدار ميل التي هي البلد والمدينه القاطنين فيها تجار المسلمين
والحكام كباقية البلاد وتلك الحاره ما بيدخلها الا قاصدها من تجار المسلمين وغيرهم
من الرعايا.

١١،٤ فمضي بي الي دير اليسوعيه فلما دخلنا وراءنا الريس بهت بمعرفته بذلك الشب لما
كان في اسطنبول فسلموا علي بعضهم ادخلنا الي بيت المايده وضيفنا ووقف في
واجنا قوي كثيرثم ساله الريس عن حالة التي هو فيها وعرّه فاحكاله بالذي جري
عليه كما سبق القول فاتوه عليه وسلاه واخد بخاطره لان كان بيعرف بان حضرة
الالجي يحبه قوي كثير وكان راس علي كل جوخداريته. اخيراً لما ردنا نمضي طلب
ذلك الشاب من الريس كام غرش يدينه وفي اسطنبول يدفعها ريس ديرهم كمثل بولصه
فاجابه تكرم وفي الحال فتح سندوق دراهم الدير وكلفه بانه ياخد بقدر ما يريد.

١١،٥ فاخد خمسة عشر غرش وكتب له ورقه في وصولها. اخيراً ودعناه ومضينا ولما
خرجنا من الدير اعطاني تلك الدراهم وقلي ابقيها معك لاجل خرجيت الدرب ومن
هناك مضينا الي دير الكبوجين فضيفنا الريس ايضاً واستقرض منه عشرة غروش
ايضاً وبعد خروجنا من الدير اعطاني هي وقلي افتكرت ليلا ما تكفانا تلك الدراهم
التي اخدنا من ريس اليسوعيه اخدت ايضاً هذه العشرة غروش حتي يفصل معنا ولا
يعوزنا.

١١،٦ فبقي معي خمسة وعشرين غرش كلها زلط ومن هناك سرنا ندور ونتفرج ونتشبرق
ونعمل كيفيه فاستقمنا علي هذا الحال بمقدار خمسة عشر يوم علي اكل وشرب وتنزه

---

١ الأصل: الدكاين.

"As long as you're with me, you won't need to worry about your next meal," said the young man the next day. "Come on, follow me."

So I did, gazing upon the sights of Izmir as we went on our way. By the harbor was a large quarter inhabited entirely by Frankish merchants and other Franks involved in commercial dealings. Their women sat in the shops just as they did in Frankish lands. It was called the Frankish quarter. The main city of Izmir was about a mile away, and that was where the Muslim merchants and the governors lived, just like any other city. The only other people who would enter the Frankish quarter were Muslim merchants or other subjects who had a reason to be there.

The young man brought me to a Jesuit monastery. When we went inside and the abbot saw us, he was stupefied because he recognized the young man, whom he'd known from Istanbul. They greeted each other, and the abbot ushered us into the dining hall, offering us refreshments and treating us most cordially. He asked the young man about the state he was in and his threadbare clothes, and the latter told him the story. The abbot then offered his consolations and sympathy, for he knew how much His Excellency the ambassador loved this young man. After all, he'd been the chief of all the embassy officials. 11.4

When it was time to leave, the young man asked the abbot if he could borrow a few piasters from him, which he would repay to the abbot of the Jesuit monastery in Istanbul, as if he were using a promissory note.

"Of course," said the abbot, opening the monastery's cashbox and inviting the young man to take as much money as he needed.

He took fifteen piasters and wrote a receipt for the abbot. Then we bid him farewell and set off. As soon as we left the monastery, the young man handed me the money. 11.5

"Keep this with you," he said. "Travel expenses."

Then we went to the Capuchin monastery, where the abbot similarly invited us in for refreshments. The young man borrowed ten piasters from him, which he also gave me after we left.

"Just in case the money we took from the Jesuit abbot wasn't enough, I thought I'd pick up another ten piasters," he explained. "That way, we'll have plenty and won't have to worry about running out."

Now I had twenty-five piasters, all in *zolota* coins. So off we went, touring the city and seeing the sights, buying treats, and having a great time. We spent fifteen days in this fashion, eating and drinking and strolling about. Finally, 11.6

الي يوم من الايام اتي مركب كبير من مصر واسق بن ورز وقماش وماضي الي اسطنبول فاتي الينا الترجمان وكلفنا باننا ننزل في ذلك المركب فنهض ذلك الشاب وقلي قوم يا اخي حتي نمضي الي المركب ونسافر فابيت وقلته باني انا بسافر الي حلب مع اول قفل فاجابني شيل من بالك يا اخي اني بقيت افارقك الا في اسطنبول.

٧،١١
اخيرًا ما امكن حتي اخذني معه فمضينا صحبة الترجمان الي ان وصلنا كمرك المينا فرايت جالس اغة الكمرك وحداه جالس قبطان ذلك المركب. حينٍذ تقدم الترجمان الي اغة الكمرك واحكي معه من طرف القنصر بانه ينزلنا في ذلك المركب ويوصي القبطان فينا والتف الترجمان وسلمنا في يد اغة الكمرك واغة الكمرك سلمنا في يد القبطان واوصاه فينا وقبضه الترجمان نولينا اعني كروتا. حينٍذ دعا القبطان البحريه الذين في القايق وامرهم بانهم ياخدونا الي المركب ويعطونا كامره علي خصتنا ويديروا بالهم علينا فمضينا مع البحريه الي القايق فاينا الترجمان ارسل لنا خمسين اقة بقصمات وخمسة اقق جبن قوالب وسمك مقلي وقلت انبيد واعطوا لكل واحد منا خمسة غروش خرجيت الدرب فمضينا الي المركب ووضعنا حوايجنا في الكامره اعني اوضه زغيره واستقمنا ذلك اليوم.

٨،١١
وتاني يوم من باكر فتح قلوعه وسافر ولا زلنا سايرين في ذلك البحرحتي اشرفنا علي بوغاز اسطنبول طويل وعريض ومنه الي مينة اسطنبول بمقدار سفر اربع خمس ايام فلما وصلنا الي البوغاز خرج ريح من البر صدنا عن الدخول فالتزم القبطان يرسي في اسكت كليبولي التي هي برات البوغاز وهي بلد زغيره فنزلنا الي البلد وسرنا ندور ونرجع ننام في المركب فاستقمنا في تلك الاسكله خمسة ايام وبعده اتانا ريح من البحر فسافرنا ودخلنا البوغاز.

٩،١١
وبعد يومين خرج ايضاً ريح من البر ومنعنا عن السير فرسينا في اسكله زغيره الي ان ياتينا الريح من البحر فبعد يومين اتانا ريح فسافرنا ووصلنا الي مينة جكك جكمجا فرسينا هناك وفي تلك الليله فاينا مركبين مقبلين الينا فظن القبطان بانهم مركبين

a large ship arrived from Egypt. It was carrying coffee, rice, and fabric, and was headed for Istanbul. The dragoman came by and encouraged us to leave on that vessel.

"Come on, brother," said the young man, rising to his feet. "Let's get on that ship and get out of here!"

I told him I was taking the next caravan to Aleppo.

"Come now, brother," he replied. "If you think I'm going to part with you before we get to Istanbul, you can forget it!"

In the end, he got his way, and we went off with the dragoman. When we arrived at the harbor's customs office, I saw the customs officer waiting, the captain of the ship seated beside him. The dragoman strode up to the customs officer and instructed him, on behalf of the consul, to allow us to embark upon the ship and to place us in the care of the captain. Then the dragoman handed us off to the customs officer, who in turn handed us off to the captain, telling him to take care of us, as instructed. The dragoman paid our *nawlūn*, which is to say our travel fare; then the captain summoned some sailors over from a dinghy, ordering them to take us to the ship and give us a private cabin, and to take good care of us.

11.7

We went with the sailors to the dinghy, and saw that the dragoman had sent over fifty *uqqah*s of hardtack, a wheel of cheese weighing five *uqqah*s, some fried fish, and a demijohn of wine. He'd also given us each five piasters of travel money. Once on board, we brought our baggage into our cabin and spent the rest of the day there.

Early the next morning, we raised the sails and set off. Soon enough, we arrived at the straits of Istanbul, which are long and broad. The journey from the entrance of the straits to the port of Istanbul was to take four or five days. But as we approached the straits, a wind blew out from the coast, preventing us from entering. The captain was compelled to drop anchor in the port of Gelibolu, a little town outside the straits.[46] Each day, we'd leave the ship and tour the town, returning by night to sleep on board. After five days, a favorable wind blew from the sea, so we raised our sails once again and entered the straits.

11.8

Two days later, another wind blew out from the coast, preventing us from going any farther. So we anchored in a small harbor for a couple of days until the wind changed and we could set off again. We soon arrived at the port of Küçükçekmece, where we dropped anchor.[47] That night, two ships appeared, heading in our direction. The captain suspected that they might be Maltese

11.9

قرصان مالطيه في الحال ارسل اخبر اهل القلعه في قدوم هذين المركبين فصار من القلعه يضربوا عليهم مدافع ومركبنا ايضاً يضرب مدافع حتي يصدهم عن الدخول الي الاسكله فاما المركبين رسوا بعيد عن القلعه ولفوا قلاعهم حتي يعطوهم اشاره بان مانهم اعدا فا امكن بان يكفوا الضرب .

١٠،١١ اخيراً علقوا فنر في الصاري علامة الصلح فا امكن ايضاً انهم يكفوا عن قتالهم وجميع الذين كانوا في مركبنا من الركيه انهزموا الي القلعه وايضاً اهل الاسكله هربوا للجبال فزعاً من القرصان. اخيراً لما نضروا اهل تلك المركبين بان اهل القلعه ما اقتنعوا منهم بتلك الاشارات حينٍ ارسلوا قايق وداخله يازجي المركب وثلاثة انفار من مدبرين المراكب فلما وصل القايق الي الاسكله في الحال ارتموا عليهم ومسكوهم واصعدوهم الي القلعه ثم سالوهم من تكونوا ولاي سبب دخلتوا البوغاز .

١١،١١ فاجابوهم نحن مراكب فلمنك دايرين منتسوق قمح من الاضاوات فا امكن انهم يبيعونا من غير فرمان من الوزير فردنا نمضي الي اسطنبول حتي ناخد فرمان فصادفونا قرصان فرنساويه في الطريق فهربنا منهم واتينا الي هذا المكان نلتجي ونحتي بالقلعه وانتوا ما بالكم بتحاربونا وبتضربوا علينا مدافع كانا اعدا لكم فا اقتنعوا من كلامهم بل حبسوهم في القلعه لهم وللبحريه الذين معهم في القايق .

١٢،١١ اخيراً اجا اغة القلعه ومعه كم واحد من اهل القلعه الي عندنا للمركب وتشاوروا مع قبطاننا كيف يعملوا فاشار عليهم باني انا وانتم منمضي الي تلك المركب وعندي في مركبي اثنين فرنج فرنساويه مناخدهم معنا لاجل الترجمي لان واحد منهم بيتكلم بالتركي فقبلوا منه هذا الشور في الحال هيوا لنا قايق فنزلنا جميعنا وقصدنا المركب الاكبر فصعدنا اليه ودخلنا اوضة القبطان فاينا القبطان وجماعته جالسين وقدامهم الشموع متقده واواني الخمر والقداح وهن في غاية الراحه والانبساط .

١٣،١١ حينٍ نهض القبطان ومن معه علي الاقدام واسترحبوا فينا ثم ضيفونا من صنوف الحلاوات والمربايات ومن الشربات اللذيذه فاستقمنا عندهم في هذه الكيفيه حكم

pirates, so he immediately sent word to the citadel, which began to fire its cannons at the two ships. Our ship joined the barrage, aiming to prevent the ships from entering the port. But the ships dropped anchor far from the citadel and lowered their sails, a sign that they had no hostile intent. But this wasn't enough to stop the cannons.

After a while, the two ships raised a banner indicating that they came in 11.10 peace, but this too didn't stop the assault. All the passengers on our ship soon retreated to the citadel, while the port's inhabitants fled to the mountains in fear of the pirates. Finally, when the people on the two ships realized that their signals of peace had not convinced the citadel, they sent out a dinghy with the ship's clerk and three officers. As soon as it arrived in the harbor, the men were seized and brought up to the citadel, where they were asked to identify themselves and explain their reason for entering the straits.

"We're two Flemish ships, and we've been sailing around, trying to pur- 11.11 chase wheat from the Province of the Islands," they explained. "But no one will sell us anything unless we have an edict from the vizier. So we decided to go to Istanbul to secure one but ran into some French pirates along the way. We fled and came here to seek refuge in the citadel. What's the matter with you, anyway? Why have you been firing your cannons at us as if we were your enemies?"

But the people in the citadel weren't convinced. They seized the men, and the sailors who had been with them in the dinghy, and threw them in jail.

Then the chief of the citadel came down to our ship along with some of his 11.12 men, and consulted with our captain about how to proceed.

"Why don't you and I go out to their ship?" he suggested. "I have two Frank-ish men from France on board whom we can bring along to act as interpreters. One of them speaks Turkish."

They agreed, and immediately prepared a dinghy to take us out. We all jumped in and headed toward the larger of the two ships. We climbed aboard, entered the captain's cabin, and found him sitting with his crew. They had before them some lighted candles, bottles of wine, and goblets, and all were in a very merry mood.

The captain and his men rose to their feet and greeted us. Then they served 11.13 us some sweets, fruit preserves, and delicious refreshments, and we spent the next couple of hours having a wonderful time together. Finally, we bid them farewell and prepared to return, resolving to have their men sent back from the

ساعتين ثم ودعناهم وردنا الرواح وصار اننا في الحال نمضي ونرسل لهم جماعتهم من القلعه وفي ذلك الوقت قبطان الفلامنكي استمن قبطاننا حتي يرسل يازجيه معه حتي يروح معه الي اسطنبول لاجل الفرمان المذكور لاجل مساق القمح كما ذكرنا فرضي قبطاننا بذلك واخد معه اليازجي الي مركبه.

١١،١٤ وبعد كام يوم جانا الريح من البحر وسافرنا ومعنا ذلك الفلامنكي ولا زلنا سايرين حتي وصلنا الي مينة بيبوك جكمجا وهناك رسينا وخرجنا ندور في البلد وجميع ما نصرفه يعطينا هو ذلك الفلامنكي فطالة المده علينا ونحن مرسيين فغدت علي ذلك الفلامنكي الطوله لان المركبين لان في استدارته فصار يسال هل يمكنه يسافر في البر الي اسطنبول فاجابوه انه يمكن وهو سفر ثلاثة ايام واقل. حينذٍ طلب بان ياتوه بناس تاخده وتسافر فيه في الحال احضروله دبه.

١١،١٥ حينذٍ التفت الينا وكلفنا باننا نسافر معه فابينا وقلنا له باننا نحن عاطيين كروه المركب والقبطان ما يتطلقنا لانه مكفل فينا حتي يوصلنا الي اسطنبول ويسلمنا لبيت الالجي. اخيرًا لح علينا كثير وقال لنا انا بعطي الكروه عنكم وانا ما يمكني اسافر وحدي ولا بعرف باللسان فلما سمعنا منه هل كلام رق قلبنا لما ساله ومضينا للمركب وابقينا حوايجنا داخل الكامره وقفلنا بابها وطلبنا اذن من القبطان حتي نسافر في البر لاجل خاطر ذلك الفلامنكي فاجابنا القبطان انا تكهلت فيكم عند اغة الكمرك وصار اني اسلمكم الي بيت الجي الفرنساويه فاجبناه ها ان حوايجنا تركاها في مركبك وحتي تصل بالسلامه مناتي الي مركبك ومناخد حوايجنا وفي ذلك الوقت منعطيك طسكره من الترجمان في وصولنا الي بيت الالجي ومناخد حوايجنا.

١١،١٦ فرضي منا هل مقال. اخيرًا ودعنا ومضينا الي عند الفلامنكي فاينا محضرلنا دبتين واخد زواد وافره لاجل الطريق. اخيرًا ركب كل منا دبته وسافرنا ولا زلنا مسافرين الي ان وصلنا الي مدينة اسطنبول ودخلنا من مكان يسما قون قبي وهو مبدا مدخول المدينه وهنا مكان يسما يدي قله فرايت في ذلك المكان حافرين طغر في الارض غماق

citadel. That was when the Flemish captain asked our captain if he would be so kind as to let the Flemish ship's clerk travel to Istanbul with us so that he could request the edict granting permission to trade in wheat. Our captain agreed, and brought the clerk back to our ship.

After a few days, the winds became favorable again, blowing from the sea, and we set sail with the Flemish clerk aboard. We soon arrived in Büyükçekmece,[48] where we dropped anchor and went to tour the town. Wouldn't you know it, the Flemish fellow covered all of our expenses! The longer we remained in the harbor, though, the more anxious he became about getting to Istanbul, because the two ships were awaiting his return. So he began to make inquiries about whether it was possible to travel to Istanbul from there by land, and was told it was a journey of three days or less. He then asked to have some people rounded up who could take him to Istanbul, and a mount was brought over right away.

11.14

The Flemish man then turned to me and my friend, and invited us to go with him, but we refused, explaining that we'd already paid our fare, and that the captain wouldn't let us go off on our own. After all, he'd been tasked with delivering us directly to the ambassador's residence in Istanbul. But the man continued to insist.

11.15

"I'll pay your fare," he said. "I can't travel by myself! I don't speak the language!"

We felt sorry for the fellow and went back to the ship to lock up our things inside our cabin and ask the captain's permission to travel the rest of the way to Istanbul by land, for the sake of the Flemish man.

"But I guaranteed the customs officer that I'd be responsible for you," the captain said. "And he insisted that I deliver you to the French ambassador's house."

"Look, we've left our bags on board the ship," we said. "Once they arrive, we'll come to the ship and give you a document from the dragoman certifying that we arrived at the ambassador's house. Then we'll take our things."

The captain was satisfied, so we bid him farewell and rejoined the Flemish fellow. He had already procured a couple of mounts for us and prepared ample provisions for the road. We climbed onto our mounts and set off. Soon thereafter, we arrived in Istanbul, coming first to a place called Kum Kapı, the entrance to the city. There was a place there called Yedi Kule, where I saw some deep holes dug into the earth.

11.16

كثير فسالت ما هذه الطغر فاجابني القاطرجي[1] الذي هو معنا بان هذه الطغر حافزينهم حتى ينكشوا على الرخام اعني المرمر لانه بيطلع في تلك الارض.

١١،١٧ فمشينا في طريقنا حكم ساعه الى ان وصلنا الى اسكلت الكبيره وهناك مكان الكمرك فلما وصلنا ونزلنا عن دباتنا حيندٍ استكرينا قايق ومضينا الى الغلطه فطلع الفلامنكي ومضى الى بيت الجي الفلامنك في بيك اغلي فانا بقيت حيران كيف اعمل والى اين اروح بما اني غريب فسالت ذلك الشاب صاحبي بانه يدلني على مكان حتى اني انزل فيه فهز راسه وقلي اتبعني الى بيت اسدادي حضرة الاجي وهناك منزولك.

١١،١٨ فامتنعت عن المضي معه فصار يجرني ويمشيني معه فمضينا جمله وصعدنا الى بيك غلي وهو مكان جميع الاجيه وجميعهم قاطنين هناك وهو مكان عالي شرح وقتنا على قط قلعه اعني قلعة البنت التي لما اتاخدت اسطنبول عصيت هذه البنت في هذه القلعه واستقامة زمان وبالجهد حتى قدروا احدوا منها القلعه وحكايتها طويله فما زلنا صاعدين حتى انتهينا الى صحن ذلك المكان وفيه معمر صرايات الاجيه. اخيراً انتهينا الى صراية الجي فرنساء وهو اجمل واوسع غير صرايات وداخله بستان مكلف وفي باب الصرايا البراني جمله انجاريه مهيين.

١١،١٩ فلما دخلنا الباب نهضوا جميعهم سلموا عليه وبعده دخلنا الى صراية الجوانيه حيث محل حضرة الاجي فلما راوه جماعة الاجي بهتوا فيه وهو في تلك الحاله فدخل منهم ناس واخبروا الاجي في قدومه فدعاه لعنده فدخل وقلي اتبعني فتبعته وامتثلنا امام حضرة الاجي فلما راه وهو في تلك الحاله تعجب وساله ما هذه الحاله التي انت فيها.

حيندٍ عمل ثمني وسجد للارض وقال له يا سيدي اذن لي حتى احكيك بالذي جرى عليّ فاذن له بالقول فعاد ايضاً وعمل ثمني واحكاه بالذي جرى عليه من حين خروجه من عنده الى حد رجوعه الى عنده كما ذكرنا سابقاً فتاسف عليه وبعده طيب خاطره وبعده ساله عني.

---

١ الأصل: القاطر.

"What are these holes for?" I asked.

"Excavating marble," our muleteer explained. "You find it in these parts."

We continued for about an hour until we arrived at the large port where the customs authorities were located. We got off our mounts and rented a dinghy to take us out to Galata. When we arrived, the Flemish man went to the home of the Flemish ambassador in Beyoğlu, while I remained where I was, uncertain what to do and where to go. I was a stranger, after all.

Turning to my friend, I asked him to point me in the direction of a place where I could stay, but he shook his head.

"Follow me to the residence of my master, His Excellency the ambassador," he said. "That's where you'll be staying."

I tried to refuse, but he grabbed me and pulled me along, and together we went up to Beyoğlu, where all the ambassadors lived. It was a spacious quarter, occupying an elevated position. We visited Kız Kulesi, the "Maiden's Tower," named for the young woman who resisted the siege of Istanbul in that fortress. She held out there for a long time, and it was only with considerable difficulty that the fortress was conquered. Hers is a long story.

We made our way higher up into the quarter until we arrived at its central square, where the palaces of the ambassadors were located. The French ambassador's palace was the grandest and most beautiful of them all, and encompassed a delightful garden. A company of armed janissaries stood at the outer gate.

As we passed through, everyone rose to greet my friend. We entered the inner pavilion where the ambassador's residence was located. When the embassy staff saw the state my friend was in, they were astonished. Some went to inform the ambassador, who summoned the young man in.

"Follow me," he said. I obeyed, and we presented ourselves before His Excellency, who was surprised to see the young man in such a condition.

"Whatever happened to you?" he asked, incredulous.

"My lord, allow me to tell you my story," the young man said, bowing so deeply that he swept the ground.

The ambassador gave him permission to speak, and the young man bowed again and launched into an account of his journey, from the time he left until the moment he arrived, as I described earlier. Upon hearing it, the ambassador commiserated with the young man and did what he could to console him.

11.17

11.18

11.19

ما هذا الغلام فاجابه يا سيدي هذا الغلام صارة حياتي علي يد الله ويده لان
هذا اتلاقاني وسلاني والبسني من حوايجه ووصل معي الي هذا المكان واحكاله
بجمروايتي وفي البخت التقى معي في مصفنتي ذلك المكتوب الذي كان اعطاني هو
ذلك الامير في بهريس توصاي في للالجي فاخرجت المكتوب واعطيته اياه فلما قري
المكتوب استرحب فيّ.

٢٠،١١

وقلي ماذا تريد افعلك خدمه فاجبته يا سيدي انكان بتريد تقبلني من احد
خدامك فاجابني بان جاني خبر من سلطان فرنسا باني ارجع الي بهريس لكن استقيم
عندي في صرايتي الي حين ما يجي الجي الجديد بخدمك عنده وبوصيه فيك والتفت
الي ذلك الشاب الذي كان معي وامره بانه يدير بباله عليّ ويعطيني اوضه ومنامه وانه
ياكل في ثاني صفره مع الجوخداريه. حينذٍ استكثرت في خيره وخرجنا من امامه
انا وذاك الشاب.

٢١،١١

وفي الحال استدعا المدبر وقال له عن لسان حضرة الالجي بان يهيي لي اوضة
منامه وهو لبس بدلته المكلفه ورجع كما كان فلما حل وقت الغدا كلفوني للغدا
بجلست مع الجوخداريه في ثاني مايده وهي قريه لمايدة الالجي فلما دخلت بجلسني
صاحبي حداه وصار يقول لرفقاته الذي يجب خاطري يكرم هذا الغلام فصار كل
واحد منهم يقطع من تلك الالوان الطيبه والطيور المشويه ويضع قدامي ونوبة الالجي
بتشتغل من وقت جلوس الالجي علي المايده الي انتهاها ووقت العشا كذلك لان هذه
عوايد الالجيه بتدق النوبه وقت الغدا ووقت العشا دايماً بالات موسوقيه مكلفه كما
رايت منهم في بهريس.

٢٢،١١

فاستقمت علي هذا الحال مدة من الزمان علي اكل وشرب وتنزه وكيفيه الي يوم
من الايام طلبت من ذاك الشب صاحبي باني بريد اروح اتفرج علي مدينة اسطنبول
فقلي تكرم فتاني يوم بعد الغدا اخدني معه ونزلنا للغلطه وفي الطريق تخلف عنيّ حتي
يريق رياقة الماء فصدفني واحد انجكاري سكران وصار يتغازل عليّ في سكره وفي

٢٣،١١

Then he inquired about me: "And who might this young man be?"  11.20

"My lord, my life was in this man's hands, as it was in God's," he said. "He found me and diverted my thoughts from my misfortune. He gave me some of his own clothes to wear, and brought me all the way home."

He told the ambassador my story. Luckily I happened to have, tucked away in a pouch, the letter of recommendation to the ambassador that the nobleman in Paris had given me. I pulled it out and handed it to him. Upon reading it, the ambassador welcomed me cordially.

"How might I be of service to you?" he asked.  11.21

"My lord, if it pleases you, perhaps you would accept me as one of your servants."

"Alas, I've received word from the king of France, summoning me back to Paris," he explained. "But you are welcome to remain here in my palace until the new ambassador arrives. I'll arrange to have you employed in his service, and I'll recommend you to him."

The ambassador turned to the young man I'd accompanied and ordered him to take care of me and give me a bedroom, and to have me dine with the embassy officials at the second table. I thanked the ambassador for his benevolence and we departed.

The young man summoned the embassy's steward and conveyed to him  11.22
the order of His Excellency that I should have a bedroom prepared. Then the young man got dressed in a magnificent suit and reassumed his former aspect. At lunchtime, they invited me to join the embassy officials at the second table, which was next to the ambassador's table. My friend seated me at his side and began to praise me to all of his companions.

"If you love me, then honor this young man!"

Everyone at the table then began to serve me, slicing pieces of those wonderful delicacies and grilled fowl, and setting them before me. Meanwhile, the ambassador's orchestra had struck up as soon as the ambassador was seated and played throughout lunch, just as it would at dinner. This was in accordance with embassy protocol, and the musicians played fine instruments, similar to those I'd seen in Paris.

I spent a period of time at the ambassador's residence, eating and drinking  11.23
and amusing myself. Then one day, I asked my friend if we could go out to see the sights of Istanbul.

ذلك الوقت وصل صاحبي فلما رآه وهو كامشني وبيريد مني حق عرق فانتهره ورفسه في رجله خلاه يقلب علي الوطاه فانا ارتعبت ليلا يصدر منه شر فتركه ملق ومضينا وخليناه مطروح علي الارض ولا التفت اليه وقلي امشي معي لا تخف.

٢٤،١١ اخيراً نزلنا الي الغلطه فاتفرجت علي الغلطه ومن هناك نزلنا في قايق ومضينا الي اسطنبول فاولاً رحنا الي خان الوالده وهو خان مكلف مبني من حجر وداخله خان الاخر وداخل خان الاخرخان وجميعه اوض بازركان وناخودات وصراف وفيه خزاين مال ما بتحصا لان هذا الخان ما بيلحقه حريق ولاجل هذا جميع التجار والصيارفه قاطنين فيه فدرنا في الخان وتفرجنا ورايت حلبيه ما عرفوني ولكن انا عرفتهم وما ردت انهم يعرفوني ومن جملتهم ابن القاري وشكري ابن شاهين جلبي وغيرهم كثيرين ما عدا واحد اسمه خواجه ازات وهو بيته قريب من بيت اخي هذا عرفني لا غير فتقدم لعندي وسلم عليّ وعرفني بذاته وعاد كلفني الي اوضته انا والذي معي فضيفنا وسقانا قهوه ووقف في واجنا قوي كثير.

٢٥،١١ ومن هناك مضينا الي سوق الطويل وهذا السوق موجود فيه من جميع الاصناف ومنه دخلنا السوق البالستان وهو ايضاً معمر من حجر لان بينوجد فيه خزاين مال شتي وايش ما طلبت بتجد فيه من امتعه وسلاحات واتواب مكلفه ومن قري صمور وقاقون وغيرهم من الفرو الثمين وداخل هل سوق موضوع سناديق لاجل صيانة المال من الحريق لان كثير ناس بيضعوا سناديق دراهمهم في ذلك السوق فزعاً من الحريق وما احد بيسكر دكانه لان المسا بيسكروا البابين ويضعوا القفال المتينه ويبقفوا الحراس من خارج الابواب متيقظين طول الليل والنتيجه انه مكان مضبوط كانه خزنة السلطان.

٢٦،١١ ومن هناك مضينا الي باب همايون اعني باب صراية الملك. حينذٍ قلي ذلك الشاب ادخل معي حتي افرجك علي الضرب خانه فدخلنا فرايت فسحه عظينه ولها ثلاثة دروب الدرب الاول الذي هو عن اليمين لما بتدخل من الباب وهو درب بيتصل الي صراية القزرار حيث موجود فيه حرم الملك وكل من فات فيه بغير معرفه بياكل عصي

"Of course," he replied, and the next day we went down to Galata after lunch. Along the way, he left me for a moment to go relieve himself. As I waited, a drunken janissary walked up and began to accost me coarsely in his inebriated state. My friend returned to the scene, where he found the janissary clutching me and demanding money for arak. Scolding the janissary, the young man kicked him in the leg, knocking him to the ground. I was suddenly afraid that this would lead to trouble, but my friend left the man lying on the ground and walked off without giving him a second glance.

"Come along," he said to me. "There's nothing to fear."

We went down to Galata and toured the neighborhood before boarding a dinghy to Istanbul. Our first stop was the Valideh Caravansary, a luxurious caravansary built of stone. Inside it was another caravansary, and inside that one yet another! The whole complex was full of rooms populated by merchants, boat skippers, and money changers, and its storehouses held an uncountable amount of money, due to the fact that the caravansary was impervious to fire. That was why all of the merchants and money changers lived there.   11.24

We toured the caravansary, admiring the sights. I spotted some Aleppans I knew, but who didn't seem to recognize me. That suited me, as I didn't want to be noticed. Among them were Ibn al-Qārī, Shukrī ibn Shāhīn Çelebi, and many others. One of them, a certain *khawājah* Azāt who lived near my brother's house, did recognize me. He strolled up to say hello and introduce himself, then invited me and my friend to his room, where he served us coffee and treated us most cordially.

From there, we headed to the grand bazaar, which contained just about every sort of merchandise one could imagine. We then visited the Bālistān souk, which was also constructed of stone, as it included many storehouses. The souk had everything you could want, from furnishings and weapons to precious fabrics and expensive furs such as sable and ermine. There were special cashboxes in the souk meant to protect money from a fire, which many people took advantage of to safeguard their wealth. No one ever bothered to lock up their shop because, when evening came, the two gates of the souk were closed and secured with strong locks. Guards were stationed outside the entrances all night long. As a result, the souk was as secure as the sultan's own treasury.   11.25

The next stop was Hümayun Gate—that is, the gate to the king's palace.   11.26

"Come in with me," the young man said. "I'd like to show you the imperial mint."

والدرب الثاني الوسطاني هو درب بينتهي الى صراية الملك الجوانيه ما بيخطره غير الوزير واكابر الدولة فقط والدرب الثالث الذي هو من الشمال الذي بينتهي الى الضرب خانه وكل من راد بيدخل فيه من غير حراج ولا خوف .

٢٧٫١١ فلما انتهينا الى مكان الذي فيه الضرب خانه فدخلنا فرايت مكان متسع وفرنين متوقدين بيدخلوا فيهم سياخ الفضه والدهب ورايت من جانب الواحد كومه كبيره وجميعها سياخ فضه ومن جانب الاخر كومه ايضاً سياخ دهب ومكان اخر جالسين ناس بيطرقوا السياخ المذكورين ويجرروهم وفي جانب الاخر جالسين بيقطعوا¹ بواسطة منكمات تلك السياخ علي البيكار من غروش ومنهم نصاف ومنهم ارباع لانه واحد يمد السيخ علي السندان والاخر بيدير المنكمه فينقطع الغرش وبيسقط تحت وفي ناس اخرين بيسكوا تلك المعاملة المقطوعه بواسطة حركه منكمه فينطبع الاسم والطغره² والتاريخ من الوجين من غير دق مطرقه .

٢٨٫١١ فخرجنا من هناك ومضينا الى كنيسة اجيه صوفيا وهي الان صايره جامع للملك لانها قريه لصراية الملك وكل نهار جمعه بيصلي الملك فيها فتفرجنا من خارج لان ما بيدعوا احد من المسيحيين يدخل اليها انما رايت عمارتها من الخارج شي بيفوق الوصف وهي عمارت ملوك المسيحيين القدما ومن هنا مضينا الى جامع الوالده وهو جامع ما له مثيل في مدينة اسطنبول وكل من راد بيدخل اليه ما عدا قبة القبله فخرجنا من هناك ومرينا علي صراية صاحب الختام اعني الوزير الاعظم وذلك الدرب ما بينشق من الدخلين والخارجين ومن المشتكيه وعطين العرزحالات وما يشبه ذلك كت اري احد الباشاوات ماشي ومعه جوخدارين لا غير ولا احد بيدير باله اليه ولا احد بيقف له كأنه احدي الناس واتفرجنا علي فج كثير المراد ما رجعنا الى محلنا لحكم المسا .

٢٩٫١١ وبعد كام يوم اجا الى حضرة الالجي خبر بان الجي البنادقه بعد ثلاثة ايام بيروح بيقابل الملك لانه وصل الى اسطنبول عن قرب وفي وصوله بيرسل الهدايا الى الملك وبعد ثلاث ايام بيمضي بيقابل الملك كمالوف عوايدهم . حينذٍ نبه الالجي علي المدبر بانه

---

١ الأصل: بيقطعوا. ٢ الأصل: والطره.

We passed through the gate into an immense courtyard, traversed by three paths. The first, which was to the right, led to the women's palace, where the king's harem was located. Anyone who entered it without warning would be flogged with a cane. The second path, which lay in the middle, led to the king's inner palace. It was accessible only to the vizier and the other nobles of the realm. The third path, on the left, led to the mint. All were welcome to visit it without fear or trepidation.

We walked over to the mint and went inside. It was spacious. There were    11.27
two glowing furnaces, which received the rods of silver and gold. On one side of the furnaces was a large heap of silver rods, and on the other a pile of gold ones. In another spot, some people sat hammering the rods to make them even, while others cut the rods into perfect piasters, half piasters, and quarter piasters with the help of presses. One person would lay the rod across the anvil while another turned the press, cutting the piaster, which fell to the ground. Some other people would then stamp the freshly cut coins with the aid of another press, marking them on both sides with the sultan's name and seal, and the date. All of this without a single hammer blow!

We left the mint and headed over to the church of Hagia Sophia. Today,    11.28
it has become a royal mosque, as it is situated near the royal palace. Every Friday, the king comes to the mosque to pray. We admired the mosque from the exterior, as Christians were not allowed to enter. But even from the outside, I could see that the church, which had been built by ancient Christian kings, was indescribably marvelous. We continued on to the Valide mosque, which had no equal in all of Istanbul.[49] It was open to all, except for the section beneath the qibla dome.

From there, we passed by the palace of the Keeper of the Seal, by whom I mean the grand vizier. The street was full of people going in and out of the palace with complaints and petitions and other such things. I saw a pasha walk by with two royal footmen and no one gave him a second glance, just as though he were an ordinary person! We spent the day regarding such remarkable spectacles, returning home in the evening.

A few days later, His Excellency the ambassador received word that the    11.29
Venetian ambassador had recently arrived in Istanbul and was to have an audience with the king in three days. Upon his arrival, he'd sent gifts to the king and would meet with him three days later, per the usual protocol. The French ambassador told his steward to prepare the costumes and notify the

يهيي البدلات وينبه علي الجوخداريه حتي يتهيوا للالاي لان عوايد الالجيه اذا مضي منهم واحد للمقابله فكل واحد بيرسل جوخداريته حتي يمشوا امام الالجي لما بيقابل ومعتاد الجي الفرنساويه بيرسل اربعين جوخدار وبيلبسوهم بدلات مرسلين من السلطنه جوخ اسقراط مجركسين كمامهم وصدورهم بتبل التون وسياخ مسقطه بصبغة دهب وبرايط مسجقه بسجاقات الطون وشعور مجعده شقر وعلي ما حكولي ثمن البدله خمسمايه غرش ونيف.

٣٠،١١ فعدما المدبر هيا الجميع نقصه من الاربعين جوخدار ثلاثه فارسل احضر ثنين والفقير الثالث وفي يوم الثالث لبسوا الجميع كما ذكرنا والفقير من الجمله ومضينا الي بيت الالجي واصطف الالاي وكان اوله من بيت الالجي واخره واصل للغلطه فلما وصل الالجي الي اسكلت الغلطه كانت وصلت جكتريات الملك فنزلوا الالجي في باش جكتريه وجماعته في غيرها ومضوا الي القرشي اعني الي اسكلت اسطنبول ومن هناك بتمشي امامه الانجكاريه والسكفات المرسلين من عند اغة الانجكاريه وغيرهم من جماعة الوزير الي ان يصل الي صرايةالملك الجوانيه.

٣١،١١ فيدخل الوزير والالجي وباش ترجمان لا غير وبيتقدموا الي عند مقصوره الملك ولها ثلاثة درجات فيصعدوا في اول درجه والثانية وقلما بيصعدوا الي الثالثه يمر الملك حتي يدخل الي ثاني مقصوره وفي ذلك المحل بيكون الوزير والالجي والترجمان الي ثاني درجه. حينذٍ بيقف الملك فيبدا الترجمان بيعمل دعا للملك من قبل الالجي مقتصر من غير طوله وفي انتها كلامه بيسال الملك للالجي كيف حال اقوانه فيرد عليه الترجمان وبعده بيدخل الملك الي مقصورته الثانيه وفي دخوله بيكون ارتمي علي كاف الالجي القفطان من عند الملك وبيرموا علي كاف جماعته القفاطين وهذه علامة الرضا والصلح من الملك.

٣٢،١١ وبيخرجوا من هناك وبيدخلوا الي صراية الديوان فيجلس الالجي علي كرسيه المخصص له في الديوان. حينذٍ بيقدموا له المشروب والضطلي والقهوه والبخاخير. اخيراً يخرج الالجي من هناك فتمشي امامه حاشية الملك من البلطجيه وحلويه وبسطنجيه وشربجيه وغيرهم كثيرين يصلوا معه الي حد الاسكله فينزل الالجي في جكتريت الملك والباقي

embassy officials to get ready for the parade. Whenever an ambassador was to be received by the king, it was customary for all the other ambassadors to send their officials to parade before him. The French ambassador would usually send forty of his own officials, all decked out in ceremonial costumes sent by the monarchy. They were made of scarlet fabric with gold embroidery on their sleeves and breasts. They wore rapiers damascened in gold and hats hemmed with gold thread, as well as curly blond wigs. According to what I heard, each outfit cost more than five hundred piasters.

Once the steward had finished making his preparations, it transpired that the company of forty officials was short three men. So he sent for three more, and I was one of them. On the appointed day, everyone got suited up as described, including me, and we headed off to the Venetian ambassador's residence. The procession lined up, stretching from the ambassador's house all the way down to Galata. By the time the ambassador reached the harbor of Galata, the king's boats had arrived. The ambassador got into the lead boat, while his entourage rode in the other ones, and they set off for Sirkeci, the port of Istanbul. From there, various ranks of janissaries, sent by their chief, along with other figures from the grand vizier's staff, paraded before the ambassador in the direction of the king's inner palace. 11.30

The vizier, the ambassador, and the chief dragoman would enter alone and make their way to the king's private pavilion, which was accessed via three steps. They would climb the first step and the second, but before climbing up to the third, the king would pass, on his way to the second chamber. At that point, the vizier, the ambassador, and the dragoman would still be on the second step. Then the king would stop, and the dragoman would present a brief request to address the king on behalf of the ambassador. When he was finished, the king would ask the ambassador for the news of his peers, and the dragoman would respond on his behalf. Finally, the king would enter the second pavilion, followed by the ambassador, who now wore a caftan on his shoulders, given to him by the king. His entourage also received caftans, a sign of the king's acceptance of their presence. 11.31

From there, they would continue on to the council hall, where the ambassador would be seated in a chair reserved for him, and served drinks, sweets, coffee, and incense. Finally, he would leave the palace, preceded by the king's retinue—harem guards, confectioners, gardeners, cooks, and many others—who accompanied him all the way to the harbor. The ambassador would board 11.32

بينزل من كل بلك كام واحد بيوصلوه الي صرايته مع جملة الجوخداريه والانجكاريه وجوخداريت الالجيه وكما ذكرنا بنصف الالاي من الغلطه الي بيك اغلي الي بيت الالجي فلما وصلنا الي بيت المذكور فرايت صامدين صمات الي الانجكاريه وللباقي يجي طوله مايه ضراع وواضعين فيه من جميع الحلاويات والمربايات وجميعها في صحون مدفوره من عروق الخيزران وفي وصولهم الي الصمات عملوه يغما وفي دقيقه واحده اخدوا الحلاوات والصحون وما بقي في الصمات شي يقال له شي.

٣٣،١١ وعاملين ثاني صمات داخل صراية الالجي لاجل جوخداريت الالجيه وموجود فيه من جميع الاكولات طرطات وسنبوسكات[١] ونخضات مشويه وغيرهم شي كثير وفي كل قزنه من الصمات راكزين برميل نبيد وحوله كثره قداح بلور . حينذِ كلفونا للاكل والشرب فطنا في تلك الاكولات وشربنا من ذلك الخمر الطيب وشربنا يسر حضرة الالجي وصرحنا جميعنا كيوبوا حتي علي حسنا برات الصرايا وبعده خرجنا من هناك وكلّ منا مضي الي محله وهذا الذي رايته من مقابلة الالجي لكن في دخوله الي صراية الملك وخروجه منها ما رايت من هذا شي انما سمعته نقلاً من الغير الذين دخلوا معه والله اعلم.

٣٤،١١ وبعد كام يوم وصل من قبل سلطان فنساء رجل عالي شان في عزلت الالجي واتسلم الصرايا وما فيها شكل متسلم ومن ذلك الوقت بطل حكم الالجي وتغيرت الامور الي حين ما يجي الجي جديد. حينذِ داقت الدنيا فيّ ولا عاد يمكنني استقيم في الصرايا لانه ضشرا كثريت الجوخداريه وقطع خرجهم وبطلت تلك الصفر والالات الموسيقيه وانا في تلك الحيره وهميت انقل حوابجي الي الاستريه الموجوده في بيك اغلي فدخل ريس اليسوعيه الذي ديره في الغلطه وكان بيني وبينه[٢] معرفه ومحبه فلما راني سلم عليّ وانا في همت الخروج من الصرايا.

٣٥،١١ فسالني لين ماضي اجته الي الاستريه فما هان عليه وقلي ما بريدك تقطن في الاستريه . حينذِ قلتله الي اين اروح يا ابانا فافتكر حصه والتفت قلي بتريد تخدم يا ابني

---

the king's boat with a few members of each company, and they'd deliver him to his own palace along with the king's footmen and janissaries, and all the embassy officials.

As I was saying, the procession of officials extended from Galata all the way up to the ambassador's residence in Beyoğlu. When we returned, I saw that a banquet table had been set up for the janissaries and other guests. It was a hundred arm spans long, and laden with sweets and compotes served upon plates of braided rattan. But as soon as the janissaries arrived, they pillaged the table, snatching up all the sweets and other plates in an instant, leaving it devoid of anything that could be called food!

However, a second banquet table reserved for the embassy officials had been set up inside the ambassador's palace. There one found a wealth of fine dishes, such as tarts and dumplings, grilled chicken thighs, and many others besides. At each corner of the table was a barrel of wine along with several crystal glasses. We were invited to eat and drink, so we dug in to the food and downed the good wine. We drank to the health of the ambassador, crying out "*Che viva!*" and the clamor of our merrymaking resounded outside the walls of the palace.[50] Then we left and each returned home.      11.33

This is what I witnessed of the ambassador's audience. Of course, I wasn't able to observe what happened between his entrance to the king's palace and his departure. I heard about it from those who were present, but God knows best!

A few days later, a high-ranking emissary arrived in Istanbul. He'd been sent by the king of France specifically to remove the French ambassador. He took control of the embassy, and assumed the role of caretaker. The former ambassador's tenure was terminated, and everything began to change in anticipation of the arrival of a new ambassador.      11.34

So I began to feel a sense of despair once again. I couldn't remain in the ambassador's mansion any longer because the emissary had dismissed most of the embassy officials and curtailed their wages. Those lovely banquets accompanied by music would be no more. Unsure of what to do, I decided to move my things to an inn in Beyoğlu. But just as I was preparing to leave the embassy, the abbot of the Jesuit monastery in Galata, with whom I'd become friends, passed by. He greeted me when he saw me.

"Where are you going?"      11.35

"To the inn."

He didn't look pleased about this.

فاجبته نعم يا ابانا لكن عند مان بتريد تخدمني فقلي في جانب دينا في الغلطه رجل بازركان بندقي وهو رجل ناس ملاح وغني وانكان بتريد حتي اكلمه من جهتك فقتلته افعل يا ابانا مثل ما بتريد وانا تحت طاعتك. حينٍ قلي استقيم اليوم في الصرايا ونهار غدي باخذك لعنده فودعني ومضي.

وثاني يوم ارسل ودعاني لعنده فقلي انا لقشت مع الخواجه وقبل بانه ياخذك لعنده كـاور امضي بنا فمضينا الي بيت ذلك الخواجه ولما امتثلنا[1] امامه قام علي اقدام واسترحب في الريس. حينٍ قله الريس ها هو ذا الغلام الذي احكيت لك عنه وانت تكون امين منه من طرف الامانه ومن طرف الخدمه فرضي ذلك الخواجه وجعلي اجره في السنه خمسين غرش ونصف مدخول البوابه التي بتدخل من الرزق الذي بينباع ونصف الاخر للطباخ وخادم اخر. اخيراً مضي البادري والخواجه سلمني جميع اواني البيت والفضي والت الصفره وسلمني مفتاح الكلار وما يشبه ذلك.

حينٍ مضيت واتيت بحوايجي من بيت الالجي الي بيت ذلك الخواجه وكان اعطاني مفتاح اوضه لمنامتي فدخلت حوايجي الي تلك الاوضه وبديت احوس في البيت فرايت وسخه عن جانب عظيم وفي الحال ابتديت اكنس الارض والبيت وادع كل شي في مكانه وهندمت فرشت الخواجه وفرشة يازجيه ومحل الغدا هندمت الصفره وجلبت الفضي والسكاكين ودخلت الي الكلار عبيت اواني النبيد وخسلت القداح واخرجت من الكلار ما يلزم مثل جبن وزيتون وهذا كله انا بفهمه من حلب لاني خدمت خواجه رنباو الكبير وبعده خواجه رمزات مدة اثني عشر سنه الي حين ما خرجت من حلب وقصدت الرهبنه فلما اجا الخواجه واليازجي للغدا وراء تلك النضافه والترتيب فانبصط قوي كثير.

فاستقمت عنده اول شهر فسالني الخواجه هل فضيت الفوجيه من النبيد فاجبته ما راح نصفها فالتفت الي اليازجي وقله علي زمان ذاك الخادم ما كان

"I don't want you to go live at the inn," he said.

"Where am I supposed to go, Father?"

He thought for a moment, then looked up at me.

"Are you willing to work, my son?"

"Yes, Father," I said. "But where can you find me a job?"

"There's a Venetian merchant near our monastery in Galata. He's a good man, and a wealthy one too. If you like, I can mention you to him."

"Whatever you think is best, Father," I replied. "I'm in your hands."

"Spend another day here at the embassy, and I'll take you to meet him tomorrow," the abbot instructed, before bidding me farewell and departing.

The next day, the abbot sent for me.     11.36

"I spoke with the *khawājah*, and he has agreed to take you on as a cellarman," the abbot said. "Let's go see him."

We went to the *khawājah*'s house, and when we presented ourselves before him, he rose to his feet and greeted the abbot.

"This is the boy I told you about," the abbot said. "You can be confident that he'll be trustworthy and hardworking."

The *khawājah* agreed to hire me, and gave me a wage of fifty piasters per year. I'd also receive half the sum of the door fee, which was earned on the basis of merchandise sold. The other half would go to the cook and another employee. Then the priest went on his way, and the *khawājah* put me in charge of all the kitchenware, silver, dinnerware, and so forth. He also gave me a key to the cellar.

I brought my things from the ambassador's house to the *khawājah*'s, plac-     11.37
ing them in my own room, to which he'd given me a key. Then I set about tidying up the house, which I discovered was quite filthy. I began by doing some sweeping and putting everything in its place. I made the beds of the *khawājah* and his clerk, and arranged the table in the dining room. Then I went down to the cellar and brought up some cheese, olives, and other necessities.

This work was familiar to me from my time in Aleppo, when I'd spent twelve years working for *khawājah* Rimbaud the elder and *khawājah* Rémuzat after him, just before I left Aleppo to join the monastic order. When the *khawājah* arrived for lunch in the company of his clerk, he saw how clean and neat everything was, and was overjoyed.

After I'd spent a month working for the *khawājah*, he asked me one day if     11.38
the demijohn of wine was empty.

يكفينا في الشهر فوجيت نبيد فسمع الطباخ وذلك الخزمتكار هذا القول من الخواجه فا هان عليهم وشربوا بغطتي من ذلك اليوم لان بانت خيانتهم وانا ما بعرف بانهم ضمروا لي السو فصرت ارا منهم عين الغدر لكني ما ابالي ولا احسب لهم حساب خصوصاً الطباخ كان ضدي علي خط مستقم فاعلمت الخواجه بذلك فني الحال ضشره.

٣٩،١١ وصار يفتش له علي طباخ فانا لما رايت الخواجه محصور لاجل ما وجد طباخ علي كيفه فقلتله لا تهكل هم انا بطبخ لك الي حين ما تري لك طباخ فقلي بتعرف تطبخ قلت له نعم فقلي بارك الله وانا كنت تعلمت الطبخ علي يد طباخ الذي كان يطبخ الي معلمي خواجه رنباو واتقق بانه طشره فصرت اطبخ مكانه وارضي الخواجكيه في طبخي وما اني كت ذلك الوقت ولد فتيعجبوا في. المراد استقمت اطبخ وذلك الخزمتكار من تحت يدي فزاد فيه البغضه والالام مني لان الخواجه كان قوي مبصوت من طبخي وما عاد فتش علي طباخ.

٤٠،١١ فصار كل البيت في يدي امر وانهي واصنع الذي بريده فليله من ذات الليالي خطر لعند الخواجه خطار وامرني باني ازيد الاكل فصرت اقول لذلك الخزمتكار امضي جيب شي الفلاني ما يجيب واعمل شي الفلاني ما يعمل علي قدر ما هو محصور مني فالتفيت ونهرته ثم شتمته فا رايت الا سحب السكين وانحدق علي بخلق وغضب شيطاني وقاصد قتلي فاستغت في ملاكي الحارس وارتميت عليه ومسكت يده واخدت السكين من يده ورميته تحتي وصرت اقتل فيه بكل قوتي.

٤١،١١ فسمع الخواجه صراخنا علي بعضنا فدخل للمطبخ فانا متكامشين ونحن بالقرع فعيط علينا وخلصنا من بعضنا بعض والتفت الي الخواجه وقلي هذا محل القتال وعندنا موجود ضيف قوم اسعي في شغلك وما تركني حتي احكي له بالذي صار بينا.

"It's not even half empty," I replied.

The *khawājah* turned to his clerk, remarking, "When the last fellow was in charge, a single demijohn of wine wouldn't last the month!"

Now, the cook happened to hear what the *khawājah* said, and so did the other servant. They weren't pleased about it, and from that day forth they harbored a bitter resentment toward me, because I'd inadvertently exposed their pilferage. However, I was unaware of the grudge they bore.

After a while, I began to notice the treacherous glances they cast at me, but I paid them no mind. It was the cook, in particular, who was dead set against me. So I told the *khawājah* about him, and he dismissed the fellow on the spot!

The *khawājah* set about searching for a new cook, but when he had trouble   11.39
finding a suitable replacement, he became frustrated.

"Don't worry," I said. "I'll cook for you until you find someone."

"Do you know how to cook?" he asked.

"Yes."

"Praise the Lord!"

I'd learned how to cook from the man who used to cook for my master, *khawājah* Rimbaud. When he was fired, I took his place. All the *khawājah*s used to love my cooking, marveling at the fact that I was just a boy. So, anyway, I started cooking for the Venetian merchant, and consequently the other servant fell under my authority. He was very upset about this, since the *khawājah* was overjoyed with my cooking and stopped looking for another cook.

The house was now my domain; I gave the orders and did as I pleased. One   11.40
night, a traveler passed by for dinner, and the *khawājah* ordered me to prepare more food than usual. But when I told the other servant to go and get something for me, or to perform some task or other, he refused. That was how much he resented me!

Angrily, I began to scold the man and ridicule him, and wouldn't you know it, he pulled out a knife and strode toward me, seething like a devil. He wanted to kill me! Appealing to my guardian angel for help, I threw myself at him and pried the knife out of his hand! Tossing it aside, I began hitting him as hard as I could.

The *khawājah* heard us shouting at each other, and rushed into the kitchen,   11.41
where he found us locked in combat. Shouting at both of us, he pulled us apart, then turned to face me.

المراد خزيت الشيطان وقت هيت العشا والخدمه كما يجب وعند الاتها بعد خروج الضيف من عنده احكيت له المجراويه كما تمت. حينٍ اخد بخاطري وقلي غدي من الصباح بدشره وانت كون في امان انا بعرف جنس هل كريكيه ناس ارديا حقودين ما لهم ذمه.

١١،٤٢ النتيجه ما طيلعني من عنده الا انا راضي. اخيرًا مسيته وذهبت الي مخضعي وقفلت الباب من داخل خوفًا بلا يغدر فيّ وانا نايم فافتكرت تلك الليله وانا في الفراش وقلت في بالي ولين الخواجه طشرني يخشا عليّ منه ليلا يصدفني في الطريق ويطعني بسكين ويقتلني لان الروم في تلك البلاد هين عليهم قتل القتيل لانهم في الحال بيسلموا وبيدخلوا في اوجاق الانجكاريه ولهذا السبب زاد عليّ الوهم وما قدرت انام في تلك الليله وانا في دهدار كيف اعمل.

١١،٤٣ فخطر في بالي باني تصادفت في كنيسة اليسوعيه في رجل حلبي ماروني يسما حنا ابن الزغبي وهذا كان صاحبي في حلب فمن بعدما سلمنا علي بعضنا دعيته بان يمضي معي الي بيت الخواجه البندقي الذي كنت قاطن فيه وهناك ضيفته ووقفت في واجبه ثم سالته عن سبب مجيه الي اسطنبول فاجابني بان سبب مجيي لهذه البلاد هو كان لاجل اني اتعلم طريقه سقال القماش لانها معدومه في حلب والان الله سهلي برجل معلم يمضي معي الي حلب واخد معه مطوية السقال التي هي من بولاد مسقي مع حركاتها وهذا كان غايه مرادي والان انا في استدار اول قفل الذي بيسافر الي حلب منزوح معه ماكد.

١١،٤٤ اخيرًا قلي بعدما كت احكيت له بالذي جري عليّ وكيف اني وصلت لهذه البلاد باني اروح معهم الي بلادي ولا تديع حالك في هذه الغربه امضي لاهلك ولا تهلك من هذا الكلام وغيره كثير فابيت وما ردت اطيع كلامه وكان يتردد عليّ كثير اوقات

"Is this any time to fight, while we have a guest in the house?" he demanded. "Go back to work!"

With no opportunity to tell him what had happened, I said a quick prayer and went back to preparing dinner and serving it. Afterward, once the guest had left, I told the *khawājah* the whole story, and he reassured me that it wasn't my fault.

"I'll throw him out tomorrow morning, you can be certain of that," he said. "I know all about these Greeks. A wicked, spiteful lot. They can't be trusted, you know."

He wouldn't let me leave him until my spirits had risen. Then I wished him good night and went up to my bedroom. I bolted the door from the inside, afraid of what treachery might come my way while I slept. But instead, I spent the night lost in thought.   11.42

"Even if the *khawājah* dismisses that troublemaker, what if I bump into him in the street and he pulls out a knife and kills me?" I thought to myself. "The Greeks in these lands wouldn't think twice about murdering someone. When they do, they turn themselves in and enlist with the janissaries, simple as that."

At this thought, my imagination ran wild, and my anxieties kept me up all night long. What was I to do?

Then a thought crossed my mind. I'd run into a friend of mine from Aleppo   11.43
at the Jesuit church, a Maronite named Ḥannā ibn al-Zughbī. After we'd greeted each other, I'd invited him over to the Venetian *khawājah*'s house, where I was living, and served him some refreshments and welcomed him as my guest. Then I asked him why he'd come to Istanbul.

"I came to this country to learn the craft of calendering textiles, a trade that doesn't exist in Aleppo," he explained.[51] "Fortunately, God led me to a master artisan, who's agreed to come with me to Aleppo, and he's bringing along his calendering machine, which is made of tempered steel. This was exactly what I'd hoped for, and I'm just waiting for the next caravan to Aleppo. We plan to be on it."

After I told him the story of how I'd ended up there, he encouraged me to   11.44
return home with them.

"Stop wandering," he'd said. "Better to be safe than sorry."

He'd gone on in that vein, but I declined to follow his advice. From time to time, he'd bring up the subject again, urging me to travel home with them,

ويلح عليّ بالمضي معهم وانا ابي فلما خطر في بالي تلك الليله كلامه حينذٍ صممت النيه في المضي الي حلب صحبتهم.

وثاني يوم دخلت عند الخواجه وطلبت منه اذن في خروجي من عنده فصار يتملقني وياخد بخاطري بقوله لي لا تخف انا الان بضشره من بيتي لا يكون خاطرك الا طيب من هذا الكلام ومامنه فما اقتنعت من كلامه بل استقمت علي رايي وطلبت الخروج من عنده فلما راني ثابت علي كلامي حينذٍ عمل حسابي بالذي خصني من الاجره ونصف البوابه كما اتفقنا واعطاني بالتمام ثم ودعته وحملت حوايجي من بعد ما سلمته جميع الذي كان تحت يدي من الفضي والة الصفره وغير امتعه وخرجت من بيته ودخلت الي دير اليسوعيه الذي هو بجانب بيت ذلك الخواجه.

ودخلت الي عند الريس واحكيت له بالمجراويه كما تمت وطلبت منه بانه يقبلني عنده في الدير الي حين ما يسافر القفل الي حلب فاجابني الريس بقوله لي يا بان يا ولدي ما يمكن نقبل في دينا احد من العوام ولا غيرهم انما بعطيك مفتاح بيت الطايفه الذي ينزلوا فيه القباطين الفرنساويه وغيرهم من عبارين الطريق والان موجود فيه واحد من البادريه بيستنا مطران من بلاد المسيحيين حتي يسافروا علي الحجم فشكرت فضله واخدت المفتاح وارسل معي خادم الدير حتي يروريني المكان وهو قريب من الاسكله.

فدخلت في ذلك البيت وهو بطبقتين وداخله اوض زغار وكل اوضه داخلها تحت وفيه فراشين ولحاف وملاحف نضاف فحطيت حوايجي داخل اوضه تحتانيه وخرجت للسوق اشتريت طنجره فخار وصحنين فخار وصرت اطبخ لحالي ما تسير والبادره يجي لعندي بعد المغرب ويصعد الي اوضته التي هي فوق اوضتي فنسامر قليلا معه وانزل الي منامتي وافيق حكم نصف الليل اسمع حس دبدبه فوق مني فانوهمت اول ليله من تلك الدبدبه وثاني ليله كذلك وفي ثالث ليله خرجت من فراشي وصعت

but I always said no. On that sleepless night following my fight with the Greek servant, however, I remembered his words and made up my mind to go to Aleppo with them.

The next day, I went in to see the *khawājah* and asked permission to leave his service. He did his best to make me change my mind. 11.45

"Don't you worry, I'm going to throw that fellow out of my house," he promised. "I want you to be happy."

Unconvinced by his entreaty, I remained resolved to go through with my plan and repeated my request. When he saw that I'd really made up my mind, he paid me the remainder of what I was owed in wages, and half the door fee, as we'd agreed. Then I bid him farewell and gathered all my things, after handing over the silver, dining utensils, and other household implements I'd been safeguarding. I left the house and went straight to the Jesuit monastery next door.

I went to the abbot, told him the story of what had happened, and asked his permission to stay in the monastery until the caravan was ready to depart for Aleppo. 11.46

"My son, we can't admit laypeople and such into the monastery," he explained. "But I can give you a key to the community guesthouse, where the French ship captains and other travelers stay. There's a priest staying there at the moment, waiting for a bishop to arrive from Christian lands so they can travel together to Persia."

I thanked the abbot and took the key. He sent the monastery's workhand along to show me the way to the place, which was near the harbor.

When I entered the house, I saw that it had two floors filled with small rooms. Each room had a bed with two mattresses, a quilt, and clean blankets. I put my things in one of the rooms on the lower floor, then went to the souk to buy an earthenware pot and two dishes, which I used to cook for myself. The priest would come by to see me after sunset, then go up to his room, which was directly over mine. Sometimes I'd chat with him upstairs for a while before going down to my own room. 11.47

On the first night, I awoke at midnight to the sounds of pacing overhead. These sounds filled me with fright the first night and the second, but on the third I got out of bed and went upstairs to see where the sound was coming from. Peering through the cracks in the door to the priest's room, I saw him kneeling on the floor. He had a crucifix in his hand, which he thumped against his chest as he prayed. Then he'd lean forward and put his head against the

حتي اري ما هذه الدبدبه فطلعت من شقوق باب اوضة البادري فرايته ركع وامامه الصلبوت وهو يصلي وبيدق علي سدره واحيان بيركع وبيضع راسه في الارض فلما رايت هذا المضهر نزلت ونمت في فراشي من غير فسع.

٤٨،١١ فرايع ليله قلت له يا ابونا انت ما بتنام ايش بتعمل. حينذٍ تنهد وتحصر من قلب حزين وقلي يا ابني لما رايت جميع اهل هذه المدينه كلهم مسلمين ونفوسهم هالكه فتاسفت علي هذه الانفس الضايعه عن الطريق المودي للملكوت والشيطان قايدهم فصرت اطلب من سيدي يسوع المسيح بانه ينور عقل المسلم الكبير اعني الملك حتي تقتدي فيه هذه الرعيه الذي ما لها راعي غير الديب الجهني والتفت قلي انت ايضاً اطلب معي لعل الله يقبل صلاتك فلما سمعت منه هذا الكلام بهت وقلتله هذا الشي ما بيقطع عقل وشي بعيد عن التصديق فاجابني كل شي الذي ما هو مستطاع عند البشر هو مستطاع عند الله فتعجبت من غيرة هذا البادري وتركته ومضيت الي منامتي وهو استقام يصلي ويتضرع طول الليل.

٤٩،١١ وهذا البادري علمني اصطناع قطره لشفا جميع اوجاع العين وصنعها امامي وقلي لا تخف اعطي منها لاي وجع كان في العين وقلي بتقدر تاكل خبزك من هذه القطره طول عمرك وعلمني غير اشيا نافعه لصحت البدن وانا تلك الايام ما كنت واعي لاكتساب العلوم بل كنت شارد وغالبه عليّ فورة الصبوه والجهل.

٥٠،١١ وفي تلك المده كنت اخرج ادور في مدينه اسطنبول واتفرج علي اماكنها واسواقها وشوارعها فاتفق بان سلطان احمد كان امر في بنا خمسة مراكب بكلك كبار وكل منهم باربع عنابر وبسبعين ثمانين طوب فسمعت من احدي الناس بان المراكب كمت وامر الملك المذكور بان يوم الخميس ينزلوا المراكب للبحر وهذه فرجه عظيمه فاتفقت انا وكام واحد من الحلبيه واستكرينا قايق حتي ننزل فيه ونتفرج.

٥١،١١ فلما حكم ذلك اليوم نزلت كل اهل اسطنبول للبحر وكنت تري انتلت الاسكله من القيق حتي كنت تقدر تمشي فوق القيق علي قدر ما لتزقوا في بعضهم وعلي ما اكدوا لي

floor. After witnessing this scene, I was able to go back down to my bed and sleep without fear.

"Father, don't you ever sleep?" I asked the priest on the fourth day. "What are you doing up there anyway?"

He let out a mournful sigh.

"My son, as I look around at all the Muslims of this city, whose souls are damned, I feel sorry for them," he said. "Satan has led them astray from the path to the Kingdom of Heaven, so I pray to Our Lord Jesus Christ to enlighten the mind of the Grand Muslim himself, the Ottoman king. Perhaps the flock will follow him. As it stands, they have no shepherd besides the Devil himself."

"Pray with me," the priest continued, turning to me. "Perhaps God will accept your prayer."

"But that doesn't make sense," I replied, flabbergasted. "Who would believe such a thing could happen?"

"What is impossible for man is possible for God," he replied.

Amazed by the fervor of this priest, I went back down to my room, leaving him to pray and beseech God all night long.

Now, this priest taught me how to make a certain type of eye-drop medicine suitable for every type of eye-related ailment and pain. 11.49

"Don't be afraid to use it for any sort of eye pain," he said as he made it in front of me. "This medicine will put bread on the table for the rest of your life."

He also taught me other useful things related to bodily health. In those days, I wasn't aware of the importance of learning new things. I was a vagabond, under the sway of youthful and foolish passions.

I used to spend my time going out and touring the city of Istanbul, admiring its buildings and souks and avenues. It so happened that Sultan Aḥmad had, at that time, ordered the construction of five large imperial ships, each with four holds and seventy or eighty cannons. I heard that the ships had been completed and that the king had ordered them to be placed in the water on the next Thursday. This was to be a grand spectacle! I joined a group of Aleppans who planned to rent a dinghy and go watch. 11.50

When the day came, all of Istanbul went down to the sea. The harbor was crammed so full of boats you could practically walk across them. I'd heard that there were twelve thousand boats in Istanbul harbor that paid taxes to the 11.51

بان موجود في اسكلت اسطنبول اثني عشر الف قايق الذين بيعطوا ميري من غير قيق الاغاوات الذي له كل واحد منهم قايقين وثلاثه لاجل سيرهم وتنزهاتهم. المراد نزلوا اول مركب للبحر بضوضه عظيمه وجميعهم يصرخوا الله الله ودبحوا القرابين وبعده نزلوا الثاني والثالث الي الخامس بحضور الملك والوزرا وكل اكابر الدوله وصار نهار يا له من نهار مفترج وهذا ما رايته في اسطنبول في نزول تلك المراكب لكن النضرما هو مثل السمع لانه شي نادر الوقوع.

٥٢،١١ وبعد كام يوم وصل ثمانية غلابين بكلك من عند سلطان فرنساء ودخل واحد بعد واحد للاسكله ولما يصل امام صرايه الملك التي من علي جنب الايسراذا دخلت من البحر الي الاسكله فيبدا يضرب المدافع لاجل السلام واصغر المراكب موجود فيه سبعين طوب ومن العسكر ينوف عن السبعمايه جندي من غير البحريه فلما انتهي الاولي من ضرب المدافع دخل الثاني وصار يضرب المدافع من الجانبين وبعده دخل الثالث وصنع مثل الاولي والثاني فارتجت اطاريف اسطنبول وضنوا بان الافرنج اخذت المدينه وكثير ناس هربوا الي الفيافي وكت تري الدخنه جللت الاسكله ولا عاد احد يري رفيقه ولا يسمع قوله.

٥٣،١١ حينذٍ ارسل الوزير من طرفه باش اغا الي عند قبطان حتي يستمنه بانه يطل ضرب المدافع لان حضرة الملك حاكم راسه راسه بيوجعه. وقتيدٍ صاروا الغلابين الاخر يدخلوا من غير ضرب المدافع ورسوا في الاسكله كالمعداد. حينذٍ نزلوا تراجمين الالجي واستقبلوا القبطان باشي بغاية الاكرام ومضوا اخبروا وزير الاعظم في قدوم هل ثمانية غلابين المرسلين من عند حضرة سلطان فرانسا وانه راسل الي حضرة الملك سلطان احمد ثمانين مرسايه لاجل مراكبه الجدد يكون يقبلهم منه هديه وانه عزل الالجي لاجل النقص الذي صدر منه.¹

٥٤،١١ فامر حينذٍ الوزير بان يحضروا القبطان باشي الي عنده ثاني يوم وفي الحال عين الي تلك المراكب زخاير وافره واهدي للقبطان باشي هدايا ثمينه وعمل له اكرام زايد

---

¹ «وانه عزل ... منه» في الهامش.

state, which didn't include the boats of the officials, each of whom had two or three vessels for personal travel and recreation.

They lowered the first ship into the water, and a great din rose from the crowd. All were shouting, "Allah! Allah!" as they slaughtered animals as ritual offerings. The other ships followed one at a time, as the king himself looked on, along with his ministers and all the grandees of the state. What a marvelous day it was! This was what I saw when those ships were launched in Istanbul. It's one thing to hear about it, but quite something else to witness such a rare event.

A few days later, eight royal galleons sent by the sultan of France arrived in Istanbul. One by one, they entered the harbor, and as they passed before the king's palace—which is positioned toward the left side of the harbor when you're entering it from the sea—the galleons fired their cannons in salute. The smallest ship had seventy cannons and more than seven hundred soldiers on board, not including the sailors. After the first ship fired its cannons, the second one entered the harbor and fired its cannons from both sides, followed by the third, which did the same.  11.52

The neighborhoods on the outskirts of Istanbul trembled at these sounds, and the people thought the Franks had captured the city. Many people fled into the wilderness. The smoke hanging over the harbor was so thick you could scarcely see the person standing next to you—or hear them, for that matter.

The minister then sent one of his chief officers to the French admiral with a request that they cease firing their cannons, because His Majesty had developed a headache. So the remaining galleons entered the harbor without firing their cannons, anchoring in the usual way. The dragomans of the ambassador came down to receive the admiral in most honorable fashion. They then went to see the grand vizier, informing him of the arrival of eight galleons dispatched by His Majesty the king of France, who had sent eighty anchors to His Majesty Sultan Aḥmad, for his new ships, which he hoped the sultan would accept as a gift. Furthermore, the king of France had dismissed his ambassador for not fulfilling his duties appropriately.  11.53

The vizier arranged to have the admiral brought to him the following day, and ordered that the French ships be reprovisioned with victuals. He presented the admiral with expensive gifts, showering him with honors on behalf of the king.  11.54

من قبل الملك وفي ذلك الوقت مناه بقوله له انضر ماذا يعوزك من امر من الامور حتي نقضي لك هو علي اتم المراد فاجابه القبطان باشي تعلم لسيادتكم بان الان بلادنا مغليه من قلة القمح فالمامول من حضرة الملك ومن حضرتكم بان تقطعوا لنا فرمان بان ندور في الاضاوات ونشتري مغل ولا احد يتعارضنا فاجابه الوزير علي الفور يكون لك ما طلبت واصرفه بسلام.

فلما الوزير اخبر الملك بمطلوب القبطان باشي فقطع الملك خط شريف من يده ٥٥،١١ وامر بان يوسقوا الثانية غلايين من القمح الجيد ولا ياخدوا منهم حقه فاستقاموا الغلايين مقدار عشرين يوم الي حينما ارسل الوزير الجكتريات الي الاضاوات وحضروا القمح المطلوب وفي تلك المده خلص من اليسرا نحو مايتين يسير لانهم كانوا يغطوا في البحر ويصعدوا الي تلك الغلايين ويخلصوا من اليسرا لان حالما اليسير مسك بيده جانب الغليون يخلص وما يقدر احد ياخده من ذلك الغليون بل يسمحوا لهم لاجل نام سلطان ونساء.

وفي تلك الايام قدم الي اسطنبول امير من امرات سلطان سويد وكان قصده ٥٦،١١ يدور ويتفرج في الاقليم وكانت جماعته تفتش علي ناس من اهل البلاد يعرفوا بلسان التلياني والتركي فجاني واحد من اصحابي وهو ذاك الجوخدار الالبي الذي اجا معي من مرسيليا[1] وراد يشبكني مع هذا الامير بصفة ترجمان فارضيت انا بذلك واعطيته قرار باني بسافر معه وصممت نيتي علي المضي مع هذا الامير لاني سمعت بانه بعد دورته بيروح الي بلاده بسفر البر وراد ياخدني ويواجهني مع الامير.

وفي ذلك اليوم الذي كنت رايح حتي اوجه الامير حضر لعندي حنا بن الزغبي ٥٧،١١ المذكور فلما سمع في رواحي مع ذلك الامير فما هان عليه وصار يوعضني وعمل كل جهده حتي يصدني عن المضي وقال لي القفل طالع بعد يومين الي حلب وانا استكريت لك دبه مع احمد القاطرجي الحلبي واعطيته رعبون.

والنتيجه لا زال يدوي علي حتي غير نيتي عن السفر مع ذلك الامير المذكور فلما ٥٨،١١ تغيرت نيتي واعطيته قرار باني عدلت عن المضي واني بروح معه الي حلب حينِد

---

١ «وهو ذاك الجوخدار . . . مرسيليا» في الهامش.

"Is there anything you are in need of that we might provide?" the vizier asked the admiral.

"Perhaps you might inform His Majesty the king that our lands are experiencing a rise in prices because of the shortage of wheat," the admiral said. "We ask that His Majesty the king might issue an edict authorizing us to tour around the Province of the Islands and purchase your crops without encumbrance."

"Request granted," the vizier replied immediately, and sent him on his way.

When the vizier brought the admiral's request to the king, the latter issued 11.55 an imperial edict in his own hand ordering that the eight galleons be loaded up with good wheat, for which they would not pay a cent. The galleons remained in port for twenty days, until the vizier sent a group of galleys off to the Province of the Islands to gather the requested wheat. In the meantime, two hundred prisoners were given their freedom, which they gained by diving into the sea and climbing aboard the galleons, because, from the moment a prisoner grasped the side of a galleon, he was officially saved, and no one had the authority to take him back once he was safely aboard. They were pardoned as a gesture of goodwill toward the king of France.

Around that time, one of the princes of the kingdom of Sweden arrived in 11.56 Istanbul. His intent was to tour the region, and his coterie were searching for local guides who spoke Italian and Turkish. One of my friends—the embassy official who'd traveled with me from Marseille—came to see me, proposing to get me a job as a dragoman for the Swedish prince. I agreed to his proposal and gave him my word that I'd travel with him. I'd heard that the prince planned to return to Sweden overland following his tour of the region, so I made up my mind to leave Istanbul with him.

The very same day, as I was about to go meet the prince, who should pass by 11.57 but Ḥannā ibn al-Zughbī. When he learned of my impending departure with the prince, he wasn't happy. He began to admonish me and did all he could to prevent me from leaving.

"The caravan is leaving for Aleppo in two days," he said. "I've already rented a mule for you from Aḥmad the Aleppan muleteer, and I gave him a deposit."

In the end, I succumbed to his protestations and decided against travel- 11.58 ing with the prince, giving Ḥannā my word that I would return to Aleppo with him.

قلي بيلزم نهي حالنا الي السفر فيلزمنا ناخد' معنا بعض اشيا التي بتنفعنا في الطريق وهي اقة فلفل وكم درهم قرنفل وجنزبيل وما يشبه ذلك من الة العطاره وايضاً كم ورقة ابروسلات وشويت صابون لان هل اشيا بتسلك في درب اسطنبول احسن من المصريات لان اهل الضيع بيعطونا مهما اعتزناه لاجل معاشنا وبيصير لنا توفير كثير .

٥٩.١١ فقبلت مقاله واخرجت واحد دهب اعطيته وقلت له اشتري الذي بتريده فذهب وانا حضرت حالي ومضيت ودعت الريس والجوخدار صاحبي واستقمت استنضر مجي حنا المذكور فبعد يومين اجا لعندي وقلي قوم بنا نسافر .

٦٠.١١ وكان خروجي من اسطنبول في اواسط شهر حزيران سنه ١٧١٠ فحملت حوايجي ومضيت معه الي الاسكله وكان استكري قايق حتي يطلعنا الي اسكدار فرأيت ذلك الاختيار معلم السقال وحوايجهم فنزلت حوايجي في القايق وسرنا الي اسكلت اسكدار فخرجنا حوايجنا من القايق ودخلنا استكرينا اوضه في الخان واستقمنا نستنا القاطرجي والقفل معاً .

٦١.١١ وفي ذلك المحل اقبل علينا اوادلق باشة افيون قري حصار' وقاطرجينا وغير قاطرجيه فسالنا القاطرجي عن سبب عوقته فاجابنا بان بعتوا يسقوا علي دوابي والزموني باني احمل للباشا طيبه غصيبه انا وغير قاطرجيه التزمنا بان نخلي احمالنا ونحمل للباشا ولكن لاجل خاطركم ابقيت من دوابي ثلاثه منشانكم واظهرت بان عندي سبعة دواب لا غير والان التزمت اسافر مع الباشا الي افيون قري حصار وان كان بتريدوا تسافروا معي فكان والا استكروا من غيري علي كيفكم .

٦٢.١١ فلما بلغنا هذا الخبر حزنا وحنا في امرنا كيف نعمل فدورنا عل غير قاطرجيه حتي نستكري معهم فما وجدنا احد انه يكرينا . حينذٍ التزمنا نسافر مع قاطرجينا الي افيون قري حصار فاستقمنا ذلك اليوم وثاني يوم اجا الباشا الي اسكدار وفي الحال

---

١ الأصل: ناخدنا .  ٢ الأصل: عصار .

"In that case, we must prepare ourselves for the journey," he said. "We'll need to bring along a few things that will serve us well on the road, like an *uqqah* of pepper; a few dirhams' worth of cloves, ginger, and other spices; some pack needles; and some soap. These things will be worth more than money once we leave Istanbul, and the people of the villages will give us whatever we need in exchange for them. This way, we'll save a lot of money."

What he said made good sense. I took out a gold piece, handed it to him, and told him to buy whatever he deemed necessary, and off he went. In the meantime, I put my affairs in order, and went to say goodbye to the abbot and to my friend the embassy official. Then I waited for Ḥannā to return. He appeared two days later.     11.59

"Let's go," he said.

I departed Istanbul in the middle of June 1710. I grabbed my bags and we went down to the harbor together, where he'd rented a dinghy to take us to Üsküdar. An old man, the master calenderer, was waiting there with their baggage. I loaded my bags into the dinghy and we crossed over to the harbor of Üsküdar, where we unloaded, and then went to the caravansary and rented a room. We waited there for the muleteer and the caravan.     11.60

The concubines of the pasha of Afyonkarahisar then arrived at the caravansary, along with our muleteer and various others. We asked our man why he was late.     11.61

"I was forced by the pasha's men to let them load up my beasts, whether I liked it or not," he explained. "We had no choice—the other muleteers and I—but to drop our other loads and carry the pasha's goods. I did manage to set aside three mounts for you by pretending that I only had seven, but I must travel to Afyonkarahisar with the pasha. If you're willing to come with me, you're welcome to. Otherwise, you should feel free to find another muleteer."

At this news, we became despondent and didn't know what to do. We made the rounds of the other muleteers, looking for someone else to hire, to no avail. So we were resigned to traveling with our original muleteer to Afyonkarahisar.     11.62

We spent the day there. The following day, the pasha arrived in Üsküdar and the concubines immediately loaded up and set off, with us close behind. When we arrived at a gulf of water blocking our path,[52] we crossed it in a dinghy

حملوا اوادلق الباشا وساروا في اثرهم الي ان وصلنا الي الديل الذي هو في
دربنا وقطعنا في القايق نحن ودوابنا الي ذلك الناح وسافرنا مع الاوادلق الي ان وصلنا
الي كاوركوي.

١١،٦٣ فلما وصلنا نزل القفل بعيد عن الضيعه مسافة ميل في مكان قفر محرف انا ورفقاتي
نزلنا تحت الضيعه في مكان مرج واسجار ونبع ماء يجري كانه روضه فلما نزل القفل
هناك اجا القاطرجي لعندنا وامرنا باننا نروح ننزل في مكان النازل فيه القفل وقال لنا
بان اهل ضيعه قوم ارديا حراميه بينزلوا في الليل بيشلوكم.

١١،٦٤ فالفقير ما قبلت اني اروح ولا رفقاتي ايضاً وقلنا له نحن ما معنا شي ايش بياخدوا
منا فما امكنه انه ياخذنا فاستقمنا تلك الليله في ذلك المكان. حينذٍ ارسل القاطرجي
اخوه ينام عندنا واوصاه بانه لما بيشيل القفل بيصرخ عليه حتي يحملنا ونمشي مع
القفل ونحن من فسعنا من اهل تلك الضيعه ليلا ياتونا في الليل وينشلوا من حوايجنا
فربطنا خراجنا وكل منا ربط حاله في خرجه ورقدنا وفي انتصاف الليل حمل القفل
والقاطرجي صرخ علي اخيه بانه يحملنا فرد عليه اخوه من عندنا وهو نايم وغير واعي
فرجع نام ونحن نايمين ما معنا خبر وبعد ساعه فاق الغلام وعطي دانه للقفل فاء ما في
طنت جراس فتحقق بان القفل سافر فصار يعيط ويشتمنا ويقول لنا هل وقت منتشلح
وبياخدوا حوايجكم والدواب معاً.

١١،٦٥ حينذٍ نهضنا وحملنا خراجنا علي الدواب وركبنا ولما وصلنا مكان الذي كان نازل
فيه القفل فما راينا احد انما راينا اثار النار فوقفنا في ذلك المكان فراينا سكتين فسالنا
الغلام من اي سكه نسافر فما عرف اينا هي السكة التي تمشي فيها القفل فوقفنا باهتين
وفزعانين ليلا يلحقونا اهل الضيعه ويشلحونا ونحن في ذلك الديق والحيره الله سبحانه
الهمني بان كُدَيْشي مراجعي الدرب وبيعرف الطريق.

١١،٦٦ حينذٍ نزلت من عليه ولفيت رسنه علي رقبته ورخيته فمشي الكديش في سكت
الفوقانيه فلما مشي تبعناه وكل منا ركب دبته وسرنا الي ان وصلنا الي اعلا مكان وكان

together with our beasts, then pressed on with the concubines until we arrived at Gavur Köy.

The convoy halted in a desolate spot, a mile from the village. Meanwhile, my companions and I made camp just below the village, in a field as lovely as a garden, with trees and a freshwater spring. Shortly after we arrived, our muleteer made his way over from the other spot and told us to make camp with the rest of the convoy.   11.63

"The people of this village are a pack of thieves," he said. "They'll rob you in the night."

I didn't want to budge, and neither did my companions.   11.64

"We don't have anything," we said. "What are they going to take from us?"

The muleteer wasn't able to change our minds, so we spent the night in that spot, and he sent his brother to sleep in our camp with us. He told his brother that when it came time for the convoy to leave, he'd shout out to him to have us load up and set off as well. Meanwhile, we tied our bags to our bodies, in fear that the village people might indeed come for us in the night, and then went to sleep.

In the middle of the night, the convoy loaded up and the muleteer called out to his brother to have us load up as well. The brother responded, but he did so while half asleep, and he then turned over and went back to sleep! Meanwhile, the rest of us slept on, oblivious to what was happening. An hour later, the young man woke up and listened for the sounds of the convoy, but he didn't hear any bells. That was when he knew it had left, and he began to shout and curse us.

"We're going to get robbed!" he yelled. "They're going to take our things, and our animals too!"

We scrambled to our feet, loaded our bags on our mounts, and galloped away, soon arriving at the spot where the convoy had been camped. There wasn't a soul to be seen, only the remains of a campfire. And two roads.   11.65

"Which road should we take?" we asked the young man.

He didn't know. We stood there, confused and afraid. What if the villagers came after us while we were so vulnerable and robbed us? Suddenly, I was struck by divine inspiration. My horse had frequently traveled this road, and surely knew which way to go!

I got off the horse and loosened its halter. It walked forward toward the upper road, and we followed behind, each mounting his horse and galloping   11.66

تحتنا ودي غميق فسمعنا من قاطع ذلك الوادي رنت جراس دواب فاتكدنا بان دربنا من هناك وصار لنا غم عظيم وهمينا علي الرجوع فصار الغلام القاطرجي يصيح علي اخوه وابنطح علي الارض وعطي دانه لعله يسمع صياح اخيه فسمع وهن يقولون ما قلنا لكم بان الدرب من فوق. حينذٍ فرحنا بان هم التايهين ما هو نحن.

١١،٦٧  حينذٍ اصطبرنا لهم حتي وصلوا لعندنا ومشينا في الطريق الصحيح الي ان اصبح الصباح وبعد ساعتين وصل الباشه الي عندنا وفات فسرنا نتبعه وحكمنا ذلك النهار مطر غزير حتي غرقت حوايجنا من كثره الامطار والسيل واستقام الغيث الي المساء وبقت حالتنا يرثي اليها فلما نضر الباشا بان المطر مستقيم حيد الي ضيعه قريه من السكه ودخل هو وخواصه الي الضيعه وضشروا اصحاب البيوت وقطعوا فيها وعسكره استقام برات الضيعه ونصبوا خيامهم والتجوا تحتها اما نحن بقينا واقفين في صحن الضيعه تحت المطر فصرنا نتدخل علي الفلاحين حتي يعطونا منزول ولوكان اخو رحتي نلتجي من ذلك السيل فاكدولنا بان عيالهم وحريمهم ملتجيين بين ارجل البقر والدواب فخرنا في امرنا.

١١،٦٨  ونحن في ذلك الوقت في التفكير وربنا له المجد بالتدبير فما راينا الا انتصب امامنا شب بهي المنضر وسال رفقاتي عني لانه راني بغير حلاس لان كنت لابس لبس فرنج وشعري مدلاء من راسي ولابس في هامي قلبق صنصار فقلت لرفقاتي قولوا له باني حكيم فلما سمع باني حكيم فرح وصار يتوسل اليهم بانهم يقولوا لي حتي امضي معه لان عنده مريض اشرف عليه.

١١،٦٩  حينذٍ رديت انا عليه بلسان التركي وقلت له انكان بتاوينا هذه الليله عندك حتي اروح اشرف علي مريضك فاجابني بتحل عليّ البركه لكن بخاف ليلا احد من جماعة الباشا يعرف داري فبلتزم انا وحريمي نخرج من الدار ويدخلوا هن فيه لكن انا بمشي بعيد عنكم فاتبعوني انتم حتي ادخلكم الي داري فقبلت وقلته امضي ونحن منتبعك عن بعد فمشي امامنا ونحن تابعينه في لفاف وري الضيعه فانتهي الي كهف ونزل فيه

on. We soon arrived at a peak. A deep valley stretched out ahead of us, and the jingling of bells could be heard far below. It dawned on us that we'd taken the wrong road, and our spirits sank. As we turned around and prepared to return the way we'd come, the young muleteer shouted out to his brother. He lay down and pressed his ear to the ground, hoping to hear a response.

"Didn't we tell you that we should have taken the upper road?" is what he heard them saying, so we felt profoundly relieved. It was they who had chosen the wrong road, not us!

We waited for the convoy to arrive at our spot, and then we all followed the correct road until morning came. Two hours later, the pasha caught up with us and passed by, and we followed behind him. It rained heavily that day, and our bags were soaked in the downpour, which lasted until the evening, leaving us in a sorry, sodden state. The pasha, faced with the incessant rain, decided to veer off into a village just off the road. He and his coterie rode into the village, kicking the people out of their houses and settling in. 11.67

Meanwhile, the troops set up camp outside, pitching their tents and huddling beneath them, while we were left standing in the center of the village, the rain pouring down on us. When we begged the peasants to give us a place to stay, even a lowly stable, to protect us from the torrent, they swore to us that their own women and children had already taken refuge there among the livestock. What were we to do?

We stood there, trying to think of a solution to our troubles, and Almighty God provided one. A handsome young man suddenly appeared before us, and asked my companions who I was. He'd noticed that I was dressed differently, like a Frank in fact. My hair tumbled loosely from my head, and I wore a calpac made of marten fur. 11.68

"Tell him I'm doctor," I said to them.

At this news, the young man implored my companions to let me go with him to visit an invalid he had at home.

"If you shelter us at your house tonight, I'll come see your invalid," I replied to him, speaking in Turkish. 11.69

"It would be a blessing to have you," the young man replied, "but I fear that one of the pasha's men might discover where I live. Then my wife and I will be forced to leave the house so they might commandeer it. Why don't you follow me at a distance?"

بنزول وغاب عنا فلما وصلنا الي ذلك المكان رايناه وهو في استدارنا فدخلنا الي ذلك الكهف فاينا باب فطرق الباب واعطاهم اشاره بانهم يفتحوا ففتحوا الباب فاينا داخله ثلاث شباب واقفين.

٧٠.١١ فانا ورفقاتي جفلنا لئلا يكون هذا المكان شرك حراميه لكن ايش عاد يفيدنا وقعنا في الشرك ونحن في تلك الفكره والا خرجوا تلك الشباب واخذوا خيلنا من يدنا ودخلوهم الي داخل وكلفونا في الدخول فدخلنا معهم الي مكان مفروش وفي صدر المكان اوجاق. حينذٍ قدموا لنا اخراجنا ولبشنا فلما راوهم نديانات في الحال عيشوا نار في ذلك الاوجاق حتي ننشف تيابنا. حينذٍ استرحب فينا ذلك الشاب الذي اتينا معه.

٧١.١١ وكان امسا المساء ونحن ننشف حوايجنا واسترحنا قليلا فامر ذلك الشاب للواقفين امامنا بانهم يجيبوا العشا فانفرد واحد منهم ومد الصمات ووضع الزاد ومد البشكير علي ركبنا وحضر شربة الماء وجنق حتي يسقينا ونحن في ذلك الوقت باهتين متعجبين من هذا الامر الذي وقع وكيف ان ربنا له المجد ارسل لنا ذلك الشاب حتي اتاوينا عنده وصنع لنا هذا الاكرام. حينذٍ قدموا لنا العشا وهوصحن كبير رز هميس ومعه صحن كبير ايضاً يخني وصحن فزارايج قزن كبابي اكل مفتخر وفتعشينا نحن وذلك الشاب.

٧٢.١١ فلما انتهينا من العشا جابوا طشت وابريق حتي خسلوا ايدينا وبعده جابوا ابريق قهوه كبير وسقونا اول دور ثاني دور قهوه طيبه. حينذٍ عبينا غلايينا وبدينا¹ نتسامر مع ذلك الشاب حصه فقلتله اين هو مريض الذي عندك حتي اراه حتي واقف في خدمته لانك طمرتنا في احسانك فاجابني كمل غليونك وكلف خاطرك معي الي عنده فبعدما كملنا غلايينا نهض ذلك الشاب وكلفني في الدخول معه فدخل في دهليز وانتهينا الي باب فطرق الباب وهو باب الحرم فامر بانهم ياخذوا درب.

---

١ الأصل: وبدبينا.

I agreed to his plan, and the young man set off. We followed him through the thickets behind the village until we came to a cave. The young man disappeared inside. We approached the mouth of the cave and found him waiting for us. Then we descended together into the cave and came to a door, which he rapped upon with a particular knock. It swung open, revealing three young men inside.

My companions and I were suddenly seized by the panicked thought that    11.70
we'd fallen into a den of thieves! As we stood there dumbstruck and fretting helplessly over this prospect, the young men came out and took hold of our horses, brought them inside, and invited us in as well. We went in: The cave had rugs on the ground and a stove in the center. When they handed our bags to us, the men discovered that they were all wet, so they fired up the stove to dry our clothes as the young man who'd led us to his home welcomed us warmly.

Night had fallen in the meantime, and we rested a little as our clothes dried.    11.71
Then the young man ordered the others standing before us to bring in some dinner. One of them went to set the table, place some bread upon it, and lay cloth napkins across our laps. He brought in a jug full of water and an earthenware cup for us to drink from as we sat there, stunned at this wondrous turn of events. It was nothing less than the work of God Almighty, who had sent us this young man to give us shelter and treat us so generously!

Dinner was served. A large platter of rice with lamb appeared, followed by a second platter of stewed vegetables and a plate of chicken cooked in the *kazan kebabı* style. It was a sumptuous meal indeed, and we dug in together with the young man.

After dinner, they brought a basin and a pitcher for us to wash our hands,    11.72
followed by a large pot of coffee. We all had a round of delicious coffee, followed by a second, then filled our pipes and sat back to chat with the young man for a while.

"Where's that sick person you mentioned?" I asked. "It's time I had a look at him, now that you've treated us so generously."

"Please finish your pipe," the young man said. "I'll trouble you to come see him when you're done."

We finished smoking, and the young man rose to his feet and invited me to follow him inside. We walked down a corridor and arrived at the door of the women's quarters. He knocked and told them to make themselves scarce, as we were coming in.

١١،٧٣ وبعده دخلنا الي حوش مكلفه ودخلني الي بيت مفروش مصود صمد مكلف ونايم في الفراش رجل اختيار وهو ابوذلك الشاب وصاحب تلك الضيعه فجلست حداه ودسيت نبطه وهو بيلهث ومتعوب كثير وما فيه يلقط نفسه وكان مرضه من كُثره الخلط الذي حاقن في معدته. حينٍ سليته وجرعته بقولي له ما فيك شي خطر لا تخاف هذا خلط متحرك عليك وانا من باكر بخرجلك هذا الخلط وبتستريح وبتقوم من فراشك لا تهكل هم وقلت لابنه بانه يامرهم يسلقوا دجاجتين في هذا الليل لان السلام بريد اسقيه شربه حتي تكون المرقه حاضره ولا يضعوا فيها ملح واوصيته بانه يفيقني سلام الغميق حتي اسقيه الشربه اخيراً ودعته ونهضت من عنده ومضيت الي عند رفقاتي.

١١،٧٤ وكان معي قراس كان معلي جايب منهم لاجل الطريق واعطي منهم لبعض من الناس ورايت فعلهم غريب عن غير شربات لان تركيبهم مفيد لاربع طبايع الانسان اعني للسوده وللبلغم والي الصفره والدم واذا احد منهم شرب واحد بيتنقي من جميع الاخلاط الموجوده فيه وما بيستقيم غير ساعتين لا غير وبعده بيستريح وبمضي الي شغله كانه ما شرب شربه وهذا رايته في ذاتي وفي غيري ايضاً فتبقي من هل قراس عشره او اثني عشرفاعطاني اياهم حتي اشيلهم فبقيوا معي ونسيهم.

١١،٧٥ اخيراً لما رجعت من عند ذلك المريض فتحت الخرج واخدت واحد منهم وصحنته ووضعته في ورقه حتي يكون حاضر وانتكيت ونمت انا ورفقاتي الي ان صار وقت السلام فاجا نبهني ذلك الشب فنهضت عاجلاً واخدت ورقة الشربه معي ومضينا الي عند المريض حيث هو نايم. حينٍ طلبة منهم فنجان مرقه ودوبت تلك الشربه في ذلك الفنجان المرقه وناولته الي ذلك المريض وامرته بشربي الي اخرنقطه منه فبعد ما شربه واستقام مقدار ربع ساعه فضاج كثيراً وداخ حتي كاد يغشي. وقيدٍ امرتهم بان يسقوه جنق مرقه.

The door opened onto a splendid interior courtyard. He led me to a luxu-    11.73
riously furnished room, where an old man lay upon a bed. It was the young
man's father, the village elder. I sat at his side and felt his pulse. He panted
weakly, unable to catch his breath. It turned out that he was suffering from an
excess of humors trapped in the stomach.

"Don't worry, you're not in danger," I said, consoling the old man. "You've
got some humors acting up inside, but I'll take care of them early tomorrow morning, and that'll give you some relief. You'll be out of your bed soon
enough, just you wait."

I turned to his son and instructed him to have two chickens boiled overnight to make a purgative that would be ready by dawn.

"No salt," I specified, and I told him to wake me up early so that I could
administer the purgative myself. Then I said good night, and returned to my
companions.

Now, I happened to have some special tablets with me, which my master    11.74
had acquired for his travels. He used to administer them to people, and I'd
witnessed their effects. They were quite unlike other purgatives, as they
were composed specifically to address the four bodily humors—namely,
black bile, phlegm, yellow bile, and blood. Within two hours after swallow-
ing a tablet, a person would be cleansed of the humors that had accumulated
inside him. Relieved of his ailment, he'd return to work as usual, feeling as
though he'd never taken a purgative! I experienced this firsthand, and also witnessed its effects in others, and I had ten or twelve of these tablets left over.
My master had given them to me to put aside for safekeeping, then forgotten
about them.

After leaving the sick man, I opened up my traveling sack and took out one    11.75
of the tablets. I ground it up and put it in a paper envelope, ready for the next
day. Then I went to sleep along with my companions. Early the next morning,
the young man came to wake me, and I got up hurriedly, taking the envelope
with the purgative in it. We went to see the sick man, who was asleep. I asked
for a cup of chicken broth, stirred the purgative into it, and handed it to the old
man, telling him to drink it to the very last drop.

He swallowed the broth. A quarter of an hour later, he suddenly became
very agitated and grew so dizzy that he seemed about to faint. I ordered that
he be given a bowl of broth.

فبعد شربه المرقه بهنيهه طلب الطشت وصار يستفرغ حتي صار نصف ٧٦،١١
الطشة من ذلك القي الذي كله صفره وبلغم وغير مواد كريهة فبعدما كمل قيه امرتهم
ايضاً يسقوه جنق مرقه فبعد شربه المرقه طلب يطلع صوب براء وفي رجوعه سقيته
ايضاً جنق مرقه وما زلت اسقيه من تلك وينطق ويتطلع بطنه حتي نضفت امعاه
من جميع تلك المواد والخلط الذي كان مستكن في جوفه. المراد من بعد ما مرساعتين
من الزمان جلس واستراح وصار يطلب غليون تتن.

حينذٍ امرتهم بانهم يرموا علي تلك المرقه قليلاً من الرز ويطبخوا له شوربا ويطعموه ٧٧،١١
قليلاً من الجبيه حتي يتقوى ويقوم من فراشه ويمضي الي حيث ما راد. اخيراً ودعته
وردت امضي الي عند رفقاتي فقلي المريض اصبر يا معلم هنينه واخرج كيس من تحت
المخده واخرج منه جملة دراهم حتي يعطيني فقلت له ما عاد الله باني احد منك شي
انت صاحب الجميل الذي قبلتنا في بيتك واطعمتنا من زادك وابنك عمل لنا قدر
اكرام ولاجل هذا ما بقدر اكافيك علي هذا الاحسان.

حينذٍ اعطي لابنه الدراهم حتي يعطيني اياها فا قبلت اخد منه شي ومضيت الي ٧٨،١١
عند رفقاتي فما رايت الا وجابوا لنا فطور وقهوه وبعده جابوا لنا اربع طيور جاج
مسلوقات ومقدار اربعين بيضه مسلوقه وجبن وخبز ووضعوهم في صفرة الاكل
التي كانت معنا وفي ذلك المحل صوت اول نفير الباشه. حينذٍ اخرجوا كدشنا من
الاخور من بعد ما كانوا علقوا عليهم الشعير اعني السلق وحملوهم اخراجنا ونحن
لبسنا جزماتنا وتهيينا للسفر فصوت تاني نفير فصوت ذلك الشاب واستكثرنا
بخيره قوي كثيره فدق ثالث نفير وركب الباشه وسرنا نحن في اثره الي ان خرجنا برات
تلك الضيعه فإينا قاطرجينا كانه مجنون وهو يفتش علينا فلما رانا بهت.

وصار يقلنا فين كنتوا واين بتوا وانا طول هذا الليل بفتش عليكم. حينذٍ احكينا له ٧٩،١١
بالمجرويايه كيف تمت ولا يبقي خاطره من جيهة دوابه كيف انهم علقوا عليهم ومن باكر

A moment after drinking the broth, he demanded a basin and began to    11.76
vomit, filling half of it with yellow bile, phlegm, and other odious fluids. When
he finished vomiting, I ordered them to give him another bowl of broth to
drink, and once he'd consumed it, he asked to be taken outside. Upon his
return, I gave him another bowl of broth, and we alternated in this way—with
him vomiting his guts out and me giving him broth to drink—until his insides
had been purged of all those foul fluids and humors. Two hours later, he sat
back, relaxed, and asked for his pipe.

I asked them to add a little bit of rice to the broth and to boil some soup to    11.77
feed the old man, along with a little bit of chicken. In that way, he would regain
enough strength to get out of bed and go where he pleased. I said goodbye to
the old man and began to head back to see my companions.

"Wait a moment, doctor," the sick man said, pulling a pouch from beneath
his pillow and extracting some coins to give me.

"God forbid I accept any payment from you, as it was you who did a great
favor for us," I protested. "You accepted us into your home and fed us at your
table, and your son treated us most honorably. I have no way to repay you for
such kindness!"

The old man gave the coins to his son to pay me, but I refused and went    11.78
back to find my companions, only to discover that our hosts were serving us
breakfast and coffee! Then they brought out four boiled chickens, forty boiled
eggs, some cheese, and bread, laying them out on the camp table we had with
us. Suddenly, we heard the first bugle call of the pasha's convoy. They brought
our horses out of the stable, having provided each with a bag of boiled barley,
and loaded them up with our bags as we pulled on our shoes and prepared
to leave.

The second bugle sounded. We mounted our horses and bid farewell to the
young man, thanking him profusely for his generosity. Finally, the third bugle
sounded as the pasha climbed onto his mount and set off, with us following
behind. As we left the village, we spotted our muleteer, who was searching
frantically for us like a madman. He was dumbstruck when he saw us.

"Where have you been? Where did you pass the night? I've spent all night    11.79
looking for you!"

We told him the whole story, and reassured him that his mounts had been
properly cared for and given their fodder in the morning.

اعطوهم السلق . حينذٍ انبسط وقال لنا يا ريتكم اخذتوني معكم ولاكت اقاسي طول ليلي تحت المطر ومن ذلك الوقت قلت لرفقاتي بان كل من سالكم عني قولوا له باني حكيم حتي نقضي هل طريق بالعز ومن ذلك اليوم طلع خبري في الارض باني حكيم وصار كثير من جماعة الباشه يدعوني حتي احكمهم وكت اصف لهم وصفات واوقات اعطيهم من عندي حب منتي . المراد سرنا صحبة الباشا بغاية العز من قبل حماعته وكانوا يتهادوني ويكرموني ويكلفوني حتي استقيم في خيمهم .

١١،٨٠ المراد ما زلنا مسافرين حتي وصلنا الي اسكي شهر وهي مدينه زغيره الا انها عامره وداخلها قبلوجه اعني ماء كبريتي سخن في الغايه ومعمرين فوق ذلك النبع الكبريتي شكل حمام وكل اهل المدينه بيدخلوا بيستحموا هناك فلما وصلنا نصب الباشا خيامه برات المدينه حكم ثلاث اميال وطلع خبر بانه بيستقيم هناك ثلاثة ايام فالتزمنا نحن نستقيم في المدينه الي حين ما يسافر الباشا فاستكرينا اوضه في قيصريه وبتنا هناك .

١١،٨١ فزارنا رجل مسيحي كان نازل في تلك القيصريه وهو من مدينة افيون قري حصار وصار يسال رفقاتي عني فاجابوه باني حكيم فتقدم الي عندي وارواني عينه الواحده وهي كانت مقرحه ومجلل عليها بياضه وصار يتوسل اليّ باني اكحله نحن قلبي عليه واخرجت من عندي حبور القطره التي مر ذكرها وقطرت في عينه وقلته يبقي يجي عندي باكرحتي اقطرله ايضًا الي ثالث يوم خرجنا من المدينه ومضينا الي الارض في البريه وكان الوقت حكم العصر لان كان معلوم عندنا بان ثاني يوم الباشا بيسافر فجلست انا ورفقاتي قريب من الارضي واستقمنا نتسامر نخطر في بالي فكر .

١١،٨٢ وقلت الي رفيقي الحلبي الذي هو حنا بن الزغبي بان جميع جماعة الباشا عرفوني باني حكيم وان اتفق بان الباشا يمرض كيف بعود اعمل وانا ما بعرف من الحكمه الا شي قليل فاجابني لا تخف ذلك الوقت الله بيدبرك ونحن في هذا الكلام والا راينا ثنين

"If only you'd taken me with you!" he said cheerfully. "Then I wouldn't have had to suffer all night in the rain!"

I told my companions that, from that moment on, they were to inform anyone who asked about me that I was a doctor. In that way, the rest of our journey would pass most gloriously! And sure enough, the news began to spread after that day, and many of the pasha's men started calling upon me to treat them. I'd prescribe remedies and sometimes give them some of my purgative tablets. Soon enough, we were traveling with the pasha's entourage, basking in the glow of their esteem. They sought out my company and treated me very generously, and invited me to stay in their tents.

The convoy arrived in Eskişehir, a small yet prosperous city. It contained a *qablūjah*, one of those springs that spouted intensely hot sulfurous water. A sort of bathhouse was built around it, where the city's inhabitants would bathe. The pasha pitched his tents about three miles outside the city, and word spread that he would remain encamped there three days. We were forced to wait in town until the pasha's convoy set off again, so we rented a room in a caravansary and spent the night there. 11.80

Staying in the same caravansary was a Christian man from Afyonkarahisar, who came by to visit us. When he asked my companions about me and they told him that I was a doctor, he came over to show me one of his eyes. It was festering and covered with a white film, and he begged me to treat it with collyrium. My heart went out to the man, and I took out the little pot of ointment I mentioned earlier. I put a few drops in his eye and told him to come back in the morning so I could give him another dose. 11.81

On the third day, we left the city and went out to the camp, arriving in the afternoon. My companions and I knew that the pasha was to travel the next day, so we sat near the camp, chatting and passing the time. Suddenly, something occurred to me.

"The pasha's men all think I'm a doctor," I said to my Aleppan friend, Ḥannā ibn al-Zughbī. "What do I do if the pasha gets ill? I know only a little about medicine!" 11.82

"Don't worry," he said. "God will guide you when the time comes."

While we were in the midst of this conversation, two of the pasha's attendants suddenly appeared, asking for the doctor. Someone pointed in our direction. They strode over to us.

"Which of you is the doctor?" they asked.

من جوخدرية الباشا بيسالوا بعض انفار اين هو الحكيم فدلوهم علينا فلما وصلوا لعندنا سالونا من منكم الحكيم فقلتله انا هو فقلي قوم كلم حرم كاخياسي الباشه.

فنهضت وقلبي بيرتجف ومضيت معهم وكان الباشا لما راء بانه مريض وسخن دخل في بيت اغة الضيعه هو وحريمه وامر بان يمضوا الي المدينه ياتوا له بجراح حتي يفصده فاجابوه بان موجود معنا في الارضي حكيم فرنجي قوي معلم فقال اتوني به وهذاكان السبب فلما وصلت الي ذلك الدار الذي الباشا قاطن فيه رايت واقف في الباب رجل اختيار وهو حرم كاخياسي فلما امتلت امامه قلي السلامه ادخل معي حتي تشرف علي حضرة افندينا لانه مريض وما له كيف.

حينِ اعتذرت له بان ما معي سندوق الحكمه لاني ارسلته مع مركب الي حلب وانا سافرت في الطريق حتي اتفرج علي هذه البلاد فاجابني باشتنا ما هو مريض انما حكمه عارض وهو ليلة انبارح دخل للقبلوجه في الليل وفي خروجه منها وهو عرقان سفقه ريح بارد فصار له ورم في وجه وسخن وامرني بالدخول فدخلت معه لعند الباشا وهو في بيت ونايم في الفراش فجلست علي ركبه ونصف امامه وجسيت مفصله فرايته في غاية السخونه كانه في حمه عظيمه ووجهه مورم وحالته بالويل وهو بينفخ مثل الثور.

حينِ قلت الي حرمكايسي بان كان لازمني شوية دهن ورد فاجابني بان الان برسل رجل الي المدينه يجيب لنا من هذا الدهن فلما سمع الباشه باني بريد دهن ورد فامر الي حرمكايسي بانه يمضي الي عند الخزنادار وياخذ قنينة دهن ورد فرنجي الذي كان ارسله هن واحد حكيم فرنجي وهن اتنتين فيجيب واحده منهم.

فلما حضرة قنينة الدهن افتكرت في اني اضع معها اجزاء حتي يبين باني وضعت مع الدهن غيرشي فمضيت الي عند رفقاتي وتاشورت انا وحنا المذكور فاجابني ما في احسن من مرهم الجادبون لانه بيفش الورم وكان معي من ذلك المرهم فقطعت شقفه

"I am," I said.

"The steward of the pasha's harem would like to speak with you," one replied. "Come with us."

Heart pounding, I stood up and went with the two men. It seemed that when the pasha had become feverish, he'd left his camp and moved, along with his harem, into the house of the village chief. He had ordered the two men to go into the city and find a surgeon to bleed him.   11.83

"But sire, we have a very skilled Frankish doctor with us in the convoy," they replied.

"Bring him to me!" he said.

And that was how I ended up standing before the house where the pasha was staying. There was an old man at the door. It was the steward of the pasha's harem.

"Greetings," he said when I presented myself to him. "Please come in, and have a look at His Excellency the effendi, who is ill and feeling indisposed."

I told the steward I was sorry, but I didn't have my doctor's kit as I had sent it ahead to Aleppo by ship while I traveled by land to see the sights.   11.84

"Our pasha isn't really ill; he's just under the weather," the steward explained. "Yesterday evening, he went to take a bath at the hot springs. When he came outside, covered in sweat, he caught a draft. As a result, his face became swollen and he developed a fever."

The steward ushered me inside. I found the pasha in a room, asleep in bed. I crouched down beside him and felt his wrist. He was very hot, apparently in the throes of a high fever. He looked terrible: His face was swollen and he was snorting like a bull.

"I need a little rose oil," I said to the harem steward.   11.85

"I'll send someone to the city to bring some right away," he replied.

When the pasha heard my request for rose oil, he ordered the harem steward to go find the quartermaster and ask him for a vial of Frankish rose oil, which the pasha had received from a Frankish doctor.

"There are two vials in all," the pasha said. "Bring one."

Soon enough, the steward returned with the vial of oil, and I had the idea of   11.86
adding some other ingredients, just to make it seem like I'd done something to the oil. I went to find my companions and consulted with Ḥannā.

"The best thing for treating swelling is *jādhbūn* ointment," he assured me.[53]

منه ورجعت الي عند الباشا وقلت لذلك الاختيار اتيني بصحن نحاس ففرغت من ذلك الدهن وقته علي النار والقيت داخله تلك قطعت المرهم حتي دابت مليح. حينذٍ دكيت راس الباشا علي ركبتي وصرت ادهن خدوده ودقنه وتحت دقنه من ذلك الدهن.

٨٧،١١ واوصيت الاختيار بانه يجي لي منديلين فبعدما دهنته لجكته في منديل الواحد والاخر ربطت فيه جبينه ورفعت راسه علي المخده فالتفت اليّ الباشا وقلي بان راسه يوجعه بزياده فاجبته الان بعطيك شي بطيب راسك وكان معي حشيشه شكل اليانسون من مصر نافعه لوجع الراس وجربه في الحال انطلقت واتيت من تلك الحشيشه ووضعتها في كف الباشا وكلفته بانه يسفها وقلت لذلك الاختيار بان يجيبوا لحضرة الباشا فنجان قهوه فبعدما شرب القهوه واتوه بغليون تتن وفي خلوص غليون التتن استراح وجع راسه وانبسط. حينذٍ قبلت اتكه واوصيت الي حرمكايسي بان لا يطعموه شي ابداً حتي اجي اشرف عليه ومضيت الي عند رفقاتي وما فات مقدار ساعه والا ارسل واحد يدعيني فلما رحت لقا لي الاختيار.

٨٨،١١ وقلي بان الباشا طلب اكل وانت اوصيتيني بالا نطعمه شي كيف بتقول فاجبته حضره له شوربه وليمونه والان بدخل بشرف عليه وبعود اقلك انكان بتطعمه ام لا فدخلت وجسيت نمطه فرايت عنده سخونه الا انها اخف من قبل. حينذٍ قلت للباشا يا سيدي ما بقدر اسمح لك في الاكل ما دام عندك سخونه اصبر قليلاً الي حين ما تمضي السخونه. حينذٍ بتاكل شوربا لا غير فامتثل لكلامي وصبر بلا اكل وانا مضيت من عنده الي عند رفقاتي وكانوا هيوا لنا العشا فتعشينا وشربنا القهوه وكان فات المغرب فجاع الباشه وصار يطلب حتي ياكل فارسل فارس الاختيار واحضرني الي عنده وقلي بان الباشا ما عاد يصبر بيريد ياكل فدخلت الي عنده فرايته محصور لانهم تعوقوا عليه في احضار الاكل فبركت علي ركبي وجسيت نمطه فرايت فلت عنه السخونه.

I happened to have some, so I broke off a little piece and returned to the pasha. I ordered the harem steward to bring me a copper plate, emptied part of the vial of rose oil into it, and placed it over a flame. I dropped the piece of ointment in and let it melt entirely. Then, resting the pasha's head on my knee, I began to spread the salve all over his cheeks, chin, and neck.

"Warm up two muslin cloths for me," I ordered the old man, and after I fin- 11.87 ished anointing the pasha with the oil, I wrapped one around his head like a scarf and tied the other around his forehead. Then I propped his head up on a pillow. The pasha turned to me and complained that he had a terrible headache.

"Let me bring you something to relieve it," I said.

I happened to have in my possession a certain herb from Egypt, similar to anise, which was a tried and true remedy against headaches. I dashed off to get it, put it in the pasha's palm, and urged him to swallow it. Then I asked the old man to bring His Excellency the pasha a cup of coffee. He drank it down, and they brought him his pipe, which he smoked until his headache dissipated and he sat back, relaxed and happy. I kissed the skirt of the pasha's robe and instructed the harem steward not to feed him a single morsel until I came back to check on him. Then I went to find my companions. Barely an hour had passed when someone came to fetch me again. The harem steward was waiting for me when I arrived.

"The pasha wants to eat!" he said. "But you told me not to feed him any- 11.88 thing. What am I supposed to do?"

"Prepare some soup for him, with a lemon on the side," I instructed. "I'll go check on him now, and come back and tell you if you can feed him or not."

I went in to see the pasha and took his pulse. He still had a fever, but it had subsided somewhat.

"Sire, I can't permit you to eat anything as long as you still have a fever," I explained. "Wait a little longer, if you will, until it subsides completely. Then you may have some soup, but nothing else."

The pasha accepted my recommendation to refrain from eating, and I rejoined my companions. In the meantime, they had prepared dinner, so we dined together and drank some coffee. The sun had set by then, and the pasha was hungry and demanded some food. The old man summoned me again and told me that the pasha couldn't wait any longer, and felt he had to eat. I went in to see him, and found him irritated about the delay in bringing him some food. I knelt down before him and felt his pulse again. The fever was gone.

حينٍ قلت للاختيار بان يحضروا الشوربا والليمونة في الحال جابوا چنق صيني كبير ١١،٨٩
شوربة دجاج وصحن صيني فيه دجاجه . حينٍ وضعت من ما تلك الليمونه شي قليل
علي الشوربا وكلفته بانه ياكل من تلك الشوربا حتي ما فضل في الچنق شي وطلب
بان نفسخ له الدجاجه حتي ياكلها فقتله مهلًا يا سيدي بخاف عليك ليلا ترجع اليك
السخونه فامتثل لقولي لكن رايته مشتق كثير للاكل فقطعت جنح من الدجاجه وقدمت
له حتي ياكله لا غير فالتفت الي حرم كيخسي .

وقله اريت كيف حكمت الفرنج بيداروا المريض . المراد بعدما اكل ذلك الجنح ١١،٩٠
خسلوا اياديه وجابوله فنجان قهوه وبعده اتوه بغليون تتن فراء بانه استراح وزالت
عنه السخونه وهذا صار بعناية الله تعالي له المجد ما هو بمعرفتي لكن بالهام الله تعالي
وجوده الذي دبرني في هل مصيبه . اخيرًا نهضت وفكيت المناديل عن وجه الباشا
فرايت الورم خف وبقي منه شي قليل فرديت سخنت الدهون وادهنت خدوده وحلقه
وربطت المناديل كما كانوا اتيك وقبلت منه وطلبت منه اذن حتي امضي الي مكاني . حينٍ
قلي حضرة الباشا بتريد اني اسافر غدا فاجبته يا سيدي من باكر بجي بشرف عليك
وبقلك انكان بتسافر ام لا ومضيت من عنده الي محلي .

فلما صار وقت السلام ارسل دعاني الي عنده فمضيت ودخلت الي عند حرم ١١،٩١
كيخسي وسالته عن كيفيت١ الباشه فاجابني بان كيفيته مليحه ونام مليح . حينٍ امرني
بالدخول معه الي عند الباشا فلما دخلنا فرايته جالس بيشرب تتن وهو بصحة العافيه
وما بقا فيه شي البته . حينٍ سالني الباشا وقلي هل بتريد اني اسافر فاجبته يا سيدي
الامر امرك ولكن اذا سافرت اجعل قناقك قصير يكون لاني بخاف عليك من حرارة
الشمس ليلا يزيد عليك التحليل فقلي مليح قشعت وامر الي حرم كيخسي بان يرسل
علي الصروبچي باشي بان ينصب الصيوان بعيد عن هل مكان بساعتين وامر بان
يدقوا اول نفير وهي علامة السفر .

---

١ الأصل: كفيت.

"Bring the soup and lemon," I said to the old man.    11.89

Immediately, a large porcelain bowl of chicken soup appeared, along with a porcelain platter with a chicken. I squeezed a few drops of lemon into the soup and invited the pasha to eat. He finished the entire bowl, then asked for the chicken to be sliced so he could eat it.

"Easy there, my lord," I said. "We don't want the fever to return, now do we?"

The pasha consented, but I could see that he was still ravenous. So I cut off a wing from the chicken and presented it to him as a lone concession. He turned to his harem steward.

"See how these Frankish doctors take care of the sick?" he remarked.    11.90

After he finished eating the wing, they washed his hands and brought him a cup of coffee and his pipe. He declared that he was feeling better and that his fever had broken. This was all thanks to Divine Providence—may God be praised! It had nothing to do with my own knowledge but rather with the inspiration I received from God, who in His goodness guided me through this crisis.

I untied the muslin cloths enveloping the pasha's face and saw that the swelling had subsided, with only a little remaining. So I warmed up the ointments again and applied them to his cheeks and throat, and tied on the cloths as before. Then I kissed the skirt of his robe and asked his permission to take my leave.

"What do you say? Am I able to travel tomorrow?" the pasha asked.

"I'll come check on you early tomorrow morning, my lord, and will give you an answer then," I said, then left him and returned to my companions.

The next morning at dawn, I was summoned to the pasha. I went to see the    11.91
harem steward and asked him how the pasha was feeling.

"He's doing fine, and he slept well during the night," the steward replied, ushering me in to see the pasha, who was sitting up, smoking a pipe, and looking right as rain.

"Well, what do you think? Am I cleared to travel?" he asked.

"The choice is yours, my lord," I said. "However, if you do decide to travel today, let this leg be a short one. I wouldn't want the sun to dissolve your humors."

"Good idea," he replied, and ordered the harem steward to send word to the chief baggage officer to set up the next camp a two-hour journey from where we were. He also gave the order to sound the first bugle call, which was the signal for departure.

حينٍ تقدمت وبست اتك الباشا ومضيت الي عند رفقاتي وانا فرحان وبشرتهم
بان حضرة الباشا استراح وهو بغاية الصحه والعافيه فشكرنا الله جميعا وحملنا
اخراجنا علي الدواب وبقينا علي هيئة السفر الي ان دق ثالث نفير وركب الباشه وبدت
النوبه تدق وسرنا الي ان وصلنا الي حيث الصيوان منصوب وهو سفر ساعتين لا
غير فنزل الباشا ودخل الي صيوانه ونزلت العسكر في خيامهم ونزلت انا ورفقاتي
قرب من خيمة الخزنادار لاننا معلومين حضرة الباشا.

فما لحقت نزلت عن دبتي والا باش جوخدار الباشا قدم لعندي ودعاني وقلي
بان حضرة الباشا يدعوك فمضيت معه ودخلت الي الصيوان فرايت حرم كايخسي
باستنداري فدخلنا معًا امام حضرة الباشا فرايته متكي بين وسادتين فتقدمت وبست
اتكه واستقمت واقفًا فامرني بالجلوس حداه ومد لي يده فدسيت نمطه وهنيته
بصحة العافيه فقلي بريد تعطيني جزء من الذي وضعته في دهن الورد لاني رايت
هل دهون نفعني وفش عني الورم عاجلًا فاجبته سمعًا وطاعه ومضيت في الحال
وقطعت من ذلك المرهم قطعه كبيره واتيت بها لحضرة الباشه وهي داخل قزظار
نضيف فقبلت اتكه واعطيته هي فانبسط. اخيرًا طلبت منه اذن وخرجت من
الصيوان فما لحقت مشيت كام قدم والا واحد من الجوخداريه امرني بالرجوع الي
عند حرم كايخسي.

فلما امتثلت امامه فقلي حضرة افندينا امرلك بقناق وارسل واحضر القبجي امامه
وامره بان يكتب للحكيم باشي قناق وعليق دواب فسالني القبجي كام نفر انتم فاجبته باننا
ثلاثه ومن ذلك الوقت لما نصل الي قصبه او ضيعه يعطيني القبجي ورقه مختومه الي
شيخ الضيعه فينزلنا ذلك الشيخ في بيت واهل ذلك البيت يقفوا في اودنا ويقدموا لنا
عشا والي دوابنا عليق.

فبعد كام يوم وصلنا الي قرب مدينة افيون قري حصار التي هي منصبيت الباشا
عليها فنزل الباشا في مكان بعيد عن المدينه سفر يوم وبلغنا خبر بانه بيستقيم في

I stepped forward, kissed the skirt of the pasha's robe, and set off to see my  11.92
companions, to whom I excitedly brought the news that His Excellency had
made a full recovery. We all thanked God, loaded our baggage on our horses,
and prepared to travel as soon as the third bugle sounded. The pasha set off,
accompanied by the sounds of a marching band. We traveled for two hours,
and arrived at the next encampment. The pasha went into his large, sumptuous tent, and the soldiers entered theirs. My companions and I were given a
tent near the quartermaster's, as we were now recognized as part of His Excellency's coterie.

No sooner had I dismounted from my horse than the pasha's chief valet  11.93
approached.

"His Excellency the pasha summons you."

I followed the valet to the pasha's tent, where I found the harem steward
waiting for me and we entered. The pasha was reclining against a couple of
cushions. I came forward and kissed the skirt of his robe, then stood at attention. He invited me to sit beside him and held out his hand. I took his pulse and
congratulated him on his recovery.

"I'd like you to give me a little of whatever you put in that rose oil," he said.
"The salves you made me were very helpful; they eased the swelling right away."

"It would be my pleasure," I replied, and went to get what he'd requested,
bringing back a large piece nestled within a clean piece of paper. Then I kissed
his robe once again and presented it to him, to his delight. I asked his permission to leave, and left the tent. But before I'd taken a couple of steps, one of the
other valets called me back in to see the harem steward.

"His Excellency, our effendi, has ordered that you be provided with proper  11.94
lodgings," he said, and summoned the convoy captain.

"See to it that the pasha's chief physician is afforded lodgings and fodder for
his horses," he told him.

The convoy captain asked me how many people were traveling in my party.
I told him there were three of us. From that moment on, whenever we arrived
in a village, the convoy captain would hand me a document affixed with an
official seal to give the local shaykh. The shaykh would then arrange for us to
be lodged in a house whose owners would wait on us, prepare our dinner, and
provide fodder for our horses.

A few days later, we arrived in the vicinity of Afyonkarahisar, which fell  11.95
under the pasha's jurisdiction. The pasha set up camp in a spot that was a day's

ذلك المكان خمسة ستة ايام لاجل تحصيل المال من الفلاحين وصاحبين الاراضي التي هناك تحت حكمه واطلق القاطرجيه[1] الذين اتوا معه من اسكدار واعطاهم كري دوابهم واصرفهم فحضر لعندنا قاطرجيا ونهنا بالمسير الي مدينة المذكوره في هذا الليل فلما سمعت من القاطرجي هذا الكلام فودت امضي واخذ اذن من الباشا في السفر فمنعني رفيقي حنا المذكور بقوله لي انكان الباشا ما رادك تساؤ وقلك استقيم عندي وانت في حكمه ايش بتقدر ترد له جواب دعنا نمضي ونخلص من هل ورطه .

٩٦،١١ فاصتصوبت كلامه وغيرت نيتي عن المضي لعند الباشا حضرًا ليلا يصدني عن السفر . اخيرًا استقمنا هناك الي نصف الليل وسافرنا الي ثاني يوم حكم الدهر وصلنا للمدينه فلما دخلنا داخل المدينه ونحن سايرين صدف في ذلك الرجل الذي كت قطرت له في عينه الموجوعه في مدينة اسكي شهر فلما راني اعتنقي وصار يقبلني واسترحب في قوي كثير وكلفني باني انزل في بيته فابيت وقلته نحن ثلاثة انفار انما بطلب من فضلك ترينا مكان يكون مليح حتي انزل انا و رفقاتي وندعيلك .

٩٧،١١ فمضي معنا ودخلنا الي قيصريه ودعا الاوداباشي حتي يعطينا اوضه تكون مليحه عمار . حينذٍ صعدنا معه في درج وفتح لنا اوضه وارسل ذلك الرجل الذي اتا معنا وجاب لنا حصيره وسباط وفرشه من بيته واوصاني باننا لا نطبخ عشا ومضي وعند المساء جابوا لنا صينيت عشاء وهو جاب معه فراغ عرق وفراغ انبيد وجلس تعشا معنا الي صار هدوي من الليل وهو يقلي ما بقدر اكافيك علي الجميل الذي صنعته معي وهو شفا عيني التي كانت تلفت وما عدت انضر فيها شي فاجبته اشكر الله يا اخي هذا صنيع ربنا معك وهو الذي اشفا عينك لاني ما كت اصدق بان عينك بتشفا من هل قطره .

٩٨،١١ اخيرًا استكثر بخيري ومضا الي بيته ونحن استقمنا تلك الليله في غاية الانشراح الي ان اصبح الصباح وشرقة الشمس كما فطرنا وشربنا قهوه وجلسنا نتصامر والا اتانا شاب مسيحي بهي المنضر والقامه وطلب مني باني اروح معه الي[2] بيته

---

١ الأصل: القاطريه. ٢ «الي» لم ترد في الأصل.

journey from the city, and we learned that he intended to remain there five or six days to collect money from the peasants and the landowners subject to his authority. The pasha paid the muleteers who had traveled with him from Üsküdar, and discharged them.

Our own muleteer then appeared, giving us notice that we would be leaving for Afyonkarahisar that very night. Upon receiving this news, I decided to ask the pasha's permission to depart. But my companion, Ḥannā, dissuaded me.

"What if the pasha doesn't want you to go?" he said. "You're under his authority now, so if he tells you to stay here, what are you supposed to say? Let's just leave now, before we get stuck here."

I saw the wisdom of his words and decided not to go to the pasha, fearing that he might prevent me from traveling. We waited until midnight and set off, traveling until we arrived in Afyonkarahisar at noon the next day. As we entered the city, I happened to bump into the fellow whom I'd treated for eye pain in Eskişehir. When he saw me, he showered me with embraces and kisses, welcoming me with great affection, and invited me to stay at his house! 11.96

"I'm sorry, I can't, as there are three of us," I said. "Instead, could you perhaps recommend a good place for us to stay, and we'll invite you over?"

The man took us to a caravansary, and told its proprietor to give us a good room. We went upstairs with him, where he opened a room for us, and the man who'd taken us to the caravansary had some furnishings brought over from his own house: a straw mat, a carpet, and a mattress. Making us promise not to prepare any dinner, he went on his way. When evening came, our dinner was delivered to us on a platter, and was followed by the man himself, who strode in with jug of arak and a jug of wine too. He sat down and we dined together as night fell. 11.97

"I'll never be able to repay the great favor you did me," he said. "You cured my eye of that squint, when I couldn't see anything out of it!"

"Don't thank me, brother, thank God—curing your eye was His work," I said. "In fact, I didn't think the medicine would work."

The man returned home after thanking me profusely, and we spent a most comfortable night at the caravansary, not waking up until the sun rose the next morning. After breakfast and coffee, we were sitting and chatting when a young man appeared. He was a Christian lad, a tall, strapping fellow. He asked me to visit his house to examine someone's eyes. 11.98

حتي اشرف علي عينين واحد فاجبته لا يا اخي انا ما بروح الي عند احد جيب ذلك الانسان الي عندي حتي اشرف علي عينه وكان السبب في هذا الشاب لما سمع من ذلك الرجل باني طيبت عينه بعدما كانت تلفت وهو الذي دله علَيّ. اخيراً صار يتوسل اليّ باني اروح معه الي بيته فابيت وما اردت امضي معه فلما عجز وقطع الامض في رواحي معه فاخدني علي جنب وقلي بان الشخص الذي احكيت لك عنه هو حرمتي وهي عروسة سنه ما يمكن انها تدخل الي قيصريه وارتمي علي ايديي ويقلي كرامة الله امضي معي ليش بتخاف نحن ناس مسيحيه.

فلما سمعت منه هل كلام التزمت باني اروح معه وكان رفيقي حنا المذكور ما بريدني ان اروح ليلا يطلع في البلد صيت حكيم ما بعود اقدر اخلص خصوصاً من الحكام لان في تلك البلاد الحكيم ما له ذكر ولاجل هذا السبب ما بريدني ارجع. اخيراً اخدت معي جنبور القطره ومضيت معه الي بيته ولما دخلنا في الحال وضع امامي مايده وكلفني اتعدا معه فبعدما اكلنا وشربنا¹ القهوه حيندٍ احضروا الصبيه وهي جميلة الحسن فتفرست في اعينها فرايتهم صحيحين النضر وما بان عليهم شي البته.

فسالت رجلها من ايش بتشكوا من نضرها وانا علي ما يلوح لي بان نضرها ما فيه كسور فاجابني الشاب بانها ما بتنضر فيها شي. حيندٍ سالتها كيف انها بتنضر الدنيا فقالت بانها بتنضرها سوده وما بتفسر الابيض من الاسود ولا الرجل من الامراه فتيقنت بان دخل بوبو اعينها ماء وهذا عديم الشفا علي راي ايمت الحكماء. حيندٍ حزنت عليها ولكن لاجل تسليت رجلها قطرت في اعينها من تلك القطره واعطيت الي رجلها جزء من تلك القطره حتي يبقي يقطر لها فيما بعد وودعتهم ومضيت الي عند رفقاتي وانا حزين علي تلك الصبيه.

فرايت عندهم ناس في استنداري منهم مرضا ومنهم في وجع اعينهم ومنهم بريدوا ياخدوني الي بيوت حتي اشرف علي مرضاهم فحرت في امري كيف اعمل

٩٩،١١

١٠٠،١١

١٠١،١١

---

١ الأصل: وشربا.

"Sorry, brother, I'm not going to anyone's house," I said. "Bring this person to me, and I'll examine his eye here."

The young man had, it seemed, heard about me from the squint-eyed fellow I'd cured, who'd sent him my way. Even after he begged me, I continued to refuse to go with him. The man became despondent, and took me aside.

"The person I told you about is my wife!" he confided. "She's a young bride—we've only been married for a year, and she can't very well enter a caravansary."

The young man pressed his face to my hands.

"For the love of God, please come with me! What are you afraid of? We're Christians!"

At this, I felt compelled to go with him, though my friend Ḥannā didn't like    11.99
it one bit. What if the news got out that there was a doctor in town? If that happened, I'd never escape, especially if the authorities found out. There were no doctors in these parts, Ḥannā reminded me, which was why he didn't want me to go with the young man.

In the end, though, I took my little flask of ointment and went to the man's house. As soon as we arrived, he led me to the dining table and invited me to have lunch with him. After we ate and had our coffee, they brought the young woman before me. She was a beauty. I peered into her eyes, and they seemed to be perfectly fine, with no indication otherwise.

"What's the problem exactly?" I asked the young man. "As far as I can tell,    11.100
her vision is fine."

"She can't see anything," he replied.

I turned to the young woman and asked her what she was able to make out of the world around her.

"I see blackness," she replied. "I can't tell the difference between black and white, or a man and a woman."

That was when I realized she had cataracts, a condition that was untreatable according to just about every doctor. I felt sorry for her, and even though I knew it would do no good, I put some drops in her eye, as a way of comforting her husband, and gave him some of the medicine to administer later. I bid them farewell, feeling terrible for the young woman, and returned to my companions.

When I arrived, a group of people was waiting for me. There were sick    11.101
people, some experiencing eye pain themselves, and others who wanted to

فصرت اقطر الي بعضهم والمرضي اوصف لهم وصفات وما شاكل ذلك واصرفهم فشاع الخبر في المدينه بان في قيصريت الفلانيه موجود حكم فرنجي قوي معلم فصارت الناس تجي وتروح وانا افضهم بالممكن.

١١،١٠٢ الي ثالث يوم من وصولي الي هناك فما رايت الا اجا الاوضا باشي ومعه اتنين من جوخدريت متسلم البلد ودعوني الي عند المتسلم وكان السبب هو ان قبجي فايت ومعه اربعين سرج وهو مرسل من قبل وزير الاعظم وفي تسليمه شاب وهو ابن اخت ناصيف باشه الذي كان وقتيدٍ باشة الحج وله صيت عظيم في الدوله لان كان جملة سنين ياخد الحجيج ويجيبهم سالمين الي الشام وكان طيع العرب وفتح الدرب ولاجل هذا صار له نام وصيت عظيم.

١١،١٠٣ فاتفق انه غضب علي ابن اخته المذكور وراد يقتله لاجل انه اختلس من ماله الذي كان موكله عليه من معبور البلاد الذي كان متروس عليها فهذا لما بلغه الخبر بان خاله امر بقتله فهرب ليلا واختفى ثم بعد ذلك سافر خفية الي اسطنبول والتجي عند الوزير واحكاله قضيته فحن عليه الوزير ولجاه ومن بعد حين سمع خاله بانه ملتجي في الدوله فغنت عليه كيف انه فلت من يده.

١١،١٠٤ فلاجل هذه النكايه مسك خزنه مصر سنتين وارسل يقول للوزير ما برسل الخزاين حتي ترسلي ابن اختي لان لي معه حساب فالتزم الوزير يرسل له ابن اخته صحبة قبجي باشي بانه يواجهه مع خاله ويرجعه معه الي اسطنبول سالم وحدد عليه هل قدر ايام في مده سفره من غير تعويق بموجب خط شريف من يد الملك فهذا الشب من فزعه ليلا في وصوله لعند خاله يقتله لانه ما كان يستهاب من الوزير ولا من الدوله فزاد عليه الوهم والرعب فمرض في الطريق وما عاد يمكنه انه يركب

take me home to examine their invalids. What was I supposed to do? I had no idea! I began going around, putting drops in some people's eyes and prescribing remedies to others, before sending them away. Soon, word got around town that there was a very skilled Frankish doctor staying at a certain caravansary. People came in droves, flowing in and out of the place as I struggled to stave them off as best I could.

Three days after our arrival, the proprietor of the caravansary suddenly 11.102 appeared in the company of two officials who served the local governor. They invited me to come with them to see the governor, for the following reason: It seemed that an imperial chamberlain was passing through town, at the head of a company of forty cavalrymen. He'd been sent by the grand vizier to deliver a certain young man to his maternal uncle, Nāṣīf Pasha, the pasha of the hajj pilgrimage. Nāṣīf Pasha was a famous and powerful man in the empire at that time. For years, he'd led the pilgrimage to Mecca and brought it back safely to Damascus. He'd brought the Bedouins to heel and kept the roads open. On account of this achievement, he'd acquired a great deal of power and fame.

Now, Nāṣīf Pasha had become enraged with his nephew—his sister's son— 11.103 and vowed to kill him. It seemed that the nephew had embezzled some funds that he was responsible for collecting from the territories under his uncle's jurisdiction. When he learned that his uncle wanted him dead, the nephew fled in the middle of the night and vanished. He traveled in secret all the way to Istanbul and sought the protection of the vizier, to whom he explained his predicament. The vizier felt sorry for him and took him in, but Nāṣīf Pasha soon learned that his nephew had found refuge at the palace, and was furious that he'd managed to escape.

Out of revenge for this injustice, the pasha seized the treasury of Egypt for 11.104 two years. He sent word to the vizier that no monies would flow to Istanbul until the nephew was released to him, as he had a score to settle. The vizier was compelled to send the nephew in the company of a chief chamberlain, who was given instructions to let the young man meet with his uncle and then to bring him back safe and sound to Istanbul. He was also told to complete the journey without delay, spending no more than a specific number of days, on the authority of an edict signed by the king himself.

The young man was terrified that he'd be put to death as soon as he arrived. He knew his uncle wouldn't be intimidated by the vizier, or even the sultanate itself. As they traveled, his anxieties grew so severe that he became sick with

نخار فيه القبجي وارسل واحد من طرفه الي عند حاكم افيون قري حصار يطلب منه بانه يرسله جراح حتي يفصد المريض الذي معه.

١١،١٠٥ فلما وصل البصطنجي المرسل دخل لعند المتسلم وطلب منه بان يرسل معه جراح واحكاه في قضيت ذلك الشاب. حينذٍ امر المتسلم بانهم يحضروا واحد من الجراحاتيه يكون معلم وبالصدفه التقا عنده في ذلك المحل امام الباشا الذي كان سبق ودخل للمدينه ونزل في صرايه الباشا في منزوله المعين له فهذا في ذلك الوقت قال للمتسلم بان اجا معنا من اسطنبول حكيم فرنجي معلم وهو الذي حكم الباشا لما مرض في الطريق وطيبه فلما سمع البصطنجي قال للمتسلم انا بروح بطلبه من حضرة الباشا فناس من جماعة المتسلم الذين كانوا وقوف هناك قالوا للمتسلم بان حكيم الفرنجي الذي اجا مع حضرة الباشا هو هاهنا نازل في فلان قيصريه فامرهم المتسلم بانهم يمضوا ويحضروه امامه.

١١،١٠٦ وهذا كان سبب مجي هل اتنين لعندي وامروني بالمضي معهم الي عند حضرة المتسلم فلما سمعت منهم هذا الكلام ارتعبت قوي كثير وضنيت بان الباشا طلبني وما راني ارسل امر المتسلم في مسكي لاني مضيت بغير اذنه. حينذٍ نهضت ومضيت معهم وانا في بحر من الافكار وكثر علي الوهم والرعب ليلا يكون امره بانه يضربني عصي او يلقيني في الجنزير وما يشبه ذلك من الافكار السوداويه.

١١،١٠٧ فلما وصلنا الي الصرايا وانا مقطوع الضهر وغايب عن صوابي فامتثلت امام المتسلم فرايت حداه امام الباشا ومن ذلك الجانب جالس رجل بسطنجي. حينذٍ سال المتسلم[١] للامام هل هذا هو الحكيم فاجابه نعم فالتفت اليّ المتسلم وقلي بان قبجي باشي فايت قريب من البلد ومعه رجل عزيز مرض في الطريق وارسل هل بسطنجي لعندنا يطلب حكيم فالتفيت انت بامرك تروح معه حتي تشرف علي هذا المريض.

---

١ الأصل: المسلم.

fright and could no longer ride. Faced with this predicament, the chamberlain was uncertain what to do. He dispatched one of his men to visit the governor of Afyonkarahisar, asking him to send a surgeon to bleed the invalid.

The imperial guard arrived and explained the situation to the governor, who immediately called for a skilled surgeon to be dispatched to treat the young man. Now, by sheer coincidence, the imam of the pasha with whom we'd traveled to Afyonkarahisar happened to have come to town and was staying in his quarters in the pasha's palace. When this fellow heard about the governor's order, he weighed in. 11.105

"There was a Frankish doctor who traveled with us from Istanbul," he said. "He was the one who treated the pasha when he fell ill en route, and brought him back to health."

"I'll ask His Excellency the pasha if we might make use of him," the imperial guard replied.

At that moment, some people in the governor's coterie who were present informed the governor that the Frankish doctor who accompanied the pasha happened to be staying at a certain caravansary. Upon learning this, the governor ordered them to bring him in.

This, then, was the reason for the appearance of those two individuals, who ordered me to come with them to see His Excellency the governor. I was stricken with terror upon hearing these words, for I assumed that the pasha must have ordered the governor to arrest me when he found that I'd taken off without his permission. I got up from my seat and went with the two men, overcome with terror and fright. My thoughts turned darkly morose and my fear mounted as I imagined being flogged with a cane or shackled in irons. 11.106

By the time we arrived at the palace, I was scared out of my wits. I presented myself before the governor and noticed that the pasha's imam was standing beside him, just as I feared. On the other side of the governor sat an imperial guard. 11.107

"Is this the doctor?" the governor asked the imam.

"Yes."

"The chief chamberlain is going to be passing close to town," the governor said as he turned to address me. "There's someone important traveling with him, and he's ill. They've sent this imperial guard to us to ask for a doctor. Since you're here anyway, would you be so kind as to go examine the sick man?"

فلما سمعت منه هل كلام رجعت روحي اليّ لاني كنت مضيع الحواس. حيندٍ ١٠٨،١١
استعدرت من حضرة المتسلم بقولي له بان ما معي سندوق الحكمه حتي احكمه ايش
هي الفايده في رواحي وهو في البريه مكان ما بينوجد شي لاجل حكمته وعلاجه فعاد
قلي المتسلم انته روح لاجل خاطر القبجي واعمل ممكنك وهذا بينوبك من خير وصار
ايضاً البسطنجي يتملقني ويوعدني بالعطا الزايد فاجتهم ما يمكنني الرواح. حيندٍ التفت
امام الباشا وقال للمتسلم بانه لا يلزمني بالمضي لان حضرة الباشا له نضر عليه.

حيندٍ امر المتسلم بان يحضروا جريحاتي وارسله مع ذلك البسطنجي واطلقني فرجعت ١٠٩،١١
الي عند رفقاي وانا فرحان كيف اني خلصت من هل ورطه واحكيت لهم بالمجراويه
كيف تمت. حيندٍ راح رفيقي حنا المذكور الي عند القاطرجي وقله انكان انت ما
بتسافر حتي نستكري من غير ناس فاجابه بان في قفل مهيا الي قونيه وانا كريت دوابي
وبعد غدي من كل بد منسافر حضروا شغلكم فاستقمنا تلك اليومين ونحن خايفين
ليلا الباشا يطلبني فبعد تلك اليومين سافر القفل ونحن صحبته الي ان وصلنا بقرب
مدينة قونيه.

ونحن سايرين في الطريق راينا قبجي باربعين سرج فايت من بعد فانفرق منه واحد ١١٠،١١
واجا الي القفل وسال عن كروان باشي من هو فدلوه علي قاطرجينا فلما وصل لعنده
قله من قبل القبجي بان الحكيم الفرنجي الذي مع القفل هو يطلبه منك في قونيه وقله
بالك ثم بالك تخليه يضيع عن نظرك لانه ان غاب بيصير لك مضره عظيمه من حضرة
القبجي فاجابه القاطرجي سمعاً وطاعه.

فمضي ذلك البسطنجي الي عند اغته ودخلوا للمدينه قبلنا لانهم راكبين كدش منزل ١١١،١١
وكان السبب هوان البسطنجي الذي اجا عند المتسلم وطلب جراح فراني وكلمني هناك
فلما مرمن علينا القبجي فعرفني ذلك البسطنجي واحكي للقبجي عني بان هذا الذي ما راد

At these words, I felt my spirit and senses come back to life, and I quickly 11.108 apologized to His Excellency the governor, explaining that I didn't have my doctor's kit with me.

"What good would it do for me to go out and see him in the middle of nowhere, a place without any of the things I'd need to treat him?"

"Go as a matter of respect for the chamberlain," the governor urged me. "Do whatever you can, under the circumstances, and there will be something in it for you."

The imperial guard also tried to talk me into it, promising I'd make a pretty penny, but I dug in my heels. That was when the pasha's imam turned to the governor and told him not to force me, since I was under the protection of the pasha.

So the governor had a surgeon summoned to be dispatched with the impe- 11.109 rial guard, and allowed me to depart. I returned to my companions, feeling overjoyed that I'd somehow managed to get out of that jam, and told them the whole story. My friend Ḥannā went to tell our muleteer that if he wasn't planning to travel soon, we'd be finding someone else to take us.

"There's a caravan ready to depart for Konya, and every one of my beasts has a rider, so we can go," the muleteer replied. "We'll be setting off the day after tomorrow, without fail. Get your affairs in order."

We bided our time anxiously over the next two days, fearing that the pasha would summon me. But they passed without incident, and we left with the caravan as planned, arriving in due course near the city of Konya.

While we were on the road, we happened to see the chamberlain pass by us 11.110 with his forty cavalrymen. One of their company peeled off and galloped over to our caravan.

"Who's the caravan chief here?" he asked when he rode up, and was directed to our muleteer.

"The chamberlain asks that once you arrive in Konya you send him the Frankish doctor who is traveling with you," he said. "Don't let him out of your sight, no matter what! If he disappears, you'll have to answer to His Excellency."

"It's as good as done, sire," the muleteer replied.

The guard then set off to see his master. They entered the city before us, as 11.111 they were riding postal horses. The reason for all of this was that the guard who had gone to the governor to request a surgeon had seen me at the palace, and had in fact spoken to me there. When the chamberlain's party passed us, the

يجي معي. حيندٍ امره القبجي بان ينبه علي الكروان باشي بانه يدير باله ليلا اغيب عن نضره الي محل ما يطلبني فلما احكالي القاطرجي هذا الكلام اخذني الرعب ايضاً كيف اني ما بخلص من واحده بقع في الاخره فاتكلت علي الله وسلمت الامور لله تعالي.

١١٢،١١ فسرنا في الطريق الي ان وصلنا الي مدينة قونيه فامرني القاطرجي باني امضي معه حيث بينزل لانه هكذا وقلي لاني انا مامور من حضرة القبجي فدخلنا معه الي اخور حيث ربط دوابه فما لحقنا وصلنا والا جاني شاويش من قبل حاكم البلد ومعه واحد بصطنجي من جماعة القبجي وامروني بالمضي معهم الي عند حضرة القبجي فسرت معهم الي ان وصلنا الي قناق القبجي فاصعدوني في درج ودخلوني امام القبجي.

١١٣،١١ فلما امتثلت امامه فنضر الي بعين الغدر وقلي لماذا ما ردت تجي مع تابعي من افيون قري حصار. وقتيدٍ ارتميت وقبلت اتكه وقلتله العفو يا سيدي ان الذي منعني عن اني اتشرف بحضرتكم هوان ما معي سندوق الحكمه وبغيره ما بقدر احكم احد وهذا كان السبب وعزيز حياتك. حيندٍ روق وامرني بالجلوس واسقوني فنجان قهوه وبعده صار يحكيلي قضيت المريض الذي هو معه مثل ما مر الكلام سابقاً. حيندٍ قلي بملاطفت الكلام وحرضني باني انزل لعند المريض وعالجه وابدل كل جهدي باني اطيبه عاجلاً لان ايامه معدوده عليّ من السلطنه فاجبته علي الله يا سيدي.

١١٤،١١ حيندٍ امر واحد من خدامه بانه يمضي معي الي عند المريض فلما دخلت وجدت هذا الشب المريض ملقي علي الفراش وهو بينفخ مثل التنين فلما تفرست فيه رايته وهو في حمه محرقه وسخونه عظيمه كانه ملقي في اتون نار نخرت في امري كيف اني بقدر اعالج هل محموم وفي ذلك الوقت الله تعالي له المجد الهمني في اشيا ما هي في بالي

guard recognized me and told the chamberlain I was the one who had refused to return with him. That was when the chamberlain ordered him to warn the caravan chief to keep his eye on me and prevent me from disappearing till they summoned me. When our muleteer told me all this, I was seized with fright again. It seemed I'd fallen out of the frying pan and into the fire! All I could do was put my trust in God and my fate in His hands.

We arrived in Konya, and the muleteer demanded that I accompany him to the place where he would be staying. 11.112

"That's how it has to be," he said. "I'm under strict orders from His Excellency the chamberlain."

We went into a stable with him, where he tied up his beasts. No sooner had we arrived than a constable appeared, representing the city's governor. One of the chamberlain's imperial guards was with him, and they ordered me to come with them to see His Excellency the chamberlain. We went to the chamberlain's lodgings, and I was escorted up some stairs and brought before the man himself.

"Why didn't you want to come with my attendant when you were in Afyonkarahisar?" he asked, regarding me with a baleful eye. 11.113

"Please forgive me, my lord!" I cried, throwing myself before the chamberlain and kissing the skirt of his robes. "It would surely have been a great honor to oblige Your Excellency's wishes, but I was unable to do so for lack of a doctor's kit! Without it, I'm unable to treat anyone. This was the reason for my response, I swear it!"

Hearing this, the chamberlain's temper eased, and he invited me to sit down. After I was served some coffee, he told me the tale of the sick young man who was with him, as recounted earlier. He said a few things to butter me up then urged me to examine the patient and treat him, and do all I could to help him recover swiftly.

"I've been granted only so many days by the sultanate to deliver him," he explained.

"I'll go if you insist, God help me!" I replied, consenting to his request.

The chamberlain ordered one of his servants to take me to the sick young man, whom I found lying on a mattress, huffing and puffing like a dragon. When I examined him, I found he had a burning fever, as hot to the touch as though he'd been thrown into a furnace. I was at a loss. How was I supposed to treat a man in his condition? Then, quite out of the blue, Almighty God—His 11.114

فطلبت من خادمه المؤتمن عليه بان يحضر لي حجر بازهر وما الورد فاجابني ما له وجود عندي واخرج اعطاني كيسملان من المعامله وقلي امضي واشتري من المدينه الذي تريده بـ.

١١٥،١١ فما قبلت اخد الكيس عنه بل قلتله اعطيه الي واحد من جماعتك يمضي معي الي السوق حتي اشتري الذي يعوزنا. حينذٍ ارسل معي اثنين من جماعته جوخداريه فمضينا الي السوق فصرت اسال لاهل السوق علي حجر بازهر فما انوجد عند احد. حينذٍ افتكرت ماذا اسقيه عوض البازهر فاشتريت جمله من البزورات وطمرهندي واجاس وما الورد ورجعت راجعاً الي القناق[١] وقبل ما اخرج من السوق فتقدم الي واحد رجل من اولاد البلد وقلي بتريد حجر بازهر قلتله نعم فقلي في موجود عند واحد ولكن لاجل الذين[٢] معك ما بيريد يظهره خوفاً ليلا ياخدوه ناقص من ثمنه.

١١٦،١١ فلما سمعت منه هل كلام اعطيت البزورات[٣] الي واحد منهم وامرته بانه يمضي الي القناق ويدقوا البزورات وينقعوا الثمرهندي والاجاس والاخر الذي معه كيس الخرجيه امرته بانه يقف من بعد يستناني فمضوا الاثنين كما امرتهم والتفيت الي ذلك الرجل وقلتله يدلني اين يوجد هذا الحجر فاجابني امشي معي فتبعته.

١١٧،١١ حينذٍ دلني علي رجل اختيار جالس في دكانه وقلي هذا الرجل موجود عنده مطلوبك ومضي فتقدمة الي عند ذلك الاختيار وطلبت منه حجر المذكور فقلي عندي لكن بتشتريه بثمنه اجابته نعم حينذٍ فتح سندوق واخرج منه علبه داخلها خمسة حجار فنقيت احسنهم وهي حجر زيتونيه فطلب في حقها خمسة عشر غرش والنتيجه فصّلتها منه باثني عشر غرش ومضيت الي ذلك الجوخدار وامرته بان يعد له المبلغ.

١١٨،١١ واخدنا الحجر ومضينا الي القناق في الحال حكيت من ذلك الحجر فنجان كبير واسقيته الي المريض وبعده استحلبت من تلك البزورات شاهكاسه واسقيته هي ووضعت

---

١ الأصل: القنان.   ٢ الأصل: اللذين.   ٣ الأصل: البزوات.

name be praised!—inspired me with an idea I wouldn't otherwise have had. I turned to the servant assigned to attend the young man and asked him to bring me a bezoar stone and some rosewater.[54]

"I don't have any," he replied, taking out a pouch full of coins. "Go into town and buy whatever you need."

I wouldn't accept the pouch and told him instead to give it to one of his 11.115 men, who should then accompany me to the souk to buy what we needed. He chose two footmen to accompany me, and we went to the souk. I asked the shopkeepers for bezoar stones, but nobody had any. What could I give the young man to drink instead of bezoar stones? I bought a bunch of seeds, tamarind, pears, and rosewater, then headed back to the chamberlain's lodgings. As I was leaving the souk, a local man approached me.

"Are you looking for bezoar stones?"

"Yes."

"I know someone who's got them," he said. "But he won't put them out for sale because he's afraid that the people you're with won't pay a fair price."

When I heard this, I handed the seeds to one of the footmen and ordered 11.116 him to return to the chamberlain's lodgings and have the seeds pounded, while the tamarind and pears were to be macerated to soften them. Meanwhile, I told the footman who was carrying the pouch of money to stand at a distance and wait for me. The two did as I asked, and I turned to the man from the souk, asking him to lead me to the bezoar stones.

"Come with me," he said.

He took me to see an old man sitting in a shop.                                      11.117

"This is the fellow who has what you want," he said, and left.

I approached the old man and asked if he had any bezoar stones.

"I do. Will you pay a fair price?"

"Yes."

He opened a case and took out a box with five stones in it. I selected the finest among them, an olive-colored one. He demanded fifteen piasters for it, and I managed to bargain him down to twelve. Then I went to find the footman and ordered him to pay the man.

The stone in hand, we headed back to the chamberlain's lodging, where 11.118 I immediately grated it into a large cup and gave it to the sick young man to drink. Then I squeezed the juice from the seeds into another large cup and gave him that to drink as well. I mixed some vinegar and rosewater in a vase

خل وما الورد في انا وامرتهم بانهم يدهنوا اطرافه بذلك الخل والما ورد وبعده نقعت من الثمرهندي والاجاس المارداني وصرت وقت اسقيه من البزورات ووقت اخر اسقيه من الماء طمرهندي ووقت اسقيه من الحجرالبازهر ولا زلت اسقيه من هذه الامياه الي حين المساء فإنته استراح وفكت عنه السخونه وفتح عينه وجلس مستوي في فراشه. حينذٍ طلب غليون تتن وفنجان قهوه فسالته عن كيفيته.

فقلي الشكرلله برا حالي اني استرحت. حينذٍ ودعته واوصيت خدامه بانهم لا يطعموه شي البته غير تلك المیات وخرجت من عنده حتي اروح الي عند رفقاتي وقبل خروجي من باب المنزول والا واحد من جماعة القبجي امرني بالرجوع الي عند القبجي فرجعت معه وصعدت في ذلك الدرج ودخلت الي عند القبجي فسالني عن حال المريض فاجبته الحمدلله استراح قوي انبسط ذلك الوقت وقلي يمكن نهارغدي نسافر اجبته باكر برد عليك الجواب انكان استقام علي ما هوالان يمكنك تسافر فيه. حينذٍ طلبت منه اذن حتي امضي الي منزولي فما رضي وامرني بالجلوس وامر بان يجيبوا لي قهوه وغليون تتن.

فبعدما شربت القهوه فصار يسالني من اي بلاد انت اجبته انا من بلاد حلب وابي حكيم في حلب واسمه بيداو فلما مات ابي وكنت ولد زغير فارسلوني الي عند عمي الذي هو في مدينة مرسيليا في بلاد الفرنساويه فلما تعلمت الحكمه هناك طلبت الرجوع الي بلادي فجيت في مركب الي مينة ازمير ومن هناك قصدت الفرجه علي مدينة اسطنبول ومن هناك رت اسافر في البر الي حلب لاجل الفرجه وسندوق الحكمه ارسلته في البحر الي حلب والان انا ماضي الي بلادي حلب.

فاجاب وقلي انا كنت كمركي في حلب وكان لي اصحاب من تجار الفرنساويه وهن خواجه سيرون وخواجه بازان وبنفاي وروس وسيمون واخص اصحابي كان واحد يسمي خواجه رنباو وكان يلقش تركي وكنت كثير اوقات ازوره واشرب من عنده عنبريه وكان عنده مخزنجي اسمه انطون كان يجبلي العنبريه فلما سمعت منه

and told the attendants to daub his extremities with it, while I macerated some more tamarind and Mardin pears. I alternated between giving the young man the juice of those seeds to drink, and the water from the tamarind and bezoar stones, and did not stop until the evening. Finally, the fever broke and the young man recovered. He opened his eyes and sat up in bed. He requested his pipe and a cup of coffee, and I asked him how he was feeling.

"I'm feeling better, thank goodness," he replied, and I bid him farewell and  11.119 instructed his attendants not to let him consume anything besides the fluids I'd prepared. As I headed out to rejoin my companions, one of the chamberlain's men met me at the door and ordered me to come and see his master. I accompanied him to the chamberlain's residence, and went upstairs to find him waiting for news of the invalid.

"He has recovered, thank goodness," I informed the chamberlain, to his great pleasure.

"Can we travel tomorrow?"

"I'll let you know tomorrow morning," I said. "If he remains in the condition he's in now, then you can travel."

I then asked permission to return to my house, but he refused, invited me to sit down, and ordered his servants to bring me some coffee and a pipe of tobacco.

"Where are you from?" he asked, after I'd had some coffee.  11.120

"I'm from Aleppo," I said. "My father was a doctor named Bidaut; he died when I was a young boy. I was sent to the land of the French to stay with my uncle in the city of Marseille. After studying medicine I wanted to return to my homeland, so I boarded a ship to Izmir, and continued on to Istanbul. From there, I decided to travel by land to Aleppo so as to take in the sights, and had my doctor's chest forwarded to Aleppo by sea. I'm on my way back to Aleppo as we speak."

"I used to be a customs officer in Aleppo!" the chamberlain said. "Many  11.121 of the French merchants were friends of mine. Let's see, there was *khawājah* Sauron, *khawājah* Bazan, Bonifay, Rousseau, and Simon. My best friend of all was a fellow named *khawājah* Rimbaud, who used to speak Turkish. I used to visit him often, and sample some of his flavored liqueur. As I recall, he had a warehouseman named Anṭūn who'd fetch it for me."

At this, my blood ran cold. For I thought he'd recognized me and seen through my lie, as *khawājah* Rimbaud had been my master and that of my

هل كلام تغيرت الوافي وضنيت انه عرفني وتباين له باني كتاب لان خواجه رنباو
المذكور هو معلمي ومعلم اخي انطون وانا الذي كنت احد له العنبريه واقف في
خدمته وفي البين تغيرت عليه وما عرفني لاني في ذلك الوقت كنت ابن اثني
عشر سنه ونيف وشكرت الله تعالي الذي ما عرفني. اخيراً طلبت منه اذن حتي
امضي الي قناقي.

١٢٢،١١ فقلي امضي ولكن اغبش في قيامك وتعال الي هاهنا حتي تشرف علي هذا المريض
حتي نسافر من كل بد فقلت له علي الراس ثم العين ومضيت من عنده الي عند ارفاقي
وكانوا في استداري وبقي بالهم عندي ثم احكيت لهم بجميع الذي جري من الاول
الي المنتهي وشكرنا جميعنا الله تعالي علي اعتناه فينا وبعده رقدنا بسلام.

١٢٣،١١ الي ان مضي من الليل نصفه او اكثر فاجاني اثنين جوخداريت المريض ونبهوني
وهن ملهوفين وقالولي اعجل في المضي لان الشاب قارب الموت فخرجت من حجرتي
ومضيت معهم وانا مضيع الحواس وصرت اسالهم والج عليهم بان يقولوا لي ما هو
السبب حتي رجعت الجه اليه فما امكن يجيبوني بالصحيح انما واحد منهم اقترب اليّ
وقال لي سرّاً بان الاغا بعد خروجك من عنده امر بان يجيبوله ثلج واكل منه مقدار
اقه والذي فضل منه وضعه علي سدره وفوق معنته فصار عندي معلوم اصل
اندكازه وبقي في يدي عدر كافي لتخليص ذاتي من القبجي.

١٢٤،١١ فلما انتهينا الي ذلك المنزول دخلت الي عند المريض فرايته في حاله يرثي اليها
وعادة اليه الجه الطاق تبين عن الاول وهو في حال التلف. حينئذ بينت علي حالي
باني متعجب كثير وسرت اسالهم ما الذي اطعمته وماذا فعل قولوا لي الصحيح فنكروا علي
جميعهم وقالوا ما اطعمناه شي ابداً. حينئذ قلت الي ذلك الذي هو موكل عليه انا ماني
بني حتي اعرف انكان ما بتصدقني والا الرجل بموت وتكون خطيته في ارقابكم.

١٢٥،١١ فلما سمع هذا الكلام اخذني علي جنب وقلي سرّاً لان اتوسل اليهم المريض بان لا
يقولوا لي وقلي بانه اكل ثلج ووضع منه علي صدره وهذا كان السبب ولكن بحياتك

brother Anṭūn. And it was I who used to bring him the aromatic liqueur and put myself at his service! It seemed, however, that he didn't recognize me after all, as I was a twelve-year-old boy at the time. I thanked God that the chamberlain had not recognized me, then asked his permission to let me return to where I was staying.

"Off you go," he said. "But be sure to rise before dawn, and return to check up on your patient. Then we absolutely must be on our way." 11.122

"Yes sir," I said, and went to rejoin my companions. They'd been waiting anxiously for me. I told them the whole story from start to finish and we all thanked God Most High for His loving-kindness, before falling into a restful sleep.

Sometime past midnight, two of the sick man's attendants came to wake me, looking stricken. 11.123

"Hurry! The boy is dying!"

I shot up, tore out of the room, and dashed off with them, frantic with worry. As we made our way back, I peppered them with questions, urging them to explain why the fever had returned. Neither would respond truthfully. Finally, one of them took me aside.

"After you left, the agha ordered some ice to be brought," the attendant confided. "He chewed an *uqqah*'s worth, and put the rest on his chest and stomach."

Now I understood why he'd relapsed, and I had a worthwhile excuse to give the chamberlain to save my own skin!

When we arrived at the residence, I went in to see the patient and found him in a pitiable state. His fever had returned—but now it was twice as severe as before—and he looked ready to succumb at any minute. Feigning shock, I turned to interrogate his servants. 11.124

"What have you given him to eat?" I demanded. "And what did he do? Tell me the truth!"

"We didn't give him anything!" they replied, denying any wrongdoing, so I turned to the servant who was responsible for the young man.

"I'm no prophet, so I don't know if you're telling me the truth," I said. "But if you're lying to me, this man is going to die and you're all going to pay the price."

At this, the attendant took me aside and quietly explained what happened. The sick young man had begged them not to tell me the truth. 11.125

لا تخبر القبجي بهذا ليلا ينتقم منا والشي صار . اخيرًا امرتهم بان يستحلبوا من البزورات واسقيته فنجان كبير من حجر البازهر وصرت اعالجه كالاول الي ان اصبح الصباح وسمع القبجي بان رجع مرضه اليه فاغتاض قوي كثير وارسل فاحدرني امامه وهو مغضب ونظر اليّ بالزجر وقال لي هل انك كذبت عليّ انبارح بقولك لي بانه استراح والان بلغني خبر بانه اشتد فيه المرض اكثر من الاول هل انك ضحكت عليّ .

۱۲۲،۱۱ فانا لما رايته مغضب وراد ينتقم مني فالتزمت حيندٍ احكي له بالذي جري في هذا الليل وكيف انه اكل تلج ووضع منه على صدره كما احكولي فلما سمع مني هل كلام اشتد بالغضب عليه وقال لي انا بسافر فيه وان مات بربطه من اجريه وبخلي يجروه مثل الكلب ولا انا بخاطر براسي . حينذٍ ارتميت على اياديه واتوسلت اليه بانه يصبر عليه ذلك النهار لعل انه يستريح شويه ثم يسافر فيه ورجعت اعالجه بالمستحلب وغيره الي ان امسا المسا فاستراح عن قبل قليل .

۱۲۷،۱۱ وكان القبجي امر بان يهيوا له تحت روان حتي يركبه فيه وبسافر ثاني يوم وارسل فاحضرني امامه وقلي حتي اروح معه الي الشام حتي اعالج المريض في الطريق فقلت له سمعًا وطاعه . حينذٍ قلي امضي الليله حضر شغلك حتي غدي تسافر معنا فمضيت الي عند ارفاقي واحكيت لهم باني بسافر مع القبجي الي الشام.

۱۲۸،۱۱ فما رضي رفيقي حنا ومنعني عن الرواح بقوله لي بان بخاف ليلا يعرض لهذا المريض في الطريق شي او انه يموت وخاله بيكون ناصيف باشه ويقولوا بان الحكيم صار سبب موته ايش بيعود يخلصك من ايدي ناصيف باشه بلا شك ما بيعاملك الا بالقتل وانكان وصل بالسلامه ما بتخاف[1] ليلا يمتحنوك الحكما هناك وانت ما بتعرف في الحكمه بشي ابدًا كيف بيسير فيك ذلك الوقت وبتكون مصيبتك اعظم .

---

۱ الأصل: بتخاو.

"He chewed some ice and put the rest on his chest, and that's why he got sick again," the attendant said. "But please, for the love of God, don't tell the chamberlain, because he'll take revenge on us! What's done is done."

Then I ordered them to extract some more juice from the seeds, and I gave the young man a large cup of bezoar water to drink. I treated him as I had the previous day, until morning came and the chamberlain received word that the illness had returned. He was furious, and summoned me before him.

"Did you lie to my face yesterday when you said that he had recovered?" he demanded, fixing me with a wrathful eye. "Now I hear that his illness is worse than before! Do you take me for a fool?"

Finding him so angry, and seeing that he was likely to take his anger out 11.126 on me, I was forced to tell him what had transpired during the night—how the young man had eaten the ice and put it on his chest, as they'd told me. He erupted again, this time at the boy.

"I'm going to make him travel anyway, and if he dies along the way I'll tie a rope to his feet and let them drag his corpse like a dog," he said. "I won't risk my own neck on account of him!"

I threw myself before him, clutching his hands and begging him to wait another day in the hope that the young man would recover slightly before traveling. I then returned to treat him with the emulsions and other medications until that evening, when he began to recover.

In the meantime, the chamberlain had ordered that a litter be prepared for 11.127 the young man to ride in when they set off the next day. He summoned me and asked me to travel with them as far as Damascus, so as to treat the patient along the way.

"My pleasure," I said, and he said, "Go pack so you're ready to leave with us tomorrow morning."

And off I went to tell my companions that I'd be accompanying the chamberlain to Damascus.

My friend Ḥannā wasn't happy about this, and warned me not to go. 11.128

"What if something happens to the sick man on the road, and he dies?" Ḥannā said. "His uncle is Nāṣif Pasha. If they say that the doctor caused his death, who's going to save you from Nāṣif Pasha? He'll kill you, without a doubt! And even if the young man arrives safely, aren't you afraid that the doctors over there will put you to the test? You don't know a thing about medicine! What do you suppose will happen to you then? You'll be in an even bigger pickle!"

١٢٩،١١ النتيجه وعظ علي في كلام وغيره وكبر علي الاوهام وانا بقيت في حيره لاني اعطيت
القبجي قرار باني بروح معه فاستقمت تلك الليله وانا في بحران كيف وايش برد جواب
للقبجي الذي هو بمقام وزير فلما اصبح الصباح سمع قاطرجينا والذين مستكرين معه
بان القبجي ماشي ومعه تخت روان لجميعهم هموا بالسفر معه وقالوا نحن منفارقه في
انطاكيه ومن هناك منمضي الي حلب وصاروا يحملوا كدشهم واخدوا زوادهم وهموا
علي السفر وفي دلك الوقت ارسل القبجي ودعاني فلما دخلت الي المنزول رايت التخت
روان والخيل مسروجه وهن علي هيئة السفر .

١٣٠،١١ فلما راني القبجي قلي فين خرجك ها انا امرت لك بفرس نشيط امضي في
الحال وجيب خرجك وحوايجك وتعال وانا في استدارك فمضيت حتي اجيب
خرجي وارجع اسافر فرايت الذين كانوا مهاين للسفر معنا بطلوا فسالت ماهو السبب
فاجابني واحد منهم وقلي في الاول عرفنا بان يمكنا نمشي مع التخت روان لكن واحد
اختيار نصحنا بقوله لنا بان القبجي بيغير في كل ساعتين كدش في اي مكان دخل
يحضروا له مركوب وبياخد سفر يومين بيوم هل كدشكم بيضاينوا يمشوا معه ولاجل
هذا السبب عدلنا عن السفر .

١٣١،١١ فلما سمعت منه هل كلام تغيرت نيتي عن السفر لاني كنت مسترجي باني افارق
القبجي في انطاكيه وبختفي عن وجهه فلما رايت اني بسافر وحدي معه فغيرت النيه
ورايت لي جه برضي فيها القبجي فمضيت الي القناق فرايت ركبوا المريض في التخت
اروان وجماعته حوله مجتمعين وهن في استنضاري . حيندٍ صعدت الي عند القبجي
وقبلت اتكه واستعدرت منه بان ما لي قوه اركب في منزل لاني بموت في الدرب
وسرت اتوسل اليه بانه يعفيني لان ما لي مقدره علي هذا السفر .

١٣٢،١١ فالله تعالي حنن قلبه علي وقلي ما بيلزم امضي في حالك وفي حال ركب جواده
وخرج من المنزول واما المريض وجماعته ساروا يملقوني بقولهم لي ها نحن جميعا
منداريك في الطريق لا تخاف واغتهم المريض اكد لي بقسم باني وصوله للشام

As Ḥannā continued to caution me against going, my anxiety mounted. 11.129
What was I to do? I'd given the chamberlain my word that I would go with
him. I spent that night in a panic, wondering what I could possibly say to an
official who occupied the rank of a vizier.

When morning came, the muleteer we'd hired received word that the chamberlain was about to depart, together with the sick man's litter. My companions decided to join the chamberlain's convoy and break off once we arrived at
Antioch, where we'd continue on to Aleppo. They loaded up their horses and
gathered their provisions, preparing to leave. Then I was summoned to see the
chamberlain, and when I arrived I saw the litter and the horses saddled up, and
everyone ready to depart.

"Where's your bag?" he asked. "I had a fast horse saddled up for you. Go get 11.130
your things, and come back at once! I'm waiting."

I returned to grab my bag and set off with the chamberlain, only to find
that the people who were preparing to travel with us had changed their minds
about going. I asked what the reason was.

"We'd originally planned to go along with the litter," one of them explained.
"But then an old man advised us not to. He said, 'The chamberlain swaps
horses every two hours. Wherever they stop, there's a new mount waiting for
him, so they travel the distance of two days in a single day. Can your horses
keep up with him?' This is why we decided not to go."

Hearing this, I changed my mind about leaving with the convoy. I'd been 11.131
willing to take the risk of leaving the chamberlain once we got to Antioch and
vanishing from sight. Then, when I learned I would be the only one traveling
with him, I had given up hope. But now I had an excuse that just might satisfy
him. I went to his camp. They'd put the sick man in the litter and his attendants
were milling about, waiting for me. I went upstairs to see the chamberlain,
knelt to kiss the hem of his robes, apologized, and begged his forgiveness.
I explained that I didn't have the strength to ride without stopping, swapping
horses as we went—I would die on the road. I begged him to release me from
my obligation, for I didn't have the ability to make the journey.

At this, the chamberlain took pity on me, thank goodness. 11.132

"You're free to go now," he said, then mounted and rode off. But the sick
man and his attendants tried to talk me into going.

"Don't worry, we'll take care of you on the road," they said.

يوهبني فرس وبيرسلني للقدس بغير كلفه وبيعطيني اجره وافوه لكن كنت فزعان من قول حنا لي ليلا يصيبني مصيبه فابيت عن الرواح فلما ايس من رواحي معه غضب وانحصر مني قوي كثير وامر العكامه بالمسير . حينذٍ التفت اليه جوخداره وقله بانه يعطيني بخشيش فمد يده الي كيس خرجيته وكش والقا الدراهم التي في يده علي الارض بحرده وغيض فلموه من علي الارض واعطوني اثني عشر تلت ابو كلب ومضوا في طريقهم.

١٣٣،١١ وانا سرت الي عند رفقاتي واستقمنا في قنيه خمسة ايام بعد رواح القبجي ثم بعده تهيا قفل الي حلب فرافقناه الي ان وصلنا الي قرب ادنه وهناك بوغاز ديق ما يجوز فيه الا واحد بعد واحد وفي ذلك المكان بيجلس اغة السبنج حتي ياخد من الورادين السبنج وهو غرشين الا ثلث علي كل انسان اتي من تلك النواحي من النصارا فقط فلما وصلنا الي ذلك البوغاز وقفوا جماعة ذلك الاغا وردونا عن المسير حتي نعطي اسبنج.

١٣٤،١١ فبعد ما اخد من رفقاتي ومن غيرهم التفت اليّ وطلب مني بان اعطيه واخد منه طسكره مثل ما اعطا للغير فاجبته علي الفور قايلًا ان كان بعطي الي سلطانك خراج بعود بعطيك اسبنج فترس في وسال عني للذين كانوا معي من يكون هذا الرجل فاجابوه هذا حكيم فرنجي فسدقهم لانه راء ملبسي وشعر راسي وحلاسي مغير . حينذٍ استرحب في وامرني بالجلوس بقوله لي ما عرفتك لا يحصل مواخده.

١٣٥،١١ وبعد انتها واحد من الجميع اطلقنا فركبنا كدشنا وسافرنا ولا زلنا سايرين حتي وصلنا الي جسر مصيص وكت انا سابق القفل فلما قربت من الجسر رايت اثنين جوخداريه تعارضوني وكلفوني باني ادخل لعند اغتهم وهو اغات مصيص فظننت بان احد تعاون عليّ بان ماني فرنجي فانهمت وما اردت ادخل معهم الي حين ما يصلوا رفقاتي واسلمهم مركوبي اعني كديشي فاصطبروا وما عملوا عليّ زور وكان

Their master, the sick man, also promised he would give me a horse once they arrived in Damascus and would send me to Jerusalem, all expenses paid, and pay me a hefty fee besides. But I was afraid that Ḥannā's prediction would come true and some mishap would occur on the road, so I declined to join them. The master lost hope of convincing me, but was not at all pleased. As he ordered the litter driver to set off, one of his footmen suggested he give me a tip of some kind. So he reached into his pouch, grabbed some coins, and threw them to the ground in a fit of pique. His attendants picked them up and handed them to me: There were twelve *abū kalb* thirds in all. Then they set off.

I returned to my companions, and we spent five days in Konya following the 11.133 chamberlain's departure. Then a caravan set off for Aleppo, which we traveled with until we drew close to Adana. There was a narrow mountain pass, only wide enough to allow one person through at a time.[55] A toll officer sat there, collecting the *isbanj* tax—a piaster and two thirds—from anyone traveling in that direction. All the Christian travelers, that is; no one else had to pay. When we reached the pass, the collector's men stopped us and demanded the toll.

After he'd collected some money from my companions and the others, the 11.134 officer turned to me and demanded that I pay in exchange for a ticket, as the others had done.

"If I paid your sultan the poll tax, I'd pay this too, but I don't, so I won't," I fired back.[56]

He studied me for a moment, then turned to my companions.

"And who might this fellow be?" he asked them.

"A Frankish doctor."

The officer believed them, as he'd seen that I looked different in my clothing and wig, so he greeted me and invited me to sit with him.

"Pardon me, sir, but I didn't realize who you were!"

Once he received payment from everyone else, he let us go. We mounted 11.135 and set off, riding until we arrived at the bridge of Misis.[57] I was riding ahead of the caravan, and when I approached the bridge, I found myself face-to-face with a pair of officials, who blocked my way and asked me to come along to their superior, the master of Misis. In my terror, I assumed that someone must have double-crossed me and let slip that I wasn't a Frank. I told them that I didn't want to go with them until my companions arrived and I could give them my horse for safekeeping.

السبب هو وان اغتهم فيه وجعه واحد خبر بان في القفل موجود حكيم فرنجي فارسل
هل اثنين حتي اذا وصلت الي عندهم يدخلوني الي عند اغتهم وبيت الاغا هو
بقرب الجسر.

فلما وصلوا رفقاتي سلمتهم كديشي ودخلت مع تينك الاثنين امام ذلك الاغا ١٣٦،١١
الذي هو حاكم البلد فلما امتثلت امامه فاسترحب فيّ وامر الخدام بان يشلحوني
جزمتي. اخيرًا دعاني حتي اجلس حداه وامر بان يجيبولي فنجان قهوه وغليون تتن
فاخدني العجب وصرت افتكر ما هو سبب هذا الاكرام والاناسيه معي من رجل عالي
شان وحاكم البلد وانا في هذه الفكره حينذٍ قلي قرب لعندي فدنيت منه وهو يقلي
امان يا معلم خلصني من هذه الوجعه وايش ما طلبت بعطيك فقلتله ما هي وجعتك
فكشف حينذٍ عن ساعده فرايت له مهري وكان ذلك الوجع قعطال هاري جسده
وامعاه وبشرته فلما رايته في هذه الحال صرت اتاوه امامه وارويته باني عرفت الدا
لكن ما هو موجود معي الدوا فزاد عليّ بالتوسل.

فاجبته لا تخاف انا بوصفلك شي تدهن فيه جسدك من خارج حتي ينشف ١٣٧،١١
جراحتك ولكن باطنك يلزمه تركيب معجون خصوصي لهذا الداء والان ما هو موجود
معي انما في حلب بركب لك هولانه من جملة عقاقير ما لها وجود في هذه البلاد فان
كان لك صاحب ارسله لعندي في حلب وانا بعطيه مرطبان من ذلك المعجون فاذا
استعملته قبل ما يخلص بتكون شفيت من هذا المرض لانه شي مجرب.

فسالني في اين بتوجد في حلب اجبته بان دكاني في خان ابرك اذا سال عني فيراني ١٣٨،١١
هناك. اخيرًا قلي ما هي الوصفه التي قلت عنها فاجبته خد من حجر الجاز الذي بيسما
بلسان التركي كوزرضاشي بمقدار خمسين درهم وانقعه في الماء داخل انا زجاج وبعد
اربعة وعشرين ساعه حتي يكون حل خد من ذلك الماء في فنجان وبل شاشه وامسح
قروحك وهذا بينشف عنك هل مواد والليله ارسل لعندي للقفل من طرفك رجل
حتي ارسلك من عندي حب تستعمله علي ثلاث مرات عند النوم وبرسلك شويت
ضرور تكبس بها قروحك.

They waited patiently, not forcing me to accede. The reason they'd come was that their master was suffering from some aches and pains, and he'd received word that a Frankish doctor was traveling with this particular caravan. So he had sent these two to wait for me to arrive and bring me to his house, which was next to the bridge.

Once my companions arrived, I handed my horse over to them and went 11.136 with the two officers to see their master, who was the governor of the town. When I presented myself before him, he welcomed me and told his servants to remove my shoes. Then he invited me to sit at his side, and ordered some coffee and a pipe for me to smoke. I was surprised at this treatment, and wondered why a man who held the high rank of local governor was being so warm and friendly. As I was mulling this over, the governor spoke.

"Come a little closer," he said, and when I obliged, he wailed, "Oh doctor, put an end to this pain of mine and I'll give you anything you ask!"

"What sort of pain is it?" I asked, and he showed me his forearm, the flesh of which was decayed. He was suffering from snail fever, which had eaten away at his body, his innards, and his skin. At this sight, I set about remonstrating that I recognized the disease but didn't have the medicine with me to treat it. This only made him plead all the more.

"Never fear," I said. "I'll prescribe an ointment for you to apply topically, 11.137 which will dry up your lesions. As for your insides, I'll have to put together a paste specifically meant to treat this illness. I don't have any with me at the moment, but I can put some together for you in Aleppo. It's composed of a group of drugs that can't be found nearby. Perhaps you have someone you could send to Aleppo. I'll give him a jar of the paste, and once you start using it, you'll be healed before the jar is finished. It's a tried and true remedy."

"Where can I find you in Aleppo?" he asked. 11.138

"My shop is in the Abrak market. Ask anyone and you'll find me."

"And what's the prescription you mentioned?"

"Take fifty dirhams' worth of blue vitriol—which they call *göztaşı* in Turkish. Soak it in a glass container full of water for twenty-four hours. Once it's dissolved, pour the water into a cup and moisten a cloth with it, then use it to wipe your ulcers. That should dry them up," I said.

"Send one of your men over to the caravan tonight and I'll give him some pills for you to take for three nights, before you go to sleep," I continued. "I'll also give him some powder for you to press on your ulcers."

١٣٩،١١ وقتيذٍ نهضت وطلبت منه اذن ومضيت حيث كان نازل القفل وهو ذلك الناح من الجسر علي حفت الماء الي عند ارفاقي ولما حان وقت المساء افتكرنا ماذا نتعشا وفي ذلك الوقت اتانا من عند الاغا صينيت عشا مكلفه ثلاثة الوان وكلفونا الخدام حتي نتقدم ونتعشي فجلسنا علي ذلك المرج امام النهر وتعشينا عشوه مشبعه . اخيراً نهضنا وخسلنا ايادينا وشكرنا الله تعالي علي ما انعم علينا.

١٤٠،١١ وبعده جانا ابريق قهوه من عند المذكور ايضاً فبعدما شربنا القهوه فقلي ذلك الجوخدار الذي جاب لنا ابريق القهوه بان الاغا بيسلم عليك وبيقلك تعطيني الذي وعدته فيه فاجبته علي الراس والعين وفي الحال فتحت الخرج واخرجت خمسة عشر حبه منقيه وكان معي مستحضر لاجل القروحه شب محروق فصريت في ورقه شويه منه واعطيته لذلك الجوخدار واعلمته كيف يعمل فيه وهو انه بعد ما يكون اندهن بذلك الماء يضع من هذا الضرور علي قروحه ويكبسهم حتي ينشفوا عليه والحب في كل ليله عند النوم يبلع خمسة حبات واطلقته.

١٤١،١١ وبتنا تلك الليله في ذلك المكان ونصف الليل سافرنا وما بعرف كيف صار في ذلك الاغا ولا زلنا سايرين حتي وصلنا الي ايلة ادنه تسما ايلة رمضان وهي في صحن جبل وذلك الجبل مشحون من الاشجار وعيون الماء وهو مكان كانه فردوس ارضي وقبل وصولنا لهذا الجبل كما مرنا علي قصبه تسما اركلي وهذه القصبه ايضاً تشبه هذا المكان كانه بستان من كثرة الاشجار والمياه الموجود فيها.

١٤٢،١١ فلما دخلنا الي تلك الايله نزلنا هناك فكنت تري كانها مدينه مسكونه لان كل صاحب عيله عامل له بين الاشجار ستار ومجلس حريمه واولاده لان في فصل الصيف من شده الحر والغم الذي يصير في مدينة ادنه يخرجوا كل اهلها الي هذه الايله بيقضوا صيفيتهم هناك وكل من هو في كاره البياعين والشراين والخياطين والنجارين وما يشبه ذلك من الاصناف حتي موجود سوق وفيه موجود كل شي مثل ما موجود في المدينه عينها.

Then I got up and asked his permission to depart, whereupon I returned to 11.139
my companions who were with the caravan, encamped across the bridge by
the water's edge. When evening came, we were wondering what we should
have for dinner when suddenly a sumptuous feast, with three different dishes,
appeared on a platter. The master of Misis had sent it, and his servants encouraged us to come right up and dig in. So we all sat down in that field overlooking the river, and enjoyed an ample supper. When we were done, we
got up, washed our hands, and thanked God Most High for the grace He had
shown us.

A pot of coffee, also sent by the master, then appeared, and we all had some. 11.140
The attendant who had brought the coffee came over to me.

"The master sends his greetings," he said. "And he asks that you give me
what you'd promised him."

"With pleasure," I said.

I opened my bag and took out fifteen purgative pills. I happened to also have
some burnt alum powder, for ulcers. I put a little in a piece of paper, gave it to
the attendant, and explained how to administer it. After daubing the ulcers
with the blue vitriol water, the master was to sprinkle some of the powder over
them and apply some pressure until they dried up. As for the pills, he was to
swallow five of them before going to sleep. I said all this to the attendant before
sending him on his way.

We spent the evening in that spot, then got on the road at midnight. I don't 11.141
know what became of the master of Misis. We kept on until we arrived at the
province of Adana, which was known as Ramazan Province. It is situated on
a mountain plateau covered with trees and freshwater springs, a veritable
paradise on earth. Before reaching the mountain, we'd passed a village called
Ereğli, which was as verdant as an orchard, full of trees and plentiful water.[58]

Once in the province, we set up camp. The countryside was full of so many 11.142
people that it looked like a fully inhabited city! Every man with a family had
put up screens between the trees, creating a place for his wives and children to
sit. During the summer, all the residents of Adana would flee the city because
of the intense heat and stifling conditions, and come to this province. They'd
spend the summer there, people of every profession: merchants, tailors, car-
penters, and other artisans. There was even a market, furnished with all the
same things one would find in the city.

١٤٣،١١ فبتنا تلك الليله في ذلك المكان ونصف الليل توجهنا الي مدينة ادنه وفي دربنا وجدنا رجال ونساء واولاد متوجهين الي الايله في هذا الليل وشاعلين فنارات كانهم في سيبانه. المراد ضحوة نهار دخلنا الي ادنه ونزلنا تحت الجسر في احد القناطر الناشفات وهذا الجسر له اربعين قنطره وعمارته ما رايت مثلها في كل دورتي لان اصغر حجر التي معمره فيه ٩ بقد قبر فرنجي شي بيفوق الوصف وكانت اعتنت في عمارته الملكه هيلانه ام قصطنين الملك وعمرت غير جسوره ايضاً ورصيف حجر من اراضي اسطنبول الي ان وصلت الي مدينة القدس الشريف وعمرت ابراج في اليمين وخبرها مستطيل نعدل عنه.

١٤٤،١١ فلما نزلنا تحت تلك القناطر وبعد حصه اجا الينا رجل نصراني ومعه واحد بكاسم جوخدار حتي يري انكان احد منا ما اعطا اسبنج في ذلك البوغاز المذكور وصار يقلنا اروني اوراقكم فكل منهم اراه ورقته وبعده اتقدم الي عندي وانا كت متكي حتي ارويه ورقتي فقالوا له جماعة القفل ارجع عنه هذا حكيم فرنجي ما يعطي اسبنج ولا اغة مصيص قدر ياخد منه بل وجبه واكرمه.

١٤٥،١١ فرجع في الحال وما عاد قرب صوبي فاستقمنا ذلك اليوم في ذلك المكان وعند غروب الشمس رادوا القاطرجيه يمشوا بنا فسالناهم لماذا بدكم تسافروا قبل الوقت فاجابونا باننا مقبلين علي باب العتم يسما قرانق قبي وهذا المكان ملطا حراميه بدنا نجوزه في هذا الليل ليلا يصدفنا احد منهم فطعنا امرهم وكل منا ركب كديشه وسرنا في هذا الليل الي ان وصلنا الي هذا الباب المذكور وهو معمر من حجر اسود وداخله مقتم عتم شديد والذي بيدخل اليه بيرتعب فهون الله وخرجنا من ذلك الباب وصرنا نزل في نزول ومن علي يميننا جبل شامخ وعرمان اسجار ومن علي شمالنا هيش عظيم وواره البحر.

١٤٦،١١ فاستقمنا نمشي ونحن فزعانين الي قرب نصف الليل. حينذٍ انحدرت البروده والندا من رطوبة البحر حتي تري الندي نازل علينا مثل الدبس ولا عدنا نقدر نفتح اعيننا من ذلك الوخم الكتيف حتي ان الراكبين يقعوا من علي ضهور خيلهم

We passed the evening in that place then took to the road again at mid- 11.143
night, headed for the city of Adana. Along the road, we came upon some men,
women, and children making their way to the countryside at night, carrying
torches as though they were parasols. By morning, we'd arrived in Adana,
and set up camp beneath the bridge there, under one of the dry arches.[59] This
bridge has forty arches, and I've never seen such an edifice in all my travels.
The smallest stones used to construct it were the size of Frankish tombstones.
The whole structure is simply indescribable. It was built by Empress Helena,
the mother of Emperor Constantine. She also built other bridges, as well as a
paved road from the outskirts of Istanbul to the city of Jerusalem, and towers
in various ports. Her story is too long for me to recount here.

Shortly after we halted beneath those arches, a Christian man came over 11.144
to us accompanied by a person wearing the uniform of an official. He wanted
to confirm that we'd all paid the toll at the mountain pass I mentioned earlier.

"Show me your papers," he demanded.

After all had shown their papers, he came over to me. I crouched, pretending to fumble around for my papers, and the other people in the caravan told
him to leave me alone.

"He's a Frankish doctor," they explained. "He doesn't need to pay the toll.
Even the master of Misis wouldn't take anything from him. In fact, he treated
him as a guest."

At this, the official pulled away and left me alone. We spent the rest of the 11.145
day there, and when the sun went down, the muleteers elected to start moving
again.

"Why do you want to leave early?" we asked them.

"We're heading for a pass called Karanlık Kapı, or the Gate of Darkness,"
they said. "It's full of bandits; if we don't want to run into them, we need to
cross at night."

We did as they asked: All of us mounted and we set off into the night. We
soon arrived at the pass. Constructed of black stone, its interior was plunged
in profound darkness, terrifying anyone who entered. With God's help, we
emerged safely, and as we continued the road began to descend. To our right
was a lofty mountain, thick with trees. To our left was a vast thicket, beyond
which lay the sea.

We pressed on apprehensively. As midnight approached, the humid sea air 11.146
became cool and we could see the dew settling on us, heavy as molasses. The

والفقير ما عدت اقدر اضاين من النعس الذي استولي علي فسقت جوادي وسبقت القفل حكم ميل ونزلت من ضهر الجواد الي الارض وحت عن السكه قليلًا ودخلت في ذلك الارمان ولفيت رسن الكديش علي زندي وانتكيت نمت غير مبالي من شي من شدة النعس.

١١،١٤٧ في الحال غرقت في النوم فمر القفل وانا نايم اما الكديش لما راء رفقاه مروا من عليه فصار يصحن وانا برا في منامي بان الكديش يصحن وانا غرقان في النوم فلما انقطع فاضج القفل وبعد عني فالكديش بيريد يلحق رفقاته الكدش. حينٍ نتر رسنه حتي يمضي ولما نتر رسنه انتبهت واعطيت داني لعلي اسمع جراس الكدش فا سمعت شي من هذا بل الكديش من كل قوته يجرني حتي يلحق رفقاته وانا متبت في الرسن وما في مكان علوه حتي اعلي علي ظهره وهولا زال يجرني وانا مرعوب من ذلك المكان لاني سمعت بيقولوا بان لصوص هل مكان بيشلحوا وبيقتلوا. المراد صرت استغيث في مريم العدري والقديسين وما بقا لي قوا اركك مع هذا الكديش.

١١،١٤٨ فخطر في بالي باني ادوس علي حياصته واركب فوقفت في وجهه حتي اهديه واركب فما كان يمكني بذلك بل كان يركد ويجرني معه فخارق قوتي ونويت ارخي رسنه من يدي وامشي علي مهلي وكيف ما صار ما صار لاني عفت حالي فما رايت الا هدي الكديش وصار يمشي علي مهله وهذه كانت عجيبه من مريم العذري التي استغثت فيها وملايكي الحارس فلما رايت الكديش هدي في مسيره حينٍ وضعت رجلي في حياصته القدامي ونهضت فركبت فلما ما عاد الكديش يتضبط بل صار يركد ضولي درزين حصه فوصلني للقفل وما احد له خبر عني. حينٍ صحيت وطار نومي وشكرت الله تعالي علي احسانه نحوي.

١١،١٤٩ ولا زلنا سايرين حتي وصلنا الي مكان مجمر فرايت في ذلك المكان شريك سهل فسقت كديشي ومشيت في ذلك الشريك بعلي باني اسبق القفل واخلص من ذلك المجمر فلما انتهيت المكان وانا تابع الشريك فوصلت الي كهف جبل . . . فسقت الكديش فا عاد ووقف . . . بالقبجه ضرب عنيف حتي يمشي فالتزم الحيوان . . .

fog was so thick we could scarcely keep our eyes open, and men were falling off their horses left and right. As for me, I was feeling too drowsy to continue at that pace, so I galloped ahead of the caravan and stopped about a mile down the road. I dismounted and went to the side of the road, into the thicket. I wrapped the horse's reins around my wrist and lay down as if I didn't have a care in the world, such was the extent of my fatigue.

I fell asleep instantly, and when the caravan passed I was still sleeping. 11.147 When my horse saw all his fellow horses passing by, he began to whinny. But I remained sound asleep, dreaming that a horse was whinnying! The caravan passed, making a din, then rumbled away. In his eagerness to join his fellows, my horse tugged on his reins. That woke me up, and I immediately pricked up an ear, listening for the caravan's bells, but didn't hear a thing. Meanwhile, the horse was pulling on the reins with all his might, trying to drag me along after his harness-mates.

I held fast to the reins, but had no way to mount him while he was pulling me forward! I ran along in terror, remembering what I'd heard about the brigands in these parts who robbed people and killed them. As I prayed to the Virgin Mary and the saints for help, my strength began to flag. How much longer could I keep running alongside the horse?

It then occurred to me to wedge my foot into the horse's surcingle and hoist 11.148 myself up. I stood in front of him and tried to calm him down but he wouldn't let me climb up. Instead, he ran off again, dragging me along! At that point I gave up and decided to let go of the reins so I could slow down and walk. Whatever happened would happen: I didn't care anymore. Wouldn't you know it, when I did that, the horse calmed down and began to walk slowly as well! This was nothing short of a miracle worked by the Virgin Mary, to whom I'd appealed for aid, along with my guardian angel. Once the horse slowed down, I put my foot in his forward surcingle, heaved myself up, and mounted him. As soon as I was on his back, he immediately set off at a gallop of his own accord, bringing me back to the caravan without anyone suspecting a thing. After being scared wide awake, I felt revived again and thanked God Most High for His beneficence.

We pressed on to[60] an area full of rocks. I spotted a smooth trail through 11.149 and steered my horse toward it. Then I proceeded down the trail, knowing

ذلك الكهف وانا ما داير بالي . . . وانحصرنا في ذلك المكان وهو تحته . . . نهر
عظيم ومن جانب اليمين فيه غير . . . فقط[1] باياس وكان دخولنا ضحوه من النهار[2]
ودخولنا من باب سوق باياس لانه من ذلك السوق مخرج برات باياس فلما تواسطنا
في السوق فما رايت الا رجل نزل من دكانه واعتنقني وصار يسلم علي سلام موده
فاعتجبت من ذلك الرجل علي هذه المحبه التي اظهرها لي من غير اني اعرفه فسالته
من يكون ومنين هذه المعرفه فاجابني اما بتعرفني يا اخي انا ماني حنا ابن ميخاييل
ميرو ومحبك وصديقك في حلب فلما سمعت منه هل كلام فعرفته حق المعرفه ثم عانقته
واستعدرت منه في قلة معرفتي له وهذا كان يجي الي حلب مع والده وينزل في خان
العلابيه وهو خان الذي نحن قاطنين فيه وكان والده عقد شريكه مع اخي انطون
وكان يراسلوا الي بعضهم ومرات عديده عزمناه الي عندنا للبيت هو وابنه المذكور
وكان بينا محبه عظيمه وهذا سبب معرفته فيّ.

والنتيجه مسكني من يدي بعدما سلم كريشي الي واحد حتي يوصله لرفقاتي في
القفل الذي نزل برات ذلك السوق المذكور فلا زال ماسكي حتي وصلنا الي بيته
واصعدني في درج فانتهينا الي ديوان خانه وتحت تلك الديواخانه بستان علي ما
تمد عينك والنضر ومزروع جميعه بكاد وليمون ورارنج شي بيفوق الوصف فجلسنا
هناك وفي الحال امر لخادمه بانه يتدارك في الغدا. حيندٍ اتوسلت اليه بانه لا يدعهم
يطبخوا زفولاني جزمت علي حالي باني ما عدت اكل زفومن دخولي الي ادنه الي حين
ما اصل الي حلب فزعًا ليلا اتوخم فلما سمع مني هل كلام امر بان يطبخوا صحن مجدره
برز ويطبخوا سمك بحري وبتاريخ وما يشبه ذلك من الاكل الطيب.

وبعده امر بانهم يجيبوا فراغ عرق من عرق العتيق فلما احضروه فسكب وناولني
فنجان فلما شربته من شدة حديته انطبيت علي وجهي حصه زمانيه ونهضت وقلته
يا اخي ما هذا العرق فاجابني بان هذا العرق بيدفع عنا الوخم ولولاه كما منقع في
الامراض الوخمه فاصطبرنا حصه فوضعوا المايده ووضعوا تلك الاكولات الطيبه فزاد

---

١ من «مكان محجر فرايت» إلى «غير . . . فقط» في الهامش ومطموس في الأصل. ٢ الأصل: النها.

I'd be leaving the caravan behind, along with the rocky terrain. I continued to follow the trail until I arrived at a mountain cave . . . I urged my horse on but it wouldn't take another step, halting in its place . . . some violent lashings to make it walk, and so the animal was compelled . . . that cave. Meanwhile, I wasn't paying attention . . . and so we found ourselves stuck in that place. Below it was . . . a great river. And on its right side, there was another . . . only . . .[61] Payas, and arrived in the morning and entered through the gate to the souk, which opened onto the space outside the walls. Lo and behold, as soon as we made our way into the middle of the souk, a man emerged from his shop and came over to embrace me, showering me with affectionate greetings. I didn't think I knew the man, so I was taken aback by his warmth.

"Don't you recognize me, brother Ḥannā?" he asked. "It's me, Ḥannā ibn Mikhāyīl Mīro, your dear friend from Aleppo!"

As soon as I heard these words, I suddenly realized exactly who he was. I gave him a hug and apologized for not recognizing him right away. This fellow used to visit Aleppo with his father and stay at Khān al-ʿUlabiyyah where we lived. His father had established a partnership with my brother Anṭūn, and they would correspond. We invited father and son over to our house on many occasions, and became very good friends. That was why he recognized me.

Ḥannā had someone take my horse to my companions in the caravan, 11.150 which was headed for lodgings outside the souk, then took me by the hand and led me to his house. He ushered me upstairs to a belvedere overlooking a vast orchard, extending as far as the eye could see. The orchard was planted entirely with citron, lemon, and orange trees; what an exquisite sight it was! We sat down and Ḥannā ordered his servant to prepare lunch for us, but I begged him not to let them cook anything greasy, as I'd made a vow not to eat any fat from the time of my arrival in Adana until I reached Aleppo, fearing I'd have indigestion. At this, he gave an order for them to prepare a plate of *mujaddarah* with rice, some saltwater fish, bottarga, and other tasty dishes.

Then he had a bottle of fine aged arak brought over, and poured me a glass. 11.151 I had a drink and was bowled over by how strong it was. At length, when I had gathered my wits again, I turned to my friend.

"Brother, what kind of arak is this?"

حينٍ يسقيني فنجان اخرٍعرق فما شربت انما شربنا مع الغدا نبيذ طيب فبعد خلوصنا من الغدا فشربنا القهوه ونزلنا نتمشي في ذلك البستان الملوكي فصار يقطعوا لنا من ذلك الكباد والليمون الحلو وبعض فواكي مثل رمان وخيار وما يشبه ذلك.

١١،١٥٢ فاستقمت عنده الي حكم العصر ثم ودعته ومضيت الي عند ارفاقي وبتنا تلك الليله علي حفت البحر الي ان مضي من الليل نصفه ومن هناك ركبنا كشنا كشنا وسرنا الي ان وصلنا الي اسكندرونه وفتنا اسكندرونه ونزلنا عند العين واستقمنا ذلك النهار هناك وبعدما قطعوا العليق الدواب مشينا ومرينا علي بيلان في الليل ولا زلنا سايرين حتي وصلنا الي خان الجديد ومن هناك الي قط قلاق ومن هناك الي جسر الحديد ومن هناك الي مدينة انطاكيه نزلنا علي حفة العاصي وبتنا هناك.

١١،١٥٣ وتاني يوم سافرنا ومرينا في سوق انطاكيه فنزلت من علي كديشي ووقفت علي فرن صوصاني حتي اشتري خبز فبعدما زان لي الخبز اخرجت اعطيته حقه مصريات ديواني فما قبل ياخدهم بل قالي بده جرقات وانا ما معي جرقات فانحصرت منه وكشته من زيقه واحضرته الي تحت وصرت اقله انا ماني راخيك الا قدام الحاكم لانك ما رضيت تاخد من معاملة السلطان بل بتريد معاملة الفرج فالتمت الناس علينا وبالجهد حتي فلتوا يدي من زيقه واخدوا مني المصريات واعطوني الخبز واطلقوني بسلام.

١١،١٥٤ حينٍ ركبت كديشي وسرت وخرجت من باب بولص حتي الحق القفل فتهت عن السكه ومشيت في غير سكه فما رايت حالي الا وانا بين البساتين وانقطعت السكه فصرت ادور بين اشجار التوت وسواقي ماء وما عدت اعرف الدرب الذي جيت منه فخرت في امري واستقمت حكم ساعه وانا بفتل بين الاشجار والقفل فاتي وبعد عني. حينٍ داقة في الدنيا وانحصرت جدًا ولكن عند الديق ياتي الله بالفرج فرايت مارر في ذلك المكان رجل فلاح فاتوسلت اليه بانه يدلني علي الطريق فجاد علي وقلي اتبعني فتبعته الي انه اخرجني من تلك البساتين الي امام باب بولص حيث كنت وارواني سكت التي يمشي فيها القفل ومضي وتركني وحدي.

"It's the sort that prevents indigestion," he explained. "If not for this drink, we'd all be suffering from bad vapors in the gut."

A little while later, they set the table and brought the delicious foods. He then tried to give me another drink of arak, but I wouldn't accept. Instead, we drank some good wine with our lunch. When we were finished, we had coffee and went for a stroll through that magnificent orchard, fit for a king. As we passed, the gardeners plucked citrons and sweet lemons for us, and other fruits too, such as pomegranates and cucumbers.

I stayed at his house until the late afternoon then returned to my compan-    11.152
ions. We spent the night on the seashore, and at midnight set off for Alexandretta. When we arrived, we pitched camp by the spring and spent the day there. After gathering some fodder for the horses, we set off again, passing Belen during the night, and continuing to Khān al-Jadīd. From there, we journeyed to Qurṭ Qulāq and Jisr al-Jadīd, and from there to Antioch. We camped on the banks of the Orontes River and spent the night there.

The next day, we set off again, passing through the souk of Antioch. I got    11.153
off my horse and made a stop at the bakery of an Armenian from the region of Sassoun, to buy some bread. After the baker weighed the bread, I took out some Ottoman coins to pay for it. But he wouldn't accept them, demanding *jarq* coins instead, which I didn't have. Annoyed, I grabbed him by the collar and forced him down.

"You'd better accept the sultan's coin or I'll drag you to a judge!" I scolded. "To think that you'd ask for Frankish coins instead!"

A crowd of people gathered around us and struggled to pry my hands from his collar. They took my money, gave me the bread, and bid me farewell.

I mounted and set out through Saint Paul's Gate in pursuit of the caravan.    11.154
Somehow I lost my way and took the wrong road. Before I knew it, I found myself on a path that ended in the middle of some orchards. I wandered for a good long while among the mulberry trees and waterwheels, with the caravan moving farther away with every passing minute, and I felt increasingly panicked. But my distress was followed by divine deliverance! It took the shape of a passing peasant, whom I begged to guide me to the road.

"Follow me," he said kindly, and led me out of the orchards and back to Saint Paul's Gate, where I'd started. He showed me the road the caravan had taken, then left me to find my way.

١٥٥،١١ وانا صرت افتكر ليلا في الطريق يصدفني احد اللصوص ويعريني من ثيابي وياخذ الكديش فاصطبرت حصه لعل اري رفقا فما احد فات فبقيت بين الخوف والرجا فالتزمت بالمسير وحدي وسلمت لله الامر وسقت الكديش علي قدر ما امكني. حينئذٍ كشفت علي رجل جايي لطرفي وهذا كان اخو قاطرجينا لانهم استفقدوني في القفل فما رووني فدق قاطرجينا القفل وارسل اخوه بانه يعاود الي انطاكيه ويري ايش صار في فلما قرب لعندي وراني فرح وصار يسالني ما هو السبب باني تخلفت عن القفل فاحكيته بالمجراويه كيف وقعت. وقيدِ ركن قلبي واستبشرت بالسلامه ومشيت معه الي ان وصلنا الي القفل واحكيت لهم سبب عوقتي.

١٥٦،١١ وسرنا مسافرين الي ان وصلنا الي وادي بيسما وادي الجن والحق انه وادي الجن لانا قاسينا في المرور فيه مشقات عظيمه ومخاطر تلك الدروب العسر المشي فيها. المراد استقمنا ذلك النهار الي ان جاز النهار حتي خرجنا من ذلك الوادي واتينا الي حريم١ وهناك بتنا تلك الليله الي ان اصبح الصباح فسافرنا من هناك ومرينا علي ضيع والاراضي شتي وبعد يومين وصلنا الي خان العسل فبتنا هناك وتاني يوم دخلنا الي حلب وقبل دخولنا الي حلب صار زنزله عظيمه ما صار مثلها علي الحكي استقامة خمسة دقايق ونيف لكن نحن ما حسينا فيها لاجل اننا كنا راكبين وفي دخولي قصدت بيت اخي الذي هو في زقاق الخل وكان ذلك في اواخر شهر تموز سنه ١٧١٠٢ ليلا اصير فرحه.

١٥٧،١١ اخيرًا سمعوا اخوتي واخواتي حضروا لعندي بالسلامه وهنوني واحضروا لي حوايج ومن هناك مضيت الي بيت اخي عبدالله وصاروا يجوا لعندي الاهل والقرايب ويهنوني بالسلامه لان كان بلغهم خبر باني غرقت في البحر لاني كت كتبت مكتوب الي اخي انطون من مرسيليا باني نزلت في مركب وماضي الي ازمير ومن ازمير الي حلب وبعده بلغهم خبر بان مركب اتي من ازمير الي اسكندرونه انكسر وغرق كل كان فيه فتيقن اخي المذكور باني غرقت من الجمله وقدسوا علي روحي لان ما عاد بين

---

١ الأصل: حيرم. ٢ «وكان ذلك في.... ١٧١٠» في الهامش.

"What if I run into thieves on the road," I thought, "and they strip me of 11.155 my clothes and take my horse?" So I stayed put for a while, hoping to catch a glimpse of someone I knew, but to no avail. Torn between fear and hope, I finally forced myself to set off on my own, entrusting my fate to God. I rode that horse as hard as I could, until I spied someone down the road coming in my direction. It was the brother of our muleteer! When they'd realized I wasn't with them, the muleteer had halted the caravan and sent his brother back to Antioch to find out what had happened to me. He was very happy to see me, and asked why I'd left the caravan. I explained the whole story to him, and my heart finally stopped racing. Relieved that I'd been saved, I returned to the caravan with him, and told everyone why I'd been delayed.

Traveling onward, we arrived at a place known as the Valley of the Jinn. It 11.156 was aptly named,[62] because we found it very challenging to traverse, full of dangers and perilous stretches of road. We spent a whole day crossing that valley, finally arriving in Harim, where we spent the night. The next morning, we set off again, passing many villages and farmlands, and arrived two days later in Khān al-ʿAsal, where we stayed the night.

The next day we entered Aleppo. Just before we arrived, there was a great earthquake, bigger than any that anyone had ever heard of. It's said it lasted more than five minutes, but we didn't sense it at all, because we were riding at the time. As soon as we entered the city, I went straight to my brother's house in Zuqāq al-Khall—this was the end of the month of July, in the year 1710—so as to avoid making a public spectacle of my homecoming.

When my brothers and sisters heard about my arrival, they all came over 11.157 to congratulate me on my safe return, and brought me fresh clothes to wear. From Anṭūn's house, I went to the home of my brother ʿAbdallāh, where I was visited by family members and relatives, who all came by to pay their respects. It seems they'd heard I'd drowned at sea, as I'd last written a letter to my brother Anṭūn from Marseille, telling him I was boarding a ship to Izmir, and planned to continue from there to Aleppo. Well, they received the news that a ship bound from Izmir to Alexandretta had been lost at sea and all aboard had perished. They were convinced that I was one of the drowned, given that they hadn't received any more news from me, and prayed for my soul's eternal rest. Of course, that was because when I traveled from Izmir to Istanbul in the company of the aforementioned embassy official, I didn't send a letter to my

مني خبر لاني لما سافرت من ازمير الي اسطنبول صحبة جوخدار الالجي المذكور انفاً ماكتبت الي اخي باني مضيت الي اسطنبول وهذا كان السبب فرحهم في قدومي الي حلب بالسلامه.

١٥٨،١١ اخيراً استقمت في بيت اخي ثلاث اربع ايام الي حين ما احضرولي حوايج حتي لبست وحلقت شعر راسي ولفيت شاش وقاووق وارسلوا طيلعولي طسكره وبعده خرجت من البيت ومضيت رديت السلام علي اهلي وعلي المحبين والاقارب. اخيراً نزلت الي المدينه ومضيت الي عند اخي في المخزن وبعد كام يوم فتحلي اخي عبدالله دكان جوخ وروس عليّ خالي شاهين غزاله الي مده حتي تعلمت طرايق بيع الجوخ واستقمت تنين وعشرين سنه جوخجي.

١٥٩،١١ وكان سببها كان اخي مرتاب ليلا اعود اسافر وكل هذا كان بتدبير الله تعالي لان في هذه المده خطبوني وتزوجت وجالي بنين ومن المبين الواضح كان سبحانه وتعالي داعيني للزيجه لان لما مضيت من حلب خفيتاً كانت ينتي ارجع الي الرهبنه فصدفني ذلك السايح المذكور وغير ينتي عن الرهبنه في ضيعة كفتين وصار النصيب وسافرت معه الي تلك البلاد المرّ ذكرهم وزجع الي ما كنّا في صدده.

١٦٠،١١ فاستقمت في دكان الجوخ وبعد سنه اجا الي حلب معلمي الذي كنت سافرت معه خواجا بول لوكاز ونزل في بيت قنصر الفرنساويه فلما سمعت في قدومه مضيت الي عنده وسلمت عليه وهو لما راني عانقني ثم بعده عاتبني قوي كثير لاجل خروجي من عنده وما اعلمته في السبب وفي ذلك الوقت دخلوا لعنده خواجكيه فقطعنا المصاحبه الي غير يوم وفيما بعد عت اختبرت سبب رجوعه الي السياحه وهو ان لما اخد خبر بان الامير المذكور راسلني حتي اسوح سياحته فرفع من عقله ارسالي واعطاه قرار بانه هو يمضي للسياحه علي خصيته عوضاً عني وهذا كان سبب مجيه الي حلب وكملت السياحه علي خصيت ذلك الامير.

١٦١،١١ فبعد كام يوم عزمته حتي يزورنا ويتعشا عندنا فقبل وبعده عزمت اخوتي حتي يتعشوا معه وفي تلك الايام كنت اعزب وفارشلي مربع علي خصيتي. حيندٍ اتداركله

brother informing him of my plans. This was why my family were so overjoyed to see me safe and sound in Aleppo.

I spent three or four days at my brother's home, until fresh clothes had 11.158 been prepared for me. Then I got dressed, shaved my head, and donned a turban. They had a certificate of safe conduct drawn up for me, and once I had that in hand, I left the house and went to repay the visits to my family, loved ones, and relatives.[63] I then returned to the city and to my brother's warehouse. A few days later, my brother ʿAbdallāh opened a cloth shop for me. He put me under the supervision of my uncle Shāhīn Ghazzālah till I had learned the cloth-selling trade. I would spend twenty-two years working as a cloth merchant.

My brother was afraid that I would go on another journey. But God's plan 11.159 for me was different. During this period, I was engaged, got married, and had children. It's perfectly evident to me now that God Most High—may He be praised—had called me to a life of marriage, for when I had left Aleppo in secret, my plan was to become a monk. It was a matter of good fortune that I encountered that traveler in the village of Kaftīn who dissuaded me from my plan, and, as fate would have it, I traveled with him to all of those lands I've described. But let me go back to what I was saying.

A year after I began working in the cloth trade, my former master, *khawājah* 11.160 Paul Lucas, the one I had traveled with, arrived in Aleppo. He stayed at the home of the French consul. When I heard he had come to town, I went to pay my respects. As soon as he saw me, he embraced me, then scolded me severely for having left him without explaining my reasons. At that moment, some other *khawājah*s came by to see him so we had to cut short our reunion, saving it for another day.

Some time later, I figured out why he was back on the road. It seemed that when he'd learned that the nobleman I mentioned earlier had sent me on a voyage of exploration in his stead, he managed to change the nobleman's mind, promising to take my place and travel on his behalf. This was why he had come to Aleppo again: to carry out his mission for the nobleman.

A few days later, I invited him to visit and have dinner at our house. He 11.161 accepted, and I invited my brothers to join us for dinner. I was still a bachelor in those days, and I had furnished a room on the second floor for my own use. I prepared a sumptuous meal, then went to fetch him from the city and brought him back to the house and my waiting brothers. They greeted him

في عشا مكلف وبعده كلفته للمجي فاجبته معي من المدينه الي البيت وكانوا اخوتي
حاضرين فاسترحبوا فيه في غايه ما يكون ولما صار الوقت جلسنا علي المايده
وبعدما فرغنا من العشا جلسنا نتصامر معه. حيندٍ خطر في بالي باني كنت احكيت
له عن مرض والدتي وكيف ان عزرت الحكما عن شفاها في ذلك الوقت دكرته عنها
فامرني في حضورها امامه حتي يرا ما هو مرضها فاحضرناها امامه فلما نضرها
عرف ما كان فيها من المرض واطلقها وقلي ابقا ذكرني حتي اعطيك شي وفيه بتستريح
من مرضها.

اخيرًا قضينا السهرانه معه الي ان صارت الساعه في العشره وكنت هيات ١٦٢،١١
له فرشه علي قدر المراد فوقد الي ان اصبح الصباح وبعدما شربنا القهوه مضينا
جمله الي المدينه وكان كثير اوقات يجي لعندي لدكان الجوخ وكنت ادور معه بعد
الاحيان في البلد كهادته لاجل انه يفتش علي اشيا قديمه من فلوس وكتب وجواهر
ثمينه قليلة الوجود وما يشبه ذلك فتاني يوم لما اجا لعندي قلي خدني اليوم الي
سوق السياغه.

فلما وصلنا صار يتفرس في الاقماص الموضوعين عند السياغ فراء في قفص واحد ١٦٣،١١
من السياغ حجر منحوشه يتشبه حجر العقيق فاشتراها من الصايغ بمصريتين فاعتجبت
منه وبعدما مرينا من تلك الدكان فسالته ما حاجتك في هذه الحجر الدنيه فاجابني باني
اشتريتها لاجل شفا والدتك وامرني باني اضم فيها خيط واعلقها في عنق والدتي علي
اللحم وهي بتشفا من مرضها فاتضحكت وقلت في بالي بان عالجوها هل قدر اطبا وما
شفيت كيف ان هل حجر بتشفيها .

المراد ما ردت اخالفه واخدت الحجر منه وفعلت كما امرني وما عدت افتكرت فيها الي ١٦٤،١١
يوم من ذلك الاسبوع لما عاودت من المدينه احكولي بان والدتك اليوم طلبت بانها
تروح للحمام بعدما غيرت حوايجها وكان لها ثلاث سنوات ما راحت للحمام ولا جلست

most cordially, and when it was time for dinner, we sat at the table. Following the meal, we sat and chatted with *khawājah* Lucas.

I then remembered that I'd once told him about my mother's illness, and how the doctors had been unable to cure her. When I reminded him of that, he told me to bring my mother out so he could determine what her ailment was. We brought her out, and as soon as he looked at her, he knew what sort of illness she was suffering from.

"Be sure to remind me to give you something for her," he said to me after letting my mother go. "It will rid her of this illness."

We spent the rest of the evening in his company, until ten o'clock. I'd pre- 11.162 pared a bed for him, as comfortable as could be, and he slept soundly until the morning. After some coffee, we went off together to the city.

He would often pass by my shop, and sometimes I'd join him for his customary tours around town, looking for antiques like coins, books, and rare and valuable gems—that sort of thing. The day after our dinner, he came by my shop.

"Take me to the jewelry market," he said.

When we arrived, he set about scrutinizing the contents of the jewelers' 11.163 cases. In one of them, he found a stone resembling a carnelian, with a hole bored through it. To my surprise, he purchased it from the jeweler for two *miṣriyyah*s.

"What do you want with that worthless stone?" I asked him after we'd left the shop.

"I bought it as a treatment for your mother," he replied, and told me to thread the stone and hang it around my mother's neck so it rested against her skin. "She'll recover," he said.

"We've had so many doctors try and fail to cure her," I thought, chuckling to myself. "How's this stone going to be any different?"

But I didn't contradict him. I simply took the stone and did as he instructed, 11.164 and didn't give it a second thought until later that week, when I came home from the old city and was told that my mother had announced that she wanted to go to the public baths that day, after she changed her clothes. She hadn't been to the baths in three years! Nor had she joined us at the table for meals. She hadn't been able to sleep and never spoke to anyone. But on that day, she sat at the table and had a good lunch, chatting with us all like she used to do, then went off to the baths. Everyone was astounded. How had she made a full recovery?

معنا في المايده وما بتقدر تنام ولا تخاطب احد فذلك اليوم جلست معهم علي المايده وتعقدت مليح ولاقشتهم كعادتها ومضت معهم الي الحمام فصاروا يتعجبوا منها كيف انها شفيت بالكليه ولما رجعت من الحمام جلست معنا علي المايده واكلت بقابليه كانها ما كانت مريضه فاعتجبنا جميعنا من هذا الامر .

فقلت لهم لا تعجبوا هذا فعل خواص الحجر الذي علقته في عنقها فما صدقوا حتي اني ١٦٥،١١
سالت معلمي واعلمته بانها استراحة حينةٍ قلي وصيها بانها تدير بالها ولا ترفع هذه
الحجر من عنقها ليلا ترجع اليها بخار السوده وترجع كما كانت لان هذا الحجر له خواص
يجبذب البخار السوداويه وصار فيها كما قال كما قال بعد سنه وقعت الحجر من عنقها في الحمام
فرجعت كما كانت¹ ودرت وفتشت حتي اري مثل تلك الحجر فما رايت واستقام فيها
ذلك الي الموت .

ويوم اخراجا لعندي وصار يعاتبني بان كيف عندكم مكان يسما كاكيه وما اخبرتني ١٦٦،١١
فيه فما فهمت كلامه وسالته ما هو المكان وكيف اخبروك عنه فاجابني بان المكان
هو سرداب بينفد الي مدينة عنتاب . حينةٍ فهمت وهي الخناقيه اعني مغارة العبد
فقلتله وما لك في هذا المكان الخطر الموهم لان ما احد دخل وخرج لان مكان مغر
متسع وعتم والذي بيدخل اليه ما بيقدر يرجع لانه معوج الدرب كثير ناس دخلوا وما
خرجوا هل انك مضيت الي هذا المكان واختبرته هل انه صحيح ام لا اجبته بان
كل الناس يخبروا² عنه علي هذه الصفه ما بعرف انكان صدق ام كذب .

حينةٍ قلي انا بريد اختبره بالمعاينه حتي اعرف حقيقته ولكن بريد منك بان ترا لي ١٦٧،١١
رجل اختيار يكون يعرف هل مكان ويدلنا عليه وانا بعطيه اجرته بالوافر ويوم الخميس
انا بمضي الي هناك تكون تجيب هل رجل معك من كل بد وسبب فاجبته علي الراس
والعين ومضي من عندي وانا ما اعتبرت كلامه وقلت في بالي يوم الخميس بمضي الي
عنده وبرفع من عقله هذا الامر .

---
١ الأصل: كأنت. ٢ الأصل: يخزوا.

When my mother returned from the baths, she joined us for dinner and showed a good appetite—as though she'd never been ill. We were all baffled.

"There's really nothing to it," I told them. "It's because of the special properties of that stone I hung around her neck."

They wouldn't believe me until I asked my master about it. When I told him 11.165 that my mother had made a recovery, he gave me further instructions.

"Tell her to take care not to remove the stone from her neck, or else the black vapor will return and she'll suffer a relapse," he said. "The stone has the special property of drawing out the black vapor."

He was right. A year later, the stone fell off her neck while she was in the baths, and her melancholy returned. I went in search of a similar stone, to no avail. She remained melancholic until she died.

Another day, he came over and started to scold me. 11.166

"How is it you've never told me there's a place here called 'the Kanakia'?"[64] he demanded. I had no idea what he was talking about.

"What is this place, and who told you about it?" I asked.

"It's an underground passage that leads to the city of Antep."

Now I understood. He was talking about al-Khannāqiyyah; it's also known as the Cave of the Slave.

"Why would you be interested in such a dangerous and frightful place?" I asked. "No one who has gone in has ever come out! It's a vast, dark cavern, full of crooked passages that send people in circles and prevent them from escaping. Many have entered; none have come out alive."

"Have you ever been?" my master asked. "To investigate whether all this is true?"

"This is how *everyone* describes it," I insisted. "Are they telling the truth or lying? I don't know."

"I want to see it for myself, to find out the truth," he said. "And I'd like you 11.167 to find me an old man who knows the place and who can guide us there. I'll pay him well. I plan to head out on Thursday, so be sure to bring him with you then, without fail!"

"Consider it done," I replied, and he went on his way.

I didn't think much of his plan, and told myself that when Thursday came, I'd go see him and put the whole affair out of his mind.

١٦٨٫١١ ولما كان يوم الخميس باكر وانا ماضي الي المدينه كعادتي فصدفت رجل اختيار
نصراني كان يسما ابو زيت وهذا الرجل قديم الايام وكان في كل مدة حياته في
البراري كان اوقات يقدم عنب للمسيحيه لاجل الكبس وفي خلوص العنب كان
صاير مطرباز حطب يلاقي الي جمال الحطب من بعد وياتي فيهم الي حلب ويبيعهم
فلما صدفته وهو واقف علي التله في استندار جمال الحطب حينذٍ خطر في بالي بان
هذا الرجل يعرف حقيقة هذا المكان.

١٦٩٫١١ فاتقدمت اليه وحيته بالسلام وسالته هل له معرفة في مغارة العبد التي هي في
الخناقيه فاجابني علي الفور انا دخلتها مرار عده ويعرف مكانها لكن ما انتهيت الي
اخرها فلما سمعت منه هذا الكلام فرحت واحكيت له بان واحد فرنجي بيريد يمضي
اليها ويختبرها امضي معي الي عنده وهو بيعطيك بخشيش بالوافر اذا اريته تلك المغاره
فاجابني حبًا وكرامه امضي بنا.

١٧٠٫١١ فمضينا جمله وكان معه رجل اخر فلما انتهينا الي الخناقيه وبعد هنيهه وصل
الخواجه ومعه جمله من الفرنج والخدام وكلهم مسلحين ومحملين حمل زخيره وخيشة تبن
فلما وصلوا الي عندنا وسالني معلمي هل رايت احد يعرف المكان فاجبته نعم ودليته
عليه فانبصط قوي كثير واستكتر بخيري وقلنا لذلك الاختيار بانه يروينا ذلك المكان فقال
لنا اتبعوني فتبعناه الي ان دخلنا الي مغاره وسيعه ومكان عالي نقر حوار بيسما قصر
التقاتين مكان العبد الذي كان عصي فيه.

١٧١٫١١ اخيرًا دخلنا من هناك الي ان وصلنا الي منتها المغاره فراينا باب زغير منقور من
جبل الحوار وداخله مغارة العبد علي ما قال لنا ذلك الاختيار فلما رايناه انوهمنا وابينا
في الدخول فصار يجرعنا الخواجه وامر الخدام بانهم يخرجوا فنوده الشمع وكان ساكب
ستة فنود شمع عسلي. اخيرًا جلسنا في ذلك المكان واخرجوا لنا ماكل ومشرب
فبعدما اكلنا وشربنا حينذٍ امر الخدام بانهم يشعلوا فندين شمع ويعبوا كيس تبن من

On Thursday morning, I was on my way to the city as usual when I happened 11.168
upon an old Christian man named Abū Zayt. Now, this fellow was very old, and
had spent his whole life in the countryside. For a time, he would bring grapes
to the Christians for their presses. When the season was over, he'd become a
wood peddler. He would meet up with the camel drivers transporting wood,
bring the drivers to Aleppo, and sell the wood. When I came upon him, he
was standing at the top of a hill, waiting for the camel drivers to arrive with the
wood. It occurred to me that this fellow might know how to find the cave.

I went up and greeted him, and asked him if he knew anything about the 11.169
Cave of the Slave, in al-Khannāqiyyah.

"I've gone inside plenty of times," he replied at once. "I know where it is,
but I've never reached its very end."

I was delighted to hear this, and told him about my master's plan.

"There's a Frankish fellow who would like to explore the cave," I explained.
"Come see him with me, and he'll give you a handsome tip if you guide him
to the cave."

"It would be a pleasure and an honor," he said. "Let's go!"

Off I went with the old man, who brought a companion along with him. 11.170
We arrived at al-Khannāqiyyah, and the *khawājah* turned up shortly thereafter with a company of Franks and their servants. They were armed and had
brought along some ammunition and a sack of straw.

"Did you find someone who knows where the place is?" my master asked
me as soon as they arrived.

"Yes," I said, and pointed to the old man. My master was overjoyed, heaping
praise on me. We told the old man to take us to the spot.

"Follow me," he said.

We did as he asked, and soon arrived at a vast cave, hollowed out of the
limestone, whose entrance was at a considerable elevation. It was known as
the Castle of al-Tamātīn, and was the hideout of a certain rebellious slave, for
whom it was named.

We entered, and made our way to the bottom of the cave. There we found 11.171
a small door, hollowed out of that mountain of chalk. Beyond it was the Cave
of the Slave, according to the old man. None of us, in our fear, was willing to
proceed any farther, but the *khawājah* tried to embolden us. He ordered the
servants to take out their candles—he had had six candles made of beeswax.
We sat down, they took out some food and drink for us, and we ate and drank.

الخيشه فبعدما انتهوا من الذي امرهم به فتقدم الي عند ذلك الباب وفرغ تبخليه مدكوكه رصاص فكت سمع حس دوي عظيم استقام حكم ثلاث دقايق .

١١،١٧٢ حينذٍ جزمنا جميعنا بان ما ندخل فلما راء الخواجه ما منزيد ندخل فدخل هو واثنين من الخدام الواحد ماسك فند الشمع والاخر حمل كيس التبن حتي يرش تبن وهو ماشي ليلا يضيع الدرب عنه فلما دخل وحده عاد صار لنا جرعه فدخلنا جميعنا ما عدا ابقينا اتنين من الخدام ليحرسوا الحوايج والباب ليلا يمسكه احد علينا .

١١،١٧٣ فلما انتهينا داخل المغاره ونحن في غاية الرعب فمشيوا اتنين امامنا بالفنود الموقوده وواحد اخر بيرش التبن في اثرنا ليلا نضيع عن الطريق . حينذٍ كل شي الذي قالوه لنا رايناه كذب لان الطريق ما فيه ولا عوجه بل ساوي سهل وعالي وعريض عرض مايتين قدم وما راينا فيه غير عظام دواب وهو منقور من حوار فاستقمنا ماشيين حكم ربع ساعه فما راينا الا الفنود اعتمت وانقطع النفس وما عدنا نقدر ناخد نفس لان غم علينا المكان بسبب ما له منفس . وقتيذٍ ارتعبنا وردنا نرجع ليلا نهلك جميعنا داخل هل مكان . حينذٍ الخواجه جرعنا وقال لنا لا تخافوا المكان وسيع ما بيغم اصبروا حتي نمشي كام خطوة اخر ومنعود نرجع فتبعنا كلامه ومشينا معه مقدار ماية قدم فرانا امامنا سد انما في علوه منقوره من الجبل مثل مسطبه .

١١،١٧٤ حينذٍ الخواجه سال ذلك الاختيار لماذا بتقولوا بان هل سرداب بينفد من عنتاب وها قد وصلنا الي منتهاه فقال ذلك الاختيار بان باب السرداب هو في هذه العلوه ودمومه بالتراب ليلا يدخل احد فيه ويهلك فلما سمع الخواجه منه هذا الكلام وكب علي الكّاف واحد من الخدام وصعد الي تلك العلوه واخرج بنياره ونكش ارض تلك العلوه فراها سد وهي تترجبل . حينذٍ تحقق بان وصلنا الي منتها تلك المغاره وان الذي قالوه عنها هو كذب وانحدر وخجل ذلك الاختيار وبان كذب القايلين بانها بتنفد من عنتاب .

Then he ordered the servants to light two candles and fill a bag with straw. He strode over to the door and fired at it a pistol full of lead powder, emitting a powerful din that echoed for three minutes.

Now we swore we'd never go in! When the *khawājah* saw our trepidation, 11.172 he forged ahead, followed by two servants, one carrying a candlestick and the other the bag of straw, sprinkling straw as he walked so they wouldn't lose their way. When we saw the *khawājah* going ahead on his own, we found the courage to follow him, leaving two servants behind to guard our supplies, and also the door, so no one could block our way out again.

We descended into the cave, terrified. Two men walked ahead with candles, 11.173 while one sprinkled straw behind us so we would not lose our way. It was plain to us that everything we'd heard about the cave was a lie. The path did not have a single twist or turn; it was straight, easy to walk along, with plenty of headroom, and two hundred feet wide. There was nothing to see but the bones of dead animals. The passage was carved out of limestone. We had walked along it for about fifteen minutes, when suddenly the candles flickered out and it became difficult to breathe. No one seemed to be able to catch their breath, and the whole place felt suffocating. It had no source of air, after all! Fearing for our lives, we started to turn back.

"Don't be afraid," the *khawājah* said in encouragement. "This is a large space, and there's no chance of suffocation. Let's press on a bit longer, then we can head back."

We did as he asked. About a hundred feet farther along, we came to a dead end. But above our heads was a sort of stone shelf hewn out of the mountain rock.

"Why do you people say that this underground passage opens onto Antep?" 11.174 the *khawājah* asked the old man. "We've just reached the end of it!"

"The entrance to the passageway is past that perch up there," the old man replied. "But they filled it in to prevent people from entering and losing their lives."

On hearing this, the *khawājah* mounted the shoulders of one of the servants and climbed up to that very spot. Using his poniard, he dug around in the earth and found that it was blocked with gravel. That was when he realized we had reached the end of the cave, and that what had been said about it was a lie. He climbed down. The old man was embarrassed, because those who had pretended that the passageway led to Antep turned out to be liars.

١٧٥،١١ اخيرًا عدنا راجعين الي ان خرجنا من ذلك الباب وصرنا ندور في الخناقيه مكان
بمكان فسالونا الذين هم هناك بيقطعوا الحواره فحكينا لهم عن مطلوبنا فدلونا عن رجل
اختيار عمره قرب تسعين سنه وقالوا لنا بان هذا الاختيار بيدلكم علي باب السرداب
الذي بينفد الي عنتاب لانه قديم هجره وبيعرف جميع هذه الاماكن فقصدناهم بانهم
يحضروا لنا ذلك الاختيار فلما حضر فاعطاه الخواجه تلت غرش وقله ارويني باب
السرداب الذي بينفد من عنتاب فقال اتبعوني.

١٧٦،١١ فتبعناه الي ان وصل الي مغاره من تلك المغاير الموجوده هناك واروانا مكان في
نزله غميقه لكنها مردومه الي فوق وقال لنا انا كنت ولد اجي مع ابي الي هاهنا ورايت
المدخل لهذا السرداب لكن فيما بعد امر حاكم البلد بان يردموا هذا المدخل ليلا يدخل
احد ويهلك وبيقول من الجمله بان جملة شباب في عرس والعريس معهم اجوا يتفرجوا
علي هذا المنفد فجرعوا بعضهم البعض ودخلوا في هذا المنفد وما عاد خرج منهم احد
فهلكوا جميعهم لانهم ضيعوا الدرب وما اهتدوا ياخذوا معهم حبل طويل يربطوا
طرفه الواحد في باب السرداب وطرف الاخر يمسكوه معهم ويرجعوا فلما تم كلامه
ساله الخواجه عن المكان الذي دخلناه ما هو .

١٧٧،١١ فقال هل مكان في اول عماره مدينة حلب كانوا يقطعوا منه الحواره ويبنوا والشاهد
هوان له قوافع ما بين كل ماية قدم قافعه يسحبوا منها قطع الحوار وهذا صحيح لانا لما كنا
داخل هذا السرداب راينا قوافع مسدودات فاثني الخواجه عليه الكلام بان هل مكان
جميعه جبل حوار لماذا دخلوا في هل مدايقه حتي يقطعوا الحوار فقال ذلك الاختيار
لهذا سببين السبب الاول هو ان حوار هذا المكان صلب بيضاين في العمار مثل
السلب والسبب الثاني وهو الاصح بان ملوك اول كانوا يستعنوا هل سراديب حتي
يمشوا العسكر من تحت الارض حتي لا احد يشعر بهم وكانوا يظهروا في الظاهر

We made our way back, emerging from the entrance to the cave. Then we 11.175 explored the rest of al-Khannāqiyyah, investigating one spot after another. Some people cutting limestone asked us what we were looking for. When we told them, they referred us to an old man who could help us. He was nearly ninety years old.

"He'll show you the entrance to the underground passageway that emerges in Antep," they said. "He's been in these parts for a long time, and knows them well."

We asked them to bring the old man to us. When he appeared, the *khawājah* handed him a third of a piaster.

"Show me the passageway that leads to Antep," he said.

"Follow me," the old man replied.

We followed him to one of the many caves in the area, whose steep, sloping 11.176 entrance had been entirely filled in with earth.

"When I was a boy, I used to come here with my father," the old man said. "The entrance to the passageway was open then, but some time later the governor ordered that it be filled in, to prevent people from going in and getting killed." He continued as follows: "Now, they say that a group of young men were once celebrating a wedding with the groom and came here to take a look at the passageway. Well, they started goading each other to go inside, and eventually they all did. Not a single one returned. They all died, lost underground. None of them thought to bring a good, long rope with them to tie to the entrance of the passageway. They could have held on to it and used it to get out again."

After he finished telling this story, the *khawājah* asked him about the passageway we'd explored earlier. What was it?

"Oh, that one," the old man said. "When Aleppo was first built, they used 11.177 to cut limestone out of it, for construction. The proof is that it has a pit every hundred feet. That was where they'd dig out the limestone."

It was true: When we were in the passageway, we saw pits like that, blocked up. The *khawājah* commended the old man. Then he pointed out that this whole area seemed to be a mountain of limestone. Why then would they put themselves to the trouble of excavating it from a cramped cave?

"For two reasons," the old man replied. "First of all, the limestone there is more solid. For construction purposes, it's as durable as granite. The second reason—and this is the truer one—is that the kings of times past used those

بانهم يقطعوا هل حواره لاجل البنا وفي الباطن كانت لاجل انهم يمشوا العسكر من تحت الارض.

فقطع لقش هذا الاختيار عقل الخواجه وسدق كلامه ايضاً بان ذاك السرداب ١١،١٧٨ المردوم بينفد الي عنتاب. حينذٍ تركاه ورجعنا وسعدنا الي كرم يسمي كرم القليعه وهناك اتغدينا واستقمنا الي المسا وكل من راح الي حال سبيله وهذا منتها خبرنا والسياحه ونستغفر الله من الزياده والنقصان.


تم ذلك في اليوم الثالث من شهر ادار سنه ١٧٦٤ مسيحيـه.


تـم

passageways to march their soldiers underground, so no one would know they were coming. They pretended they were excavating the limestone for construction, but the secret purpose was to be able to move their troops underground."

The old man's words fascinated the *khawājah*, who found them believable. 11.178 He also accepted the old man's claim that the filled-in passageway emerged in Antep. We left him then, and returned the way we'd come. Climbing up to the vineyard known as al-Qulayʿah, we had lunch and spent the rest of the day there. When evening came, each went on his way.

This is the end of my story, and of my wanderings. I ask God's forgiveness for any undue additions or omissions.

Completed on the third of March in the year 1764 of the Christian era.

# Afterword: Ḥannā Diyāb and the *Thousand and One Nights*

## Paulo Lemos Horta

Scholars of the *Thousand and One Nights* have long known that a Syrian Maronite named Ḥannā Diyāb played a role in the genesis of some of the most famous stories added to Antoine Galland's early-eighteenth-century French translation of the story collection. However, before the identification of Diyāb's *Book of Travels*, evidence for the Aleppan traveler's distinctive contribution was frustratingly slim. Galland's diary offers a brief glimpse of his first meeting with Diyāb in the Paris apartment of Paul Lucas, a French collector of curiosities, in 1709. There, Galland discovered that the young traveler "[knew] some very beautiful Arabic tales."[65] The French translator also took notes on a series of sessions from May 5 to June 6, during which Diyāb told him fifteen fantastical stories. Although Galland requested manuscripts of these stories from Diyāb, references in his journal suggest that he received only one: "Aladdin and the Wonderful Lamp." Such were the meager resources available to researchers of the *Nights*, and for decades they seemed content to relegate Diyāb to a footnote in their analyses of a story collection whose impact on Western literature has been extensive.

The publication of Diyāb's *Book of Travels* at last offers the opportunity to rescue the author from the margins of *Nights* scholarship and to revise our understanding of the origins of Galland's most popular tales, including "Aladdin and the Wonderful Lamp," "'Alī Bābā and the Forty Thieves," and "The Ebony Horse." A mixture of memoir and travelogue, *The Book of Travels* is dominated by the author's journey from Aleppo to Paris in the service of Paul Lucas, a shady procurer of curiosities for the court of Louis XIV. Looking back on that journey fifty years later, Diyāb notes that while in Paris he met with an unnamed translator, recognizably Galland, who was working on the *Thousand and One Nights*, and that he supplied the man with enough new stories to allow him to finish the collection. There is no evidence that Diyāb offered stories he thought belonged to the *Thousand and One Nights*. Like the storytellers who plied their trade in the coffee shops of Aleppo, he may have retold old tales or created new ones from familiar elements. Although his stories were soon to become popular, Diyāb does not seem to have learned of the impact of his intervention in literary history.

*The Book of Travels* offers an opportunity to explore the resonances that emerge when Diyāb's narrative is examined alongside the tales that passed into Galland's *Nights* through his agency. Diyāb's memoir reveals his ability to weave anecdotes and story motifs into a compelling tale of a life shaped by ambition and curiosity. Its pages offer clear evidence of his attraction to religion, magic, and mystery; his thirst for adventure; and his willingness to break from what was conventionally expected of a junior member of an Aleppan merchant family. His lasting contribution to the Western storytelling corpus known as the *Arabian Nights* can now be viewed through his fascination with difference, strangeness, and wonder. As Diyāb comes to the fore as a personality and as a narrator, his encounter with Galland in Paris can no longer be dismissed as a mere footnote to the history of the *Nights*. The so-called orphan tales—that is, the tales with no extant Arabic original—can no longer be seen as authorless.[66] Their origins lie not only in the French literary practice of Galland but in the imagination and narrative skills of the Syrian traveler who first told them in 1709.

The opportunity for Diyāb to insert his tales into the extensive corpus of stories of the *Thousand and One Nights* arose from the fundamental mutability of the original Arabic collection, which had always invited storytellers to continue the sequence of tales in a potentially infinite demonstration of the possibilities of invention and recombination. In the early Arabic manuscripts of the *Nights*, only the frame tale and a few early story cycles remain constant. These are nocturnal stories told by the brave Shahrazad to save her own life and the lives of the other women of the kingdom—an attempt to use the lure of "what happened next" to prevent her husband, Shahriyar, from having her killed the next morning. As the frame story explains, King Shahriyar has been cuckolded by his queen and, having dispatched her and her lover, has resolved to marry a virgin each evening and to promptly execute her the next day. When Shahrazad volunteers to be his next victim, the string of stories begins, each more marvelous and astounding than the one before. No authentic Arabic collection of *Thousand and One Nights* tales offers the mythical number of 1,001 nights of storytelling, but each offers new additions and variations that build on the central core of the tales' oldest components. As the stories entered Western literature through French, this pattern continued. When Galland's Arabic manuscript ran out of stories, his publisher, and then Galland himself, added new tales intended to continue the pattern of ever more wondrous stories to meet French readers' insatiable appetite for Shahrazad's tales.[67]

Diyāb's arrival in Paris with Paul Lucas in 1709 was therefore providential for Galland. Of the sixteen stories Diyāb offered him during their meetings, the French translator inserted ten into his version of *Les mille et une nuits*.[68] These ten tales have proven to be among the most influential *Thousand and One Nights* tales and have been repeatedly translated, adapted, and republished in various formats. It is not just that Diyāb's tales were the most widely read: As French scholars have argued, their impact on European languages was so great that they ultimately influenced how the story collection as a whole was received and interpreted.[69] Despite having many affinities with tales contained in Arabic manuscripts of the *Thousand and One Nights*, the tales added by Galland and Diyāb seem more consistently otherworldly and marvelous. Their emphasis on supernatural elements—embodied in the powerful jinni of the lamp in "Aladdin" and the flying carpet in "Prince Aḥmad and the Fairy Perī Bānū"—has colored perceptions of the *Nights* as a whole. So too has the greater attention in their tales to precious jewels, luxurious materials, and elaborate ceremonies. In literary scholarship, these elements have been attributed, in too facile a manner, to the particular assumptions of the European Orientalist, as epitomized by Galland. Given the absence of information on Diyāb, it was Galland who was seen as adding elements he thought representative of Islamic culture, such as superstition and love of luxury, to inform and entertain his readers. It was also Galland who was credited with the literary skill needed to elevate "mere folklore" into a text deserving of a place on European bookshelves.[70]

While neglecting Diyāb's distinctive contribution to Western versions of the *Nights*, several literary critics have lauded Galland as the de facto author or creator of the *Thousand and One Nights* as a work of world literature.[71] In evaluating his achievement as a translator of one Arabic manuscript of the *Nights*, critics often stress that he reworked the original tales instead of merely translating them. This emphasis implies that the Arabic text from which he worked was merely raw material requiring the literary intervention of a French master to become worthy of European attention. When critics turn their attention to Galland's versions of Diyāb's tales, the achievement of the French Orientalist appears even more impressive, and the Syrian storyteller is confined to obscurity. In this reading of the "orphan tales," Galland, taking only the bare outlines of plot from his Syrian informant, drew on his own travels in the Orient and his research as an Orientalist to fill in the fabulous details of voyages, palaces, and magical objects. The French translator is placed within the long line of creative storytellers who have contributed to the making and remaking of the stories attached to the *Thousand and One Nights*. The credit for stitching and weaving—even when this involved plot elements that Galland's notes indicate came from Diyāb—and for making tales sing on the page has gone to Galland.[72] Diyāb, meanwhile, is either forgotten completely or credited only with providing the material that Galland's sophistication transformed into a literary product worthy of being consumed in Enlightenment Paris.

Galland has been credited not only with making the *Nights* more marvelous, but also more modern. In adapting the tales to the conventions of prose writing in vogue in eighteenth-century France, Galland, it is claimed, gave greater psychological richness and depth to the characters. The French translator was able to transform sparse notes from Diyāb's oral performances into compelling tales of ordinary characters caught up in extraordinary predicaments, according to Sermain, editor of the most recent edition of Galland's *Les mille et une nuits*. Drawing on French literary conventions, Galland invented dialogues and inner monologues, and gave narrative coherence to the rudimentary story elements offered by Diyāb. Characters were developed with more sympathy, and the hero of humble origin was developed as a moral example to French readers.[73] Galland is understood to have done more than feed the appetite for fairy tales in and beyond the French salons of the early eighteenth century. He is also said to have opened up the tales in terms of character and technique so they could resonate with mainstream literary trends in French prose throughout the eighteenth century, which coincided with the greatest penetration of the *Nights* in cultural consciousness. To this day, it is axiomatic in French scholarship that the modernity of the *Nights* tales is a result of their handling by Galland, and subsequently Diderot and Voltaire, and their circulation in both overt and subterranean currents of European modernity.[74] If the stories appealed in Europe, it was because they had become more modern, and Galland and Paris were the agents of their modernity.

A careful consideration of Diyāb's *Book of Travels* should disrupt this narrative of Galland's authorship and allow us to recognize Diyāb's distinctive contributions to the tales added in French to the corpus of the *Nights*. These contributions include his creative agency as a storyteller and the modernity of his narration of the eighteenth-century world. The narrative skill he reveals in *The Book of Travels* lends credence to the argument that the "beautiful" tales he related to Galland in 1709 contained more than mere fragments that had to be stitched together by the European translator to achieve their effect. If Diyāb's account of his journey is made up of some forty embedded anecdotes and stories, as Johannes Stephan has suggested,[75] then the author demonstrates considerable facility in weaving them together to form his own narrative. Like other travel accounts from the period, the text can be seen as a particular mixture of fact and fiction that partakes of both Arabic and European storytelling traditions. Throughout the manuscript, descriptions of foreign lands mingle with entertaining anecdotes that Diyāb has heard or read to create an engaging account of a life composed of stories. Diyāb's effort to integrate elements familiar from other contexts can be recognized in the presence of motifs from the tales of Nizami and Boccaccio. Examples include the tale of the woman buried alive and the story of the jilted painter who is promised and then denied the hand of a beautiful young woman in marriage. The memoir thus confirms Galland's journal notes, which reveal Diyāb's ability to combine existing story elements into new tales.[76]

Diyāb's *Book of Travels* shares motifs and themes with the added French *Nights* tales, as well as a manner of telling. In his memoir, the Syrian author mixes elements from different sources or embeds stories to build suspense. This skill is equally evident in the tales Diyāb offered to Galland for the *Nights*. When Diyāb tells the story of his arrest in Paris, for instance, he builds suspense by frequently interrupting the narrative, as he interpolates tales about unusual characters and their struggles with the backdrop of Enlightenment Paris.[77] The use of such embedded stories is central to the construction of tales in the Arabic corpus of the *Nights*. Some of the stories Diyāb told Galland—most importantly the three stories interlinked in "The Caliph's Night Adventure"—adopt this structure as well. Other Diyāb stories demonstrate the creative possibilities that result from linking or mixing elements from the rich storytelling culture of his homeland. The tale of "'Alī Bābā and the Forty Thieves," which began its life as the "Tale of Hogia Baba" in Diyāb's first narration to Galland, demonstrates the power of linking existing motifs to create a tale of intrigue and suspense. Diyāb's version combines three popular story elements—the magical cave, the gang of thieves, and the clever slave girl. All of these elements existed in some form prior to his intervention, but it was his telling of the tale to Galland that first brought them together into a new tale. Galland's rewriting alters the name of the main character and drops the food motif from the story of the magical cave.[78] Even so, it preserves the balance between the elements contributed by Diyāb, and it is these elements that are central to the story's appeal.

Creating tales by combining motifs is central to Diyāb's narrative practice, as it was for the many storytellers who contributed to the constantly mutating *Nights*. The author of *The Book of Travels* proved to have precisely the skills and talent necessary to give him a place among the many storytellers, compilers, and editors of the *Nights* tales over the centuries. There is no doubt that Galland made some additions to the stories he received from Diyāb and incorporated into *Les mille et une nuits*. The additions to "Prince Aḥmad and the Fairy Perī Bānū" are obvious, and add to the exotic quality of the three princes' travels in search of a marvelous artifact to win the hand of the beloved princess.[79] However, these interpolations drawn from Galland's academic work fail to demonstrate the kind of literary inventiveness that critics would like to attribute to him. More than these opportunistic insertions, Diyāb's mixing of story elements to create a compelling narrative deserves pride of place. Within the modern history of storytelling, the impact of Diyāb's tales is remarkable, as their plots and motifs have been codified two hundred years later as tale types by researchers. The folk-narrative historian Ulrich Marzolph has argued that Ḥannā Diyāb introduced more tale types to the narrative repertoire of the Western world than any other storyteller. Marzolph has found no fewer than four international tale types whose first appearance can be traced to the stories Diyāb told Galland.[80] If these tale types now strike us as some of the most basic plots in world literature, then it is time to acknowledge that this is a result of Diyāb's creative abilities.

Diyāb's imprint on the tales transmitted to Galland may transcend the deployment of techniques already in evidence in the core tales of the original collection. Some of the distinctly "modern" qualities attributed to the Diyāb stories appear to have echoes in *The Book of Travels*, raising the question of whether it was Diyāb who imparted this particular sensibility to the *Nights*. If the Diyāb-Galland stories indeed display more self-reflection and psychological depth than other *Nights* stories, *The Book of Travels* may explain why, as Diyāb's approach to narration in that work involves a great interiority. *The Book of Travels* is written in the first person and the narrator asserts his individuality as an observer, even hoping to spare his readers the disappointments he experienced in his life.[81] The narrator seeks to impose his authority on the work as an author rather than relying on the collective authority of a chain of guarantors, or expressing his subjectivity by quoting poetry as other travelers had.[82] The work is remarkable in capturing the emotional qualities of Diyāb's younger, more naive self, and comments in a thoughtful way on the choices that determined his path through life.[83] His description of the sense of alienation he experienced as a novice monk is striking. He writes about himself freely, confessing his difficulties and self-doubt, and when he is laid low, he feels that the world has shrunk before his eyes.[84]

In the journey that takes Diyāb from Aleppo to Paris and back, his conscious self-fashioning is evident in moments of disguise and deception. Diyāb admits to the lies and deceits that play a critical role in facilitating his journeys, as the text's French translator has noted. When on his return voyage he confidently claims to be a doctor like his father before him, and that he studied in Marseille, he is admitting to deliberate deceit. For the French translator, these are the moments where Diyāb most clearly reveals his modernity—when he demonstrates his understanding of social expectations but refuses to be bound by those constraints.[85] This distinctive stance is signaled at beginning of the memoir in an episode in which he ignores his family's order to return to Aleppo, clearly asserting his right to choose his own path in this narrative.

Life on the road with Paul Lucas offered Diyāb the opportunity to reinvent himself and provided an apprenticeship in the life of the merchant-traveler, including an immersion in a barter system defined by ruses. Paul Lucas was the consummate self-made man, who registers in the courtly correspondence of more erudite rivals and patrons as a "marvelous" autodidact.[86] What earned him this moniker was an almost preternatural ability to gauge the value of ancient coins and medallions by a combination of touch and experience, which left them baffled by his ability to bring back hundreds of coins for the cabinets of the court without a forgery among them. Doubtless, the unacknowledged labor of servants such as Diyāb helped him secure his hoard of treasures, among them manuscripts in languages he did not claim to know. But one should not discount the possibility that the self-taught Lucas accumulated a substantial store of practical knowledge that had long allowed him to survive as a jewel merchant and thrive within trading routes and markets of the Levant, the experience that recommended him to his patrons at court.

Lucas adopts the guise of a medical doctor to facilitate their passage through the lands along their Mediterranean route, and Diyāb describes the ruses of his mentor without censure. His own efforts to mirror these subterfuges later in the journey show Diyāb acting as the agent of his own destiny. Though the young Diyāb was complicit in the subterfuges Lucas deployed to swindle locals out of precious objects, his admiration for Lucas's practice of medicine was genuine, and he regrets not having learnt more when he presents himself as a physician on his return journey. Pontchartrain's instructions governing the commission given Lucas during this journey explicitly prescribed his adoption of the guise of a physician to deflect attention from his real aim of collecting items for the French court's cabinets of curiosities. To this end, a passport was drawn up in Lucas's name that identified him as a doctor, and Lucas was advised not to reveal he traveled to acquire coins, medallions, and manuscripts for the French monarch (for fear this knowledge might drive up prices and invite hostility).[87] Lucas himself describes adopting the title of physician in his previous voyage for the purpose of avoiding suspicion.[88] Diyāb had cause to take the Frenchman for a doctor. The Richelieu collection at the National Library in France preserves Lucas's commission from a naturalist at court to procure herbs and learn about medicine not native to France.[89] As part of his guise, Lucas may have traveled with common remedies to pass for a doctor in his travels.[90] Some success in this regard must have been evident (as Diyāb attests), for in this, as in his other voyages, Lucas traveled on a tight budget and relied greatly on bartering his cures for information, hospitality, and goods.

Diyāb's memoir is also notable for its interest in the testing of social boundaries, displaying an increased awareness, relative to previous Arabic travelogues, of social distinctions between Christians and Muslims, and between Maronites and other Christians.[91] These issues emerge at several points on his journey to Paris with Lucas, and again when he attempts to gauge where he fits into a social hierarchy with regard to other Maronites and Eastern Christians in Paris. At one point, he must weigh an offer of marriage into the family of a café owner that would offer him a foothold in the French capital against Lucas's elusive promise of an appointment as the king's Arabic librarian. In some cases, this attentiveness to social distinction involves navigating gendered assumptions, as in an early episode in which Diyāb is enlisted in an effort by a Maronite husband to convince his wife to cease veiling. Diyāb's comments attributing differences in women's behavior to the state of girls' education indicate a willingness to include consideration of social practices within a narrative marked by dramatic and marvelous events.

Diyāb's writing self-consciously explores efforts at shaping his identity, attentive to the roles and constraints that shaped the lives around him. In light of this evidence, literary critics should be cautious about ascribing any modern qualities in the *Nights* tales to Galland as translator, or indeed "author." Judged only from the rough notes on his meetings with Galland, the stories Diyāb told in 1709 offer moments in which the characters seem to possess a complex inner life. In "The Ebony Horse," characters are plagued by internal conflicts at several critical moments in the story, as when the king of Persia wonders whether he really ought to trade the princess for the wondrous flying horse. In "The City of Gold," a Diyāb story that Galland chose not to insert into the collection, the third prince is described in the diary notes as having "a more open, more lively, and more penetrating mind than those of his two elder brothers." Understanding that his father would never permit him to journey beyond the kingdom to satisfy his desire for adventure, he is careful to dissimulate and keep his travel preparations a secret. Even some elements of interiority in "'Alī Bābā and the Forty Thieves" attributed by at least one scholar to Galland himself, including the moment when Cassim forgets the words he needs to speak in order to escape the cave, are part of Diyāb's original telling of the story, as the notes from Galland's journal prove.[92]

Diyāb's interest in the lives of ordinary characters caught up in dangerous events that they are helpless to control resonates with the greater stress on characterization in the added *Nights* stories, when compared to the scholarly preoccupations that dominate Galland's work outside the *Thousand and One Nights*. Looking back on his time in Paris in *The Book of Travels*, Diyāb is attentive to the predicament of the economically marginal as the capital experienced the effects of economic crisis and harvest failure in the winter of 1708–9. While Galland makes no comment on the bread riots that occurred in his neighborhood on the day Diyāb delivered the conclusion of "Aladdin," Diyāb's record of his time in the city mentions beggars at cathedral doors and former soldiers forbidden to ask for alms. In *The Book of Travels*, Diyāb is particularly sympathetic to the plight of the condemned he finds in the broadsides advertising their executions. In one episode, a young man takes debt titles from his father's shop to his own through a misunderstanding and ends up on the scaffold despite the protestations of his family. Diyāb lingers over this public and private tragedy, detailing the execution and the lamentations of the assembled crowd. This story of an everyday tragedy played out on the streets of Paris offers an obvious thematic link to the plight of a young protagonist like Aladdin.[93] There is nothing like it in Galland's journals.[94]

If greater attention to social life and material culture are indeed a distinguishing feature of the Diyāb-Galland tales,[95] then *The Book of Travels* suggests that Diyāb was more likely than Galland to have nurtured those concerns. Diyāb's dreams of advancement in Paris as a servant of the royal court share a certain affinity with the fantastic journey of Aladdin, while other stories told to Galland offer a darker perspective on the possibilities of social ascent. In "Khawājah Ḥasan al-Ḥabbāl," two friends try to change the fortune of a poor rope maker by giving him money but are unable to alter his circumstances (though he does find fortune via other means). Diyāb's oral telling of the tale included details about how valuable coins might be hidden in the head garments of the rope maker at the center of the experiment ("[he] hid it in his turban as all the poor people do").[96] The particular social circumstances of women also serve as a significant element in the Diyāb stories described in Galland's notes. In "The Two Sisters Who Envied Their Cadette," the princess is given the same education as her elder brothers, with instruction in reading and writing, the sciences, riding, spear throwing, and playing musical instruments, and proves herself superior when the characters are tested. In "Qamar al-Dīn and and Badr al-Budūr," which Galland left out of the *Nights*, there is comparable stress on the significance of a woman receiving the same education as a man, and the female protagonist succeeds in rescuing her beloved cousin by outsmarting the servants of the sultan's court and beating his favorite at chess. Despite the long interval that separates them, the Diyāb who narrates *The Book of Travels* shows significant affinities in interests and approach with the storyteller who offered tales of wonder to a French translator in Paris.

When these examples are considered against the evidence regarding Galland's own literary efforts, the case for seeing Diyāb as a significant contributor to the distinctiveness of the added *Nights* stories appears even stronger. Galland did indeed spend time in the Ottoman world and achieve success as an Orientalist scholar, but his other writings include little evidence that he was adept at the kinds of literary flourishes French critics have attributed to him. If Diyāb broke with the convention of the Arab travelogue by embracing the first-person pronoun in *The Book of Travels*,[97] Galland's journal of his time in Constantinople in 1672–73 seems determined to erase his own voice and perspective.[98] Although Galland had a French tradition of journal writing to draw upon, his own journal of this formative period in his life barely registers events in his life, or interest in the lives of others. It does little to construct a narrative,[99] and shows no interest in the kinds of interiority deemed new to the added *Nights* tales. Instead, it is given over to the cataloging of the manuscripts and books that were his main scholarly interest at the time. Scholars have fixated on the journal's rare and vivid description of an army heading out for battle in May 1672 as a sign of how Galland's personal experience of the Orient would have informed his retellings of the stories offered by Diyāb.[100] Yet Galland's journal generally eschews the kind of elaborate descriptions of the settings and customs of Constantinople that are assumed to be a part of the translator's literary repertoire. The same is true of his *Nights* translation as a whole. Despite Galland's gesture toward the ethnographic goal of explaining the Orient to his readers through his translation of the *Thousand and One Nights*, he did little to follow through with this program in the text (and he supplies very few notes). The translation reveals a literary approach to anthropology, rather than an anthropological approach to literature, as Madeleine Dobie aptly puts it.[101]

If Galland's diaries are any guide, the intellectual interests he pursued while translating the *Nights* and meeting with Diyāb are the same as those he pursued during his time abroad. In Paris, Galland devoted the bulk of his day to the Greco-Roman interests and numismatic projects that were his primary passion. He spent his most intense hours of study on lectures and writing projects related to the Greco-Roman classics, while his evenings were spent on translating the *Nights*, a task that required less energy and attention.[102] His diary reflects a clear preference for translation from a text rather than the exercises in expansion and development that he is presumed to have undertaken with Diyāb's outlined stories. Galland notes in his journal that he asked Diyāb to write out the stories he had told him. He records that he did indeed receive a text of "Aladdin," which is the one he presumably used in the creation of the published version of the story. While it has not yet been proven, there remains the intriguing possibility that Galland was not attempting to replicate the stories he heard from Diyāb using the shorthand notes from his journal, but was working, rather, from fuller manuscripts that contained some of the distinctive elements identified by scholars of the *Nights*.[103]

Little in Diyāb's Paris diaries reveals Galland to be capable of the kind of literary creativity and empathy necessary to create the depth of character or the "modern" interiority that some scholars perceive in the Diyāb-Galland tales. Immersed in the Greco-Roman classics, Galland evinces no curiosity about the world around him, not even in the tragic events that still held Diyāb's interest fifty years after they occurred. In many ways, the critical edition of Galland's diaries only deepens the mystery surrounding the personality at their center. The editor's notes, but not the entries themselves, point to the workings of history just outside Galland's door as war, famine, and bread riots brought suffering to many Parisians.[104] But the Orientalist preferred the world of fixed texts to the infinite stories beyond his doorstep. In his editorial work on travelogues or the *Bibliothèque orientale*, or his translations from the Qur'an and of a history of coffee, Galland preferred to let the work speak for itself. His writings over the decades do not suggest the voice of an emerging storyteller capable of providing psychological depth to the protagonists of the *Nights*.

Viewed against the labors of the French Orientalist, Diyāb's *Book of Travels* offers more convincing evidence of a narrator immersed in the lore of story-telling and attuned to the power of a carefully constructed fiction. Despite the fifty-year gap between Diyāb's journey to Paris and the production of the travel-ogue, the figure of Paul Lucas casts a long shadow over the tale it contains. Lucas was himself the author of popular French travelogues.[105] His quest for treasures and curiosities for the French court determined the itinerary of Diyāb's travels from Aleppo to Paris,[106] and his penchant for the marvelous resonates with both *The Book of Travels* and the stories Diyāb would contribute to the *Nights* in Paris. Lucas's journeys through the Mediterranean to Egypt, Constantinople, and Persia were not connected to any practice of scientific inquiry. He was neither a geographer nor an archaeologist, and he had no training in ancient or foreign languages. In essence, he was an old-fashioned treasure hunter with an insatiable appetite for precious objects and fantastic stories. The son of a merchant from Rouen, he had made his reputation traveling through the Mediterranean and Ottoman world to procure precious stones, medals, and manuscripts for his patrons at the court of Louis XIV. Drawing on the conventions of the French picaresque novel, Lucas styled himself in the mode of a fictional character. In his third travelogue, he declares, "Nothing resembles more the life of errant knights than the life of travelers, and the situation I found myself this night, and where I have found myself a hundred times, reminds me of the pleasant notions of Don Quixote de la Mancha." The travelogues he produced from these journeys were full of exotic landscapes, marvelous objects, and fantastic adventures, and could include sketches of entire cities that Lucas had never visited, including Mecca and Medina.[107]

When in 1707 Diyāb met Lucas in a caravan departing from Aleppo, he attached himself to a master who believed that fantastical tales were no less valuable than precious artifacts. For Lucas, travelers who sought to know the essence of a foreign culture needed to seek out the folktales and legends that cir-culated among the common people. Having lost his last interpreter, and unable to communicate with the leader of the caravan out of Aleppo, Lucas was in need of Diyāb's linguistic skills. Traveling with Lucas through the Mediterranean and on to Paris, Diyāb would have played a critical role in the gathering of marvelous tales and the objects with which they were associated. In his account of their time together, Diyāb captures the power of personality that Lucas brought to his pursuit of the treasures and curiosities he gathered on commission from the French crown. Aware of the lies and ruses Lucas used to navigate these uncertain territories and to acquire items with little concern for the destruction this caused, Diyāb is still willing to trust the Frenchmen enough to follow him to Paris in the hope of securing a position for himself at the royal court.

Beyond the interest in precious objects that drove Lucas's and Diyāb's travels together, the two men shared an abiding interest in tales of miracles and magic. In the Levant and throughout the journey to Paris, Diyāb's experiences were shaped by Lucas's preference for traveling with priests and relying on a network of religious sanctuaries.[108] Lucas possessed a genuine interest in the material remains of the Christian past in Cairo. He and Diyāb together visited the site where the Holy Family was said to have taken refuge, and both describe it in their respective travelogues. In Greece, Lucas was fascinated by the Christian marvels of the Orthodox Church, and he shared Diyāb's interest in the material culture of Marian devotion.[109] Diyāb's *Book of Travels* parallels these interests in recounting an intense religious experience in Tunis and in recording the many miracles associated with the Blessed Virgin of the Black Mountains.

Diyāb also incorporates episodes of miraculous healing into his travelogue—healing effected by the marvelous power of amulets and secret potions or the intercession of the Virgin herself. Similar motifs appear in the tales Diyāb told Galland, most notably in "Prince Aḥmad and the Fairy Perī Bānū," where the princess is healed by a magic apple that can cure any illness. The supernatural power of the elixir of life contained in the philosopher's stone, and wielded by Lucas himself, is dramatized in stories included in the travelogues of both men. Lucas spins a wild tale of finding the secret of the philosopher's stone by meeting with an Uzbek dervish in Anatolia and retracing the steps of Nicolas Flamel in Paris. Diyāb recounts the use of the elixir to save the life of a desperately ill Lucas during a stop on their journey in Tunis. Such fantastical tales were part of the storytelling repertoire of magic, medicine, and miracle that were shared by Diyāb and his French master for the critical months during which they journeyed to Paris.[110]

One might justly ask how much this common enthusiasm for marvels both natural and material would have informed Diyāb's storytelling preferences after he arrived in Paris and found an avid listener in Antoine Galland. After a journey of many months, Diyāb would certainly have gained a sense of the kinds of stories that would attract a French collector of curiosities. In his *Book of Travels*, he recalls paying meticulous attention to Lucas's note-taking as he accumulated the observations and anecdotes that would go into his own popular travelogues. Even if his personal preferences had not run parallel to those of Lucas and the growing reading public clamoring for more stories in the mode of the *Nights*, Diyāb would have been well prepared to deliver tales of marvels to the French translator who asked him for stories.

An examination of Diyāb's narrative of his experiences during the year and a half of his journey with Lucas before his encounter with Galland in Paris allows us to speculate about how they might have shaped specific elements within the stories that were later circulated through versions of the *Nights*. The resemblance of the magician from "Aladdin and the Wonderful Lamp" to Lucas, also noted by Bernard Heyberger,[111] leads me to further specify ways in which this story parallels elements of Diyāb's putative memoir.[112] Both "Aladdin" and *The Book of Travels* relate a tale of youthful adventure and feature a young man bred in the streets of a mercantile center. If Aladdin is too lazy to learn his father's trade as a tailor, Diyāb makes a more conscious decision to depart from the path of his brothers. Both young men are shaped by an absent father (dead in the case of Aladdin and presumed dead in the case of Diyāb) and a melancholic mother. In both stories, the youth falls under the sway of a mysterious father figure, a man in possession of magical objects or abilities. And Lucas, I would add, was taken in his travels in the Levant for a magician. Just as the Maghrebi magician enlists Aladdin in his quest for riches, Diyāb is drawn in to Lucas's quest for marvelous objects and stories with the promise that he would secure him a royal appointment to the library of Arabic manuscripts. Just as Aladdin wields the power of the magician's ring and discovers the jinni of the lamp, Diyāb relates tales of Lucas's amulets that can heal and speaks of the miraculous power of his philosopher's stone. Though Diyāb's tale of his younger self offers the doubled vision of an older narrator and a stronger note of skepticism, he has constructed it using a classic narrative pattern visible also in the tales he told Galland.

The self-fashioning that speaks to the "modernity" of the Diyāb-Galland tales is evident in Diyāb's portrait of Lucas. *The Book of Travels* is filled with moments that highlight the performative aspect of the French traveler's authority on the journey. At their first meeting, Lucas is traveling in his favored disguise of a physician. After one of the caravan's first stops on the road to Tripoli, his declaration that two skulls near the ruins of an old church and convent must belong to ancient kings has no grounding in any archaeological procedure. When he recruits a young goatherd to lower himself into a small cave to retrieve a ring and a lamp, Lucas resembles a tomb raider rather than a scholar. Such masquerades are as much a part of the story of Aladdin as the pursuit of fabulous riches and the use of magical objects. Diyāb, like Aladdin, would follow his roguish father figure in spite of his skepticism about his credentials and intentions. While it may be too much to imagine that Diyāb saw himself in the figure of Aladdin, the story of his travels with Lucas contains thematic parallels that may be the work of a shared creator. Both stories contain the marvelous motifs of supernatural and precious objects associated with the tales added to the *Nights*, and issues of identity that have been perceived as modern. In *The Book of Travels*, Diyāb explores the possibilities of cultivating a new identity on the model of Lucas, and himself assumes the guise of a physician on his return journey to Aleppo. For his part, Aladdin will slowly grow into the new persona created artificially through the power of the jinni of the lamp—a young man at last worthy of the trappings of wealth and power.

As *The Book of Travels* moves on to chronicle Diyāb's experiences in Paris and his visit to the Palace of Versailles, it offers an even more powerful riposte to those who seek to attribute the marvels of the added *Nights* stories solely to Galland.[113] In the travelogue, Diyāb evokes the grand spectacle of elaborate ritual and excessive luxury that accompanied his presentation to King Louis XIV. His descriptions of the radiant beauty and luxurious attire of the ladies of Versailles are reminiscent of the descriptions of the princesses in the tales of "Aladdin" and "Prince Aḥmad." An encounter in the palace with a lovely woman wearing a diadem studded with diamonds, rubies, emeralds, and other precious stones leaves Diyāb convinced he has encountered the king's daughter. Such details will recur in the tale of Prince Aḥmad when the titular character meets the fairy princess Perī Bānū emerging from her palace, adorned with jewels.[114] In describing her throne, Diyāb will use the same list of precious stones that appears in *The Book of Travels* decades later.[115] The women of Louis XIV's court may have appeared marvelous enough to inspire the description of a fairy princess in a tale later spun for Galland. Yet it is just as likely that these are stock phrases that signal Diyāb's attempt in both instances to capture the splendor and wealth of a marvelous realm. Diyāb's fascination with the rapid construction and excessive luxury of the Palace of Versailles is another clear link to the stress on magnificent material settings in the stories he related to Galland. Given the elaborate description of Versailles's gardens and glittering dome, it is unlikely that a French Orientalist scholar was needed to make Diyāb's tales more appealing to readers hungry for the wonders of the *Nights*.

The notes Galland jotted down during Diyāb's 1709 performance of his "beautiful" tales provide evidence of the Syrian storyteller's gift for combining old elements to form new tales half a century before he displayed the same skill in *The Book of Travels*. Three centuries later, literary historians are finally beginning to understand that the tales Diyāb gave Galland are not "orphan tales," as defined by the absence of an Arabic manuscript source, but rather "Diyāb's tales,"[116] the work of a gifted and curious young man who continued to exercise his narrative skills throughout his life. We also need to reevaluate how our underlying assumptions about the "modern" and the "marvelous" have been shaped. In seeking to identify what differentiates the Diyāb-Galland tales from the rest of the stories in the *Nights*, critics have failed to disentangle the marvelous from associations with the fabulous luxuries of the Arab world, or to decouple modernity from images of a literary Paris.

Beyond Galland's presumed modern sensibility, Diyāb's own fascinating journey through the Mediterranean in Lucas's service and his explorations of the spectacular facades and social mores of Paris and Versailles demonstrate a sophisticated narrative command. At the level of storytelling and technique, we cannot limit our understanding of Diyāb's contribution to new tales included in Galland's *Nights* to the conveying of a repository of marvels or recombining of folktales. Nor should we limit it to the possible imprint of autobiographical experiences. In light of *The Book of Travels*, Diyāb is equally likely to have contributed to the inner monologues and self-reflection that mark out the new added tales from those of the original story collection. The added tales have been seen as essentially French, but as we reflect upon the author that emerges from *The Book of Travels*, we may learn to read them as the product of a more complex Syrian-French genesis—shaped as much by Ḥannā Diyāb as by Antoine Galland.

# Notes

1   This section is not numbered in the manuscript, nor is it called a chapter. There is, however, an indentation in the text block, which suggests a break in the narrative.

2   Correcting Diyāb's February 1709, which is inaccurate, just as it was at the beginning of Chapter 8. Based on the report Lucas made upon his return (Omont, *Missions archéologiques*, 347), it seems the pair arrived in Paris on October 25, 1708.

3   Diyāb refers here to several jerboas that Paul Lucas acquired during the North African leg of their voyage. See Volume One, §5.109–10.

4   That is, slate.

5   This word is illegible, but is likely *al-ṣayd* ("the hunt").

6   In *Deuxième Voyage*, 198, Lucas claims he had brought seven of these animals from the town of Fayoum.

7   It was through Diyāb's mediation that *jarbūʿ*, the Arabic word for *jerboa*, entered the French lexicon (Elie Kallas, "Gerboise: L'entrée du terme arabe ǧerbūʿ à la cour de Louis XIV").

8   This view on the history of the sect gained currency among renowned Maronite clerics and historians beginning in the fifteenth century. This does not mean that Lucas did not say what is attributed to him: He may have simply been repeating something that Diyāb (or other Maronites) had told him.

9   In fact, she was the wife of Louis XIV's grandson, Louis le Petit Dauphin.

10  The word shouted by the princess may have been *turc*, as this was the common French designation for Muslims at the time.

11  The princess referred to here is Françoise Marie de Bourbon, one of Louis XIV's illegitimate children. Her governess, the future Madame de Maintenon, would become Louis's second wife.

12  Following this point, the narrative appears to shift to Diyāb's voice rather than Lucas's.

13  Diyāb here describes the Machine de Marly, a hydraulic system built between 1681 and 1685 to supply water to the Palace of Versailles from the River Seine. The engineer, Arnold de Ville, in reality obtained the task by competition (Thompson, *The Sun King's Garden: Louis XIV, André le Nôtre and the Creation of the Garden of Versailles*, 247ff.).

14  The Bosquet du Marais, commissioned in 1688, contained a fountain shaped like "a bronze tree with tin leaves that sent forth water from the tips of its branches"

(Thompson, *The Sun King's Garden*, 157–58). The bosquet was destroyed in 1705, a few years before Diyāb arrived in Versailles, but similar tinworks may have existed elsewhere on the grounds.

15 By the 1680s, Louis XIV had indeed completed the transfer of his chief residence to Versailles, though the reason was not his illicit marriage to Françoise d'Aubigné, marquise de Maintenon.

16 The marriage was a secret one, as the marquise was the king's second wife.

17 We were not able to identify this trompe l'oeil painting.

18 The motif of drawing a fly on the portrait to dupe other artists is a legend known from the life of Giotto di Bondone, who tricked his master Cimabue as recounted in Vasari, *Lives*, 35. It appears as international tale type H.504.1.1 in the Aarne-Thompson Index.

19 On this episode see Nicholas Dew, *Orientalism in Louis XIV's France*, 1–3. His source is Antoine Galland, who records the incident in his journals.

20 The inscription is the *shahādah*, the Muslim profession of faith: "There is no god but God, Muhammad is the Messenger of God."

21 This is Christofalo (Christophe) Maunier, who was one of Antoine Galland's competitors for the position of professor of Arabic at the Collège royal; see Galland, *Journal*, vol. 1, 256n256 and 266n282.

22 Diyāb mistakes the word *hôtel* (hotel, hostel) for *autel* (altar).

23 Louis XIV established juvenile detention centers (*maisons de correction*) in the late seventeenth century at the hospitals of Bicêtre and La Salpêtrière. See Gossard, "Breaking a Child's Will: Eighteenth-Century Parisian Juvenile Detention Centers."

24 This is the Edict of Fontainebleau, signed by Louis XIV in 1685, which ordered that the Huguenots be expelled from French territory on pain of death.

25 This sentence twice uses the word *niẓām*, which Diyāb uses to refer to various forms of propriety, good order, and good management. This passage suggests that he (or at least the Ottoman ambassador whose views he is communicating) saw the domains of city planning, household management, and political leadership to be linked.

26 The piaster was a silver coin used in the Ottoman Empire. Diyāb may have been referring to the French silver ecu, which weighed only slightly more than the piaster.

27 The identity of the theatrical production attended by Diyāb is uncertain. The translators of the French edition believe it to have been the opera *Atys*, by composer Jean-Baptiste Lully and librettist Philippe Quinault, which premiered in 1676 (Diyāb, *D'Alep à Paris*, 299–306). However, the description provided by Diyāb does not match the plot summary of that opera, nor is the title he supplies that of any French opera known to us. There are similarities between his account and the plot of *Sémélé*, an opera by composer Marin Marais and librettist Antoine Houdar de la Motte, which premiered at the Théâtre

du Palais-Royal on April 9, 1709. It was performed twenty-five times between its premiere and its final performance on May 21, 1709, and was never revived (Pitou, *The Paris Opéra*, vol. 1, 310–11).

28 The principal characters in the well-known shadow puppet plays once performed throughout Ottoman lands.

29 Presumably, they carried her in this way so her feet would not have to touch the ground.

30 As noted by Fahmé-Thiéry et al., Diyāb probably had in mind the cross of Saint Andrew, which is shaped like an X (Diyāb, *D'Alep à Paris*, 322n).

31 This grisly torture method involves weaving the body through the spokes of a wagon wheel once the bones have been broken, while the person is still alive.

32 This story combines elements drawn from different sources. Geneviève, according to her hagiographers, distributed bread among the poor but did not work as a maid for a rich man. Diyāb's retelling features the famous "miracle of the roses," probably taken from the hagiography of Elisabeth, queen of Portugal. The hagiographic collection, of which he probably possessed a copy, contains both stories (*Kitāb Akhbār al-qiddīsīn*, vol. 3, fol. 20r, on the roses; and vol. 1, fol. 40r–42v, the vita of Geneviève).

33 The winter of 1709, known in England as "The Great Frost" and in France as *le grand hiver*, was the coldest European winter in five hundred years (Luterbacher et al., "European Seasonal and Annual Temperature Variability, Trends, and Extremes since 1500").

34 This is Antoine Galland, the first European translator of the *Thousand and One Nights*.

35 Diyāb makes several appearances in Antoine Galland's journal; see *Le journal d'Antoine Galland*, vol. 1, 286, 290, 320–34, 346–63, 373–76, 378, 483, 504. The stories he told Galland include "Aladdin and the Enchanted Lamp" (May 5, 1709), "The Blind Man Bābā 'Abdallāh" and "Sīdī Nu'mān"(May 10), "The Ebony Horse" (May 13), "Prince Aḥmad and the Fairy Perī Bānū" (May 22), "The Two Sisters Who Envied Their Cadette" (May 25), "'Alī Bābā and the Forty Thieves" (May 27), "Khawājah Ḥasan al-Ḥabbāl" (May 29), and "'Alī Khawājah and the Merchant of Baghdad" (May 30).

36 This was very likely François de Camps, abbot of Signy (Galland, *Le journal d'Antoine Galland*, 1:483n938).

37 This individual is identified by Antoine Galland in his *De l'origine et du progrès du café*, 51–52, as one Étienne of Aleppo, who opened a café in the Rue Saint André des Arts facing the Pont Saint-Michel, close to Lucas's apartment in Paris. In his account of a fair at which Étienne sold his wares, Diyāb presumably conflates the story of Pascal, which he had also heard in Paris, with that of his neighbor and Aleppan friend in Paris.

38 Here, Lucas expresses the view that the Christian communities of the Ottoman Empire were oppressed by their Muslim rulers, a feeling that Diyāb admits to sharing later in the journey.

39   An expensive woolen broadcloth.

40   Diyāb is referring here to an Ottoman minister, perhaps the grand vizier himself.

41   For other possible readings of the ship's name, see Diyāb, *D'Alep à Paris*, 359n1.

42   The Comte de Ferriol served as ambassador in Istanbul from 1699 to 1711. His refusal to present his rapier is recorded by other historical sources, which call it *l'affaire de l'épée* (*D'Alep à Paris*, 362n1; Bóka and Vargyas, 'Le marquis Charles de Ferriol ambassadeur de France à Constantinople (1699–1703),' 93ff.). Since the incident took place in January 1700, it is unlikely that Diyāb met the messenger in 1709.

43   Ambassadors were received by the sultan just inside the Gate of Felicity (*Bab-üs Saadet*) of Topkapı Palace, which opened onto the Third Courtyard of the palace, the sultan's private domain.

44   At the time of Diyāb's travels, Sicily was in fact under the rule of Savoy. The Austrians were given the island in 1720 in exchange for Sardinia.

45   It appears that Diyāb neglected to mention a third ship that had left Marseille at the same time as his and the other vessel.

46   Gelibolu (Gallipoli) is not at the entrance of the Dardanelles Strait but at the end. Diyāb appears to have misremembered its location.

47   All Ottoman place names are given here in their modern Turkish form.

48   Diyāb has mixed up these stages of the journey, as Küçükçekmece would have come after Büyükçekmece, not before (Diyāb, *D'Alep à Paris*, 369n2).

49   This mosque, known today as Yeni Cami (New Mosque), was completed in 1665, and so would have been relatively new at the time of Diyāb's visit.

50   The toast to the ambassador's health was deciphered by Fahmé-Thiéry et al. (*D'Alep à Paris*, 381n1).

51   Calendering is a process used to thin, coat, or smooth a material such as paper or fabric, in order to produce different sorts of finishes. Calendering machines achieved their effects by passing material through sets of pressurized rollers.

52   This is the Gulf of Izmit, an arm of the Sea of Marmara.

53   Fahmé-Thiéry et al. (*D'Alep à Paris*, 402) suggest this is saffron.

54   Bezoars are undigested masses produced in an animal's gastrointestinal system. They were once thought to have medicinal properties, for example as an antidote against various poisons.

55   These are the Cilician Gates.

56   As Diyāb is pretending to be a Frankish doctor, his argument is that he is not a subject of the Ottoman Empire and therefore should not have to pay the toll that Ottoman Christians pay.

57 Here again it would seem that Diyāb has mixed up the stages of his journey, as he would have arrived at this bridge after passing Adana (see Diyāb, *D'Alep à Paris*, 422n3).

58 Diyāb has probably mixed up the stages of his journey again, as this town comes before the Cilician Gates (Diyāb, *D'Alep à Paris*, 425n2).

59 Diyāb is referring here to the ancient Roman bridge spanning the Seyhan River in Adana, known today by the name Taşköprü.

60 The manuscript here reads: "We pressed on to Payas . . ." However, a symbol before the word "Payas" indicates the insertion of a marginal note. The note is partly illegible, which accounts for the lacunae in the translation.

61 This marks the end of the marginal note.

62 *Jinn* (genies, demons) were thought to inhabit desolate and treacherous territories.

63 Christians living under Muslim rule frequently required "safe-conduct" documents.

64 Paul Lucas appears to have struggled with the sounds *kh* and *q* in Arabic: Diyāb hears his attempt to pronounce Khannāqiyyah as "Kanakia," which he does not recognize. Lucas himself describes his visit to the grottos and refers to this location as "Connaquie," (*Troisième Voyage*, 101).

65 Galland, "M. Diyab quelques contes Arabes fort beaux," in *Le journal d'Antoine Galland*, 1:290.

66 Mia Gerhardt's term in *The Art of Story-Telling: A Literary Study of the Thousand and One Nights*, 14.

67 Galland sought out other sources and manuscripts even before he had finished the tales in his manuscript of the *Thousand and One Nights*.

68 "Aladdin," "The Caliph's Night Adventure," "The Blind Man Bābā ʿAbdallāh," "Sīdī Nuʿmān," "The Ebony Horse," "Prince Aḥmad and the Fairy Perī Bānū," "The Two Sisters Who Envied Their Cadette," "ʿAlī Bābā and the Forty Thieves," "Khawājah Ḥasan al-Ḥabbāl," and "ʿAlī Khawājah and the Merchant of Baghdad."

69 For Jean-Paul Sermain, Galland's revision and elaboration of the added tales served to alter European interpretations of the entire corpus of the *Nights*. Through these added stories, Sermain argues, Galland taught the reader how to read the *Nights* as a whole. Sermain, "Notice," in Galland, *Les mille et une nuits*, i–xiv.

70 Mohamed Abdel-Halim (*Antoine Galland: Sa vie et son oeuvre*, 283) argues that Diyāb contributed "primitive" elements acculturated through their expression in Galland's hand.

71 See May, *Les "Mille et une nuits" d'Antoine Galland, ou, Le chef-d'oeuvre invisible*; Schwab, *L'auteur des "Mille et une nuits": Vie d'Antoine Galland*; and above all, Larzul, "Les Mille et une nuits de Galland," *Les traductions françaises des "Mille et une nuits,"* and "Further Considerations on Galland's *Mille et une Nuits*: A Study of the Tales Told by Hannâ."

72 "If Galland pieced and patched together from other stories," Marina Warner ventures, "he was only doing what storytellers have always done, before and since" (*Stranger Magic: Charmed States and the Arabian Nights*, 77).

73 Sermain, "Présentation," in Galland, *Les mille et une nuits*, 1:xvii–xxxii.

74 A view also expressed in Warner, *Stranger Magic*.

75 See introduction to *The Book of Travels*, p. xxiii.

76 See Stephan on the possible influence of Nizami's retelling of *Majnūn Laylā*, vol. 2, note 225 to the main text, on Boccaccio in note 168; and Heyberger on Boccaccio in the introduction to Dyâb, *D'Alep à Paris*.

77 Horta, *Marvellous Thieves: Secret Authors of the Arabian Nights*.

78 As first noted in Chraïbi, "Galland's 'Ali Baba' and Other Arabic Versions."

79 In the first prince's journey, for instance, Galland inserts a description of Indian temples from the work of a Persian historian he has translated, and in the journey of the third prince he inserts a short description of the Sodge Valley taken from the *Bibliothèque orientale d'Herbelot*. Abdel-Halim, *Antoine Galland*, 235, 280–82. Larzul, "Further Considerations," 261.

80 Ulrich Marzolph, "The Man Who Made the Nights Immortal." See Marzolph's discussion of Diyāb's contribution to international folk narrative in *101 Middle Eastern Tales and Their Impact on Western Oral Tradition*.

81 See Stephan, Introduction, p. xxvi ff; Fahmé-Thiéry, "Ecriture et conscience de soi."

82 *Interpreting the Self: Autobiography in the Arabic Literary Tradition*, ed. Reynolds, 72ff.

83 Fahmé-Thiéry, "Ecriture et conscience de soi."

84 Such moments of introspection and sadness are not unprecedented in the premodern Arabic travelogue, as Michael Cooperson has reminded me—one need only think of Ibn Battuta's arrival in Tunis, when he despairs that he alone knows no one there to greet him. Gibb, *The Travels of Ibn Battuta in Asia and Africa, AD 1325–1354*, 1:12.

85 Fahmé-Thiéry, "Ecriture et conscience de soi."

86 Henri Duranton, editor of modern scholarly editions of all three of Lucas's published travelogues, provides the most precise portrait of Lucas in his introduction to the first volume. He cautions against the bias of accounts by some of the traveler's more erudite but less popular contemporary and near-contemporary authors. A good primer on some primary sources on Lucas is provided in Omont, *Missions archéologiques françaises en Orient aux XVIIè et XVIIIè siècles*. Omont corrected the misperception that Lucas was a purported archaeologist or scholar. Note that Omont only reproduces a small fragment of the sources on Lucas in French archives.

87 Comte de Pontchartrain (Louis Phélypeaux) to Marquis de Ferriol, French ambassador to Constantinople, letter dated April 1, 1704, Bibliothèque Nationale de France, ms.

franc. new acq. 801, fol. 3–6, reproduced in Omont, *Missions archéologiques*, 330. These instructions were likely written up for the minister by the court numismatist Jean-Foy Vaillant, since in the draft manuscript they refer in the first person to Vaillant's own experience of collecting ancient coins in Italy in the guise of a doctor in the 1670s.

88  *Voyage du Sieur Paul Lucas dans le Levant: Juin 1699–juillet 1703*, ed. Duranton, 64.

89  Undated memorandum to Lucas from Mr. Juillien, professor of botany at the Royal Garden, *Correspondance et papiers de Paul Lucas, voyageur et antiquaire français,* Richelieu Collection, Bibliothèque Nationale de France, Monnaies et Médailles, carton 1, dossier 27. (Not reproduced in Omont.) Among other natural marvels, the memorandum details medicines to be sought, notably opium. Lucas is admonished to "examine above all the familiar remedies which they use to recover from illnesses; what ingredients they employ and with what preparations," and to remark "on the effects produced by the drugs they take, and the drinks they use, whether by necessity or for amusement." My translation.

90  When, in the voyage related in his first travelogue, Lucas's dragoman cautions him that he will be asked to produce remedies if he is introduced as a doctor, Lucas reassures him that he has some. *Voyage du Sieur Paul Lucas dans le Levant: Juin 1699–juillet 1703*, 64.

91  Here I follow Fahmé-Thiéry, "Ecriture et conscience de soi."

92  Sermain, in Galland, *Les mille et une nuits*, 1:xxix–xxx. The suggestion that Cassim is too dazzled to recall the password is already in Diyāb's performance of the tale as recorded by Galland in his diary: "he no longer remembers the words, so much was he occupied by what he had just seen." Marzolph and Duggan, "Ḥannā Diyāb's Tales, Part II," 442.

93  Recall that after the disappearance of his palace the crowds do not want to see him summarily executed.

94  Horta, *Marvellous Thieves*, 43–44.

95  Dobie, "Translation in the Contact Zone: Antoine Galland's *Mille et une nuits: Contes arabes*," 35.

96  In the translation by Marzolph and Duggan, "Ḥannā Diyāb's Tales, Part II," 445.

97  Fahmé-Thiéry, "Ecriture et conscience de soi."

98  Galland, *Voyage à Constantinople (1672–1673)*.

99  "You will not find any of these adventures that engage the attention of readers," Galland wrote of his Constantinople journal to a correspondent. "I was no doubt not born for these unusual things, and my personality inclines me even less to fictions." Quoted in Horta, *Marvellous Thieves*, 32.

100  Madsen, "'Auf, Auf, ihr Christen': Representing the Clash of Empires, Vienna 1683," 83–84.

101  Dobie, "Translation in the Contact Zone," 32.

102 In their edition of *Le journal d'Antoine Galland*, Bauden and Waller detail the lectures on Homer and other classical authors Galland would attend, and sometimes reference, in their notes to his diary.

103 For more on the topic of Diyāb's manuscript of "Aladdin," see the forthcoming book by Ibrahim Akel, who has recently verified the authenticity of such a manuscript. Akel writes that at this point it is too early to confirm the same with regard to "'Alī Bābā." (Personal communication, email dated May 5, 2020). One should recall further the ambiguity of Galland's diary entry ( January 10, 1711) that affirms he finished his tenth volume rendering an Arabic text given to him by Diyāb—this could refer to "Aladdin," which ends in that volume, or possibly to "The Caliph's Night Adventure."

104 *Le journal d'Antoine Galland*, ed. Bauden and Waller.

105 Available in Henri Duranton's modern editions from l'Université de Saint-Étienne: *Voyage du Sieur Paul Lucas dans le Levant: Juin 1699–juillet 1703* (1998), *Deuxième Voyage du Sieur Paul Lucas dans le Levant: Octobre 1704–septembre 1708* (2002), and *Troisième Voyage du Sieur Paul Lucas dans le Levant: Mai 1714– novembre 1717* (2004). Duranton cautions against accepting the dismissal of Lucas by more erudite contemporaries jealous of his commissions and the success of his travelogues, which ran to several editions and were translated into German.

106 Lucas was not on this journey strictly in charge of his own itinerary; Pontchartrain's instructions advised him where to go, and even the order of the stops to be made. Lucas's first travelogue made evident his love of Persia, yet on this journey it was to be avoided because it would not yield Greco-Roman antiquities.

107 The above quote is in my translation. The three travelogues were edited for length by members of the French Academy, who also inserted references to Greek and Latin classics. What was picaresque, marvelous, and fanciful in the texts—including the portraits of the never-visited holy cities of Islam—originated with Lucas, as can be corroborated with reference to a partial manuscript that survives, *Voyages de Paul Lucas*, MS 3820, Bibliothèque nationale de France. Bibliothèque de l'Arsenal (consulted March 2019).

108 In addition to the consular network his commissions urged him to rely on. Lucas's interest in the historical and material culture of Marian devotion exceeds the terms of the many court commissions he traveled with. In his first travelogue, he recounts gifting a chalice to the chapel of the Virgin in Old Cairo.

109 Lucas shared with Galland as one of his most prized personal possessions brought back from the Levant—in his journey with Diyāb—a sculpture of the Virgin, as Galland recorded in his diary shortly after first meeting Diyāb at Lucas's apartment (Monday March 18, 1709): "a portrait of the Virgin in sculpture of around six inches in height and five in width in which the face, the throat, and the hand are of chrysolite, and the

coat that serves her as a veil is of jasper. The material clothing is of amethysts and the background of a dark oriental agate, all exquisitely worked." My translation. *Le journal d'Antoine Galland*, ed. Bauden and Waller, 287.

110 Horta, *Marvellous Thieves*, 70–71.

111 In relation to their first excursion, where Lucas and Diyāb retrieve from an underground vault two skulls, a ring, and a lamp. Heyberger, introduction to Diyāb, *D'Alep à Paris*, 29.

112 See "The Storyteller and the Sultan of France," in Horta, *Marvellous Thieves*, 44–54, and "Tales of Aladdin and Their Tellers, from Aleppo to Paris."

113 Larzul sees as new to and characteristic of Galland's prose in the added tales the use of superlatives for the "creation of his marvelous environment," citing the example of "Aladdin" ("Further Considerations," 267). But she did not know Diyāb's *Book of Travels*. Invited into a princess's private residence, Diyāb sees "the wives of the princes, as radiant as moons, wearing dresses that glittered so luminously from all of the jewels set into them. The sight was just indescribable." Aladdin observes of the jewels in the vault, in Yasmine Seale's translation: "their size was unimaginable and their beauty without description" (*Aladdin: A New Translation*, 18).

114 Horta, *Marvellous Thieves*, 47. Larzul ("Further Considerations," 268), in contrast, assumes only Galland could have specified the jewels in this portrait of Perī Bānū.

115 Johannes Stephan notes the parallel: see Chapter 1 of his dissertation, "Spuren fiktionaler Vergegenwärtigung im osmanischen Aleppo," 31–33.

116 As I suggested at the concluding session of the second international workshop on Ḥannā Diyāb, "New Perspectives on the 'Orphan Stories' in the *One Thousand and One Nights*," convened by Christina Vogel and Johannes Thomann at the University of Zurich, February 28–29, 2020.

# Glossary of Names and Terms

Names and terms appear as they do in the translation.

*abū kalb*   name given to the Dutch lion dollar, a coin that circulated in the Ottoman Empire.

*Adana*   a large city in southeastern Anatolia, home to some thirty-five thousand people in the late seventeenth century.

*Afyonkarahisar*   a city in central-west Anatolia, named for a nearby citadel (Turk. *kara hisar*, "dark fortress") and for its cultivation of opium (Turk. *afyon*).

*agha*   "chief" or "master," a title given to Ottoman government officials, mostly those associated with the military.

*alājah*   a luxury fabric made of a mixture of silk and cotton.

*Aleppo*   a city in northern Syria, home to a large community of European merchants during the seventeenth and eighteenth centuries.

*Alexandria*   a major port city on Egypt's Mediterranean coast and home to a large European trading community in Diyāb's time.

*Antep*   modern-day Gaziantep, an important town in southeastern Anatolia.

*Antioch*   a city in what is now Turkey, about fifty-five miles west of Aleppo.

*Arabic Library*   the collection of Arabic manuscripts in the French Royal Library (the *Bibliothèque du Roi*).

*Asyūṭ*   an Egyptian town that was a center for cotton and linen weaving. Linen from Asyūṭ was exported to Europe.

*Bālistān souk*   likely a reference to the oldest section of the Grand Bazaar, known as the Bedesten, built by the Ottoman emperor Mehmed II in 1455.

*Barbary*   a common Western European name for Northwest Africa, designating Morocco and some western Ottoman provinces, including Tripoli and Tunis (see Maghreb).

*barjādāt*   a type of clothing or fabric.

*Bey of Tripoli*   Khalīl Pasha, ruler of the Ottoman province of Tripolitania from 1702 to 1709; deposed and executed by Qaramānlī Aḥmad Bey in 1711.

*Bey of Tunis*    al-Ḥusayn ibn ʿAlī (r. 1705–35), the bey of Tunis and the founder of the Husaynid Dynasty.

*bey*    a Turkish title bestowed on dignitaries of the Ottoman Empire, especially rulers of provinces.

*Beyoğlu*    a quarter in Istanbul, on the European side, north of the Golden Horn; during the period of Diyāb's visit mostly inhabited by Christians and foreign diplomats.

*Bsharrī*    a village in the province of Tripoli adjoining the Qadisha valley, in present-day northern Lebanon.

*Būlāq*    Ottoman Cairo's principal port on the Nile.

*Cairo*    the largest city in the Arabic-speaking lands of the Ottoman Empire, today the capital of Egypt.

*Callimeri, Antonio*    a Cypriot interpreter, protégé of France, and graduate from the Greek college in Rome.

*calpac*    (Ottoman Turkish) a form of headgear covered in sheepskin or fur, in Diyāb's time worn mostly by non-Muslims and Europeans.

*çelebi*    an honorary Ottoman Turkish title given to persons of high status or good education.

*cheramide*    a brick-colored precious stone.

*chevalier*    knight; a French title of nobility conferred during the seventeenth and eighteenth centuries upon members of influential families such as the Khāzin clan of Kisrawān (Lebanon).

*Christofalo*    see *Zamāriyā*.

*Cilician Gates*    a pass through the Taurus Mountains, which has been used for millennia to travel between the lowlands of Cilicia and the Anatolian plateau.

*Damietta*    a port city at the eastern end of the Nile Delta, about one hundred miles from Cairo. Along with Rosetta, it is one of the two principal Nile ports on the Mediterranean Sea.

*de Camps, François*    (1643–1723) French historian, theologian, antiquarian, numismatist, and abbot of Signy.

*diligence*    a large, public, long-distance stagecoach that could carry up to sixteen people. They were common in France and England during the eighteenth and nineteenth centuries.

*dirham*    an Ottoman silver coin and a unit of weight, equivalent to one-tenth of an ounce during the seventeenth century.

*dīwānkhāna*   an audience hall, sitting room, or guest quarters. In Diyāb's use, mostly an outdoor seating area meant for social gatherings and recreation.

*Djerba*   an island off the coast of Tunisia, captured by the Ottomans from the Spaniards in 1560. The island's main town is Houmt Souk, which was called Djerba in Diyāb's time

*ecu*   a French silver coin.

*effendi*   Ottoman title of respect for a member of the civil administration.

*Fagon, Guy-Crescent*   (1638–1718) botanist, physician to Louis XIV, and director of the Royal Gardens at Versailles.

*Farḥāt, Jirmānūs*   (1670–1732) Aleppan Maronite cleric, poet, grammarian, lexicographer, and traveler active in spreading knowledge of Arabic among Christians; he was made bishop of Aleppo in 1725.

*Fayoum*   an Egyptian town located southwest of Cairo in the Fayoum Oasis and linked to the Nile by a canal.

*fils*   a coin whose value varied between eight and eighteen for one *pāra*; known in Ottoman Egypt as a *jadīd*.

*Frank*   (Ar. *franjī*, pl. *franj*) a European (distinct from *fransāwī*, pl. *fransāwiyyah*, "French").

*Frankish*   (Ar. *franjī*) the Mediterranean lingua franca, a hybrid idiom used among seamen, traders, and other travelers. When used as an adjective, equivalent to "European" (e.g., "Frankish lands").

*Galata*   a quarter of Istanbul on the northern shore of the Golden Horn, south of Beyoğlu; today called Karaköy.

*Galland, Antoine*   (1646–1717) a French Orientalist and scholar of classical languages, an expert in numismatics, and a traveler to the Ottoman lands. He contributed to the encyclopedia *Bibliothèque orientale d'Herbelot* and was the first translator of the *Arabian Nights* into a European language.

*Gate of the Janissaries and the al-ʿAzab Gate*   two of the three main gates to the Cairo Citadel, one of the city's main monuments, dating to the Ayyūbid period.

*ghuzzī*   an Ottoman functionary of Egypt; the term derives from *ghuz*, "the Oguz," the Turks claimed as ancestors by the Ottomans.

*Grand Vizier of the Ottoman Empire*   the chief minister of the empire and the second most powerful figure in the political hierarchy.

*Greek (Ar. rūmī, pl. rūm)*   a speaker of Greek, usually of Greek Orthodox (*krīkī*) denomination; sometimes also a Latin Christian; distinct from *yūnānī*, "Ancient Greek."

*Ibn al-Zughbī, Ḥannā*   an Aleppan Maronite, and a friend of Diyāb's who accompanies him during his Anatolian journey.

*Ifrīqiyah*   a region of North Africa with indistinct borders. Diyāb's usage suggests that he took it to encompass present-day Tunisia and western Libya.

*isbanj*   (Turk. *ispenç*, "a fifth") a tax paid by non-Muslims for pasturage, e.g., of swine.

*Isṭifān the Damascene*   an Armenian who at the end of the seventeenth century opened one of the first coffeehouses in Paris.

*jadīd*   see *fils*.

*jakhjūr*   (Turk. *chāqshīr*) a type of trousers fastened around the waist with a band, and sewed to light leather boots around the ankle hems.

*janissary*   an elite Ottoman infantryman.

*jarq*   (Turk. *charkhī*, a five-piaster piece) a coin worth four *'uthmānī*s, or two soldi.

*jūkhadār*   (Turk. *chohadar*) originally a lackey, footman, or valet; for Diyāb, an attendant, bureaucrat, or high-ranking embassy official.

*Kaftīn*   a village in northern Syria, close to Aleppo and to several ruined Byzantine cities.

*Karanlık Kapı (Gate of Darkness)*   a pass in the Nur Mountains of southeastern Anatolia (the Amanus range in Ancient Greek), along the Cilician highway to Syria.

*kazan kebabı*   a type of meat dish, cooked in a large pot.

*khan*   a caravansary, i.e., a roadside staging post with lodging for travelers and their mounts; also, a warehouse and hostel, often built in the outskirts of cities; for Diyāb, also a market or marketplace, and, in one case, a dormitory for prisoners.

*Khan Abrak*   a marketplace in Aleppo, found in the Sūq al-Qaṣābiyyah.

*Khan al-'Asal*   a town on the western outskirts of Aleppo.

*Khan al-'Ulabiyyah*   a monumental sixteenth-century caravansary near Bizzeh Square in southern Aleppo.

*khāṣṣāt (sing. khāṣṣah)*   a type of fine, tightly woven cotton.

*khawājah*   an informal honorary title given to foreign or Christian merchants during the Ottoman period; Diyāb's first designation for Paul Lucas, later replaced by *mu'allimī* ("[my] master," "boss,").

*Khāzin family*   a Maronite landowning family of Mount Lebanon whose members wielded considerable economic and political power between the sixteenth and nineteenth centuries. Beginning in the seventeenth century, they gained political privileges through close economic collaboration with French authorities, for which some members were awarded the title of chevalier.

*Kız Kulesi (Maiden's Tower)* a small tower that stands on an island in the Bosphorus, near the coast of Üsküdar. The tower dates to the twelfth century.

*Konya* a city in central Anatolia.

*Larnaca* (Ar. Milāḥah) a coastal city in southeastern Cyprus.

*Lemaire* a family of diplomats originally from Joinville in the province of Champagne; one member, Claude, was French consul in Tripoli and later in Aleppo.

*Livorno* (Ar. Līkūrnā, from Genoese Ligorna) a coastal town in the Italian province of Tuscany and a commercial center in the early modern period.

*londrin* a type of lightweight, fulled woolen cloth, made in France and England and exported to the Levant.

*Lucas, Paul* (1646–1734) traveler, adventurer, and antiquarian in the service of Louis XIV; the son of a Rouen goldsmith and the author of three travelogues covering the period between 1699 and 1717; known during the European Enlightenment for his fanciful reports of distant places.

*Madame d'Orléans* (1677–1749) Françoise Marie de Bourbon, the youngest daughter of Louis XIV with his mistress the Marquise de Montespan; wife of Philippe II, the Duke of Orléans and Regent of France during the minority of Louis XV.

*Madame de Bourgogne* (1685–1712) Marie Adélaïde of Savoy, wife of Louis XIV's grandson, Louis le Petit Dauphin, Duke of Burgundy, and mother of Louis XV.

*Madame de Maintenon* (1635–1719) Françoise d'Aubigné, second wife of Louis XIV.

*Maghreb* the "West," i.e., the western territories of North Africa, including present-day Morocco, Algeria, Libya, and Tunisia.

*miṣriyyah* a coin of Egyptian origin normally worth one-fortieth of a piaster, or half a piece of silver.

*Messina* a city on the northeastern tip of Sicily, just across the narrow strait separating the island from the south of Italy.

*mīrī* a tax on land owned by the Ottoman sovereign.

*Misis* a town in southeastern Anatolia, about seventeen miles east of Adana. Also called Mopsuestia.

*mithqāl*   a measurement of weight equivalent to one and a half dirhams; in Diyāb's time, around four and a half grams.

*Monseigneur the Dauphin*   (1661–1711) Louis le Grand Dauphin, son of Louis XIV and heir to the French throne, father of Philip V of Spain, and grandfather of Louis XV of France.

*Morea*   the region now referred to as the Peloponnese.

*Mouski quarter*   a district in central Cairo, in the seventeenth and eighteenth centuries home to many European consuls and merchants (and thus also called the Frankish quarter), as well as several Jewish families.

*mujaddarah*   an ancient Near Eastern dish composed of lentils, rice or bulgur, spices, and onions. It remains a staple of many local cuisines, especially in the Levant.

*L'Opéra*   the Paris Opera (known at this time as the Académie Royale de Musique) was housed in the Théâtre du Palais-Royal on the rue Saint-Honoré from 1673 to 1763.

*pāra*   a silver Ottoman coin first issued in the early eighteenth century.

*Paulo Çelebi*   see *Zamāriyā*.

*Peloponnese*   see *Morea*.

*piaster*   see *qirsh*.

*Pontchartrain*   Jérôme Phélypeaux (1674–1747), a French politician who served as secretary of state for the Maison du Roi and for the navy under Louis XIV.

*Province of the Islands*   a province comprising all the major islands of the Ottoman Mediterranean, with the exception of Crete; also known as the Eyalet of the Archipelago.

*qabiji*   (Turk. *qapuči*) originally a gatekeeper or porter, then a palace guard or chamberlain, later a senior palace official or eunuch who guarded the sultan's harem; for Diyāb, also a French royal border guard, or a cavalry commander.

*qinṭār*   a measurement of weight equivalent to one hundred *raṭl*s, variable according to time and place; in seventeenth- through nineteenth-century Aleppo, probably between 487 and 564 pounds.

*qirsh*   (piaster) a heavy silver coin worth forty *pāra*s.

*raṭl*   a measurement of weight whose value varied according to time and place; in seventeenth- through nineteenth-century Aleppo, probably between 4.87 and 5.64 pounds.

*rayyis*   chief, captain, boss, superior.

*Rémuzat* (or Rémusat) a famous merchant family of Marseille with long-lasting ties to cities in the Ottoman Empire. One member, Auguste Rémuzat, was France's deputy consul in Aleppo, and apparently also the young Diyāb's second patron and employer.

*Rimbaud* a merchant family from Marseille that supplied many deputies or principal merchants of the French nation in Aleppo during Diyāb's lifetime.

*riyāl* an originally Spanish silver coin (*real*) of considerable value, widely used in Ottoman lands until 1714, when the Ottomans in Tunis banned its use and began to mint their own. Also called *riyāl qurūsh* (*riyal quruş*).

*Rosetta* a port city at the western end of the Nile Delta, about one hundred miles from Cairo. Along with Damietta, it is one of the two principal Nile ports on the Mediterranean Sea.

*Rūm, Rūmī* see *Greek*.

*Saint Elishaʿ* a monastery on the hillside below the village of Bsharrī, and the main residence of the Maronite Lebanese order during the time of Diyāb's stay.

*Saint Geneviève* the patron saint of Paris, according to the Roman Catholic and Eastern Orthodox rites.

*Samatan* a French merchant originally from Marseille, prominent in Aleppo between 1698 and 1708.

*sanjaq* an administrative subdivision of an Ottoman province (Turk. *eyalet* or *beylic*), administered by a *sanjaq bey*.

*Sauron* a prominent French merchant in Aleppo during the first two decades of the eighteenth century.

*Sfax* a commercial city on the coast of what is now Tunisia.

*shāhbandar* an Ottoman term meaning "harbormaster" (literally "king of the port"); in Diyāb's use the main representative of a group of merchants or the manager of a trading port.

*shāhiyyāt* (Ar., sing. *shāhī*) An Ottoman silver coin.

*shāsh* a long strip of cloth used to wind a turban.

*soldi* (It., sing. *soldo*) An Italian silver coin worth half a *jarq* or two *ʿuthmānīs*.

*Sousse* a coastal town in what is now Tunisia.

*Sultan Aḥmad* (1673–1736) the twenty-third Ottoman sultan, known as Aḥmad III.

*thulth* in Diyāb's use, a coin worth a third of a piaster; also a third of a dinar, or a third of a *pāra*.

*Tripoli*   a city in northern Lebanon, situated on the Mediterranean coast.

*Tripoli (of the West)*   the capital of present-day Libya, situated on the Mediterranean coast.

*Tunis*   the capital of present-day Tunisia, situated on the Mediterranean coast.

*ūqiyyah*   a measurement of weight whose value varied according to time and place. In Diyāb's Aleppo, it was equivalent to one-twelfth of a *raṭl* or one-sixth of an *uqqah* (around seven and a half ounces; see Barthélémy, 905).

*uqqah*   a measurement of weight whose value varied according to time and place; in Diyāb's Aleppo, it was equivalent to four hundred dirhams, half a *raṭl*, or six *ūqiyyah* (about 2.8 pounds).

*Üsküdar*   an ancient city on the Asian side of the Bosphorus, today a district of Istanbul.

*ʿuthmānī*   another word for *akče*, a silver coin worth a third or a quarter *pāra*.

*Yūsuf Çelebi*   see *Zamāriyā*.

*zolota*   a coin worth thirty *pāra*s, or three-quarters of a piaster (*qirsh*). The name comes from the Polish *złoty*, a currency exported to Ottoman lands during the seventeenth century.

*Zamāriyā*   a French family residing in Aleppo, some of whose members held important diplomatic posts. The head was Pierre Maunier. Diyāb met Maunier's son Christofalo (Christophe) in Paris, where he served as the steward of Cardinal de Noailles. Diyāb knew Christophe's brothers, Paulo Çelebi (Paul) and Yūsuf Çelebi (Joseph), in Aleppo. The oldest brother, known as Zamāriyā, served as syndic of the Holy Land in Istanbul.

*Zūq Mīkāyīl / Zouq Mkayel*   a village in Kisrawān, between Jounieh and Beirut in what is now Lebanon, in Diyāb's time administered by the Khāzin family and inhabited, perhaps exclusively, by Maronites.

*Zuqāq al-Khall*   (Vinegar Alley) a predominantly Christian quarter on the northern edge of Aleppo. In Diyāb's time, it served as a point of entry to the Christian suburbs.

# Bibliography

## Manuscripts

*Bibliothèque nationale de France*
*Voyages de Paul Lucas*, MS 3820. Bibliothèque de l'Arsenal.
"Comte de Pontchartrain (Louis Phélypeaux) to Marquis de Ferriol, French Ambassador to Constantinople," MS franc. Nouv. acq. 801.

*Gotha, Forschungsbibliothek*
Arab. 1548: *Riḥlat Saʿīd Bāshā*
Arab. 1549: *Riḥlat al-Ab Arsāniyūs Shukrī*
Arab. 1550: *Riḥlat al-shammās Ḥannā al-Ṭabīb*

*Syrian Catholic Archdiocese of Aleppo*
Ar 7/25: *Kitāb Mufīd fī ʿilm al-niyya*

*Université Saint Joseph (USJ), Bibliothèque Orientale*
BO 29: *Kitāb Siyāḥat al-ḫūrī Ilyās al-Mawṣilī*
BO 594–597: *Kitāb Akhbār al-qiddīsīn*
BO 645: *al-Durr al-nafīs fī sīrat al-qiddīs Fransīs*

*Vatican Apostolic Library*
Sbath 108: *Kitāb Siyāḥat al-ḫūrī Ilyās al-Mawṣilī* and *Riḥlat Saʿīd Bāshā*
Sbath 254: [*Kitāb Siyāḥat Ḥannā Diyāb*]

## Works Cited

Abdel-Halim, Mohamed. *Antoine Galland: Sa vie et son oeuvre*. Thèse en lettres, Paris: A. G. Nizet, 1964.
Addobbati, Andrea. "Hanna Dyab, il mercante di storie." *Quaderni Storico* 3 (2016): 830–42.
Al-Asadī, Khayr al-Dīn. *Mawsūʿat Ḥalab al-muqāranah*. Ḥalab: Jāmiʿat Ḥalab, 1981–88.

Barthélemy, Adrien. *Dictionnaire arabe-français: Dialectes de Syrie: Alep, Damas, Liban, Jérusalem.* Paris: Geuthner, 1935.

Bauden, Frédéric and Richard Waller, eds. *Le journal d'Antoine Galland (1646–1715): La Période Parisienne.* Vol. I. Leuven, Belgium: Peeters, 2011.

Blau, Joshua. *On Pseudo-Corrections in Some Semitic Languages.* Jerusalem: The Israel Academy of Sciences and Humanities, 1970.

Boase, Thomas S. R. "Ecclesiastical Art." In *A History of the Crusades,* edited by Kenneth M. Setton, 165–95. Madison, WI: The University of Wisconsin Press, 1977.

Bóka, Éva, and Katalin Vargyas. "Le marquis Charles de Ferriol ambassadeur de France à Constantinople (1699–1703)." *Acta Historica Academiae Scientiarum Hungaricae* 31, nos. 1–2 (1985): 87–112.

Bolte, Johannes. "Die Sage von der erweckten Scheintoten." *Zeitschrift des Vereins für Volkskunde* 20 (1910): 353–81.

Bottigheimer, Ruth B. "East Meets West: Hannā Diyāb and *The Thousand and One Nights.*" *Marvels and Tales* 28, no. 2 (2014): 302–24.

Brednich, Rolf Wilhelm. "Frau: Die tote F. kehrt zurück." In *Enzyklopädie des Märchens: Handwörterbuch zur historischen und vergleichenden Erzählforschung,* Vol. 5, edited by Rolf Wilhelm Brednich and Hermann Bausinger, 199–203. Berlin: de Gruyter, 1987.

Chraïbi, Aboubakr. "Galland's 'Ali Baba' and Other Arabic Versions." *Marvels and Tales* 18, no. 2 (2004): 159–69.

Commission des Antiquités. "Note sur Paul Lucas." *Bulletin de la Commission des Antiquités de la Seine-Inférieure* 10, no. 3 (1897): 338–40.

Davidson, Linda Kay, and David M. Gitlitz. *Pilgrimage: From the Ganges to Graceland; An Encyclopedia.* Santa Barbara, CA: ABC-Clio, 2002.

Dew, Nicholas. *Orientalism in Louis XIV's France.* Oxford, UK: Oxford University Press, 2009.

Diyāb, Ḥannā [Hanna Dyâb]. *D'Alep à Paris: Les pérégrinations d'un jeune syrien au temps de Louis XIV; Récit traduit de l'arabe (Syrie) et annoté par Paule Fahmé-Thiéry, Bernard Heyberger et Jérôme Lentin.* Paris: Actes Sud, 2015.

———. *The Man Who Wrote Aladin.* Translated by Paul Lunde. Edinburgh: Harding Simpole, 2020.

———. *Von Aleppo nach Paris: Die Reise eines jungen Syrers bis an den Hof Ludwigs XIV.* Translated by Gennaro Ghirardelli. Berlin: Die Andere Bibliothek, 2016.

Dobie, Madeleine. "Translation in the Contact Zone: Antoine Galland's *Mille et une nuits: Contes arabes.*" In *The Arabian Nights in Historical Context: Between East and West,* edited by Saree Makdisi and Felicity Nussbaum, 25–49. Oxford, UK: Oxford University Press, 2008.

# Bibliography

Dozy, Reinhart P. A. *Supplément aux dictionnaires arabes*. Beirut: Librairie du Liban, 1968.

Duranton, Henri. "Paul Lucas." In *Christian-Muslim Relations: A Bibliographical History*. Vol. 13 (1700–1800), edited by David Thomas and John Chesworth, 548–55. Leiden, Netherlands: Brill, 2019.

Fahd, Buṭrus. *Tārīkh al-rahbāniyyah al-lubnānīyah bi-farʿayhā l-ḥalabī wa-l-lubnānī, 1743–1770*. Vol. 4. Jūniyah, Lebanon: Maṭbaʿat Kuraym, 1966.

*EI2* = Bearman, P., Th. Bianquis, C. E. Bosworth, E. van Donzel, and W. P. Heinrichs, eds. *Encyclopaedia of Islam*. 2nd ed. 13 vols. Leiden, Netherlands: Brill, 1960–2009.

*EI3* = Gaborieau, Marc, Roger Allen, Gudrun Krämer, Kate Fleet, Denis Matringe, John Abdallah Nawas, and Everett K. Rowson, eds. *Encyclopaedia of Islam, Three*. Leiden, Netherlands: Brill, 2007–.

Fahmé-Thiéry, Paule. "L'arabe dialectal aleppin dans le récit de voyage de Hanna Dyâb." In *Arabic Varieties: Far and Wide; Proceedings of the 11th International Conference of AIDA—Bucharest, 2015*, edited by George Grigore and Gabriel Bițună, 223–30. Bucharest: Editura Universității din București, 2016.

———. "Ecriture et conscience de soi: Récits de voyage et accès à la modernité chez Bûlus ez Zaïm et Hanna Dyâb." Presented at the Kiev colloquium "Sous l'oeil de l'Orient: L'Europe dans les sources arabes," September 22–23, 2015.

Farḥāt, Jirmānūs. "Tārīkh taʾsīs al-rahbāniyyah al-Lubnāniyyah." In *Bidāyāt al-rahbāniyyah al-Lubnāniyyah*, edited by Jūzīf Qazzī, 111–78.

Gagliardi, Isabella. "'Ave maris Stella': Il santuario mariano di Montenero presso Livorno." In *Dio, il mare e gli uomini*, edited by Luciano Fanin, E. Ferrarini, and A. Galdi, 185–213. Verona: Cierre edizioni, 2008.

Galland, Antoine. *De l'origine et du progrès du café*. Paris: Poisson/Lance, 1836.

———. *Les mille et une nuits: Contes arabes*. 3 vols. Edited by Jean-Paul Sermain. Paris: Éditions Flammarion, 2004.

———. *Le journal d'Antoine Galland (1646–1715)*. Edited by F. Bauden and R. Waller. Leeuven, Belgium: Peeters, 2011–15.

———. *Voyage à Constantinople (1672–1673)*. Edited by Charles Schefer. Paris: Maisonneuve et Larose, 2002.

Gemayel, Nasser. *Les échanges culturels entre les Maronites et l'Europe: Du collège Maronite de Rome (1584) au collège de ʿAyn-Warqa (1789)*. Beirut: L'imprimerie V. & Ph. Gemayel, 1984.

Gerhardt, Mia. *The Art of Story-Telling: A Literary Study of the Thousand and One Nights*. Leiden, Netherlands: Brill, 1963.

Ghobrial, John-Paul A. "Stories Never Told: The First Arabic History of the New World." *The Journal of Ottoman Studies* 40 (2012): 259–82.

———. "The Secret Life of Elias of Babylon and the Uses of Global Microhistory." *Past and Present* (2014): 51–93.

———. "The Life and Hard Times of Solomon Negri: An Arabic Teacher in Early Modern Europe." In *The Teaching and Learning of Arabic in Early Modern Europe*, edited by Jan Loop, Alastair Hamilton, and Charles Burnett, 310–31. Leiden, Netherlands: Brill, 2017.

Gibb, H. A. R. *The Travels of Ibn Battuta in Asia and Africa, AD 1325–1354*. 5 vols. Cambridge, UK: Cambridge University Press, 1958.

Göçek, Fatma Müge. *East Encounters West: France and the Ottoman Empire in the Eighteenth Century*. New York: Oxford University Press, 1987.

Görner, Florian. "Das Regulativ der Wahrscheinlichkeit: Zur Funktion literarischer Fiktionalität im 18; Jahrhundert." PhD diss., Universität Köln, 2011.

Gossard, Julia M. "Breaking a Child's Will: Eighteenth-Century Parisian Juvenile Detention Centers." *French Historical Studies* 42, no. 2 (2019): 239–59.

Graf, Georg. *Geschichte der christlichen arabischen Literatur*. Vols. 3 and 4. Vatican City: Biblioteca Apostolica Vaticana, 1949–51.

———. *Verzeichnis arabischer kirchlicher Termini*. Louvain, Belgium: Imprimerie Orientaliste L. Durbecq, 1954.

Hayek, Michel. "Al-Rāhibah Hindiyyah (1720–1798)." *Al-Mashriq* 9 (1965): 525–646, 685–734.

Heyberger, Bernard. *Hindiyya: Mystique et criminelle 1720–1798*. Paris: Aubier, 2001. English translation: *Hindiyya, Mystic and Criminal, 1720–1798*. Translated by Renée Champion. Cambridge, UK: James Clarke, 2013.

———. *Les chrétiens du Proche-Orient au temps de la réforme catholique (Syrie, Liban, Palestine, XVIIe–XVIIIe siècles)*. Rome: Ecole française de Rome, 2014.

———. Introduction to Hanna Dyâb: *D'Alep à Paris; Les pérégrinations d'un jeune syrien au temps de Louis XIV; Récit traduit de l'arabe (Syrie) et annoté par Paule Fahmé-Thiéry, Bernard Heyberger et Jérôme Lentin*, 7–47. Paris: Actes Sud, 2015.

Horta, Paulo Lemos. *Marvellous Thieves: Secret Authors of the Arabian Nights*. Cambridge, MA: Harvard University Press, 2017.

———. "Tales of Aladdin and Their Tellers, from Aleppo to Paris." *Words without Borders*, April 16, 2020. Accessed October 7, 2020. https://www.wordswithoutborders.org/dispatches/article/tales-of-aladdin-and-their-tellers-from-aleppo-to-paris-paulo-lemos-horta.

Ibn al-Ṣāyigh, Fatḥallāh Ibn Anṭūn. *Riḥlah ilā bādiyat al-Shām wa-Ṣaḥārā l-ʿIrāq wa-l-ʿajam wa-l-Jazīrah al-ʿArabiyyah*. Edited by ʿAbdallāh Ibrāhīm al-ʿAskar and Muḥammad Khayr Maḥmūd al-Biqāʿī. Beirut: Jadawel, 2012.

İnalcik, Halil. *An Economic and Social History of the Ottoman Empire, 1300–1914*. Vol. 1, 1300–1600. Cambridge, UK: Cambridge University Press, 1994.

———. "A Note on the Population of Cyprus." *Journal for Cypriot Studies* 3, no. 1 (1997): 3–11.

Jennings, Ronald. *Christians and Muslims in Ottoman Cyprus and the Mediterranean World, 1571–1640*. New York: New York University Press, 1992.

Juillien (professor of botany at the Royal Garden). Undated memorandum to Paul Lucas. *Correspondance et papiers de Paul Lucas, voyageur et antiquaire français*. Richelieu Collection, Monnaies et Médailles, carton 1, dossier 27. Bibliothèque Nationale de France, Paris.

Kahane, Henry Romanos, Renée Kahane, and Andreas Tietze. *The Lingua Franca in the Levant: Turkish Nautical Terms of Italian and Greek Origin*. Urbana, IL: University of Illinois University Press, 1958.

Kallas, Elie. "The Aleppo Dialect According to the Travel Accounts of Ibn Raʿd (1656) Ms. Sbath 89 and Ḥanna Dyāb (1764) Ms. Sbath 254." In *De los manuscritos medievales a internet: La presencia del árabe vernáculo en las fuentes escritas*, edited by M. Meouak, P. Sánchez, and Á. Vicente, 221–54. Zaragoza, Spain: Área de Estudios Árabes e Islámicos, 2012.

———. "Gerboise: L'entrée du terme arabe ǧerbūʿ à la cour de Louis XIV." In *Approaches to the History and Dialectology of Arabic in Honor of Pierre Larcher*, edited by Manuel Sartori, Manuela E. B. Giolfo, and Philippe Cassuto, 342–61. Leiden, Netherlands: Brill, 2017.

Kilpatrick, Hilary, and Gerald J. Toomer. "Niqūlāwus al-Ḥalabī (c. 1611–c. 1661): A Greek Orthodox Syrian Copyist and His Letters to Pococke and Golius." *Lias* 43, no. 1 (2016): 1–159.

Krimsti, Feras. "The Lives and Afterlives of the Library of the Maronite Physician Ḥannā al-Ṭabīb (c. 1702–1775) from Aleppo." *Journal of Islamic Manuscripts* 9 (2018): 190–217.

———. "Arsāniyūs Shukrī al-Ḥakīm's Account of His Journey to France, the Iberian Peninsula, and Italy (1748–1757) from Travel Journal to Edition." *Philological Encounters* 4, nos. 3–4 (2019): 202–44.

Al-Labbūdī, Tūmā. "Sīrat al-ḥibr al-ṭayyib al-dhikr ʿAbdallāh Qarāʿalī al-Marūnī al-Ḥalabī." In *Bidāyāt al-rahbāniyyah al-Lubnāniyyah*, edited by Jūzīf Qazzī, 75–105.

Larzul, Sylvette. "Further Considerations on Galland's *Mille et une Nuits*: A Study of the Tales Told by Hannâ." *Marvels and Tales* 18, no. 2 (2004): 258–71. Reprinted in *The Arabian Nights in Transnational Perspective*, edited by Ulrich Marzolph, 17–31. Detroit, MI: Wayne State University Press, 2007.

———. "Les Mille et une nuits de Galland; ou, L'acclimatation d'une 'Belle étrangère.'" *Revue de littérature compare* 3 (1995): 312–18.

———. *Les traductions françaises des "Mille et une nuits": Études des versions Galland, Trébutien et Mardrus.* Paris: Harmattan, 1996.

Lentin, Jérôme. "Recherches sur l'histoire de la langue arabe au Proche-Orient à l'époque moderne." PhD diss., Université de la Sorbonne Nouvelle—Paris III, 1997.

———. "Middle Arabic." In *Encyclopedia of Arabic Language and Linguistics*, edited by Lutz Edzard and Rudolf de Jong. Leiden, Netherlands: Brill, 2011. http://dx.doi.org/10.1163/1570-6699_eall_EALL_COM_vol3_0213.

———. "Note sur la langue de Hanna Dyâb." In *D'Alep à Paris: Les pérégrinations d'un jeune syrien au temps de Louis XIV; Récit traduit de l'arabe (Syrie) et annoté par Paule Fahmé-Thiéry, Bernard Heyberger et Jérôme Lentin*, 48–51. Paris: Sindbad/Actes Sud, 2015.

Lucas, Paul. *[Premier] Voyage du Sieur Paul Lucas dans le Levant: Juin 1699–juillet 1703; Présenté par Henri Duranton.* Saint-Étienne, France: Publications de l'Université de Saint-Étienne, 1998.

———. *Deuxième Voyage du Sieur Paul Lucas dans le Levant: Octobre 1704–septembre 1708; Présenté par Henri Duranton.* Saint-Étienne, France: Publications de l'Université de Saint-Étienne, 2002.

———. *Troisième Voyage du Sieur Paul Lucas dans le Levant: Mai 1714–novembre 1717; Présenté par Henri Duranton.* Saint-Étienne, France: Publications de l'Université de Saint-Étienne, 2004.

Luterbacher, Jürg, Daniel Dietrich, Elena Xoplaki, Martin Grosjean, and Heinz Wanner. "European Seasonal and Annual Temperature Variability, Trends, and Extremes since 1500." *Science* 3, no. 5 (2004): 1499–1503.

Madsen, Peter. "'Auf, Auf, ihr Christen': Representing the Clash of Empires, Vienna 1683." In *Empires and World Literature*, edited by Piero Boitani and Irene Montori, 83–95. Milan: Albo Versorio, 2019.

Martin, Maurice. "Souvenirs d'un compagnion de voyage de Paul Lucas en Égypte (1707)." In *Hommages à la mémoire de Serge Sauneron. Tome II: Égypte post-pharaonique, 1927–1976*, edited by Jean Vercoutter, 471–75. Cairo: Institut Français d'archéologie orientale, 1979.

Marzolph, Ulrich. *101 Middle Eastern Tales and Their Impact on Western Oral Tradition.* Detroit, MI: Wayne State University Press, 2020.

———. "The Man Who Made the Nights Immortal: The Tales of the Syrian Maronite Storyteller Ḥannā Diyāb." *Marvels and Tales* 32, no. 1 (2018): 114–29.

Marzolph, Ulrich, with Anne E. Duggan. "Hanna Diyab's Tales, Part II." *Marvels and Tales* 32, no. 2 (2018): 435–56.

# Bibliography

Masters, Bruce. *Christians and Jews in the Ottoman Arab World: The Roots of Sectarianism.* Cambridge, UK: Cambridge University Press, 2001.

Matar, Nabil. *In the Lands of the Christians: Arab Travel Writing in the Seventeenth Century.* London: Routledge, 2003.

Mattern, Joseph. *A travers les villes mortes de Haute Syrie: Promenades archéologiques en 1928, 1929, 1931.* Beirut: Imprimerie Catholique, 1933.

Al-Mawṣilī, Ilyās. "Riḥlat awwal sā'iḥ sharqī ilā Amirkah. [Taḥqīq Anṭūn Rabbāṭ.]" *Al-Mašriq* 8, no. 2 (1905): 821–34, 875–86, 931–42, 974–83, 1022–33, 1080–88, 1118–1028.

May, Georges. *Les "Mille et une nuits" d'Antoine Galland, ou, Le chef-d'oeuvre invisible.* Paris: Presses universitaires de France, 1986.

McKenzie, Judith. *The Architecture of Alexandria and Egypt, 300 B.C. to A.D. 700.* New Haven, CT: Yale University Press, 2007.

Morison, Antoine. *Relation historique d'un voyage nouvellement fait au Mont de Sinaï et à Jerusalem.* Paris: A. Laurent, 1704.

Omont, Henri. *Missions archéologiques françaises en Orient aux XVIIè et XVIIIè siècles: Documents.* Paris: Imprimerie Nationale, 1902.

Ong, Walter J. *Orality and Literacy: The Technologizing of the World.* London: Routledge, 2002.

Ott, Claudia. "From the Coffeehouse into the Manuscript: The Storyteller and His Audience in the Manuscripts of an Arabic Epic." *Oriente Moderno* 22, no. 2 (2003): 443–51.

Özay, Yeliz. "Evliyâ Çelebi's Strange and Wondrous Europe." *Cahiers balkaniques* 41 (2013): 61–69.

Pamuk, Sevket. *A Monetary History of the Ottoman Empire.* Cambridge, UK: Cambridge University Press, 2000.

Patel, Abdulrazzak. *The Arab Nahḍah: The Making of the Intellectual and Humanist Movement.* Edinburgh: Edinburgh University Press, 2013.

Peucker, Brigitte. "The Material Image in Goethe's *Wahlverwandtschaften.*" *The Germanic Review: Literature, Culture, Theory* 74, no. 3 (1999): 195–213.

Pitou, Spire. *The Paris Opéra: An Encyclopedia of Operas, Ballets, Composers, and Performers.* Westport, CN: Greenwood Press, 1983.

Pococke, Richard. *A Description of the East and Some Other Countries.* London: W. Bowyer, 1743.

Qarā'alī, 'Abdallāh. "Mudhakkirāt." In *Bidāyāt al-rahbāniyyah al-Lubnāniyyah,* edited by Jūzīf Qazzī, 23–71.

Qarā'alī, 'Abdallāh et al. "Qawānīn al-rahbāniyyah al-Lubnāniyyah." In *Bidāyāt al-rahbāniyyah al-Lubnāniyyah,* edited by Jūzīf Qazzī, 179–210.

Qazzī, Jūzīf, ed. *Bidāyāt al-rahbāniyyah al-Lubnāniyyah*. Kaslik, Lebanon: Markaz al-Nashr wa-l-Tawzīʿ, 1988.

Raymond, André. "An Expanding Community: The Christians of Aleppo in the Ottoman Era (Sixteenth–Eighteenth Centuries)." In *Arab Cities in the Ottoman Period*, edited by André Raymond, 83–100. Aldershot, UK: Ashgate, 2002.

Redhouse, James W. A. *Turkish and English Lexicon*. Istanbul: A. H. Boyajian, 1890.

Reynolds, Dwight, ed. *Interpreting the Self: Autobiography in the Arabic Literary Tradition*. Berkeley, CA: University of California Press, 2001.

Russell, Alexander. *The Natural History of Aleppo*. Vol 1. Revised by Patrick Russell. London: G. G. and J. Robinson, 1794.

Sadan, Joseph. "Background, Date and Meaning of the Story of the Alexandrian Lover and the Magic Lamp: A Little-Known Story from Ottoman Times, with a Partial Resemblance to the Story of Aladdin." *Quaderni di Studi Arabi* 19 (2001): 137–92.

Sbath, Paul. *Bibliothèque de manuscrits: Catalogue*. Vol. 1. Cairo: H. Friedrich, 1928.

———. "Les manuscrits orientaux de la bibliothèque du R. P. Paul Sbath (Suite)." *Échos d'Orient* 23 (1924): 339–58.

Schwab, Raymond. *L'auteur des "Mille et une nuits": Vie d'Antoine Galland*. Paris: Mercure de France, 2004.

Seale, Yasmine, trans. *Aladdin: A New Translation*. Edited by Paulo Lemos Horta. New York, NY: Liveright Publishing, 2019.

Stephan, Johannes. "Von der Bezeugung zur Narrativen Vergegenwärtigung: Fokalisierung im Reisebuch des Syrers Ḥanna Dyāb (1764)." *Diegesis* 4, no. 2 (2015).

———. "Spuren fiktionaler Vergegenwärtigung im Osmanischen Aleppo: Narratologische Analysen und Kontextualisierungen des Reisebuchs von Hanna Dyāb (1764)." PhD diss., Universität Bern, 2016.

Teissier, Octave, ed. *Inventaire des archives historiques de la Chambre de Commerce de Marseille*. Marseille: Barlatier-Feissat, 1878.

Thompson, Ian. *The Sun King's Garden: Louis XIV, André le Nôtre and the Creation of the Garden of Versailles*. New York: Bloomsbury, 2006.

Touati, Houari. *Islam et voyage au Moyen Âge: Histoire et anthropologie d'une pratique lettrée*. Paris: Seuil, 2000.

Van Leeuwen, Richard, and Ulrich Marzolph, eds. *The Arabian Nights Encyclopedia*. Santa Barbara, CA: ABC-CLIO, 2004.

Vasari, Giorgio. *The Life of the Artists*. Translated by Julia Conaway Bondanella and Peter Bondanella. Oxford, UK: Oxford University Press, 2008.

Wahrmund, Adolf. *Handwörterbuch der neu-arabischen und deutschen Sprache*. Beirut: Librairie du Liban, 1974.

Warner, Marina. *Stranger Magic: Charmed States and the Arabian Nights.* London: Vintage, 2012.

Winter, Stefan. "Shiite Emirs and Ottoman Authorities: The Campaign against the Hamadas of Mt Lebanon, 1693–1694." In *Archivum Ottomanicum*, edited by György Hazai, 209–45. Wiesbaden, Germany: Harrassowitz, 2000.

Zotenberg, Hermann. "Notice sur quelques manuscrits des *Mille et Une Nuits* et la traduction de Galland." *Notices et extraits des manuscrits de la Bibliothèque nationale et autres bibliothèques* 28 (1887): 167–235.

# Further Reading

The literature on Ḥannā Diyāb's travelogue and its textual environment is still rather scarce. Due to its conspicuous features and history, *The Book of Travels* will always remain connected to at least four fields of scholarship. The first and most important of these involves studies related to the *Arabian Nights* and the orphan stories, which are Ḥannā Diyāb's contribution to world literature. The second involves research on travelers and travelogues during the early modern period. The third involves studies related to historical linguistics of Arabic. Finally, in recent years scholarship has emerged on the mobility and the textual production of Eastern Christians in the early and middle Ottoman periods, which includes Diyāb's book and similar narrative literature. Autobiographical artifacts such as *The Book of Travels* have yet to be included in the vast research on the history of the early modern Ottoman world and its entanglement with Western Europe.

In the 1990s, *The Book of Travels* drew attention from the field of linguistics, notably in Jérôme Lentin's dissertation, "Recherches sur l'histoire de la langue arabe au Proche-Orient à l'époque moderne," and in other studies of his. In the past seven years, Ruth Bottigheimer and Ulrich Marzolph have published important work regarding Ḥannā Diyāb's connection to the *Arabian Nights*. Bernard Heyberger's introduction to the French translation (2015) and some of his other works, as well as John-Paul Ghobrial's research on the traces of Middle Eastern Christians around the globe, have helped place Ḥannā Diyāb's book in the social context of the Christians of the Ottoman Empire and their entangled histories.

Selected works from these research areas that are not already mentioned in the bibliography to this volume are listed below.

# Literary and Cultural History of the Levant in the Early Modern Period

ʿĀnūtī, Usāma. *Al-Ḥarakah al-adabiyyah fī Bilād ash-Shām khilāl al-qarn al-thāmin ʿashar.* Beirut: Manshūrāt al-Jāmiʿa al-Lubnāniyya, 1971.

Dakhlia, Jocelyne. *Lingua franca.* Arles, France: Actes Sud, 2008.

Hanna, Nelly. *In Praise of Books: A Cultural History of Cairo's Middle Class, Sixteenth to the Eighteenth Century.* Syracuse, NY: Syracuse University Press, 2003.

Kilpatrick, Hilary. "From *Literatur* to *Adab*: The Literary Renaissance in Aleppo around 1700." *Journal of Eastern Christian Studies* 58, nos. 3–4 (2006): 195–220.

Masters, Bruce. *The Arabs of the Ottoman Empire, 1516–1918: A Social and Cultural History.* Cambridge, UK: Cambridge University Press, 2013.

Sajdi, Dana. "Decline, Its Discontents and Ottoman Cultural History: By Way of Introduction." In *Ottoman Tulips, Ottoman Coffee: Leisure and Lifestyle in the Eighteenth Century,* edited by Dana Sajdi, 1–40. London: I. B. Tauris, 2007.

———. *The Barber of Damascus: Nouveau Literacy in Eighteenth-Century Ottoman Levant.* Stanford, CA: Stanford University Press, 2013.

Van den Boogert, Maurits. *Aleppo Observed: Ottoman Syria through the Eyes of Two Scottish Doctors, Alexander and Patrick Russell.* Oxford, UK: Oxford University Press, 2010.

# Antoine Galland and the Orphan Stories

Akel, Ibrahim, and William Granara, eds. *The Thousand and One Nights: Sources and Transformations in Literature, Art, and Science.* Leiden, Netherlands: Brill, 2020.

Bauden, Frédéric, and Richard Waller, eds. *Antoine Galland (1646–1715) et son journal: Actes du colloque international organisé à l'Université de Liège (16–18 février 2015) à l'occasion du tricentenaire de sa mort.* Leeuwen, Belgium: Peeters, 2020.

Bottigheimer, Ruth B., and Claudia Ott. "The Case of the Ebony Horse: Part 1." *Gramarye* 5 (2014): 8–20.

Bottigheimer, Ruth B. "The Case of the Ebony Horse: Hannâ Diyâb's Creation of a Third Tradition; Part 2." *Gramarye* 6 (2014): 6–16.

———. "Reading for Fun in Eighteenth-Century Aleppo: The Hanna Dyâb Tales of Galland's *Mille et une nuits*." *Book History* 22 (2019): 133–60.

Marzolph, Ulrich. "A Scholar in the Making: Antoine Galland's Early Travel Diaries in the Light of Comparative Folk Narrative Research." *Middle Eastern Literatures* 18, no. 3 (2015): 283–300.

Further Reading

## Early Modern Travel Literature

Elger, Ralf. "Arabic Travelogues from the Mashrek 1700–1834: A Preliminary Survey of the Genre's Development." In *Crossing and Passages in Genre and Culture*, edited by Christian Szyska and Friederike Pannewick, 27–40. Wiesbaden, Germany: Reichert, 2003.

———. "Die Reisen eines Reiseberichts: Ibn Baṭṭūṭas Riḥla im Vorderen Orient des 17. und 18. Jahrhunderts." In *Buchkultur im Nahen Osten des 17. und 18. Jahrhunderts*, edited by Tobias Heinzelmann and Henning Sievert, 53–98. Bern: Peter Lang, 2010.

Göçek, Fatma Müge. *East Encounters West: France and the Ottoman Empire in the Eighteenth Century*. New York, NY: Oxford University Press, 1987.

Heyberger, Bernard and Carsten Walbiner, eds. *Les européens vus par les libanais à l'époque ottoman*. Würzburg, Germany: Ergon, 2002.

Kallas, Elie. "Aventures de Hanna Diyab avec Paul Lucas et Antoine Galland (1707–1710)." *Romano-Arabica* 15 (2015): 255–67.

———. *The Travel Accounts of Ra'd to Venice (1656) and Its Aleppo Dialect According to the MS. Sbath 89*. Vatican City: Biblioteca Apostolica Vaticana, 2015.

Kilpatrick, Hilary. "Between Ibn Baṭṭūṭa and al-Ṭahṭāwī: Arabic Travel Accounts of the Early Ottoman Period." *Middle Eastern Literatures* 11, no. 2 (2008): 233–248.

Muhanna, Elias. "Ilyās al-Mawṣilī." In *Essays in Arabic Literary Biography: 1350–1850*, edited by Joseph E. Lowry and Devin J. Stewart, 295–299. Wiesbaden, Germany: Harrassowitz, 2009.

Salmon, Olivier, ed. *Alep dans la littérature de voyage européenne pendant la période ottomane (1516–1918)*. Aleppo: El-Mudarris, 2011.

Walbiner, Carsten-Michael. "Riḥlat 'Ra'd' min Ḥalab ilā al-Bunduqīya." In *Mélanges en mémoire de Mgr Néophytos Edelby (1920–1995)*, edited by Nagi Edelby and Pierre Masri, 367–83. Beirut: Université St. Joseph, 2005.

Yirmisekiz Çelebī Efendi, Meḥmed. *Le paradis des infidèles: Relation de Yirmisekiz Çelebi Mehmed efendi, ambassadeur ottoman en France sous la Régence*. Paris: François Maspero, 1981.

## Near Eastern Christianities

Ghobrial, John-Paul A. "The Ottoman World of 'Abdallah Zakher: Shuwayr Bindings in the Arcadian Library." In *The Arcadian Library: Bindings and Provenance*, edited by Giles Mandelbrote and Willem de Bruijn, 193–231. Oxford, UK: Oxford University Press, 2014.

———. "Migration from Within and Without: In the Footsteps of Eastern Christians in the Early Modern World." *Transactions of the Royal Historical Society* 27 (2017): 153–73.

Further Reading

Heyberger, Bernard. "Livres et pratique de la lecture chez les chrétiens (Syrie, Liban) XVIIe–XVIIIe siècles." *Revue des mondes musulmans et de la Méditerranée* 87–88 (1999): 209–23.

Khater, Akram Fouad. *Embracing the Divine: Gender, Passion, and Politics in the Christian Middle East, 1720–1798*. New York, NY: Syracuse University Press, 2011.

Walbiner, Carsten-Michael. "Monastic Reading and Learning in Eighteenth-Century Bilād al-Šām: Some Evidence from the Monastery of al-Šuwayr (Mount Lebanon)." *Arabica* 51, no. 4 (2004): 462–77.

# Index

# Index

Index

# About the NYU Abu Dhabi Institute

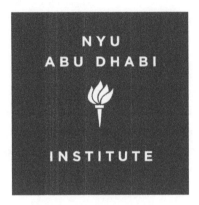

The Library of Arabic Literature is supported by a grant from the NYU Abu Dhabi Institute, a major hub of intellectual and creative activity and advanced research. The Institute hosts academic conferences, workshops, lectures, film series, performances, and other public programs directed both to audiences within the UAE and to the worldwide academic and research community. It is a center of the scholarly community for Abu Dhabi, bringing together faculty and researchers from institutions of higher learning throughout the region.

NYU Abu Dhabi, through the NYU Abu Dhabi Institute, is a world-class center of cutting-edge research, scholarship, and cultural activity. The Institute creates singular opportunities for leading researchers from across the arts, humanities, social sciences, sciences, engineering, and the professions to carry out creative scholarship and conduct research on issues of major disciplinary, multi-disciplinary, and global significance.

# About the Typefaces

The Arabic body text is set in DecoType Naskh, designed by Thomas Milo and Mirjam Somers, based on an analysis of five centuries of Ottoman manuscript practice. The exceptionally legible result is the first and only typeface in a style that fully implements the principles of script grammar (*qawāʿid al-khaṭṭ*).

The Arabic footnote text is set in DecoType Emiri, drawn by Mirjam Somers, based on the metal typeface in the naskh style that was cut for the 1924 Cairo edition of the Qurʾan.

Both Arabic typefaces in this series are controlled by a dedicated font layout engine. ACE, the Arabic Calligraphic Engine, invented by Peter Somers, Thomas Milo, and Mirjam Somers of DecoType, first operational in 1985, pioneered the principle followed by later smart font layout technologies such as OpenType, which is used for all other typefaces in this series.

The Arabic text was set with WinSoft Tasmeem, a sophisticated user interface for DecoType ACE inside Adobe InDesign. Tasmeem was conceived and created by Thomas Milo (DecoType) and Pascal Rubini (WinSoft) in 2005.

The English text is set in Adobe Text, a new and versatile text typeface family designed by Robert Slimbach for Western (Latin, Greek, Cyrillic) typesetting. Its workhorse qualities make it perfect for a wide variety of applications, especially for longer passages of text where legibility and economy are important. Adobe Text bridges the gap between calligraphic Renaissance types of the 15th and 16th centuries and high-contrast Modern styles of the 18th century, taking many of its design cues from early post-Renaissance Baroque transitional types cut by designers such as Christoffel van Dijck, Nicolaus Kis, and William Caslon. While grounded in classical form, Adobe Text is also a statement of contemporary utilitarian design, well suited to a wide variety of print and on-screen applications.

# Titles Published by the Library of Arabic Literature

For more details on individual titles, visit www.libraryofarabicliterature.org

**Classical Arabic Literature: A Library of Arabic Literature Anthology**
Selected and translated by Geert Jan van Gelder (2012)

**A Treasury of Virtues: Sayings, Sermons, and Teachings of ʿAlī**, by al-Qāḍī
al-Quḍāʿī, with the **One Hundred Proverbs** attributed to al-Jāḥiẓ
Edited and translated by Tahera Qutbuddin (2013)

**The Epistle on Legal Theory**, by al-Shāfiʿī
Edited and translated by Joseph E. Lowry (2013)

**Leg over Leg**, by Aḥmad Fāris al-Shidyāq
Edited and translated by Humphrey Davies (4 volumes; 2013–14)

**Virtues of the Imām Aḥmad ibn Ḥanbal**, by Ibn al-Jawzī
Edited and translated by Michael Cooperson (2 volumes; 2013–15)

**The Epistle of Forgiveness**, by Abū l-ʿAlāʾ al-Maʿarrī
Edited and translated by Geert Jan van Gelder and Gregor Schoeler
(2 volumes; 2013–14)

**The Principles of Sufism**, by ʿĀʾishah al-Bāʿūniyyah
Edited and translated by Th. Emil Homerin (2014)

**The Expeditions: An Early Biography of Muḥammad**, by Maʿmar ibn Rāshid
Edited and translated by Sean W. Anthony (2014)

**Two Arabic Travel Books**
  **Accounts of China and India**, by Abū Zayd al-Sīrāfī
    Edited and translated by Tim Mackintosh-Smith (2014)
  **Mission to the Volga**, by Aḥmad ibn Faḍlān
    Edited and translated by James Montgomery (2014)

**Disagreements of the Jurists: A Manual of Islamic Legal Theory**, by al-Qāḍī al-Nuʿmān
Edited and translated by Devin J. Stewart (2015)

**Consorts of the Caliphs: Women and the Court of Baghdad**, by Ibn al-Sāʿī
Edited by Shawkat M. Toorawa and translated by the Editors of the Library of Arabic Literature (2015)

**What ʿĪsā ibn Hishām Told Us**, by Muḥammad al-Muwayliḥī
Edited and translated by Roger Allen (2 volumes; 2015)

**The Life and Times of Abū Tammām**, by Abū Bakr Muḥammad ibn Yaḥyā al-Ṣūlī
Edited and translated by Beatrice Gruendler (2015)

**The Sword of Ambition: Bureaucratic Rivalry in Medieval Egypt**, by ʿUthmān ibn Ibrāhīm al-Nābulusī
Edited and translated by Luke Yarbrough (2016)

**Brains Confounded by the Ode of Abū Shādūf Expounded**, by Yūsuf al-Shirbīnī
Edited and translated by Humphrey Davies (2 volumes; 2016)

**Light in the Heavens: Sayings of the Prophet Muḥammad**, by al-Qāḍī al-Quḍāʿī
Edited and translated by Tahera Qutbuddin (2016)

**Risible Rhymes**, by Muḥammad ibn Maḥfūẓ al-Sanhūrī
Edited and translated by Humphrey Davies (2016)

**A Hundred and One Nights**
Edited and translated by Bruce Fudge (2016)

**The Excellence of the Arabs**, by Ibn Qutaybah
Edited by James E. Montgomery and Peter Webb
Translated by Sarah Bowen Savant and Peter Webb (2017)

**Scents and Flavors: A Syrian Cookbook**
Edited and translated by Charles Perry (2017)

**Arabian Satire: Poetry from 18th-Century Najd**, by Ḥmēdān al-Shwēʿir
Edited and translated by Marcel Kurpershoek (2017)

**In Darfur: An Account of the Sultanate and Its People**, by Muḥammad ibn ʿUmar al-Tūnisī
Edited and translated by Humphrey Davies (**2 volumes; 2018**)

**War Songs**, by ʿAntarah ibn Shaddād
Edited by James E. Montgomery
Translated by James E. Montgomery with Richard Sieburth (**2018**)

**Arabian Romantic: Poems on Bedouin Life and Love**, by ʿAbdallāh ibn Sbayyil
Edited and translated by Marcel Kurpershoek (**2018**)

**Dīwān ʿAntarah ibn Shaddād: A Literary-Historical Study**
By James E. Montgomery (**2018**)

**Stories of Piety and Prayer: Deliverance Follows Adversity**, by al-Muḥassin ibn ʿAlī al-Tanūkhī
Edited and translated by Julia Bray (**2019**)

**The Philosopher Responds: An Intellectual Correspondence from the Tenth Century**, by Abū Ḥayyān al-Tawḥīdī and Abū ʿAlī Miskawayh
Edited by Bilal Orfali and Maurice A. Pomerantz
Translated by Sophia Vasalou and James E. Montgomery (**2 volumes; 2019**)

**Tajrīd sayf al-himmah li-stikhrāj mā fī dhimmat al-dhimmah: A Scholarly Edition of ʿUthmān ibn Ibrāhīm al-Nābulusī's Text**
By Luke Yarbrough (**2020**)

**The Discourses: Reflections on History, Sufism, Theology, and Literature— Volume One**, by al-Ḥasan al-Yūsī
Edited and translated by Justin Stearns (**2020**)

**Impostures**, by al-Ḥarīrī
Translated by Michael Cooperson (**2020**)

**Maqāmāt Abī Zayd al-Sarūjī**, by al-Ḥarīrī
Edited by Michael Cooperson (**2020**)

**The Yoga Sutras of Patañjali**, by Abū Rayḥān al-Bīrūnī
Edited and translated by Mario Kozah (**2020**)

**The Book of Charlatans**, by Jamāl al-Dīn ʿAbd al-Raḥīm al-Jawbarī
Edited by Manuela Dengler
Translated by Humphrey Davies (**2020**)

**A Physician on the Nile**, by ʿAbd al-Laṭīf al-Baghdādī
Edited and translated by Tim Mackintosh-Smith (**2021**)

**The Book of Travels**, by Ḥannā Diyāb
Edited by Johannes Stephan
Translated by Elias Muhanna (**2 volumes; 2021**)

English-only Paperbacks

**Leg over Leg**, by Aḥmad Fāris al-Shidyāq (**2 volumes; 2015**)

**The Expeditions: An Early Biography of Muḥammad**, by Maʿmar ibn Rāshid
(**2015**)

**The Epistle on Legal Theory: A Translation of al-Shāfiʿī's** *Risālah*, by
al-Shāfiʿī (**2015**)

**The Epistle of Forgiveness**, by Abū l-ʿAlāʾ al-Maʿarrī (**2016**)

**The Principles of Sufism**, by ʿĀʾishah al-Bāʿūniyyah (**2016**)

**A Treasury of Virtues: Sayings, Sermons, and Teachings of ʿAlī**, by al-Qāḍī
al-Quḍāʿī, with the **One Hundred Proverbs** attributed to al-Jāḥiẓ (**2016**)

**The Life of Ibn Ḥanbal**, by Ibn al-Jawzī (**2016**)

**Mission to the Volga**, by Ibn Faḍlān (**2017**)

**Accounts of China and India**, by Abū Zayd al-Sīrāfī (**2017**)

**A Hundred and One Nights** (**2017**)

**Consorts of the Caliphs: Women and the Court of Baghdad**, by Ibn al-Sāʿī
(**2017**)

**Disagreements of the Jurists: A Manual of Islamic Legal Theory**, by al-Qāḍī
al-Nuʿmān (**2017**)

**What ʿĪsā ibn Hishām Told Us**, by Muḥammad al-Muwayliḥī (**2018**)

**War Songs**, by ʿAntarah ibn Shaddād (**2018**)

**The Life and Times of Abū Tammām**, by Abū Bakr Muḥammad ibn Yaḥyā
al-Ṣūlī (**2018**)

**The Sword of Ambition**, by ʿUthmān ibn Ibrāhīm al-Nābulusī (**2019**)

**Brains Confounded by the Ode of Abū Shādūf Expounded: Volume One**, by
Yūsuf al-Shirbīnī (**2019**)

**Brains Confounded by the Ode of Abū Shādūf Expounded: Volume Two**, by
Yūsuf al-Shirbīnī and **Risible Rhymes**, by Muḥammad ibn Maḥfūẓ al-Sanhūrī
(**2019**)

**The Excellence of the Arabs**, by Ibn Qutaybah (**2019**)

Light in the Heavens: Sayings of the Prophet Muḥammad, by al-Qāḍī al-Quḍāʿī (2019)

Scents and Flavors: A Syrian Cookbook (2020)

Arabian Satire: Poetry from 18th-Century Najd, by Ḥmēdān al-Shwēʿir (2020)

In Darfur: An Account of the Sultanate and Its People, by Muḥammad al-Tūnisī (2020)

Arabian Romantic, by ʿAbdallāh ibn Sbayyil (2020)

The Philosopher Reponds, by Abū Ḥayyān al-Tawḥīdī and Abū ʿAlī Miskawayh (2021)

# About the Editor

**Johannes Stephan** earned his Ph.D. at the University of Bern. Currently, he holds a postdoc in the ERC project *Kalīlah and Dimnah*—AnonymClassic at the Freie Universität Berlin, scrutinizing the early Arabic reception (eighth to thirteenth centuries) of the *Book of Kalīlah wa-Dimnah* and elaborating on the concepts of narrative framing and fictionality. His forthcoming monograph, *Vergegenwärtigendes Erzählen: Das Reisebuch (1764) des tausendundeine-Nacht-Erzählers Ḥannā Diyāb im Rahmen einer inklusiven arabischen Literaturgeschichte*, analyzes and contextualizes the literariness of Diyāb's *Book of Travels*.

# About the Translator

**Elias Muhanna** is Associate Professor of Comparative Literature and History at Brown University. He is the author of *The World in a Book: al-Nuwayri and the Islamic Encyclopedic Tradition* and translator of Shihāb al-Dīn al-Nuwayrī's fourteenth-century encyclopedia, *The Ultimate Ambition in the Arts of Erudition.*